Bruce Borthwick
Albion College

COMPARATIVE POLITICS

OF

THE MIDDLE EAST

An Introduction

PRENTICE-HALL, INC. ENGLEWOOD CLIFFS, NEW JERSEY 07632

Library of Congress Cataloging in Publication Data

BORTHWICK, BRUCE.
    Comparative politics of the Middle East.

    Bibliography: p.
    Includes index.
    1. Near East—Politics and government.   I. Title.
DS62.8.B67   320.9'56'04   79-24018
ISBN 0-13-154088-2

Editorial production and interior design by Serena Hoffman
Cover design by Wanda Lubelska
Manufacturing buyer, Harry P. Baisley

Printed in the United States of America

10   9   8   7   6   5   4   3   2   1

PRENTICE-HALL INTERNATIONAL, INC., *London*
PRENTICE-HALL OF AUSTRALIA PTY. LIMITED., *Sydney*
PRENTICE-HALL OF CANADA, LTD., *Toronto*
PRENTICE-HALL OF INDIA PRIVATE LIMITED, *New Delhi*
PRENTICE-HALL OF JAPAN, INC., *Tokyo*
PRENTICE-HALL OF SOUTHEAST ASIA PTE. LTD., *Singapore*
WHITEHALL BOOKS LIMITED, *Wellington, New Zealand*

To my mother and father

Helen Maynard Borthwick

and

George Borthwick

Contents

Preface

In 1967, while spending a very fruitful summer in France studying French and examining research facilities on the Middle East and North Africa, I decided to write a textbook on the politics of the Middle East. I envisioned a book based on contemporary methods in the field of comparative politics that was written in clear felicitous prose, a book that the neophyte could read and understand. As every author knows, such an undertaking is long and arduous, and is punctuated with disappointments and pleasant surprises. The people who give you advice, criticism, and support are numerous.

I was inspired by *Les Régimes Politiques des Pays Arabes* (Paris: Presses Universitaires de France, 1968) written by Maurice Flory and Robert Mantran. I admired the conciseness of this work and its analytical approach, combining history, sociology, and political science. At an early stage I decided that what Professors Flory and Mantran had done for French students, I would like to do for American ones.

Two persons at Albion College have encouraged me: G. Robina Quale, in the Department of History, author of *Eastern Civilizations* (2nd ed.; Englewood Cliffs, N.J.: Prentice-Hall, 1975), and Richard Rosser, formerly Dean of the Faculty, now President of DePauw University, Greencastle, Indiana, author of *An Introduction to Soviet Foreign Policy* (Englewood Cliffs, N.J.: Prentice-Hall, 1969). Both urged me on when I was discouraged and gave me much helpful advice about the steps involved in writing a book.

To Ronald M. Sirkin of Wright State University, I am particularly indebted, because he was the first to read the manuscript and say that if it was published, he would adopt it. To Arthur Goldschmidt, Jr., of Pennsylvania State University, I owe a special debt, because he read the manuscript two or more times, sharpened the prose, and checked it for historical accuracy. Also, he used it in manuscript form in one of his courses and received much helpful student feedback. Other individuals read chapters in their area of expertise: Scott Johnston, Hamline University, Israel; Carl Leiden, the University of Texas at Austin, Egypt; James Bill of the same university, Iran; and Arnold Leder, Southwest Texas State University, and Metin Heper, Harvard, for the chapter on Turkey. The chapter on Lebanon owes much to the informative lectures on the Lebanese civil war given by Halim Barakat at the University of Texas during the summer of 1977, where he was a visiting professor from Georgetown University.

Much of my insight into the Jewish people and the nation of Israel comes from two seminars I attended at Princeton Theological Seminary organized by Rabbi Solomon Bernards of the Anti-Defamation League of B'nai B'rith, and from two colleagues at Albion, Judith Elkin, a specialist on the history of Jews in Latin America, author of *Jews of the Latin American Republics* (Chapel Hill: University of North Carolina Press, 1980), and Frank Frick, a professor in the Department of Religious Studies, specializing in Jewish history and religion.

Joseph Irwin, retired professor of English at Albion, and my father, George Borthwick, a retired Presbyterian minister, have read the manuscript with an eye to improving the prose. The assistance of the latter was most appreciated in the final revision and in prodding me to get the job done.

Also, I must acknowledge the guidance and assistance of John Pickering, Editorial Director of the Pennsylvania State University Press, who nursed the manuscript along for several years, and George Grassmuck, my mentor in graduate school at the University of Michigan, who gave me the foundation upon which the book is written.

Numerous typists have worked on the several revisions, but probably the most important is Evelyn Herrick, secretary in the political science department of Albion College.

This book would not have been possible without several fellowships and grants: the Relm Foundation of Ann Arbor, Michigan, for making possible the trip to France during the summer of 1967; the Great Lakes Colleges Association for awarding me some money during the summers of 1968 and 1969; the Associated Independent College and Universities in Michigan, which gave me a grant partially funded by the Kellogg Foundation so I could take a leave of absence, 1971-1972, to live in Ann Arbor and do research and writing there. Also, I must acknowledge the National Endownment for the Humanities, which gave me the opportunity to attend a seminar on Middle Eastern political systems directed by James Bill at the University of Texas, Austin, during the summer of 1977.

Finally, I am grateful to Paul English and James Bill, Director and Assistant Director respectively of the Center for Middle Eastern Studies at the University of Texas, who allowed me to be a faculty research associate and visiting scholar there during the fall semester, 1977, while on a sabbatical leave from Albion College. They provided access to all the resources of the center and the university library, introduced me to many of the faculty, and treated me with the friendliness and hospitality for which Texas is world famous. Gary Menges, Assistant Director for Public Services of the University of Texas Library, was also most helpful.

Any book on the Middle East has to deal with the question of transliteration. There are four major languages in the region (Arabic, Turkish, Persian, and Hebrew), and three use non-Latin alphabets, while Turkish, the fourth, employs the Latin alphabet but with diacritical marks not used in English. An author thus has to decide whether to transliterate using a system that designates every letter in the foreign alphabet, resulting in signs and marks that only someone who knows the language can understand, or a system that approximates the original. I have opted for the latter. My rule has been to keep the spelling as simple as possible, so the nonspecialist can read and pronounce the word easily. Wherever there are common spellings in English, I have used them. If a word appears in the unabridged edition of *Webster's Third International Dictionary,* I have considered it to have passed into the English language and have not placed it in italics. I have used English plurals and not those of the language *(waqf, waqfs,* not *awqāf; za^{c}īm, za^{c}īms,* not *zu^{c}amā')* except where the foreign plural is common in English (kibbutzim, fellaheen). For Turkish words, I have left out the diacritical marks.

Bruce Borthwick
Albion, Michigan

Part I

THE MIDDLE EAST

AS A WHOLE

Chapter 1

Introduction

The Middle East, a region vital to the economies of Western industrialized countries and critical to the peace of the entire world, is undergoing rapid and traumatic social and political change. Throughout the region educational systems are being expanded quickly, producing large numbers of young men and women with heightened expectations that often cannot be met. Education also leads to increased awareness of the outside world and greater consciousness of the indignities their nations have suffered at the hands of the great powers, whether Great Britain, France, the Soviet Union, or the United States. Often these young people feel an intense devotion to and appreciation of their own culture and religion, a longing for the "good life" that people in the developed nations live, and a desire to end the poverty and injustice prevalent in their own societies. Many are dedicated to the revolutionary ideologies of Karl Marx, Mao Tse-tung, and Fidel Castro.

Radio broadcasting blankets the region. The inexpensive battery-operated transistor radio has made it possible for the peasant to be connected to the outside world as he plows or eats his noonday meal. A blaring radio, with its lilting Oriental music, news broadcasts, and religious homilies, dominates the din of traffic and conversation in the bazaars and shopping streets. Television is prevalent in coffee houses, restaurants, and middle-class homes, showing the comings and goings of local officialdom, sports competitions, locally produced melodramas, and reruns of American and Western European television programs. The numerous movie theaters show films produced in the Middle East and other parts of the world.

The major cities of the Middle East are linked to each other by airlines, and many have excellent connections to India, the Orient, Europe, and the United States. Businessmen from South Korea, Japan, Taiwan, Europe, the United States, and from the Middle East travel to and fro making deals, and government officials from these countries do the same, encouraging and promoting the trade of their country. Hundreds of thousands of Turkish workers are temporarily employed in Western Europe, especially West Germany, and the same holds true for Algerians in France. Middle Eastern students attend secondary schools, colleges, and universities in Germany, France, Britain, and the United States.

Two-thirds of the entire world's known reserves of petroleum lie in the Middle East, and oil is bringing about startling and highly visible change. While fields in Iran, Bahrain, and Iraq were discovered and exploited prior to World War II, most of the exploration and discovery has taken place since then. Some enormous finds have been made in Saudi Arabia, Kuwait, Qatar, the United Arab Emirates, Libya, and Algeria. Nations that formerly were barely known to the Western world are now oil powers, and their leaders control huge amounts of capital that give them increasing influence in international monetary diplomacy.

These rapid changes in education, communication, transportation, and in the exploitation of natural resources are creating stresses in the social and political system. The old elites, who have ruled for decades and sometimes centuries, are constantly struggling to maintain their position, sometimes using brute force and heavy-handed political repression, other times employing the more subtle techniques of co-opting potential radicals into the establishment or providing them with opportunities to make large amounts of money. With oil revenues, these elites sometimes provide modern social welfare services, such as free education and medical care. Yet still they are threatened. In Iran, they were swept out of power by the 1978-79 revolution; in Saudi Arabia and the numerous small states along the periphery of the Arabian Peninsula, they are very insecure.

Since World War II, a group called by social scientists the *new middle class* has arisen. Possessed of a modern education at secondary or university level, they are skilled in engineering, economics, management, public administration, law, or technology. Also part of this class are the military officers, who are trained in science, technology, and modern military tactics, and who operate advanced weapons made in the developed nations. Essential to the administration of the state, the well-being of the economy, and to a strong national defense, the members of the new middle class now have a great deal of power and status. Yet leftist revolutionaries say that they are removed from the people and bent more on the preservation of their power and relatively high standard of living than on the improvement of the lot of the peasant and worker.

Rapid change has severely fractionized society. The old ruling elites are threatened by the new middle class, and both groups are attacked by the radicals, who operate underground and employ violence and terror. Traditional merchants and craftsmen are threatened by the new businessmen who have made money through imports and affiliation with foreign companies. The Islamic clergy feel that much that comes under the name of modernization is destructive of faith, morality, and the Islamic way of life. Military officers sometimes feel that they do not have the respect or support of the rest of the society. Students want jobs that will utilize the skills they have learned, and workers simply want regular employment. Peasants want steady prices for agricultural products and freedom from the arbitrariness of government officials. These demands are in conflict, and the government has the nearly impossible job of trying to please all.

Added to these disruptive social and political changes are numerous international and ethnic conflicts. On several occasions since World War II, the United States and the Soviet Union have confronted each other in the Middle East, often working through client states. Turkey and Greece have fought over Cyprus. Israel has fought four full-scale wars with its neighboring Arab states and has been engaged in continuing battles and skirmishes with Palestinian guerillas since 1967. Morocco and Algeria have been locked in a war over the former Spanish Sahara since 1976, the Kurds have fought the armed forces of the Iraqi and Iranian governments, and different religious communities in Lebanon have fought almost continuously since 1975.

The pace of social and political change has varied. In some places it has been quite rapid, and in other areas it is almost nonexistent, making for sharp and startling contrasts. Some Middle Eastern societies are almost unchanged from medieval times; others are as modern as any you can find. Some political systems are mostly tribal and operate according to unwritten codes of human conduct; others are centered around the modern state and have functioning political parties, interest groups, and a modern bureaucracy. In some economies the wheel is unknown; others have space-age scientific research institutes and technologically advanced industries.

These contrasts and vignettes could be continued, but that is not the purpose of the introductory chapter. In short, the Middle East is a region worthy of comparative political study because it has enough cultural homogeneity to make comparisons possible, and enough diversity to make it meaningful.

COMPARATIVE POLITICS

Comparative politics is a contrast of the political processes of different societies for the purpose of learning their unique and universal characteristics. Just as human beings possess both common and individual characteristics, a political system (the political process within a society) has both universal qualities and singular ones. Through comparative politics we learn of the immense diversity in the contemporary political universe that stems from the different cultures and historical experiences of today's world. We also come to the startling conclusion that underlying this worldwide diversity there are basic similarities.

Categories are necessary for comparison. Up to the 1960s, it was common practice to compare countries and their governments in terms of land, people, political parties, legislature, executive, judiciary, and administration. However, these concepts proved inadequate in studying the developing nations, where a legislature did not always exist, yet the people obeyed written and unwritten laws; the judicial system was not always formally organized with officially appointed judges and imposing court buildings, yet the responsibilities and claims of different parties were determined. The problem was that the categories that worked in describing and explaining European or American political systems were too narrow and too focused on the formal institutions of government to be effective in comparative studies of the developing nations.

In the 1960s a revolution took place within the academic discipline of comparative politics. Numerous books and articles were written laying out new analytical categories for the comparative study of politics. Their common quality was a search for a system that was universal and not bound to Western culture, that was dynamic, that could show political systems undergoing change and transformation. Of the numerous systems devised, I have chosen one suggested by Samuel P. Huntington because of its simplicity and its incorporation of change into the model. Huntington says that "a political system can be thought of as an aggregate of components, all changing, some at rapid rates, some at slower ones."[1] The components he selects are: (1) culture, (2) structure, (3) groups, (4) leadership, and (5) policies. He points out that "in any political system, all five components are always changing, but . . . the rate, scope and direction of change in the components vary greatly within a system and between systems."[2] In order to understand this better, we will first need to define the components one by one.

Culture

Everyone carries around in his or her head ideas, attitudes, opinions, and values regarding the fundamental character of the political system, the nature of justice, the policies that should be instituted by the government, and the qualities of good political leaders. For example, most Americans support the constitution and the system of liberal democracy that it established, believe in the free enterprise system, dislike socialism, regard competition as good, praise individualism, and distrust concentrated power. These attitudes and beliefs produce the Ameri-

---

[1] Samuel P. Huntington, "The Change to Change: Modernization, Development and Politics," *Comparative Politics*, 3 (April 1971), 316.
[2] Ibid.

can political culture, something that is vague and amorphous, yet exists and is passed on from one generation to the next.

The political culture of all Middle Eastern states except Israel is rooted in Islam. Although Jews and Christians have lived in the area from the time of Abraham and Christ to the present, since the seventh century Islam has been predominant. Its political philosophy and legal system, along with the customs and practices that have arisen in Muslim countries, set the tone of the society and determine the attitudes and beliefs of the people. It influences what people think about the kind of person who should rule, the type of laws that should be enacted, the form of justice, and the rights and duties of every person.

No culture is static. Witness the United States, where attitudes of whites towards blacks have changed quite dramatically since the early 1950s, and opinions about women's role in society have changed significantly since the late 1960s. The same is true, probably more so, for the Middle East. In the nineteenth century and the first half of the twentieth century, most Middle Eastern nations came under the domination of the European powers. Members of the top layer of society in cities close to Europe or on the major trade routes, such as Istanbul, Beirut, Cairo, and Tunis, were greatly influenced by European intellectual and political movements. They became fervent advocates of civil liberties guaranteed by a constitution, parliamentary government, competitive political parties, and civic equality of all men, regardless of religion. They had faith in science and technology and a desire for progress. The attitudes of some changed so much that they came to regard the Islamic social and political system as unjust and archaic, and they felt that it should be replaced in totality by a European one. Others argued for selective incorporation of some European practices and institutions into the Islamic system. Still others were convinced that little was wrong with the Islamic system and that it should be fervently defended from attack.

Since World War II, this revolution in attitudes has spread. In places that in the nineteenth century were considered remote and backward, people are challenging old myths and beliefs, and it is not simply the top layer of society that is being affected. Also, the current stimuli for change come not only from Western Europe, but also from the United States, China, the Soviet Union, and from some nations in Africa, Asia, and Latin America. Liberal democracy, the democratic socialism of Western Europe, the viewpoints of Western European Marxists, the "scientific socialism" of the Soviet Union, the thought of Mao Tse-tung, the workers' self-management and socialist market economy of Yugoslavia, are all studied, analyzed, debated, and imitated.

However, Islam remains the primary source for the culture. With the spread of literacy, books on faith and practice, Islamic law and history, the life of Muhammad and great Muslim leaders, written in both the popular and scholarly vein, have multiplied enormously. Popular religious magazines abound that have in them simple exegeses of Koranic passages, letters to the editor on religious subjects, and articles with titles such as "Islam and . . . ," "The Islamic

Viewpoint towards . . . ," and "What Does a Good Muslim Do When . . . ." The mosque, the network of religious schools that teach children and adults, the circles for prayer and study that meet in people's homes, the sermons given at communal worship service every Friday, and the religious radio broadcasts all influence the attitudes and beliefs of the people.

What is being discussed is the role of Islam in modern society and the place it should have in each person's life. The debate is so widespread and so far reaching that one can truly say that it has the dimensions of a reformation, the greatest since Muhammad.

Structure

Though the stranger may not recognize them, every society has its political structures—regularized patterns of action whereby authoritative decisions are made. In the developed nations such structures tend to be highly visible and constitutionally or legally established, such as the American Congress, Supreme Court, President, and the multiple federal agencies and departments. In the developing nations, the tendency is more towards informal structures.

The difference is not one of dichotomy but of continuum. While the formal and legal tend to predominate in the developed nations, and the informal and nonlegal in the developing, there is a mix in both. In the United States the two-martini lunch, the smoke-filled room, the working breakfast, and the 6 o'clock cocktail party supplement the workings of Congress and federal executive agencies. In the developing nations the formal bureaucracy frequently conceals a complex web of personal and family relations in which the really important decisions are made. The differences are not in kind but in the proportions of the mix.

Lebanon is one example of the predominance of informal nonlegal structures over formal legal ones. It possesses a constitution, political parties, a parliament, prime minister, cabinet ministers, a president of the Republic, and a bureaucracy; yet operating behind these and intermeshed with them is an elaborate and complex network of religious sects, sectarian organizations, political bosses, and private militias. The latter are far more important in the political process than the former.

Iran is another example. Under the shah it had a constitution, parliament, one or two political parties, a cabinet, and government ministries; yet more important was the web of family ties and personal connections, relationships of trust and mutual benefit, that centered on the shah. Since the 1978-79 revolution such informal politics has continued, but with a new man at the center— the Ayatollah Ruhollah Khomeini. Around him is a network of confidants and loyal followers who supervise a system of revolutionary committees that have important decision-making powers and exist side by side with the government ministries.

In the Middle East in the nineteenth century, it was quite common for an autocratic ruler to modify the system of administration by establishing European-style ministries, particularly in the areas of Finance, Defense, Foreign Affairs, and Public Works. European legal codes were introduced to cover matters of commerce and trade and were gradually expanded to cover more areas, thus restricting the authority of the Sharia, the Islamic law. Some rulers promulgated constitutions and experimented with parliaments, generally not for very long, because they were used as a basis to challenge the ruler's absolute authority.

These changes have continued in the twentieth century, sometimes with dizzying rapidity, as in Egypt, which has had five constitutional documents since the revolution of 1952. However, these changes in the formal legal structures usually have not affected the informal nonlegal ones. The network of personal, family, and group relations and the structure of power have frequently stayed the same.

The change in structure has been much more rapid than the change in culture. It takes only a decree from the king or president to reorganize the administration. A new constitution can be put into effect through pronouncements by the head of state, followed by a controlled national debate and a referendum in which it is approved almost unanimously. The head of state and the cabinet can decide to introduce a European-style legal code. They can create new ministries, nationalized companies, and executive agencies. The army can be reorganized and equipped with the most modern weapons from Europe, the United States, or the Soviet Union.

Yet the leaders cannot so easily change the political culture. Frequently the result is that the structures are modern while the culture is traditional. The attitudes, values, and beliefs of the people are attuned to the Middle East and to Islam, while the structures are attuned to the West and are derived from Western rational-legal secular culture. The structures frequently have a short life span simply because they are not in congruence with the culture.

Groups

In every political system, there are groups that participate in politics and make demands on the political structures. Their leaders act as advocates and spokespersons vis-à-vis the government. They are of four types: (1) associational, (2) nonassociational, (3) institutional, and (4) anomic.[3]

Commonly called interest groups or pressure groups, *associational groups* comprise organizations specifically created to articulate an interest in the political process. They try to mobilize public opinion behind their particular political

---

[3]Gabriel A. Almond and James S. Coleman, eds., *The Politics of the Developing Areas* (Princeton, N.J.: Princeton University Press, 1960), pp. 33-34.

stand through traveling speakers, brochures, paid political advertisements, seminars, workshops, rallies, and conventions. They attempt to get elected to public office persons who share their viewpoints. They have "friends" in the bureaucracy whom they telephone frequently and with whom they eat lunch and correspond. Their representatives sit on government commissions and boards. Labor unions, professional associations, manufacturing syndicates, and organizations espousing a humanitarian cause are examples.

Except in Israel and Turkey, associational groups are still rather weak in the Middle East. Industrialization is just beginning, and a large, strong working class has not yet come into existence, so labor unions, when they are not prohibited by the government, are small, weak, and poorly organized. Professionals, such as engineers, economists, technicians, teachers, and doctors, are overwhelmingly government employees and are absorbed into the massive bureaucracy. Censorship is quite common, so interest groups do not have the opportunity to mobilize opinion through the press. The radio and television networks are government-owned and operated, so these channels of communication are not available. Elections are often supervised by a powerful national leader, and thus interest groups cannot use them legitimately to get "their man" into office.

Nonassociational groups form the second category. They are communities of people tied together by kinship, race, nationality, language, or religion. Persons are born into the group and, for the most part, identify with it their entire life. They associate primarily with members of the group, defend it from criticism, and sometimes take up arms in its defense.

In the contemporary world, political conflict rooted in racial, national, or religious differences is a problem that confronts developed and developing nations alike. In the United States there is discord between Blacks and Whites, in Canada between the French-speaking and English-speaking segments of the population, in Northern Ireland between Catholics and Protestants.

The Middle East has a multiplicity of such conflicts: between the Greeks and Turks, the Armenians and Turks, and between the Kurds and the Turks, Arabs, and Iranians. The Israelis and the Palestinians are extremely hostile to each other. The dominant group in Lebanon is the Maronites, a Christian Community affiliated with the Roman Catholic Church; since 1975 they have been locked in a violent civil war with the Palestinians and the Lebanese Muslims. In both Syria and Turkey a Muslim minority (called in Arabic the *Alawis* and in Turkish the *Alevis*) has been in conflict with the Sunni Muslim majority. In Israel, there is social strife between Jews of European ancestry (Ashkenazim) and those who come from Mediterranean and Middle Eastern areas (Sephardim). In this same country the Jewish majority is at odds with the Arab minority. In Iran there is tension between the dominant nationality group, the Persians, and such minorities as the Kurds and the Turks.

Social change often exacerbates these group cleavages. One group will become more modernized or Westernized than the others. Its members will be more educated and prosperous, and they will hold a higher percentage of the important positions in government and the economy, thus producing resentment among other groups. Two conspicuous examples of this are the Maronites in Lebanon and the Ashkenazim in Israel.

Institutional groups are the third category. They are composed of professionally qualified persons and are formally organized for a purpose other than politics, yet they do articulate interests and make demands on the political structures. The military and the civil bureaucracy are prominent examples. Though the mission of the former is national defense and of the latter the administration and implementation of policies made by the political leaders, both compete for larger government appropriations and more power and authority. This phenomenon is aptly labeled "bureaucratic politics."

In most Middle Eastern states, the armed forces and the civilian bureaucracy are large and powerful. Their members are well paid and highly educated; they have the security of lifetime employment, and they enjoy high social status. Large numbers have lived in Western nations, and they know how to operate the sophisticated technological machinery of the Western world. The growth and influence of the military and the bureaucracy can be attributed to the Soviet-American rivalry and each side's cultivation of client states in the Middle East, the numerous international conflicts in the region, and the desire of most states of the region to modernize and develop their economies. Given these factors, it is not surprising that many of the states in the Middle East are dominated by the military and the civil bureaucracy.

The fourth type are *anomic groups*. They are spontaneous, unplanned, and largely unorganized outbreaks in the political system, such as riots, demonstrations, strikes, and armed guerrilla activity. Though disruptive, such groups are a means by which dissatisfied people can articulate interests, and frequently they do result in startling reversals of government policies or changes in the political leadership. A crippling strike of oil workers and government employees, massive demonstrations, and urban guerrilla robberies, threats, and assassinations were primary factors leading to the collapse in Iran of the regime of the shah. Demonstrations and protest marches are a principal means that the Palestinians living on the West Bank use to vent their grievances against the Israeli authorities. Nationwide demonstrations and riots have taken place in Egypt at sporadic intervals, a serious one occurring January 1977 over a government decision to end subsidies on staple foods and basic consumer items, a decision which was reversed. Assassinations, robberies, and civil disturbances emanating from conflicts between rightist and leftist paramilitary organizations have been common in Turkey since the 1960s.

Leadership

In all political systems there are some persons at the top who have more influence than others in the determination of policies and the allocation of resources. Popularly referred to as the power elite, the establishment, oligarchy, and ruling circles, they exist in democratic and authoritarian, developed and developing societies.

Sociologists and political scientists analyze the leadership stratum to determine the degree of continuity and change in it. They want to know whether it is closed or open, whether new persons are able to join it, and how. They are interested in the number of military officers, both on active duty and retired from the service, who hold important positions. They examine the list of people who have filled cabinet positions to find out if they are traditional leaders of a nationality or religious group, leaders of a modern political movement or party, or nonpolitical technocrats from the bureaucracy and the free professions.

Middle Eastern elites are, for the most part, quite insecure. Monarchs are rapidly becoming extinct, and except for the sheiks of small states in the Persian Gulf, only three are left: King Khalid of Saudi Arabia, Hussein of Jordan, and Hassan of Morocco. The military leaders who sometimes accede to power in their place have no greater stability, and one army clique follows another.

Changes in leadership often result in drastic alterations in a country's domestic and foreign policies. A less pro-Western stance is taken, the negotiating position with the international oil companies and the consuming countries becomes tougher, or land reform and the nationalization of businesses are instituted at home. The state adopts one or another of the various forms of socialism, Marxism, or modern Islam.

Policies

Governments make basic decisions, not in the issuance of one decree, the enactment of one law, the institution of a new regulation, but in the *stream* of decrees, laws, and regulations that emanate from them over a significant period of time involving matters such as: Is the state to be officially designated as socialist, democratic, Islamic, or something else? Shall it have a one-party or multi-party system, or shall it function without political parties? Shall the state support and defend religion, be neutral towards it, or militantly combat it? What shall be the role of the private and public sectors in the economy, and which shall the government favor? What shall be the form of taxation, and who shall be heavily taxed? What type of weapons shall the country buy, whom shall it be prepared to fight against, and with whom shall it ally itself?

Decisions on questions such as these affect one or another group adversely or favorably. The military officer corps may receive higher salaries and fringe benefits and may get new weapon systems with which to work. State funds may be used to support mosques and religious schools, thereby enhancing the status and influence of the clergy. State capital may be poured into industry rather than agriculture, to the benefit of engineers, technicians, and workers, and the detriment of peasants and farmers. In each case one group has benefited and another has lost out.

Policy decisions also affect the structures of the society. An old constitution is abolished and a new one instituted; the bureaucracy is reorganized; a modification or change is made in the legal system. And the culture is altered, for policies determine what the official ideology of the state is to be. That ideology is then pronounced over the state radio and television, taught in the schools, and indoctrinated into the soldiers.

CONCLUSION

In all political systems, but particularly in the Middle East, no component is static. The culture that is a part of the warp and woof of the society, the structures through which authoritative decisions are made, the groups that participate in politics, the leaders who make decisions, and the policies that they institute are in a continuing state of flux.

Middle East politics is not a calm, picturesque pond, well-contained with-in its banks and nonthreatening to people and land, but rather it is a turgid, noisy, rapidly moving stream that can barely be contained within its banks and menaces people and property. To portray this system requires the perspective of the motion-picture photographer, who wants the viewer to see the movement of objects and people, rather than that of the still photographer, who tries to capture the essence or charm of a given moment.

With this understanding of the region, we proceed to examine it. Part I of this book deals with the common phenomena that influence politics in all Middle Eastern countries. Part II examines in depth the politics of five well-known and closely studied states: Israel, Lebanon, Egypt, Iran, and Turkey. They represent the major nationalities of the area (Jewish, Arab, Iranian, and Turkish), include some of the top military and economic powers (Turkey, Iran, Egypt, and Israel), and encompass the three largest states in terms of population (Turkey, Egypt, and Iran). They are representative, but not exhaustive, and some obviously important states have been left out.

Chapter 2

The Influence of Geography on Society and Polity

A photo of the Middle East taken from a space satellite reveals with brilliant clarity seven large bodies of water, great expanses of desert, high mountains, and wide plateaus. The Atlantic Ocean, the Mediterranean Sea, the Black Sea, the Caspian Sea, the Persian Gulf, the Arabian Sea, and the Red Sea are highly visible. The Sahara and the desert of the Arabian Peninsula are dominant, as are deserts in Syria and Iran. Piercing the photo are the Atlas Mountains of Morocco, the Pontic and Taurus Mountains of Turkey, the Elburz and Zagros Mountains of Iran, the Lebanon Mountains in Lebanon, and high mountains in Yemen. The two major plateaus are situated in Turkey and Iran.

If you look for people and greenery, you discover that both are heavily concentrated, like tiny islands in the desert or thin strips along the coasts of the Mediterranean Sea, Aegean Sea, Black Sea, and the southern shore of the Caspian Sea. The greenery and the people are also concentrated in the valleys of the Nile, Tigris, and Euphrates Rivers, and next to the mountain ranges.

If the space camera were capable of seeing underground, it would detect enormous pools of oil and natural gas around the Persian Gulf, the city of Mosul in Iraq, and in the Sahara in Libya and Algeria.

Just as the insular nature of Britain has influenced its social and political development, these geographic features have influenced the society and politics of the Middle East. For Britain, the oceans protected it from foreign conquerors and provided a sense of security that made military government unnecessary and allowed for the development of the fragile systems of common law and parliamentary democracy. They also enabled Britain from the sixteenth through the twentieth centuries to establish an overseas empire that girdled the globe.

In the Middle East, the desert has easily been traversed by conquering armies from different nations (Persians, Arabs, Mongols, Turks), making the region a melting pot for all of the world's civilizations. The desert has also divided the region, separating Iraq from Egypt, Egypt from Tunisia, and Tunisia from Morocco. The mountains of the Middle East have served as a refuge for persecuted minorities and the plateaus have protected the Turks and Iranians from national fragmentation. The plethora of oil in very limited areas has brought much wealth to a few states, producing dangerous rivalries and disrupting centuries-old social and political patterns.

Straddling three continents at the very doorstep of powerful neighbors such as Western Europe, the Soviet Union, and China, the Middle East has experienced conquest in the past, and its residents have a fear of being conquered in the future. The reality and the dread of conquest have caused them to create political systems that have defense as their all-pervading goal rather than orderly improvement of society itself, and caused them to see in their powerful neighbors' actions greedy machinations rather than creative growth and movement. But the reality of conquest has also infused the Middle East with new peoples and ideas, producing a productive cross-fertilization, and the fear of it has stimulated Middle Easterners to engage in a healthy competition with their powerful adversaries.

"MIDDLE EAST" OR "NEAR EAST"

The very terms *Middle East* and *Near East* indicate the central location of the area in the geography of the Eastern Hemisphere. Both terms came into use in the days when "the sun never set on the British Empire." Great Britain was at one end of this planet, and China (the "Far East") was at the other end, with the area under study in this book in the "Middle," or "Near"-er to Britain than the Far East. *Near East* was the term used prior to World War II, especially in the nineteenth century, when it referred to relations between the European powers and the Ottoman Empire. During World War II, the term *Middle East* came into common usage, and it is now used interchangeably with *Near East*, although the former is predominant. Unlike terminology elsewhere in the Afro-Asian world, where the Gold Coast has become Ghana and the Far East has become East Asia in order to remove imperialist connotations, the term *Middle East* has not been dropped in favor of a term without an imperialist origin. The nations of the Middle East could not agree on another term, because any available historic one would connote the former dominance of one Middle Eastern people over another.

DEFINITION OF THE MIDDLE EAST

Wide differences of opinion exist among scholars and statesmen over what territory is included within the Middle East. These differences exist because this is an area spanning three continents that is defined by culture, not by geography. Cultural regions do not have distinct borders, as do geographical areas, which are delimited by mountain ranges, oceans, and rivers. Culture is a way of living that transcends geographical barriers whenever people feel the superiority of its ways and put it into practice in their lives. *Western Europe*, a geographical expression, denotes a fairly definite part of Europe, but *the West*, denoting the part of the world in which the culture of western Europe predominates, is far harder to define. In common usage it includes Canada, the United States, Australia, and New Zealand—all regions geographically separate from Western Europe; but normally it is not clear whether it also includes the Soviet Union, eastern Europe, and Latin America—all regions of the world where Western culture is strong.

The same problems are encountered in defining the Middle East. Scholars and statesmen agree that it is an area of the world in which Islamic culture predominates, but they divide into two camps in regard to the extent of the area. The "minimalists" say that it is the triangle formed by Turkey, Iran, and Egypt and all the countries inside it. This is the region of the world in which Islam was born and in which all the great Islamic empires had their capitals. It excludes the fringe areas of the Muslim world, in which Islam has only recently become established or which, throughout history, have only been loosely attached to the center of the Muslim world, if at all.

The "maximalists" start with this area and add to it all the Muslim areas of the world that are continguous to it: North Africa, Soviet Central Asia, Afghanistan, Pakistan, Cyprus, the Sudan, and Somalia on the Horn of Africa. However, they exclude Indonesia, Malaysia, and the Muslim regions of West Africa, because of their distance from the center of the Muslim world.

To this author, the Middle East comprises the Arab states plus Israel, Turkey, and Iran. This region includes all countries populated by the Arabs, the first believers in Islam, plus the homelands of the Turks and the Persians, two nations that have given Islam some of its greatest power and glory. The names of the countries included can be seen in Table 2-1 and in Map 1.

The Jewish state of Israel would appear to be left out of a definition of the Middle East that is based on the culture of Islam. However, when Islam is thought of as a civilization more than as a religion, such is not the case. Christian and Jewish minorities have lived in Muslim countries since the time of Muhammad, and while they have not believed in the faith he proclaimed, they have adopted the culture that emanated from it and have made major contributions to it in

TABLE 2.1. THE MIDDLE EAST: OIL, NATURAL GAS, LAND AREA, AND POPULATION

	Estimated proved reserves (1/1/1979)			
	Oil (thousand) barrels)	Gas (billion cu. ft.)	Area (sq. miles)	Population (1978 Estimates)
USA[a]	28,500,000	205,000	3,540,939	218,525,000
USSR[a]	71,000,000	910,000	8,649,489	260,750,000
Algeria	6,300,000	105,000	919,595	18,500,000
Bahrain	250,000	7,000	240	280,000
Egypt	3,200,000	3,000	386,661	39,500,000
Iran	59,000,000	500,000	636,296	34,200,000 (1977 E)
Iraq	32,100,000	27,800	167,924	12,350,000
Israel	10,000[b]	60[b]	8,019[c]	3,700,000
Jordan	—	—	37,738	2,080,000 (1977 E)
Kuwait	66,200,000	31,300	6,880	1,190,000
Lebanon	—	—	4,015	3,165,000
Libya	24,300,000	24,200	679,362	2,600,000 (1977 E)
Morocco	125	30	172,414	18,675,000
Neutral Zone[d]	6,480,000	5,000	3,560	—
Oman	2,500,000	2,000	82,030	850,000
Qatar	4,000,000	40,000	4,274	200,000
Saudi Arabia	165,700,000	93,900	829,995	9,800,000
Sudan	—	100	967,494	16,550,000 (1977 E)
Syria	2,080,000	1,500	71,498	8,000,000
Tunisia	2,300,000	6,000	63,170	6,400,000
Turkey	360,000	500	301,380	43,120,000
United Arab Emirates[e]	31,316,000	21,600	32,278	656,000
Yemen[f]	—	—	75,290	7,300,000
Yemen[g] Democratic	—	—	111,074	1,850,000
Totals for Middle East	406,096,125	868,990	5,561,187	230,966,000
World Totals	641,607,825	2,502,010	58,473,000	4,044,000,000 (1976 E)

SOURCES: For oil and gas reserves, *The Oil and Gas Journal* (Tulsa, Oklahoma), December 25, 1978, pp. 102-3; for area and population, *Information Please Almanac, 1979,* 33rd ed. (New York: Information Please Publishing, Inc., 1978), pp. 112-13.

[a] *Included for comparative purposes.*
[b] *Includes portion of Gulf of Suez formerly occupied by Israel.*
[c] *Excluding territory occupied in 1967 war.*
[d] *A territory along the coast of the Persian Gulf, formerly jointly owned by Kuwait and Saudi Arabia. In 1966, it was partitioned between them, and an agreement was reached to share its oil wealth equally.*
[e] *A confederation of seven sheikdoms on the Persian Gulf, formerly known as the Trucial States. It includes Abu Dhabi, Ajman, Dubai, Fujairah, Ras al-Khaimah, Sharjah, and Umm al-Quwain.*
[f] *Yemen Arab Republic (capital Sana), North Yemen.*
[g] *People's Democratic Republic of Yemen (capital Aden), South Yemen.*

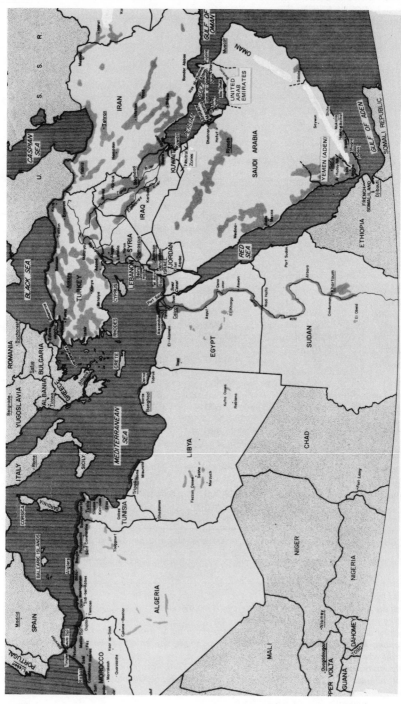

MAP 1. COUNTRIES AND POPULATION DENSITIES IN THE MIDDLE EAST. Population density above 40 per square mile is shown in gray tint. (Adapted from Manfred Halpern, *The Politics of Social Change in the Middle East and North Africa*, copyright © 1963 by the Rand Corporation. Reprinted by permission of the Princeton University Press.)

literature, philosophy, and science. In Lebanon, Christians are numerous and are economically and politically strong. Lebanese Christians speak Arabic, yet many also speak French or English and are very Westernized.

More than half the Jewish population of Israel consists of Oriental Jews who have migrated there from Morocco, Algeria, Tunisia, Egypt, Yemen, Iraq, and Syria since the establishment of the state in 1948. Their mother tongue has been Arabic, and their way of life has been similar to that of their former Muslim neighbors. Today they are living in Israel, speaking Hebrew, and adopting some aspects of the dominant European Jewish culture. However, as a result of their presence, Israel may, in fifty or a hundred years, be a predominantly Western state in its economic, social, and political structures, but markedly Middle Eastern in its language, cuisine, art, architecture, music, social life, and religion—a synthesis of the West and Middle East.

The mixing of cultures is not new in the Middle East. The Arabs absorbed the culture of Byzantium and Persia, the Turks that of the Arabs and the Persians, and the Persians (Iranians) that of the Mongols. In modern times all of them absorbed elements of the cultures of the French, the British, and the Americans.

Islam as a culture and civilization gives the Middle East its unity. Yet this is a civilization that has always been eclectic and has included nationality groups other than the Arabs who first believed in Islam and religious groups other than the Muslims. Jews have been a part of this civilization, and today a majority of the Jews in Israel have their ancestral roots in Muslim countries. Israel is Eastern and Western; in this sense it is no different from Lebanon, Egypt, Turkey, and Algeria. When Islam is thought of as a civilization and not so much as a religion, then Israel is a part of the Middle East on such a basis.

AN ARCHIPELAGO OF DESERT

The Middle East is a giant archipelago of desert and islands of population stretching 4,150 miles from Casablanca, on the shores of the Atlantic, to Mashad, Iran, on the border of the steppes of Central Asia. About 231 million people live here. However, they are not spread out evenly but are clustered together in "islands" surrounded by an uninhabited sea of desert. Some of the population islands such as the Nile Valley are equal in density of habitation to the most densely populated areas of the world. Off these islands, there live only a handful of the legendary bedouins, "the seafarers of the desert." These islands can be clearly seen on Map 1.

Fresh water created the population islands. It is the most valuable commodity in the Middle East, more necessary for life than oil, and people have settled where it is available either from rain or rivers. It comes in the form of rainfall in the Atlas Mountains of Morocco, the mountains of Yemen, and along the coast of the Mediterranean in Algeria, Tunisia, Israel, Lebanon, Syria, and Turkey. Along the coast of the Black Sea in Turkey and the southern shore of the Caspian Sea in Iran, the rain is extremely heavy and produces a humid climate and dense vegetation.

Rivers and streams are another source of water. Rivulets form in the high mountains, become mighty rivers that flow through hundreds of miles of desert unfed by any tributaries, and grow smaller and smaller, more and more saline, till they finally reach the sea or disappear in the desert. The largest, the Nile, is typical; it originates in the heights of Uganda, and from there flows thirty-five hundred miles to the Mediterranean Sea, the last nineteen hundred miles, from Kartoum northward, being through total desert. Along the banks of these rivers people have been settled since the beginning of human civilization, cultivating the rich soil by means of irrigation.

THE DESERT AS A CAUSE OF UNITY AND DISUNITY

As the sea in an archipelago separates and unites the islands, the desert in the Middle East separates and unites the population islands. The sea isolates the islands of an archipelago, yet with a small amount of preparation and some care, persons can navigate it in small boats. The desert is almost the same; by the storing of provisions and with careful planning, people can traverse it. Thus, the desert or the sea is both a barrier to, and an avenue of, contact. While mountains are sometimes an almost insuperable barrier, deserts and the sea are formidable but passable barriers.

The desert has brought a certain unity and a certain disunity to the Middle East. The people live apart, but the adventurous or ambitious can leave their homes and "see the world." The duty of Muslims once in their lifetime to make the pilgrimage to Mecca and Medina has been a powerful spur to travel. Well-equipped armies have always been able to cross the desert and carry out conquests. Desert caravans carrying spices, silks, precious metals, and gems are part of the lore and history of the region. For the adventurous person or the dynamic state, the desert is no barrier, but for the population as a whole, the desert is a barrier, producing provincialism and regional differences, suspicions and rivalries.

However, the mountains of the Middle East have only brought disunity to the area. In their heights resistant populations have been able to preserve either their language or their religion against the onslaught of Islam or Arabism. As an example, the Iranian plateau has been a major factor enabling the Iranians to keep their own Persian language, stemming back thousands of years prior to Islam. The mountains of northern Iraq, eastern Turkey, and northwestern Iran have enabled the Kurds to preserve their own language while accepting the religion of Islam, and the high mountains of Lebanon have helped the Maronites to maintain their own distinctive Christian faith while adopting the Arabic language. In North Africa, the Berber language has been preserved in the mountains, while Arabic has taken over in the lowlands, even though both areas have changed to the religion of Islam. Both Islam and Arabism originated with Muhammad in the lowlands of Medina and have spread across the plains of the Middle East, only to meet resistance when they have met the mountains.

The present-day borders of the Middle Eastern states are in part natural divisions between the different population islands, and in part they are unnatural divisions, being simply compromises made by the imperialists in their scramble for colonies in the nineteenth and twentieth centuries. The borders of Turkey and Iran lie fairly close to the natural boundaries of great plateaus. Iraq and Egypt consist primarily of the population islands formed by great river valleys, and Morocco is clustered around the Atlas Mountains. However, in the Levant,[1] the borders of Palestine (now Israel), Trans-Jordan (now Jordan), Syria, and Lebanon conform to no natural barriers and can only be explained by the imperialist scramble for colonies just after World War I.

France desired control of the region approximating present-day Syria and Lebanon. The basis of its claim was its close association for centuries with some Christian minorities in this area. The British desired a buffer zone west of the Suez Canal, so the two sides agreed during World War I upon a line between Acre and Tyre eastward and then northeastward, with the French taking the region to the north and the British, the region to the south. France then divided its territory into Syria and Lebanon, the latter being set up as a country that the Christians could control. Britain separated its domain at the Jordan River into Palestine and Trans-Jordan, allowing Jews to settle in the former but not in the latter.

Of all the states of the Middle East, Jordan is the least "natural." It is a part of the sparsely populated desert that spreads from the Taurus mountains in Turkey to the Arabian Sea, and logically belongs to Syria or Saudi Arabia. Historically, it has never had an independent identity. After World War I British authorities created Trans-Jordan and put on its throne an Arab ruler, Abdallah, who had aided them in the struggle against Turkey, an ally of Germany and Austria.

The creation of borders in the Levant without much regard for the interests or desires of the local people has contributed greatly to the instability of domestic and international politics in this region. The citizens of each state have had difficulty accepting the "naturalness" of their own state and the right of other states to exist. This is one of the root causes of the Arab-Israeli conflict.

---

[1] The lands bordering the eastern coast of the Mediterranean, especially Lebanon, Syria, and Israel, are known as the Levant.

THE MIDDLE EAST: CROSSROADS OF
THE EASTERN HEMISPHERE

The Middle East is at the center of the Eastern Hemisphere and touches each of its continents: Europe, Asia, and Africa. On its periphery are powerful nations that have throughout history conquered portions of it. In the eleventh and twelfth centuries, the Crusaders came from western Europe; from the eleventh through the fourteenth centuries, the Turks immigrated from Central Asia; in the thirteenth century, the Mongols swept in, also from Central Asia; and in the nineteenth and twentieth centuries, the Russians moved down from northeastern Europe, and the French and British came across the Mediterranean from western Europe.

While the Middle East has suffered from destruction wrought by its conquering neighbors, it also has benefited from the infusion of fresh ideas, dynamic leadership, and new institutions. For example, the Mongols destroyed the irrigation system of the Tigris-Euphrates Valley and sacked Baghdad, but they brought a strong administration, mighty armies, and a Chinese influence on Islamic art and architecture. The British and the French extracted huge profits from the Middle East through the exchange of its raw materials for their industrial products, the granting of loans to the local governments, and the establishment and operation of businesses, but they also brought to the region technical knowledge, modern systems of administration and law, new principles of government, and different social and literary ideas.

At the present time, the two greatest powers of the world converge on the Middle East—the United States through its fleet in the Mediterranean, its troops in western Europe, and its dominant role in NATO and CENTO, and the Soviet Union through its extensive borders on the Middle East, its Black Sea and Mediterranean fleets, its economic and military aid to some Arab states, and its influence over Bulgaria and Rumania. Prior to World War II, the West had nearly absolute sway in respect to forms of government, political ideology, economic systems, and social institutions, and it directly or indirectly controlled the political processes in almost all of the countries of the Middle East. Since World War II, Western nations have been involved in a struggle with the Soviet Union to maintain a remnant of political influence and to preserve the supremacy of the social and political institutions and ideals which, with modifications, many of the local countries have adopted.

PETROLEUM AND POPULATION

As can be seen in Table 2-1, oil is the natural mineral resource that the Middle East has in superabundance. In 1978, it possessed 63 percent of the world's proven reserves. Saudi Arabia alone has more than five times the proven reserves of the United States. With respect to natural gas, Iran's reserves are second only to those of the Soviet Union, and they are more than double those of the United States.

Oil is not evenly distributed; generally it is discovered where there is no fresh water. Since the population and civilization of the Middle East have been concentrated near water, oil is found in the least populated and most backward areas. For example, Saudi Arabia is the Middle Eastern state richest in oil reserves, but has a population of only 9.8 million; and Kuwait, the second richest in oil, has a population of only 1.190 million (see Table 2.1). Both are desolate desert, and while Saudi Arabia has some rainfall and oases, Kuwait has absolutely no fresh water and must obtain it by desalinizing sea water.

Since oil tends to be where people are not, several states have more capital than they can fruitfully consume and invest internally. With their surplus they buy bonds, notes, certificates, and real estate in Western Europe and the United States, and increasingly they are using it to promote economic development in the Arab world and in some selected countries in Asia and Africa.

Established in 1961 for this purpose, the Kuwait Fund for Arab Economic Development has become a model. It gives out development loans for projects that will improve the infrastructure or the industrial and agricultural base of the recipient country's economy, such as oil and gas pipelines, electric generating plants, and large-scale irrigation projects. It also gives grants for economic surveys and technical assistance programs. Its staff is composed of economists and financial experts from many Arab countries, not just Kuwait. Saudi Arabia, Abu Dhabi, and Iraq have followed the example of Kuwait and have established similar funds.[2]

In addition, regional international organizations award development loans. The Arab Fund for Economic and Social Development was founded in 1968 and began its operations in 1973. It is affiliated with the League of Arab States but has a separate administrative structure. It has its headquarters in Kuwait, which aids in coordination of policies and interaction of personnel between it and the Kuwait Fund. There are also the Islamic Development Bank, established in 1974 with headquarters in Jiddah, Saudi Arabia, and the Arab Bank for Economic Development in Africa, established in 1974 with headquarters in Khartoum, Sudan. Capital from the oil-rich states is the primary source of money for all of these funds.

The capitals of states with large oil reserves are now financial centers of power rivaling the old centers of political power on the population islands. Kuwait, Riyadh, and Abu Dhabi are now as important as Cairo, Damascus, and Baghdad. No longer are they backwaters under the hegemony of the latter; rather, they are international capitals in the world of oil, finance and politics, making decisions that have a traumatic effect on the economics of the non-communist world. Sometimes they act like kind, rich uncles to their less well-off Arab nephews and nieces; at other times they behave like younger brothers who are jealous of the political and military power of their older Arab brothers and eager to overtake them.

---

[2]For a study of the Kuwait Fund in particular, see Robert Stephens, *The Arabs' New Frontier* (Boulder, Colorado: Westview Press, 1976).

Chapter 3

The Nations
of the Middle East

Prior to modern times, Muslims viewed the world as consisting of two parts: the House of Islam and the House of War. The former included the territories that had Muslim rulers and in which the Sharia (Islamic law) prevailed. The latter denoted those territories that had not accepted Islam, that were perversely resisting it, and even fighting against it. The "believers" were obligated to wage a jihad ("religious war") against these territories until they were brought under the rule of Islam. Arabs, Iranians, Turks, Kurds, all participated, and it did not matter that they spoke different languages or had different cultures; they were all Muslims united behind their Muslim ruler, fighting against the heretics.

Islamic civilization had as its common core the faith communicated to mankind by Muhammad, but it also had cultural diversity. Each nation that adhered to Islam added to the wealth of knowledge and insights of the others, producing a civilization that was transnational in scope but Islamic in substance. An educated Muslim learned Arabic, the language of religion; Persian, the language of philosophy and literature; and, in the days of the Ottoman Empire, Turkish, the language of administration. He did not bother himself with a European language, the medium of communication of a heretical religion and an alien civilization.

Today this feeling of cultural universality centered in a common religious identity is lost. Most Arabs regard the Turks as heretics because they have secularized their state and greatly reduced the social role of Islam, and the Arabs still have bitter memories of their four centuries of eclipse under Ottoman rule. The Iranians feel that their imperial and cultural grandeur, extending back several centuries before Islam, makes them unique. It is rare for an Arab to study in a Turkish university or a Persian in an Arab one, but only a century ago this was common. Clearly, there is not much unity today in the House of Islam, and the separate nations are each becoming the font of culture, the focus of individual loyalties, and the creator of social order.

NATION AND STATE

John Stuart Mill said that a nation is a portion of mankind "united among themselves by common sympathies, which do not exist between them and any others, [and] which make them co-operate with each other more willingly than with other people . . . ."[1] There is a feeling of oneness among the people, most often produced by a common language, which enables them to communicate with each other to the exclusion of others. It produces a feeling of "we" and "they."

Another factor that can produce a feeling of oneness is a territory that a people believe is theirs by right, because it is the place where their ancestors were born and where they have lived from as far back as history reaches. This place is called the fatherland or homeland, words expressing the familial myths that reinforce national feeling. Further elements strengthening the feeling of oneness are a culture that the people have created and preserved, a history that they have all shared, and possibly a common religion. But all of these elements need not be present, as can be seen in Switzerland, where the people speak four different languages, Israel, which prior to 1948 did not possess its homeland, and Germany, where the people adhere to the Protestant and Catholic faiths.

A state is something different from a nation. It is a legal entity, recognized by other states as being equal to them and sovereign, and possessing a government that rules over a people in a clearly defined territory. In international affairs, states, not nations, carry on relations with each other; they exchange ambassadors and send representatives to the United Nations; they make treaties with one another, and they declare war and make peace.

The ideal of nineteenth- and twentieth-century nationalist authors and leaders has been the *nation-state*, an entity in which nation and state live together in a symbiotic relationship. The state, through its government, perpetuates the language, history, and culture of the nation in the public schools and state-

---

[1] John Stuart Mill, *Considerations of Representative Government* (New York: Holt, Rinehart & Winston, 1882), p. 308.

supported museums; it defends the fatherland with its army, and it frequently protects the dominant religion. The nation causes the people to identify with the state and be loyal to it.

One of the strengths of Turkey, Iran, and Israel is that they combine nation and state, while the crucial weakness of the Kurds is that they are a nation without a state and are living in four states not their own: Turkey, Syria, Iraq, and Iran. A source of weakness for Lebanon, Jordan, and Syria is that many of their citizens have little attachment to the state, because they regard themselves as Arabs, not Lebanese, Jordanians, or Syrians. For a long time, Egypt has struggled with the question of whether it is Arab or Egyptian, and within the past two decades the state has been successively named the Republic of Egypt, the United Arab Republic (even after the breakaway of Syria), and is now the Arab Republic of Egypt.

The distinction between nation and state is rather important in the Middle East. From 1919 to 1938, Kemal Ataturk led the Turkish people in a movement whereby they abandoned the multinational Ottoman Empire and formed the nation-state of Turkey. In 1948, the goal of Zionists to establish a state for the Jewish people in their homeland was realized. Since achieving independence, the Arabs have struggled with the question of whether they constitute a nation that should be united into one state. Numerous plans have been put forward for a united Arab state or a union of two or more Arab states; one attempt towards this end was the United Arab Republic, a union of Syria and Egypt, which lasted from 1958 to 1961. Since 1975, a civil war has been raging in Lebanon, and one major issue is whether there is a "Lebanese nation" and whether a state can be formed among the diverse and antagonistic peoples who inhabit the territory called Lebanon.

In the negotiations between Israel and the Arab states over a peace settlement, a crucial issue is whether the Palestinians are a people who should live in a sovereign state of their own on the West Bank of the Jordan, or whether some other type of political entity should be formed there for them.

In summary, a state is an entity that has formal sovereignty and is so recognized by other states. A nation is something around which collective emotions revolve and may or may not be united within a state. Country is a much looser term and is used to refer to both nations and states.

THE ARAB NATION

The Arab people belong to various races and religions, and live from Morocco to Iraq and from Syria to Oman and Yemen. They are bound together by the Arabic language and civilization. Prior to Muhammad, they inhabited only the

Arabian Peninsula and were of one ethnic stock, but after his death, they conquered peoples from the shores of the Atlantic to the edge of the Iranian plateau and became a mélange of all races, from the deepest black of some Sudanese to the purest white of some Levantines. Many of the areas conquered had been strongholds of Christianity and also had contained large Jewish communities. Over the centuries, many Christians and some Jews became converts to the new Islamic faith, but large numbers did not. While the Jews and Christians rejected the religion of Islam, they adopted the Arabic language and were assimilated into Arab civilization.

Prior to Muhammad, Arabic was used only by the tribes of the Arabian Peninsula and was, for all practical purposes, a spoken language only. However, with the revelation to Muhammad of the Koran, the Arabic language underwent a development that made it significant as a medium of literary and scholarly expression. Arabic was regarded by Muslims as the language of God. According to Muslims, God revealed the Koran to Muhammad in the Arabic language. Since it is literally God's word, they believe that it should not be translated. To them, it became absolute dogma that both the form and the content of the Koran were perfect, and they memorized and studied it to learn both. Arab non-Muslims studied it for form alone. Muslims and non-Muslims praised and imitated the Arabic in the Koran and regarded deviations from it as poor style and irreverence towards God. The nearest equivalent in the English language would have been to so venerate the style of the King James translation of the Bible that it would have been slavishly followed by all subsequent writers.

While the perfection of the language of the Koran introduced a rigidity into Arabic, it also preserved it from linguistic fragmentation. Dialects of Arabic had developed in the population islands of the Arab world, but because of the feverish commitment of Muslims to preserve the Koran in its God-given form, these dialects never became written languages. Today, although the Arab nation is divided by dialects, some of which are mutually unintelligible, it is still united by one written language derived from the Koran.

For roughly seven hundred years, from about A.D. 700 to 1400, the Arab world was a center of political power, military might, international commerce, religious and philosophical inquiry, scientific discovery, and technological advance. Persons from all over the world came to Arab universities to study. The refinement of the Indian-derived Arabic numeral system, the preservation of the classics of Greek literature and philosophy and the writing of commentaries on them, the expansion of the world's knowledge of pharmacy and medicine, the development of the sciences of astronomy and mathematics, the creation of new art forms in poetry, calligraphy, and architecture were major accomplishments of the Arabs of this period. They are a source of pride for contemporary Arabs, who want to make similar contributions to the civilization of the world in the present.

Arab Nationalism and Islam

Prior to modern times, Arab national identity and Islamic religious consciousness were hardly distinguishable. Muhammad brought unity to the Arab tribes of the Arabian Peninsula for the first time in their history, and revealed to all mankind God's message in the Koran. Arabic was the spoken and written language of the Arabs, as well as the scriptural and liturgical language of Muslims, whatever their mother tongue. The first Arab national heroes were men such as Khalid ibn al-Walid, who died in 648; he conquered Syria from the Byzantines, not for the cause of Arabism but for Islam.

In the latter part of the nineteenth century, Christian Arabs in particular began to distinguish between Arab national identity and Islam. Some Christian intellectuals led an Arab literary revival that reawakened awareness of Arab literature, poetry, and philosophy from the period prior to the Turkish ascendance over the Middle East. These intellectuals felt themselves to be Arab in culture and Christian in religion; for them Muhammad was not a religious personage but the first national leader of the Arabs who revealed a religion that influenced every aspect of Arab culture. For them the submersion of Arab national identity in Islamic universalism was a typical pattern of the medieval period, as was also true in Europe where Christianity prevailed over French, British, English, or other national identities. But they believed that in modern times religion and nationalism should be separate, and allegiance to the nation should prevail over loyalty to a religious group.

However, this secular-nationalist position has not become dominant. In almost all Arab states, Islam is constitutionally the religion of the state and is supported by it. Laws exist prohibiting conversion from Islam to another faith, but not vice versa. Islam is taught in the state schools, sometimes to non-Muslims. The mosques, Islamic seminaries, and clergy are financially supported and supervised by the state. Often a nation's constitution requires that the head of state be a Muslim. For centuries the Muslim formula has been "religion and state," and, except in Lebanon, this continues to be in effect today.

Arab Unity[2]

It is puzzling that Arab nationalism is very strong, yet the possibilities for the political unity of the Arab states are very weak. Books and pamphlets on Arab nationalism proliferate; the advocates of nationalism abound; the words "Arabism," "Arab unity," "Arab nationalism," and the "Arab nation" are among the most common in the Arabic vocabulary. The Arabs speak the same language, are mostly of the same religion, and have a shared history and culture.

[2]Joel Carmichael, *The Shaping of the Arabs: A Study in Ethnic Identity* (New York: Macmillan, Inc., 1967), pp. 371-74.

They appear to be more unified than Western Europeans, though the latter have more institutions that unify them politically and economically than the Arabs. Why?

The reasons are numerous: geography, which divides the Arab world into population islands; the maldistribution of oil wealth, which splits it between "have" and "have-not" states; and the gross disparities in social and political development between the "traditional" states and the "modern" ones. There is also outside intervention. In the nineteenth century Britain forced Muhammad Ali, ruler of Egypt from 1805 to 1849, to surrender his conquests in Syria. If this had not been done, he might have established a greater Arab state through military might, as Bismarck did in Germany. On March 8, 1920, the Arabs proclaimed an independent kingdom in Syria, with Damascus as its capital and Faisal as its monarch, but five months later it was destroyed by the French, who took Lebanon and Syria under their rule. Since World War II the United States has been protecting King Hussein and his Kingdom of Jordan, because it feels that he brings more stability to the area than would a state controlled by the Palestinians. Israel gives its approval to this policy.

Other reasons for Arab disunity are that unity has been a cause to which politicians repeatedly proclaim their devotion, but for which they are unwilling to sacrifice some of their power, wealth, or independence. Efforts at bringing about unity in nonpolitical spheres, such as economic integration, improvement of intraregional communication and transportation, unification of armed forces, development of a common arms industry, and unification of the legal systems have produced few tangible results. Also power is highly centralized and personalized in the Arab states, and personality differences create insurmountable obstacles to unification. Currently President Sadat of Egypt and President Qaddafi of Libya have a deep personal dislike of each other. President Nasser (1918-1970) of Egypt and King Faisal (born circa 1906, died 1975) of Saudi Arabia found each other similarly distasteful.

THE TURKISH NATION

The Turks speak Turkish and live in Turkey. They formerly lived in central Asia, but beginning in the eleventh century migrated in successive waves into Anatolia; in the fourteenth century they began to move into Europe. A Turkish dynasty, the Ottomans, founded an empire that included Greece and the Balkans, North Africa (except Morocco), Egypt, the Arabian Peninsula, the Tigris-Euphrates Valley, Syria, and Palestine. When the Turks lived in central Asia, they were infidels, but as they moved westward, they adopted Islam as their religion.

The Ottoman Empire encompassed people of many nationalities and of three major religions: Islam, Christianity, and Judaism. The Empire lasted from about 1300 until just after World War I. Its ruling class was Muslim, and the ruler called himself "sultan," which means "power." Until the late sixteenth century, the sultans were able and vigorous, attentive to the details of administration, and capable of inspiring in their subordinates the enthusiasm that could build and maintain a great empire. After that time, their ruling ability declined, their armies lost battle after battle, and they had to cede territory piece by piece. In the nineteenth century, the Empire was known as the "sick man of Europe," and finally collapsed during and shortly after World War I.

Turkish Nationalism and Islam

The Ottoman Empire's reason for being was Islam, but for modern Turkey it is the Turkish nation. The man who vigorously promoted this transition from a religiously-based empire to a secular nation-state was Kemal Ataturk (1881-1938). He wanted to destroy the influence of religion and of the ulama (Islamic religious scholars, teachers, preachers, and judges) over the social attitudes of the Turks and the political institutions of the country. The ulama were educated only in traditional religious subjects, such as classical Arabic, Koran interpretation, and the Sharia. For these men the modern world was strange and hostile —strange because it was largely Christian in its foundation, and hostile because it represented the ancient enemy of Islam. Ataturk wanted to modernize the Turkish society, economy, and political system. He felt that the ulama would oppose his reforms, so he closed their schools, brought them under the complete control of the government, and introduced a repression of Islam that did not end until 1950.

For Ataturk and his followers, Islam represented Arab cultural imperialism and Ottoman decadence. The Prophet of Islam was an Arab; the prayers, liturgy, Holy Book, and Holy Law were in Arabic, and pious Muslims would not translate "what God had written." The Turkish vocabulary was about one-third Arabic and Persian, and the Turks wrote their language in the Arabic script. Islam also had been intimately associated with the Ottoman Empire, which in its final days was weak and corrupt.

Ataturk desired to erase the cultural imprint of Islam and Arabism on the Turkish nation and restore it to its "pure" pre-Islamic status. The script in which Turks wrote was changed from the Arabic to the Latin, and an attempt was made to purge the language of its Arabic and Persian words. A law was passed requiring that the language of the call to prayer and of the worship service in the mosque be Turkish rather than Arabic.

These attempts to create a "pure" Turkish language and nation were strongest in the 1930s, but in the next decade, especially after World War II, they faltered. In the 1950s the government permitted the call to prayer to be said in Arabic once again, allowed Koran recitations on the state radio, and authorized the use of public funds for the building of mosques. In general it relaxed religious oppression. Since then a return to the militant secularism and nationalism of the Ataturk era has not been attempted.

Secularists who feel that Turkish nationalism should have nothing to do with Islam are still numerous and occupy powerful positions in Turkey, but probably a majority of the people feel that the Turkish national spirit cannot be divorced from Islam. The two groups constantly argue, debate, and attempt to impose their will on one another.

THE IRANIAN NATION[3]

The Iranians (Persians) live on a plateau fifteen hundred to sixty-five hundred feet high, which is hemmed in by the Zagros Mountains on the southwest, the Elburz Mountains on the north, and great deserts on the east. As is the case throughout the Middle East, the mountains and desert have been a barrier to the invasion of outside forces, but they have not been an insurmountable one, and the Iranians have preserved a distinct national identity, while participating in the universal civilization of Islam.

They have a strong feeling of being one people on the basis of race. The Iranians are descendants of the Indo-European Aryans who settled in this area thirty-five hundred years ago, and they maintain that they have undergone far less racial intermixing than other Middle Easterners.

One way in which they distinguish themselves from the Arabs and the Turks is in their administration of powerful empires prior to their conversion to Islam. The two most famous empires were the Achaemenid and Sassanid. Under the Achaemenid Dynasty (550-330 B.C.), the Persians ruled from the Nile Valley and the Bosporus to the Indus River valley in contemporary Pakistan, and to the Amu Darya River in the present-day Soviet Union. The Achaemenid monarchs developed a noteworthy system of public works, a distinctive architecture, and an excellent imperial administration. The most famous kings were Cyrus the Great (died 529 B.C.) and Darius I (died 486 B.C.).

The Sassanid Dynasty arose in the third century A.D. and lasted until the Muslim conquest between 637 and 651. Under these rulers, the Persians once again controlled an extensive empire that included the Tigris-Euphrates Valley, the Iranian plateau, and the valleys of the Amu Darya and Indus Rivers. Under them, the Zoroastrian religion prospered and became the religion of the state. Its essential dogma was that the universe was ruled by two spirits: *Ahura Mazda*, the good spirit of light; and *Angra Mainyu*, the evil spirit of darkness.

[3] Much of this section is derived from Richard W. Cottam, *Nationalism in Iran* (Pittsburgh: University of Pittsburgh Press, 1964), pp. 23-32.

Under the Sassanids, Iranian art enjoyed a renaissance, and there are rock sculptures on limestone cliffs and ruins of palaces extant in Iran that testify to this.

A primary contributor to Iranian national consciousness has been the great epic poem *Shah Nameh* ("The Chronicle of Kings"), written about A.D. 1000 by Ferdosi. It is a collection of stories about the outstanding kings and national heroes of Iran and their struggles against the forces of evil. Battles, skirmishes, and single combats are vividly described, all in a patriotic way. There are splendid love stories in which paroxysms of passion alternate with those of despair. Ferdosi used very few Arabic words, since he was trying to revive the Persian language after three centuries of Arabic ascendancy. His efforts were successful, for his romantic, nationalistic poem is sung and recited in every village and city of Iran by persons of every social class, literate and illiterate.

The Safavid Dynasty (1501-1736), the first independent Persian dynasty since the Arab conquest in the seventh century, was the one most responsible for creating the conditions under which Iran could become a modern nation. It established Shiite Islam as the state religion, and elevated the shah to a semi-divine status. Persian poetry, literature, art, and philosophy were cultivated; dissident groups that threatened to fragment the country were kept under control; and the assaults of the Ottomans upon the nation's territory were kept to a minimum.

The most illustrious Safavid monarch was Shah Abbas I (1587-1629). He resembled the strong European monarchs prior to the French Revolution, such as Henry VIII, Louis XIV, and Peter the Great, who unified and strengthened their countries for personal and dynastic reasons, but whose actions laid the foundations of later national states. Shah Abbas glorified the former Persian empires and their great military achievements, a practice that Iran's recent ruler, Muhammad Reza Shah Pahlavi, continued.

Iranian Nationalism and Shiite Islam

Shiism, one of the two major divisions of Islam, is the national religion of Iran. Shiites believe that the Caliph, the successor of Muhammad and the leader of the community of Muslims, should be a lineal descendant of Ali, Muhammad's cousin and son-in-law. As a scion of the Prophet, they affirm that the Caliph receives from his predecessors a mysterious power and knowledge that make him infallible and enable him to be an intermediary between God and man.

By being Shiites, Iranians are different from other Muslim Middle Easterners. Most Arabs and almost all Turks adhere to Sunnism, the other major division of Islam. They have been the national enemies of the Iranians; in fighting against them, Iranians have also been opposing Sunnism.

Religion has thus been a way for the Iranians to show their national distinctiveness. In this respect they resemble the Poles, who have been hemmed in by two old enemies, Russia and Germany, one Orthodox, the other Protestant. The Poles remained Roman Catholic, and very fervent ones.

THE JEWISH NATION

Of all the nations in the Middle East, the Jews are among the smallest, yet have one of the longest and most turbulent of histories. They were enslaved in Egypt but escaped and settled in Palestine. They fluorished under a monarchy with such kings as Saul, David, and Solomon, but in 586 B.C. their capital city, Jerusalem, was razed along with its Temple and they were carried off in captivity to Babylon.

Roughly fifty years later, the Jews were freed by Cyrus, the Persian monarch, and allowed to return to their homeland, where they rebuilt Jerusalem and the Temple. In 332 B.C. they were conquered by Alexander the Great, and from then till A.D. 70 they were under the influence of empires and cultures centered in Greece or Rome. Several revolts took place under Roman rule, but the last and most important one began in A.D. 66 and by A.D. 70 resulted in the destruction of the Temple in Jerusalem and the razing of the city.

Most Jews left Palestine, though some remained; A.D. 70 marks the beginning of the *Galut* (exile), when Jews were dispersed throughout the Middle East and Europe with only a handful remaining in Palestine, or Eretz Israel. In the medieval and renaissance periods (sixth through seventeenth centuries), small numbers migrated back to the ancient homeland, but did so individually and as a religious act in order to live and die in the Holy Land. Collective migration to Palestine in order to reestablish a functioning Jewish community there began in the late nineteenth century and increased considerably in the 1930s and 1940s because of the persecution and slaughter of the Jews by the Nazis. In 1948 the modern state of Israel was established, and the Galut came to an end.

In exile the Jews were divided into three major groups. The first was the Ashkenazim, who lived in present-day Germany, Poland, and the USSR and spoke Yiddish, a German dialect written in Hebrew script. The second was the Sephardim, who dwelt in the Iberian Peninsula but were expelled by the Christians during the Grand Inquisition of the fifteenth century. They then settled in many areas of the world, particularly North Africa, France, and the Balkans, and spoke Ladino, a mixture of Spanish and Hebrew. The third group was the Orientals, who lived in the area from Iraq to Algeria and spoke Arabic.

The Jews did not speak their national language, Hebrew, using it only as a liturgical tongue. They were partially assimilated into the cultures in which they lived and mastered the local languages. Ashkenazim, Sephardim, and Orientals each formed their distinct Jewish cultures. Whever the Jews lived they were a minority group, continually under the threat of conversion, discrimination, and persecution.

Jewish Nationalism and Religion

Religion was the primary factor preserving Jewish national identity in exile. Although the Jews were located far apart from one another in places such as Poland, Germany, Morocco, Egypt, and Iraq, and although they had adopted many of the customs of the countries in which they lived, they practiced a common faith centered in the Torah, their most sacred book. Written in Hebrew, it was the medium that preserved the Hebrew language during the centuries that it was not spoken except in the synagogue. The Torah, along with other sacred writings, formed the Jewish Bible. It told stories of Jewish kings, gave accounts of Jews in battle, offered warnings by Jewish prophets, furnished the laws of the Jewish people, provided inspiring poetry and philosophy. All of these preserved a sense of Jewish national identity. Many of the religious holidays commemorated events in the history of the nation: Passover celebrated the deliverance of the people from slavery in Egypt, and Purim marked the escape of the Jews in Persia from a general massacre planned by an evil prime minister.

These factors, along with increased persecution by the Czarist government as manifested in numerous pogroms in Russia in the 1880s and 1890s, and the continuance of anti-Semitism in western Europe, as evidenced by the Dreyfus Affair in France (1894-1906), led to the development in the late nineteenth century of Zionism, the movement among Jews to return to Eretz Israel and establish a state there. Zionism was the Jewish counterpart of similar nationalist movements in Europe that were awakening oppressed peoples such as the Poles, Hungarians, Czechs, and Serbians. The difference was that the homeland for the Jews was outside Europe. Some Zionists were religiously motivated and looked upon the return to Israel as a part of God's divine plan. Others regarded it simply as a way to escape persecution and live safely in a nation-state of their own.

In present-day Israel, the role of religion in national life is highly controversial. Religious Jews believe that the state should enforce the Jewish religious laws. They have succeeded in having laws passed requiring that the Sabbath be observed as a day of rest, restricting the sale of nonkosher food, and placing marriage and divorce under the control of Orthodox rabbis. Secular Jews feel that the observance of religious laws should be a matter of voluntary compliance and resent the restrictions on individual liberty caused by them. The religious minority would like to go further to make Israel into a state that supports, preserves, and defends the Jewish religion, but the secularists resist. The result is a compromise, with neither able completely to get its way.

CONCLUSION

Formerly the political order in the Middle East was seen as having been ordained by God for the purpose of defending and furthering the Faith. In the Islamic system the true "citizens" were the "believers," and persons who did not believe

—Christians and Jews—were given secondary status. The heathen were even worse off. Individuals gained their sense of community from religion, and they gave their loyalty to the political structures that served their faith. A person was a Muslim, Christian, or Jew—not an Arab, Turk, or Iranian.

Today national consciousness is replacing religion as the source of political identity, but has not banished it totally from the political scene. Rather, religion is undergoing a metamorphosis and in some nations is emerging as a secondary element of nationalism. Individuals now think of themselves primarily as Arab, Turk, or Iranian, and secondarily as Muslim or Christian. They give their loyalty to a state that serves their nation, not to some supranational "divinely guided realm." Nationalism is supreme, but religion remains—reinterpreted and transformed, performing new political roles.

Chapter **4**

Social, Political, and Economic Development Since 1798

Geography, nationality, and religion give the Middle East both immense diversity and some uniformity. The people live on population islands in the midst of a sea of desert that divides and separates them, but also enables them to have a limited amount of contact. They speak different languages, believe in different religions, apply their religion to contemporary problems in contrasting ways, have dissimilar national histories and opposing conceptions of their nation's destiny.

In addition, different levels of social, political, and economic development contribute to the diversity of the Middle East. In 1798, the date historians agree is the beginning of the modern era in the Middle East, all of the countries in the region were roughly at the same level of development, but today they are not. Saudi Arabia is still partly a nomadic society in which the bedouin's mores, customs, and sense of justice predominate. Egypt, Turkey, and Iran are heavily urbanized, possess many modern industries, have large standing armies equipped with the latest weapons, and are amply supplied (perhaps oversupplied) with well-trained administrators. Their legal systems are based on those of Europe, though in Egypt and Iran a few concessions have been made to Islamic law.

While in most respects Israel is modern, there are aspects of the society and culture that are traditional. It has excellent universities, and its people excel at science and technology. They have formed labor unions, political parties, and professional, business, and commercial associations. Most Israelis live in cities or towns, and the minority who are engaged in agriculture inhabit modern communal settlements, not poverty-ridden villages. Israeli industry is advanced and highly technological, as are its armed forces. Yet the schism in the country about whether the state should enforce the Jewish religious law, and the economic and social gaps between Western and Oriental Jews and between the Jewish majority and the Arab minority are problems more typical of developing nations. Composed of peoples of diverse origins, Israel is both a developed and a developing nation.

The disputes between Turkey and the Arab states, between Israel and the Arab states, between Saudi Arabia and Egypt are as much the result of different levels of social, political, and economic development as of differences of nationality, religion, or history; the same factors are among the primary reasons why the Arab states themselves are unable to unite.

These different levels of development are mostly the result of varying degrees of contact with the West during the nineteenth and twentieth centuries. In certain countries the contact came early and has been deep and long-lasting. Because Turkey and Egypt straddle the Bosporus and the Isthmus of Suez respectively, they have been prime targets for European control, and Europe's influence has been extensive in the politics, economy, and culture of these Middle Eastern countries. Approximately half the inhabitants of Lebanon are Christians in whom European nations have for two centuries taken an interest, protecting them through special treaties, establishing schools and universities that catered to them, and giving them the opportunity to work for or enter into commercial relations with European companies. Algeria is close to France, and in 1830 France established a deep and enduring presence there, doing the same in Tunisia in 1881. Half of the Jewish population of Israel is of European origin, and they or their ancestors were in Europe when it was moving out of the medieval into the modern era. Countries such as Libya, Saudi Arabia, Syria, Iraq, and Iran have been less influenced by Europe, because they were less valuable strategically, had fewer natural resources, presented a smaller potential market for European goods, or were more inaccessible.

THE SEARCH FOR MODERNITY AND IDENTITY

In 1798 a French army under the command of Napoleon invaded and conquered Egypt for the purpose of cutting the British lifeline to India. By 1801 the army had completely evacuated Egypt, but its short stay had such a monumental impact on that country and on the Middle East that 1798 marks the beginning of the modern era in Middle Eastern history. Napoleon came to Egypt, not under the cross of Christ as did the Crusaders, but under the tricolor of the

French Revolution. His invasion was not another attack by Christendom, but rather the beginning of the penetration into the Middle East of the modern intellectual, social, and political ideas of Europe: the rational thinking of the Enlightenment, the scientific spirit that produced the Industrial Revolution, the glorification of the nation that was characteristic of the French Revolution, and the faith in the individual, belief in equality, and fear of authority that distinguished liberalism and democracy.

Prior to 1798 Islamic society had an identity and a self-sufficiency that gave a common purpose to all of its social and political institutions. Ruler and ruled accepted the Koran and the Sharia as the foundation of the social and political order. The overwhelming majority of the people believed in Islam, and fought and died for it. Every aspect of the people's daily life was touched by Islamic belief and practice.

But this society proved incapable of sustaining itself against the steady intellectual, economic, and military onslaught of the modern West. By 1920 every Middle Eastern country, except for "worthless" desert kingdoms, was under European economic or political control. The indigenous society was deprived of its independence but, more important, had lost its intellectual unity and the ability to sustain itself. The local rulers were not legitimate. The religion could not provide a code of ethics or a social order for modern living. Injustice and privilege were rampant, with either resident foreigners or the indigenous elite living above the law and in great luxury. The economic system could not satisfy the material needs of the people. The political system could not reconcile the conflicting interests and demands of the various groups in the society. Social development was haphazard, fragmented, and without a sense of direction.

Today the situation is only slightly improved. Formal independence has been gained, and the resident foreigners have left, but many of the states are still dependent on outside powers. The material wants of the people are more than the economy can provide. A privileged class still exists—no longer resident foreigners or indigenous landlords and capitalists, but a new class: the military-bureaucratic-technocratic elite. Governmental instability is endemic, and many governments can only maintain internal peace through authoritarian control and heavy doses of force. The sense of unity, wholeness, and self-sufficiency that characterized Islamic society prior to 1798 has not been regained.

A MODEL OF DEVELOPMENT

In order to analyze the social, political, and economic change that has been taking place in the Middle East since 1798, I have drawn up a four-stage model based on the components of a political system introduced in Chapter 1. An economic element has also been added. In each stage the elite in power attempts to produce a viable social, political, and economic order and in some respects fails, only to be succeeded by a new elite representing a new social group, which tries again. The change of elites and the advance to a new stage is always caused by an external "shock," a humiliating military defeat or some other "insult" to the national "honor." The old elite is discredited, and a new one takes over, trying to restore the national honor by rebuilding the military and reforming the social system, so that both will return power to the state. Since the Middle East is a crossroads where great powers meet and clash, and because of the Arab-Israeli struggle, Middle Eastern countries are more prone to these "shocks" than other countries in the world. Outlines of this model follow.

PERIOD 1: TRADITIONAL ISLAMIC SOCIETY

Economy　　Subsistence agriculture and crafts industry.

Culture　　Transcendental Islamic values and beliefs that assert that people, society, and politics must conform to God's will, as revealed in the Koran.

Structure　　Two separate sets of structures:

1. Despotic rulers (kings, shahs, sultans), separate from the people, with little interest in their welfare, and exercising only minimal authority over them. The major responsibility of these rulers was defense of the country and maintenance of Islam as the ruling faith.

2. Largely self-governing autonomous communities such as urban guilds, villages, tribes, and Christian and Jewish millets.[1] They had the major responsibility for maintaining social stability, allowing for orderly change, reconciling disputes, and airing grievances.

Groups　　Traditional kinship groups such as families, clans, tribes, villages, millets, and urban guilds.

Leadership　　Hereditary leaders such as kings, shahs, sultans, khans, and sheiks, or else usurpers who seized power by force.

Policies　　1. Of the despotic rulers: aggrandizement of their own wealth, and maintenance of their power.

2. Of the autonomous communities: maintenance of the status quo, particularly their autonomy vis-à-vis other communities and the ruler.

Shock　　Military defeats in the eighteenth and nineteenth centuries at the hands of the Europeans.

[1] A millet was a non-Muslim community organized under a religious head of its own who also exercised civil functions.

PERIOD 2: MODERNIZING AUTOCRATIC SOCIETY

Economy	Introduction of some cash crops, attempts at industrialization, construction of a few railroads, roads, and canals.
Culture	Same as Period 1.
Structure	Autocratic rulers (kings, shahs, sultans) who exercised considerable authority over the people since they possessed a modern standing army, a modern police force, and the ability to tax people directly. By appointment of the communal heads and by direct taxation, they deprived the urban guilds and villages of their former autonomy. They established the rudiments of a modern bureaucracy, especially in the areas of defense, finance, and foreign affairs.
Groups	1. Traditional kinship groups. 2. The Western-educated class such as military officers, lawyers, journalists, and writers.
Leadership	The autocratic rulers.
Policies	Aggrandizement of the military and economic power of the state.
Shock	Continued European interference in the affairs of the Islamic countries, and the outright conquest of some.

PERIOD 3: COLONIAL SOCIETY

Economy	Construction of more railroads, roads, and canals. Production of raw materials for export to the colonial power, and the importation of manufactured goods from it.
Culture	Two cultures in conflict: 1. The traditional Islamic culture of Periods 1 and 2. 2. A Western secular culture, which had as its hallmarks rationality, humanism, efficiency, and technology.
Structure	Two systems of administration existing side by side, with the first having authority over the second: 1. The colonial bureaucracy, in which all the top positions were held by foreigners. It was concerned with defense, internal security, finance, economic affairs, public works, and relations with the mother country. 2. The native bureaucracy. It dealt with all matters in which the colonial power had no particular interest, such as religion, culture, and education.
Groups	1. Traditional kinship groups. 2. The Western-educated class.

3. Colonial groups and associations, such as the French, British, or Greek communities, the large foreign companies, and chambers of commerce with foreign connections.

Leadership
1. Leaders of traditional kinship groups.
2. Leaders from the Western-educated class.
3. Colonial administrators.

Policies
The protection of the security of the colonial empire, the provision of a market for the mother country's manufactured products, the export to it of raw materials, and the spread of its civilization.

Shock
World Wars I and II, which weakened the power of the European colonial states.

PERIOD 4: THE BUREAUCRATIC POLITY[2]

Economy
Attempts at rapid industrialization through state planning and ownership of key industries. Nationalization or acquisition of the foreign-built oil industry.

Culture
Same as Period 3.

Structure
A large modern bureaucracy which controls the high points of the economy and subsumes within itself almost all political activity.

Groups
1. Traditional kinship groups.
2. The new middle class, persons with a modern education employed by the government, particularly army officers and bureaucrats.

Leadership
A modern monarch, a charismatic leader, or the leader of the latest coup, and leaders from the new middle class.

Policies
1. Economic development of the country.
2. The increase of the military power of the state.
3. The modernization of the society.
4. Tangentially, the increase of the prestige, status, and wealth of the bureaucrats and army officers.

Shock
Middle Eastern states are either in this period or have not yet arrived at it. A major military defeat or the collapse of an overstrained economy might cause a state to pass on to another period.

---

[2] A political system in which the bureaucracy and a powerful leader are dominant, with political parties, interest groups, the legislature, and the judiciary subordinate.

TRADITIONAL ISLAMIC SOCIETY

In the eighteenth century the Middle East was divided among two empires and one kingdom. At the far western extreme of the Middle East was the independent kingdom of Morocco. In the center was the Ottoman Empire, whose territories then included: in Europe—Bosnia, Serbia, Rumania, Bulgaria, Greece, the Caucasus, and Rumelia; in Asia—the Levant, Mesopotamia, and parts of the Arabian Peninsula; in North Africa—Egypt, Tripoli, Tunis, and Algiers. To the east was the Persian Empire, which at that time included present-day Iran, Afghanistan, and the Turkman, Uzbek, and Azerbaijan Republics of the USSR. In the capital of each—Rabat, Istanbul, or Tehran—was a dynasty that tried as best it could to control its domains, but was forced to cede much authority to regional and local leaders. Political unity within each of these two empires and one kingdom, and across the Middle East was only of the loosest sort.

However, there were many common qualities in the societies of all three. An educated Ottoman gentleman knew three languages: Turkish, the language of the bureaucracy; Arabic, the language of religion; and Persian, the language of belles-lettres. An educated Persian knew his own language and Arabic. It was not unusual for a person of education or means to live during his lifetime in several cities under several rulers. Even in the nineteenth century Jamal al-Din al-Afghani (1838-1897), a famous Muslim religious reformer, spent his life moving from one center of Islamic culture to another, Qazvin and Tehran in Iran, al-Najaf in Iraq, Istanbul, Cairo, and cities in Afghanistan and India. For him the Islamic world was one unit with a common social order, and common interests and problems.

The main division in traditional Islamic societies was between the rulers and the ruled. Sultans, beys, pashas, and shahs felt that authority gave them privilege, and that society existed to provide them with a life of luxury. Their demeanor was haughty and arrogant. They contributed nothing to society or government. All the hard work, such as maintaining an adequate military force, collecting taxes, administering justice, was carried on by underlings. They lived in the cities, secluded in their palaces, in association with their peers and isolated from the cares of the world.

The ruled lived, figuratively and literally, as far away from the rulers as possible. Contact with them could only mean trouble in the form of taxation, impressment into the army, or compulsory unpaid labor. The tribes, villages, and urban guilds were subsocieties and subcultures, a world apart from the high society of the cities.

The villages had their own folk religion, centered around a local saint whom people believed could perform miracles. His tomb was a place of pilgrimage, and his birthday was an occasion for much festivity. The village lands were owned communally, and periodically were reassigned by councils of elders to inhabitants for cultivation. The authorities taxed each village as a unit, and the more prosperous villagers paid more than their fair share in order to compensate for the lack of funds from the poorer people. Where irrigation was important, the responsibility of maintaining the dikes and canals was the community's. The network of social relations was within the village, and there were seldom contacts with people in the neighboring ones.

The urban guild was the social unit within which the common people of the city lived, and it was a community in every sense of the word. Its members lived in one quarter of the city and practiced a trade or craft, such as goldsmith, cobbler, saddle-maker, or weaver. It set standards for the craft and prices for products, insured the flow of raw materials, admitted apprentices, and gave licenses to masters. Its members married into each other's families, sometimes to produce business mergers, and they loaned money to each other when it was needed. The guild also had its own culture and society. Invariably it had a folk religion of its own, often centered around a Sufi order (an Islamic mystical fraternity). Initiation into the guild as a master craftsman was a semireligious ceremony which included many prayers and recitations from the Koran. The members of the guilds lived together, frequented each other's shops or work-places in the daytime, and visited each other in the evening. As in the villages, the community as a whole was responsible for the payment of taxes.

In the villages and in the cities, society was based on a triple relationship: (1) between the individual and his community, (2) among communities, and (3) between the community and the state. Birth established where one belonged, and it determined one's occupation, wealth, and status. Except for commercial dealings, one had no contact with the members of other communities, and one married within one's own group. A sheik, appointed by the ruler but always coming from a prominent family, headed the community. He was the point of contact between the ruler and the ruled; he collected taxes that were due and passed them on to the appropriate authorities; he gave to his fellow members all orders from on high; if any member of the group wanted a favor or special dispensation from the ruler, he was the intermediary.

In the community the individual found security and protection from the harshness and capriciousness of the rulers. The sheik was a person whom people could trust, and he was readily available for help or consultation. Members of the community provided each other with the warmth of fellowship, aid in adversity, and protection from the hostile acts of outsiders. Rulers and ruled had respect for this deeply set network of relations, and it survived eight centuries of dynastic vicissitudes and conquering armies.

Assessment

For centuries this social and political system succeeded in holding together peoples of diverse nationalities and religion. Its success was due to its loose structure and to the autonomy it allowed the many groups within it. The average ruler was not an admirable person in respect to personal integrity and fairness, nor was he in any sense of the word progressive. But he did stand aside from the communal affairs of his subjects, even when villages or tribes were fighting with each other, and he did promote the construction of public works, such as canals and dikes. From time to time, as an act of personal piety and charity, he built a mosque or established a religious foundation.

But precisely these characteristics proved to be the crucial weakness of the Middle Eastern empires and kingdoms when they confronted the West in the nineteenth century. The gulf between rulers and ruled, the contempt, fear, and hatred between them, meant that the system could not meet the requirements of the modern age—the age of nation-states, in which rulers and ruled share a common identity and mission. It could not provide mass armies composed of hundreds of thousands of citizens (the "nation in arms") and did not have industrialized economies able to furnish modern weapons and the tax revenues to pay for them. The system could not create political structures in which the masses could somehow participate, enabling them to believe that the government was theirs. It could not furnish leaders who could capture the popular imagination or lead the people to greater deeds in the service of the nation.

In the nineteenth century, some pashas and sultans raised large armies and established arms industries in an attempt to defend their domains against the West, but large armies without a concomitant popular spirit of patriotism were regarded as a form of slavery. Industries, established in a society that gave no encouragement to experimentation and innovation and no prestige to manual labor, atrophied. A sultan or a pasha who mobilized the people and brought the economy under state control to defend his domains was considered a tyrant. His counterpart in Europe might have the same authority, but he would be called a national hero and have popular support.

MODERNIZING AUTOCRATIC SOCIETY

Because of their strategic location, Istanbul and Cairo were the focus of the European attack on the Middle East in the nineteenth century. The Bosporus was the gateway that could give Russia an outlet to the world, and the Isthmus of Suez was the land bridge between the many British colonies in the Far East and the mother country. Britain wanted to prevent Russia from reaching the Bosporus, and jockeyed with France over which would control Egypt, the passageway to India.

The rulers in Istanbul and Cairo realized that simply putting up a good fight on the battlefield would not be enough to save themselves from being overthrown, nor would it save their territories from dismemberment. Major changes needed to be made in the institutions of the state and society.

They concentrated on the army, since that would make them a better match for the Europeans. They believed that the secret of European success lay in the power of its artillery, the discipline of its soldiers, and the resourcefulness of its military tactics. If these secrets could be learned and if the Ottoman and Egyptian armies could be rebuilt along modern lines, then the Muslim societies would be able to protect themselves.

In Egypt the ruler who almost perfectly fitted into this pattern was Muhammad Ali. He came to the country in 1801 as the commander of a contingent of Albanian soldiers which the Ottoman sultan had sent in an attempt to defeat Napoleon. After the French withdrawal, Muhammad Ali stayed on, and in 1811 he massacred the rulers of Egypt at a banquet in the Citadel of Cairo to which he had invited them. From that moment until his death in 1849 he was the absolute ruler of Egypt. He built a military machine that was able to capture the Levant from the Ottomans and hold it for eight years; on two occasions he could have marched on Istanbul, if it had not been for the intervention of the British.

A near contemporary of Muhammad Ali was Mahmud II, the Ottoman sultan from 1808 to 1839. Mahmud II instituted many internal reforms that strengthened his own personal power and introduced modern institutions and practices into the empire. His most significant act was to destroy the Janissaries. They made up an elite institution that provided the sultan with his best soldiers and top administrators. Originating in the fourteenth century, the Janissaries had become a state within the state by the nineteenth century, with power to make and unmake sultans. When they protested Mahmud's establishment of a new Western-style unit in the army, he killed them in their barracks in Istanbul in 1826.

Both Muhammad Ali and Mahmud II were autocrats in every sense of the word. They brooked no challenge to their authority and attempted to make every province and every person in their empires subservient to their will. Every reform was designed to increase the power of the state. Change was introduced by them, and people "reformed" out of fear and a sense of obedience to them.

The Reforms of Muhammad Ali

In the first half of the nineteenth century both Egypt and the Ottoman Empire experienced these changes under the leadership of their modernizing autocrats, Muhammad Ali and Mahmud II. While the reforms of Muhammad Ali in Egypt were more far-reaching than those of the latter, a discussion of the former will serve essentially as an analysis of both.

Since the fourteenth century, Egypt had been ruled by a class of mamluk beys.[3] Each bey had control over a fief, the revenues from which he used to maintain a contingent of troops under his command. In times of crisis, these

---

[3] Mamluk (Arabic) literally means "owned" and has come to designate a dynasty of Egyptian rulers (1250-1811) who were originally slaves. Bey is a Turkish title of respect widely used in the Ottoman Empire meaning "lord."

contingents were called up by the ruling bey in order to defend the country. The system had the advantage of being cheap and flexible; the state did not have to maintain either a large bureaucracy to collect taxes or a standing army that was expensive and tended to meddle in politics when it was not fighting. These troops, whose training was haphazard, whose discipline was of the rough and ready type, and whose weapons were few and very basic, were adequate for the defense of the country before the advent of the modern age.

The French attack on Egypt brought home to Muhammad Ali the lesson that this type of military establishment was inadequate to defend the country against the new mass-recruit technological armies of Europe. In its place he built a standing army and navy, organized in the same manner as the European ones and trained by French officers who, after the Bourbon Restoration in 1814, were without employment in France. The soldiers were Egyptian peasants and the officers Egyptians, Albanians, Circassians, and other Muslims from the different lands of the Ottoman Empire. The army and navy were the focus of Muhammad Ali's attentions, and he developed around them a host of auxiliary organizations that became the first modern industries and bureaucracies in Egypt: textile mills to produce cloth for uniforms, cannon foundries, rope factories, and shipyards. A college of medicine was founded so that members of the armed forces would be cared for by doctors knowledgeable in the latest medical practices, and a ministry of war was created to direct all these enterprises. The new armed forces sent ripples throughout the society.

Muhammad Ali also destroyed the old system of land ownership and agricultural production known as the *iltizam* system. The beys were the legal owners of state land grants, but neither performed supervisory functions on them nor farmed them. They delegated these responsibilities to *multazims* (tax farmers) and to the peasants. The former had the responsibility of extracting from the peasants certain designated amounts in taxes and then passing them on to the beys; anything over the designated amounts the *multazims* could keep for themselves. Often the *multazims* were sheiks or other local notables. The system had the obvious advantages that it saved the state from getting involved in the collection of taxes and in the production of agricultural goods, it gave the chief ruler of the country the opportunity to reward some of his faithful lieutenants with land, and it encouraged the decentralization of Islamic society in this period. The system's disadvantages were that the amount of revenue the state could collect was limited since much went into the pockets of the *multazims*, and that it produced local wielders of power who often conspired to overthrow the ruler of the country.

Muhammad Ali was determined to be absolute master of the country and to significantly increase the sources of revenue for the armed forces. When he massacred the beys in 1811, he effectively wiped out the *iltizam* system of which they were the chief beneficiaries. He personally took over the ownership of all land in the country, and then gave to some peasants and to some of his loyal officials the right to farm certain small portions. They paid taxes directly into the coffers of the state, eliminating the middle man (*multazim*) and his profits. Tax revenues went up significantly, and a new class was created, dependent upon and loyal to Muhammad Ali.

The cultivation of cotton on a massive scale was introduced into Egypt by Muhammad Ali. Toward the end of the eighteenth century, when the machinery to weave textiles and the factory system were developed in Europe, there was an increased demand for raw cotton. The cotton gin eliminated the problem of separating the cotton seeds from the fibers. Muhammad Ali was quick to see increased opportunity for him and for Egypt. He instituted the production of cotton on a large scale and under state control. Cotton was exported to Europe, with the revenues from its sale used to buy weapons, machinery, and the other accoutrements of modernity that Muhammad Ali needed. The money that trickled into private hands often was used to purchase European consumer goods, which were heavily taxed.

All this had a revolutionary effect on the rural society and the economy of Egypt. The autonomous self-sufficient village disappeared, and the peasant became subordinate to the absentee landlord, to the state, and to the price of cotton, which fluctuated drastically on the international market. Formerly a peasant and his fellow villagers had grown or made almost everything they used. Now they had to buy many foodstuffs and simple consumer products, such as cloth, often at very high prices and of low quality. The sheik, who formerly had represented the village to the government, was now an employee of the state or a lackey of the landlord.

The effect of modernization was similar in the urban areas. Muhammad Ali encouraged the immigration of Greeks, Italians, French, and English into the country, whom he licensed to undertake large-scale commerce. The manufactured European goods these merchants imported pushed the local products off the market and killed the economy on which the guilds rested. When modern factories were established, they were controlled by the state or by foreigners. The traditional craftsmen who survived became purveyors to the state, forced to make their goods for its marketing organizations at prices the latter set. As a result an indigenous industrial and mercantile middle class did not develop.

Assessment

Muhammad Ali and Mahmud II were acutely aware of the threat the European powers presented to their countries and were determined to bring them into the modern age in order to avert disaster. However, their understanding of modernity was limited. It was their naive belief that certain institutional changes could be introduced that would produce strong states capable of defending the eternally veritable Islamic society. They failed to realize that the modern European institutions they introduced—the army, a rationally organized bureaucracy, factories, secondary schools, and universities—were products of centuries of social and cultural change in Europe. These leaders were blind to the fact that such institutions functioned in an intellectual and social environment that accepted the individual as the end of society, believed in reason, saw the nation as the overarching unit of human existence, and viewed science as a means to understand and master the natural world. Traditional Islamic society and a modern state could not live together as these men hoped.

These two modernizing autocrats concentrated their energies on changing the state while ignoring many segments of the society, particularly the role of the family, the role of women, and the social function of religion. The extended family continued as before. In it the father, mother, unmarried sons and daughters, married sons and their wives and children, lived together in a single house or apartment building. The father owned all of the family property, controlled the family income, and determined where and how the family members were to work. Parents arranged the marriages of their sons and daughters. There was a definite deference of younger people to older ones, and of women to men.

Men and women were still strictly segregated, with women subservient to men. In the cities and among well-to-do peasants women continued to wear the veil. A man could easily divorce his wife, but she could not do the same to him. Polygamy was common, and the modernizing autocrats set the example by maintaining large harems.

Although modern legal codes were established to deal with commerce and crime, matters of personal status (marriage, divorce, adoption, guardianship, inheritance) were regulated by the Sharia and by its courts. Sufi orders, which were strong in the villages and cities, provided a framework for social gatherings and popular festivals, all of which had a religious content. The veneration of local saints, pilgrimages to their tombs, and frenzied celebrations of their birthdays continued.[4]

Reform came from the top. The absolute monarch ordered the establishment of a new army, sent young men to study in Europe, decreed that all his ministers were to wear Western dress, established factories, and employed the services of European experts. This was the predecessor of twentieth-century revolutions from above: the secular, nationalist one of Kemal Ataturk in Turkey, the "White Revolution" of Muhammad Reza Shah Pahlavi in Iran, and the transformation of Egypt into an "Arab socialist society" by Gamal Abdel Nasser.

There had always been a social gap between the rulers and the ruled, but under the modernizing autocrats it became a chasm. Until the nineteenth century, the aristocracy consumed the finest products of Muslim craftsmen: beautiful inlaid furniture, sumptuous costumes made from silk brocades, and exquisite hammered copper, brass, and silver utensils. They collected the greatest works of Islamic art, such as beautifully hand-written and illustrated books and magnifi-

---

[4]Gabriel Baer, *Studies in the Social History of Modern Egypt* (Chicago: University of Chicago Press, 1969), pp. 210-12.

cent carved wooden screens. Their palaces had courtyards resembling paradise; these contained fountains, flowers, and vases. The walls of their rooms were covered with beautiful glazed tiles, and the floors with mosaics. The most learned ulama and the finest poets lived near the courts of the wealthy. Islamic culture and civilization truly reached their culmination in the top ranks of society.

Starting with the reigns of the modernizing autocrats, the aristocracy began to live in a world apart from the Islamic Middle East. Its members wore European clothes and lived in villas resembling those of Paris or Milan. They considered the local handicrafts to be junk and imported all kinds of knick-knacks from Europe. Their libraries were filled with impressive leatherbound and gold-stamped volumes by European authors. Europe became for them the standard to emulate, and they turned their backs on Islamic culture. It had always been difficult for the rulers and the ruled to identify with one another; now it was impossible.

Turkey and Egypt are only two countries in the Middle East, but because of their size and central location they have had an influence beyond their borders. The significance of the reigns of Muhammad Ali and Mahmud II is not only in the changes they made in their own countries, but also in the forces they set in motion throughout the whole Middle East. Many of their reforms were ephemeral because the culture and society could not sustain them, and because they conflicted with the interests of the imperialists, who insisted that they be dismantled. By the end of the nineteenth century, Turkey and Egypt still did not have armies that could measure up to those of the Europeans; neither did they have industrial economies or political systems that could maintain harmony among the people and efficiently mobilize their energies. However, Muhammad Ali and Mahmud II had set into motion social and political movements of lasting significance. They made the bureaucracy, including the army, into the most modern sector of the society. They created elites whose education and outlook were Western, and who in the nineteenth century became the most powerful social and political class, leading the movements that fostered nationalism and tried to establish liberal democracy. These two rulers inadvertently widened the gap between the rulers and ruled, the former becoming modern and the latter remaining traditional.

COLONIAL SOCIETY

From 1798 to 1971, when Qatar and the United Arab Emirates received their independence, every country in the Middle East, except Saudi Arabia and Yemen, knew a colonial presence in one of several forms. In those countries that had had modernizing autocrats, colonialism reinforced the modernized state structures and perpetuated the social division between the rulers and the ruled. Where there had been no modernizing autocrats, colonialism established similar state structures and created analogous divisions. With the colonists change also came from the top, and it was only instituted in those sectors of society that benefited the colonists' interests. Social development was spotty and variegated, and there was no genuine revolution throughout the whole society.

Forms of Colonialism

Colonialism in the Middle East assumed four forms: (1) annexation, (2) protectorates, (3) mandates, and (4) indirect control.

Annexation was the most drastic procedure. It was practiced by the Russians in the Caucasus and central Asia, and by the French in Algeria. The objective was to assimilate totally the territory and its people into the mother country. Large numbers of Europeans were encouraged to settle in the territory, and they dominated its political, social, and economic life. The assumption was that the civilization, society, polity, and economic system of the mother country were superior, and that "enlightened" persons in the territory would welcome annexation and assimilation.

Protectorates were a looser form of control. The fiction of formal independence was maintained, but a treaty was signed in which the imperial power agreed to take up the responsibility of "protecting" the subject country in exchange for certain privileges necessary to this end: control of foreign affairs, finance, and defense. The practical effect of the treaty was that the "protecting power" kept the existing dynasty in power against local contenders and prevented other foreign powers from "interfering" in the internal affairs of the country. Britain, whose interests in the Middle East mostly involved protecting its trade routes to India and the Far East, used this system extensively in places such as Egypt and the Persian Gulf. France established protectorates over Morocco and Tunisia.

Mandates were an anomaly that grew out of contradictory claims made by various parties during World War I. In 1915 and 1916, a correspondence was carried on between Sir Henry McMahon, British High Commissioner for Egypt, and Hussein, Grand Sharif of Mecca, whereby the former made some ambiguous promises to support the independence of the Arab nation. In 1916 Britain, France, and Russia signed the Sykes-Picot Agreement, which specified how the Ottoman Empire, an ally of Germany, was to be divided among them when victory was achieved. In November 1917, the British cabinet issued a "declaration of sympathy with Jewish Zionist aspirations" favoring the "establishment in Palestine of a national home for the Jewish people." In addition, Britain occupied the Levant and Iraq, provinces of the Ottoman Empire. Woodrow Wilson, president of the United States, in his Fourteen Points proclaimed that all nations had the right to self-determination.

These conflicting demands, ideals, and interests were resolved through the mandate system. The League of Nations issued to a mandatory such as Britain or France a mandate to rule a certain piece of territory. This was a legal document specifying how the mandatory was to govern the mandated territory. Under the supervision of the League, the former was supposed to lead the latter to independence, but the League had no way of enforcing its will. It was no idle coincidence that France received mandates for Lebanon and Syria, and Britain received them for Palestine, Trans-Jordan, and Iraq—territories that had been assigned to both in the Sykes-Picot Agreement. The events of World War II— not the mandate system or the League—brought independence to these territories.

Indirect control was another form of colonialism. One of its primary mechanisms was the system of capitulations. These were treaties between European states and the Ottoman or Persian Empires by which the latter granted privileges of extraterritoriality to the citizens of the former. Begun in the sixteenth century, capitulations allowed Europeans residing in the Middle East to be subject to their own laws and to be tried in the consular courts of their own states. This meant that an English or French businessman living in Egypt, Iran, or Turkey was not under the jurisdiction of the local law and courts but under those of his mother country. The large foreign communities residing permanently in Egypt and Turkey controlled almost all of the commerce and industry in those countries. Their members could engage in shady business practices and be free from prosecution by the local government. The European consular courts usually did nothing to restrain them.

Under the protection of the capitulations, Europeans were able to obtain from the Ottoman and other Middle Eastern governments important and extensive concessions, particularly permits for the exclusive operation of some business or for the exploitation of some natural resource. Of great importance were the foreign banks, which came to dominate the money markets of the Middle East and thereby to determine in what economic sectors investment was to take place. In some cases a foreign bank was given the exclusive right to issue currency; one such case is the Ottoman Bank, which retained this right in the Ottoman Empire until World War I. Concessions were granted to foreign companies to build, own, and operate railroads, and the concessions often carried the provision that the company could exploit any mineral resource it discovered in the strip of land twenty kilometers on each side of the right-of-way. All shipping companies to and from the Ottoman Empire were controlled by foreigners, who also managed those engaged in the coastal traffic. Ports, electric power companies, tramways, telegraphs, telephones, and urban water supply companies were under alien domination. Probably the most famous foreign concession was the Suez Canal Company. It was incorporated in Egypt and had its headquarters in Paris, a majority of its board of directors were French, and after 1875 the largest single stockholder was the British government.

Titular sovereignty meant little if the economy was controlled by foreigners, if resident aliens were above the law, and if outside powers intervened to protect their economic interests. As late as 1956, Britain and France landed troops in Egypt to guarantee free passage through the Suez Canal, but this was the last effort of their imperialism.

The Colonial Economic System

The economic enterprises initiated by the colonialists in the Middle East in the nineteenth century and the first half of the twentieth were impressive: the Suez Canal; railways from Istanbul to Baghdad, throughout Egypt, across North Africa, and up and down the coast of the Levant; tramways and electric companies in every big city; vineyards for wine in Algeria; vast fields of cotton in Egypt; tobacco in Turkey; oil wells and refineries in Iran, Iraq, and Bahrain. These represented the beginning of economic modernization, but only the beginning.

Every such enterprise served to tie the Middle Eastern country to the colonial power, and to hinder the self-development and economic integration of the area. The Suez Canal was an avenue of commerce through the region and not within it. The cotton that Egypt produced was sold to Britain; the wine that Algeria made went to France; the oil of Iran was shipped to Britain. The railroads were built from the ports into the interior so that European goods could be brought into the country and the raw materials taken out.

The modern sectors of the economy, those that produced 20 percent, 30 percent, and sometimes more than half of the national income, were owned and run by Europeans. The companies kept their headquarters in Paris or London. In the Middle East, large staffs of European executives and technicians were attracted to these posts by high salaries and fancy villas. Qualified men could not be found locally, said the companies, who for a long time made little effort to train them. Some benefit came to the Middle Eastern countries from these enterprises, but when they were owned and run by Europeans, when they controlled large segments of the economy, when the profits went back to Europe, when almost no local people were employed at the higher technical and managerial levels, Middle Easterners began to see them more as an instrument for their oppression than as a means to their economic development. Profitable investment under the conditions of imperialism did not produce a viable, diversified modern economic system, but rather a few islands of economic modernity separated from the rest of the local economy and tied to Europe.

The Colonial Social System

The division that characterized the colonial economy carried over into the colonial society. In many countries of the Middle East there were large communities of Europeans who lived apart from the Muslims and the local Christians, spoke their own languages, attended their own schools and churches, and frequented their own cafés and bars. They considered the Middle Eastern country to be their permanent home and had no intention of leaving it. The French people lived in Algeria, Morocco, and Tunisia; Italians in Libya; Greeks in the big coastal cities of Turkey; and Greeks, Italians, French, and English in Egypt. Some found employment with the European firms and the colonial administration; others were small businessmen and shopkeepers; some owned farms, which they ran with the assistance of local laborers. A few were rich, but most eked out a very modest living. At the top was a small class of administrators who spent ten to twenty years in the colonies and then returned to their mother countries.

Jewish and Christian minorities, such as the Copts in Egypt and the Greek Orthodox in Turkey, formed another class. In respect to status and privilege, they were between the Muslim masses and the European minorities and rich Muslims. Because they practiced religions akin to those of the Europeans, they tended to be more receptive to Westernization. They learned to speak French and English, went to European schools, and sought employment with European firms and colonial administrations, which favored them over their Muslim compatriots since they were considered more dependable and "civilized." Never accepted as social equals by the European minorities, regarded as subject but protected peoples by the Muslim majority, they were truly caught between two societies.

The Muslim masses formed the third class of colonial society. They bore the brunt of the colonial impact and reaped few of its benefits. They were the messenger boys in the European offices and the laborers who built the railroads or worked in the fields owned by the European farmers. They lived in fetid and decrepit slums and casbahs, or else in dismal villages off the beaten track. They were either the passive observers of modernization or its victims, but never its beneficiaries.

A small class of Westernized Muslims, sons of pashas or of village sheiks, did develop, but its fate in colonial society was not enviable. Its members might become as French as the French or as English as the English, but this did not gain them entry into the sporting and town clubs of the Europeans. Neither did it persuade the Europeans to give them political power or the ownership and management of the big companies. In the 1930s and 1940s it became apparent to many of these Muslims that simply becoming Westernized would neither enable them to become free in their own country nor leaders of its destiny, so they turned to agitation and revolution in the name of independence.

The Colonial Political System

Under colonialism the Middle Eastern countries were run by alien administrators to further the interests of the colonial powers, on the assumption that what was good for the colonial powers was good for the colonies. The demands of local leaders for freedom, autonomy, or independence were labeled as naive and unrealistic, and these leaders were said to be misguided and self-serving. The colonial master believed that the people were on his side, because he gave them honest and efficient administration in place of the corruption and oppression of former times.

The primary objective of the colonial administrators was to defend and advance the strategic interests of the colonial power. The colonialists' troops were stationed in the country for purposes of defense, with those of all other foreign powers excluded; its businessmen and their economic interests were favored, and its trade routes and lines of communication protected. Partially out of humanitarian concerns, but also because they aided the colonial power, the administrators vigorously defended the rights and interests of the resident Europeans and the indigenous Christian minorities.

Under the leadership of a governor-general, pro-consul, or ambassador, there was an extensive colonial bureaucracy. Foreign troops and native levies commanded by Europeans were stationed at strategic bases around the country. The police and gendarmerie had European officers or "advisors" in their top ranks. Foreigners dominated the ministry of finance, which dealt with taxation and economic affairs, and the ministry of public works, which supervised the construction of roads, dams, and bridges. The colonial government issued passports for travel abroad and permits to import and export, to set up a business, or to publish a newspaper. The regulations and bureaucracy were bewildering to the colonized people, because they were complex and extensive, were alien to their culture, and because the bureaucracy was led by brusque, efficient Europeans.

Good administration did not satisfy the needs and wants of the colonized people. Dams, roads, railroads, excellent public health facilities, modern, European-language schools, honest judges, and incorruptible police were no substitute for a truly independent nation ruled by indigenous leaders who could promote its interests. When independence was gained, the colonial rulers, their troops, and the European minorities went home, and indigenous people took over the positions vacated by the Europeans in the bureaucracy.

Assessment

The colonialists assumed that modernization was a process of aiding their subjects to become like them. They urged the colonized peoples to adopt their language, abide by Western etiquette and mores, and put into practice European legal codes, constitutions, and systems of social organization. Some of the more romantic colonialists, such as Lawrence of Arabia, admired the bedouin Arabs in their pristine state. However, such foreigners operated only on the fringes, in the desert sheikdoms of the Arabian Peninsula. The real colonial masters in Cairo or Algiers relaxed in Europeans-only sporting clubs, lived apart from the natives, and felt that they were authorities on Eastern societies. Actually they knew very little about them. The controversies in Muslim society about national identity and the reconciliation of Islam and modernism were beyond their comprehension or interest, and the Europeans focused on the fact that many of the leaders of these movements were anti-British or anti-French.

The ethnic pluralism and social fragmentation that already existed in the Middle East were accentuated by the colonialists. Europeans were encouraged to immigrate into several Middle Eastern countries, thus adding new nationality groups and new social classes to the existing confusion and the cultural mosaic. Jews were permitted by the British to immigrate into Palestine, expanding and strengthening the Jewish community already there and leading to conflict with the Arab community. Christian minorities in all colonies were given preferential treatment, and Jews outside Palestine, while not as favored as the Christians, were granted a status above that of the Muslims.

The modernization affected only small segments of the indigenous population. Nowhere did elementary education extend to more than 10 percent of the people, and only a handful received a secondary or university education, and then not in their own language, but in French or English. Large commercial enterprises and extensive public works were built, but the development of local industry was ignored and even hindered. The cities became impressive centers of commerce and administration, yet the towns and villages were completely untouched by the modern world. The masses continued to live in primitive houses, farming a few meager acres or existing as semiemployed day laborers.

Bureaucracy was supreme, and the political activity of the colonized people was kept under strict control. The colonial regimes knew that if they allowed the indigenous peoples to engage in politics, the former would soon be asked to leave. The bureaucrats thought they knew what was best for the people, and with firmness they carried out their "responsibility." Native politicians, viewed as "self-serving rabble rousers," only hindered them in their service to the people. Programs for social reform were instituted by the colonialists, since only then could their soundness be assured and undesirable consequences be prevented. The eighteenth-century Ottoman rulers believed society existed to grant them privileges and wealth, the modernizing autocrats manipulated it in order to give more power to themselves and the state, and the colonialists controlled it because they thought they knew what was best for the people.

Colonialism continued the modernization and social development begun by the modernizing autocrats, but inherently it could not bring this process to completion. It was responsible for building roads and dams, but not a modern diversified economy. It educated an elite, but not the masses. It instituted Western legal codes but was incapable of adapting them to Islamic culture or vice versa. It created a bureaucracy but did not develop political institutions and processes that could control and give direction to it.

THE BUREAUCRATIC POLITY

Enormous, nearly impossible tasks confronted those who succeeded the colonialists at the helm of the Middle Eastern states. The business to which they gave priority was the strengthening of the military.

Colonialism and recent experiences have created in the minds of the leaders real and exaggerated military dangers. During and immediately after World War II, the Soviet Union demanded that Turkey accede to joint control of the Bosporus and the Dardanelles. In light of the power realities between the two states, this would have meant Russian control, so Turkey rejected the Russian demands. It then entered increasingly into an alliance with the United States, fighting with it in Korea from 1950 to 1952, and joining NATO in 1952. During World War II Iran was occupied by British, American, and Soviet troops; at the end of the war the Russians established Soviet-dominated "republics" in northeastern Iran. These collapsed when Soviet troops left in 1946. The Egyptian, Jordanian, Syrian, and Iraqi armies suffered defeat in the 1948 Arab-Israeli war. After that, all Arab states came to regard Israel as a threat.

Because of these real and perceived threats, most Middle Eastern states have come to funnel very high percentages of their national income and skilled manpower into the armed forces. Encouraging them in the process have been the United States and the Soviet Union, which have introduced into the region some of the world's most technologically sophisticated weapons—these into societies decades, perhaps centuries, away from any capacity to produce them. In social terms the cost has been high, because the army is now a rich, privileged institution, and its officers constitute a rich, privileged class in societies still mired in poverty. Politically it means that the states are often run by the military.

The post-colonial leaders are also confronted with herculean tasks of economic development. The first is relatively simple: to gain control of the European or American-owned economic enterprises by nationalization or by purchasing shares in the company. The purpose is to set up more local management and to retain a greater share of the profits within the affected Middle Eastern country.

A second major task is to produce a diversified, productive economy, and this is not so simple. It involves the creation of the multitude of industrial and commercial enterprises which are common in the Soviet Union, Europe, and North America, and in which goods and services are produced plentifully through technology at a low cost in terms of work hours.

The third task of the new leaders is social development. The modernizing autocrats and the colonialists disrupted the cohesion of the traditional communities, that of a shared culture permeated by religion and reinforced by kinship. They produced deep social cleavages: between rulers and ruled, among ethnic groups, among social classes, and between those who were Westernized and those who were not. The new leaders must bring about some cohesiveness, especially between the more privileged and less privileged classes. In place of the old society, which centered on communities, they must erect a new one based on organizations. In the latter the people trust one another, cooperate, abide by commonly agreed-upon rules, and give responsibility to persons who have experience and training.

The fourth task is political development, and it has several aspects. A new sense of political community must be created to replace that of the Islamic community. It will inevitably be based on the nation, but the key question is how Islam is to be integrated into it. Also the new rulers must have legitimacy; that is, the people must believe that their leaders rule by right and not by might. The government must be able to bring its authority to bear in all parts of the country and among all sectors of the population; it must be able to tax them, to recruit them for the armed forces, to mobilize them for economically productive activity, and to make sure they obey the laws. A sense of social justice and equality must be created, a feeling among the people that none get more than their fair share of the nation's wealth, that no one is above the law, that no one has more rights and privileges than others. Finally, institutions must be established that enable people to believe that they are participating in their own government: political parties, or a single "party of the people," labor unions, youth groups, student organizations, business associations—organizations that can channel the demands of various groups up to the rulers. These problems of political development can be summarized as identity, legitimacy, penetration, equality, and participation.[5]

Definition and Description[6]

As a legacy from the modernizing autocrats and the colonial rulers, and in facing the tasks we have outlined, the bureaucratic polity has emerged as the predominant type of political system in the Middle East. In a bureaucratic polity the bureaucracy is the dominant institution in the society and the economy, and

---

[5] See: Leonard Binder and others, *Crises and Sequences in Political Development* (Princeton, N.J.: Princeton University Press, 1971).

[6] This concept has been developed by Fred Riggs, who has made a case study using it in *Thailand: The Modernization of a Bureaucratic Polity* (Honolulu: East-West Center Press, 1966); for another case study, see Marvin Zonis, *The Political Elite of Iran* (Princeton: Princeton University Press, 1971). Anouar Abdel-Malek, an Egyptian Marxist who has been living in France since 1959, reaches essentially the same conclusion in respect to Egypt in *Egypt: Military Society: The Army Regime, The Left, and Social Change Under Nasser*, trans. Charles Lam Markmann (New York: Random House, Inc., 1968), and in respect to all of the Arab World in *La Pensée politique arabe contemporaine* (Paris: Editions du Seuil, 1970). On Morocco, Alberia, and Tunisia, see the excellent monographs in Charles Debbasch and others; *Pouvoir et administration au Maghreb: études sur les élites maghrebines* (Paris: Editions du Centre National de la Recherche Scientifique, 1970). For an excellent study by an Israeli that focuses on the military alone, see: Eliezer Be'eri, *Army Officers in Arab Politics and Society*, trans. Dov Ben-Abba (New York: Praeger, 1969).

all significant political activity takes place away from public view, inside it. Political parties and interest groups are either nonexistent or created and controlled by the bureaucracy. Public opinion is guided; the parliament, if it exists, is quiescent; and elections are manipulated by the authorities. Standing above and outside the bureaucracy, defining the rules of political competition and assuring their observance, is a powerful personal leader, a monarch, a charismatic leader, or a dominant army officer.

Because economic and social development have not advanced sufficiently to produce corporations, private universities, independent research institutes, and other autonomous institutions, and because most of the regimes are dedicated to socialism, the government is the major employer in bureaucratic polities. Young persons with good education and skills can find jobs only in the bureaucracy, and in order to prevent them from becoming unemployed and a dangerous revolutionary class, the political leaders create new positions, often unneeded, to employ them. Since modernization is the objective of the government, the leaders can always argue that the more skilled persons there are in the bureaucracy, the more the country will develop.

The distinctions between a bureaucratic polity and a totalitarian state are subtle but important. In the latter the state, through its bureaucracy, attempts to control all aspects of the citizen's life and to have total control over every organization in the society. Every factory, store, restaurant, and barbershop is owned and run by the state. The government creates and controls youth outing clubs, workers' cultural clubs, housewives' associations, learned societies for physicists and philosophers, labor unions, and political parties. However, in the bureaucratic polity the state controls only the high points of the economy, such as banks, modern industries, and big stores, and the major social and political organizations, such as labor unions, student organizations, and political parties. Small shopkeepers, petty entrepreneurs, and small informal social groups are allowed to remain independent.

Causes for Development

The expansion of bureaucracies in the Middle East and their development into institutions of immense power have proceeded apace during the last century and a half. Muhammad Ali and Mahmud II wanted to modernize their states, and they did this by sending young men to Europe to study, and installing them in newly-created bureaucracies when they returned. The colonial regimes established additional bureaucracies and filled them with their own nationals and some indigenous people. Since World War II, American and Russian military assistance programs have introduced jeeps, armored personnel carriers, tanks, airplanes, helicopters, and radar, all of which require military bureaucracies to maintain and operate them. The technical assistance programs of these two countries and of others have had the same effect. They train young people to be agricultural experts; these experts invariably wind up behind a desk, not behind the wheel of a tractor. New seeds or new breeds of chickens are introduced, and government agencies are created to insure their proper use.

Not to be neglected as an explanation for the expansion and rise in power of the bureaucracy are the prestige, wealth, and power that have always been accorded to bureaucrats by Middle Eastern society. Prior to the impact of the West, bureaucrats were virtually the only persons who could live in fancy houses, possess fine clothing, and command large numbers of people. In contemporary Middle Eastern society, where the overwhelming majority of people live a hand-to-mouth existence, the bureaucrats have the security of a stable income, the ability to buy luxuries such as a TV set, refrigerator, membership in a sporting club, or maybe a car, and the assurance that their standard of living is above average.

More profoundly there is widespread agreement that development is the sole path for the future and that open political debate and competition, often rancorous and divisive, hinders it. In order to conquer underdevelopment, all national energies must be oriented in one direction, and the decision-making power essential to encourage development must be given to those who are competent. Building up industries, expanding the educational system, and engaging in negotiations with the oil companies are tasks for technocrats within the bureaucracy. In modern international society, technical values are exalted to the detriment of philosophical or cultural ones, and the prestige of the expert is greater than that of the thinker or of the priest. The bureaucrats of the Middle East are the beneficiaries of this attitude.

Assessment

All the evidence is not in, but there are many indications that the bureaucratic polity cannot bring about the development which is its very reason for being. Bureaucrats who have a passion for consumer goods cannot lead the country through the period of austerity necessary to achieve the beginning levels of economic development. Bloated bureaucracies staffed by individuals holding M.S.s and Ph. D.s in a society lacking foremen, technicians, and machinists often produce plans that cannot be implemented. The insecurity that comes from the fear of incurring the wrath of the monarch or national leader, the continual shirking of responsibility, the pushing of decisions upward, the kow-towing to superiors, and the jockeying for power, all produce immobility. Plans are drawn up to "revolutionize the society," and money is poured into their fulfillment, but the only revolution is one of rising consumption for the bureaucracy and of dashed expectations for the people.

If the bureaucratic polities cannot handle the military threats from outside their borders and cannot carry on a social revolution inside, forces will arise demanding a change. In Iran, Turkey, Egypt, and Morocco, there are rumblings of discontent in the form of attempted coups, assassinations, demonstrations, strikes, and guerilla activity. Another defeat by the Arabs at the hands of the Israelis could be the blow that brings down some of the existing regimes.

Many of the revolutionary movements at work in the Middle East are Marxist, and they look to a new time beyond the bureaucratic polity, a time of the "people in arms," inspired by the National Liberation Front in Vietnam and by Castro's movement in Cuba. In the words of one Marxist, "For the first time, it will permit the tackling of the problems of liberation and of revolution in a radical manner."[7]

CONCLUSION

In eighteenth-century Middle Eastern society there were no intellectuals attacking the ruling dogmas, no new classes challenging old ones, no social revolutionaries wanting to erect a new order. The society was at peace with itself—to the point of stagnation.

Eighteenth-century Middle Eastern countries were sovereign. No outside powers dominated or influenced them; no European capitalists exploited their natural resources, or held their governments in a state of fiscal servitude; no foreign armies had been able to penetrate the House of Islam—a sovereignty based on delusion.

In the nineteenth and early twentieth centuries, the Middle Eastern states were attacked and invaded and their societies thrown into turmoil. By 1971, independence had been regained, but this was only a partial victory, for the battle now involves regaining the power the states once possessed, the self-sufficiency and prosperity their economies once provided, and the harmony their societies once enjoyed.

[7] Abdel-Malek, *La Pensée*, p. 36.

Chapter 5

Ideological Change
Since 1798

In the past 175 years, the material impact of the West on the Middle East has been significant. The big cities now have office and apartment buildings, and the streets are filled with cars and buses. There are cinemas, large stores, and European-style cafés. When the army stages a parade with tanks, jeeps, trucks, and armored personnel carriers, it looks like any European nation's. One finds daily newspapers, weekly magazines, monthly and quarterly journals, and radio and television too.

The Western impact has also been impressive in regard to the structures of the political system. There are presidents and prime ministers, republics and constitutional monarchies, parliaments and political parties, where there were none before. The law is modeled on that of the European continent, as are the courts and the legal processes. The bureaucracy is rationally organized and composed of many knowledgeable experts who hold advanced degrees.

This change is impressive and highly visible, and was relatively easy to bring about. It requires no social or intellectual revolution to import material products from the West; witness Saudi Arabia, where harems have air conditioners and sheiks ride in air-conditioned Cadillacs. It is quite easy for an autocratic ruler to decide to change his court advisors into a council of ministers, the royal treasury into a ministry of finance, or to impose from above a constitution and a new legal code.

These changes, brought about during the reigns of the modernizing auto-crats and of the colonialists, are highly visible; but the values and beliefs of the society, which are invisible, were altered less dramatically. In fact, in face of the material invasion from overseas and the structural change imposed from above, the tendency among Islamic peoples was to protect and defend the values and beliefs they had held for millennia. The political culture remained traditional while the political structures were modernized.

In Chapter 4 we examined the changes in social and political institutions; here we shall explore the continuing search for a belief system or ideology to undergird the new institutions and to give society purpose and direction.

For political inspiration, Middle Easterners have generally looked outside their region and have adapted ideologies popular elsewhere to their own con-ditions. From the French Revolution until World War II, liberal democracy was the major system of government of the Western world. After World War I and up to the defeat of Germany and Italy in 1945, fascism was strong in Europe. Following World War II, the welfare state became the norm in western Europe, and "scientific socialism" was consolidated in the Soviet Union and Eastern Europe. In 1949 Marxism as interpreted by Mao Tse-tung emerged victorious in China. In 1954 a Marxist movement led by Ho Chi Minh won out in North Vietnam and extended its control in 1975 to South Vietnam. In 1959 Marxism as interpreted by Fidel Castro triumphed in Cuba. Each of these movements has spawned an equivalent in the Middle East, which has risen and fallen accord-ing to the fate of its counterpart outside the area. The four most popular ide-ologies have been liberal democracy, Islamic fundamentalism, socialism, and Marxism.

LIBERAL DEMOCRACY

At its peak in the Middle East, from about 1860 to just after World War II, liberal democracy appeared to be the answer to the political repression of some backward and unyielding shahs, sultans, and kings. The reforms of the moderniz-ing autocrats had destroyed the numerous autonomous communities that had formerly buffered the harshness of the government. The building of telegraphs and railroads had made it easier for a ruler to move his troops around to suppress revolts. Technology had brought improved methods of government snooping and a more effective police force. The advocates of liberal democracy felt that a constitution, parliament, political party system, free press, and a democratic electoral process could alleviate much of this.

They also felt that liberal democracy was a way out of the oppression and insults of colonialism. The capitulations, financial bondage of the governments to European bankers, harsh and severely discriminatory treaties, foreign domi-nation of the local economies, and continual military threats and occupations were humiliating. The proponents of liberal democracy argued that if Middle Eastern countries adopted this form of government and some of the other European practices the colonialists would consider them "civilized" and cease their interference.

Finally, liberal democracy appeared to be the means to promote technological progress and bring economic prosperity. Its advocates argued that Europe had prospered through freedom and security, which allowed scientific and technological experimentation to take place and encouraged investment in business and industry, bringing prosperity for all.

Influence of the French Revolution

Middle Eastern liberal democracy was inspired by the French Revolution, which ushered in a fresh era for Frenchmen and all of humanity. It allowed persons of any race, religion, or nationality, using reason and knowledge, to construct a new social order. Liberty, equality, and fraternity spilled over national borders and were applicable to all.

The Middle Easterners who observed French society in the nineteenth century were impressed by the fact that the church still functioned in a secular state. The faithful worshipped as they pleased; the bishops continued to govern church affairs; and in Catholic schools, nuns, priests, and monks taught children religious and secular subjects. People were free to be religious or nonreligious and apparently the existence of the latter did not harm the former. Some Muslim observers wanted to establish a similar system in the Middle East, so that religion and a secular state would coexist, and the high ethical standards of Islam and the liberty and prosperity of democracy could be combined.

Islam had always been an equitable and tolerant faith, Muslims thought. It proclaimed the absolute equality of all believers, called for fair and just government, protected Christians and Jews, and urged that all rulers govern by means of consultation with their subjects. These ideals might be the bases on which to build liberal democracy. Certainly they did not contradict Islamic ideals.

Constitutional Movements in the Middle East

In the century roughly between 1860 and 1960, liberal democratic constitutions were promulgated in some countries of the Middle East. In 1861 the Bey of Tunis proclaimed a constitution. In 1866 the Egyptian monarch, Ismail, created a consultative assembly composed of seventy-five delegates elected for three-year terms by a system of indirect collegiate elections. In 1882 this assembly prepared and promulgated a constitution establishing a parliamentary democracy, but it was abrogated when the British occupied the country in the same year. In 1883 another constitution was put forward, and this provided for two quasi-parliamentary bodies, which were merged in 1913 to form a parliament.

In 1876, under pressure from the European powers and political groups within the empire, the Ottoman sultan promulgated a constitution. It provided for complete equality of all Ottoman subjects; freedom of worship, the press, association, and education; and freedom from arbitrary intrusion, extortion, arrest, or other unlawful violations of person, residence, and property. A senate was nominated and a chamber of deputies elected. Executive power was in the hands of the sultan, and legislative power was shared by the sultan and the parliament. However, the effective life of the constitution was short. After general elections, the first parliament met in March 1877. Further elections were held, and a second parliament met in December. It displayed considerable independence and audacity, and on February 14, 1878 was dismissed by the sultan, not to meet again for thirty years.

A revolution in Iran in 1906 forced the shah to convene a national assembly, which drafted a liberal constitution formally in effect until 1979. In 1908 the Young Turk Revolution brought about the restoration of the 1876 Ottoman constitution. In 1923 a new constitution, enshrining the highest principles of liberal democracy, was promulgated in Egypt. After World War II several countries received independence from France and Britain, and each started out its new life with a constitution based on the liberal democratic values of the former mother country.

By the 1960s almost all of the attempts by the Western European powers and some local elites to create in the Middle East liberal democracy had failed. Only in Israel and Turkey did it take root, and in the latter its life was sometimes precarious. In the sections that follow, the reasons for this state of affairs will be examined.

Popular Versus Divine Sovereignty

The foremost problem in the establishment of liberal democracy was the contradiction between the widely accepted Islamic view that God should be supreme over state and society, and the Western secular outlook that the people should be sovereign. Devout Muslims believe that God determines the social and political order and that humans can only attempt to fathom from his inscrutable mind the specific structures and rules that apply to various historical times and circumstances. They assert that people cannot, by free and willful acts of their own, create a social and political order, for to do so is to defy God's sovereignty. Also it is unnecessary to do so, because God has provided in the Koran and the Sharia the design for a just and equitable society and polity.

Turkey is the only Muslim Middle Eastern state that has clearly and unequivocally opted for popular sovereignty. Its constitution states: "The Turkish State is a Republic," and "sovereignty is vested in the nation without reservation and condition,"[1] In other Islamic countries the issue has been artfully

[1]"Constitution of the Republic of Turkey, July 9, 1961," in *Middle Eastern Constitutions and Electoral Laws*, ed. Abid A. Al-Marayati (New York: Praeger, 1968), p. 337.

avoided and obfuscated. Constitutions guarantee religious liberty on the one hand, but on the other hand declare Islam to be the religion of the state and the Sharia to be "a source," "the source," or "the major source" of all legislation.

Focus on Political Norms Rather than on Political Procedures

Overlooking the subjection of working people, the maldistribution of wealth, and the rigidity of the class system in Europe in the nineteenth and early twentieth century, Middle Eastern liberal democrats saw there the rule of law, the reign of justice, the equality of opportunity, and the dedication to public service of civil servants. An aim of Islam had always been a just and equitable political system, so on a moral basis alone liberal democracy was worthy of being transplanted to the Middle East.

However, Middle Eastern liberal democrats failed to realize that the mechanics of democracy were important for the realization of its ideals. They did not understand that politics is often the choice of the lesser of two evils, and that it involves bargaining and compromise. They failed to see the importance of political parties for maintaining contact between the elite and the masses, and the necessity of commitment to democratic institutions and process by the population as a whole. They frequently sang the praises of democracy, while in practice they undermined it.

Legalism

Rather than emphasizing the practice of democracy, the educated stressed knowledge of the law and of the constitution. Students were required to learn them by rote, even though the practice of politics was different from what they prescribed. Lawyers proliferated, and scholarly books on constitutional law abounded. Politics as taught in schools and universities emphasized law.

In a civics text formerly used in Egyptian high schools, a constitution was defined in purely formal terms:

> The constitution . . . is the fundamental principles determining the political regime, the power of government, the rights and obligations of individuals, the distribution of government's power and the way it should be used . . . [It] is issued by the power which possesses effective sovereignty in the state, so that if the state has a democratic inclination, the nation possesses the sovereignty, and it has the right to issue the constitution . . . But if sovereignty belongs to the hereditary possessor of the throne, it is for him to grant his state a constitution . . . [2]

---

[2]Quoted in Nadav Safran, *Egypt in Search of Political Community: An Analysis of the Intellectual and Political Evolution of Egypt, 1804-1952* (Cambridge, Mass.: Harvard University Press, 1961), p. 149.

From this perspective, constitutions could be instituted and abrogated, ignored and circumvented, according to who was the "power which possesses effective sovereignty in the state."

Foreign Interference and Internal Stress

In order that the delicate institutions of democracy may be slowly put together and its values and habits spread among the people, the society that is embarking upon this path needs an incubation period free from external attack, foreign interference, internal strife, and economic depression. In the Middle East these conditions did not prevail because at the same time that the attempt was being made to establish liberal democracy, the British, French, Russians, and Germans were cementing their imperial hold. By their actions, if not so much by their words, they undercut liberal democracy.

For example, in the nineteenth century Europeans were very concerned about protecting the non-Muslim minorities in the Ottoman Empire, and stories of discrimination, persecution, and atrocities against the Armenians, the Maronites, and the Greek Orthodox were common in the European press. The royal decrees guaranteeing equal rights to all Ottoman subjects and the Ottoman constitution of 1876 were partly the result of European pressure. But protection of the minorities was often a rationalization for imperialism rather than a motive. The British, French, and Russians continued to control important spheres of the Ottoman economy and to interfere in the decisions of the government, actions that undermined the liberal reformers and the reforms they supported. Bernard Lewis has called this "imperialism of interference without responsibility."[3]

Democracy was accepted in the Middle East more for what people expected it to bring than for what it was. Once a constitution was declared and a parliament convened, freedom was supposed to rule, prosperity reign, and social justice come into existence; somehow the imperialists would disappear. Of course none of this happened, and more often the constitutional regimes were beset by economic depression and increased imperialistic machinations. World War I, the Great Depression of 1929, and World War II all produced their stresses and strains. The Israeli victory in the war of 1948 was a blow to the Arabs. Since the commitment to democracy had never been great, under these conditions the majority of people looked to other forms of government to satisfy their wants and fulfill their needs.

ISLAMIC FUNDAMENTALISM

The Muslim masses had never understood or benefited from liberal democracy. Peasants were hardly free when they owned no land, had to work on the estate of a large landlord, and were subject to the landowner's arbitrary exactions.

---

[3] Bernard Lewis, *The Middle East and the West* (Bloomington: Indiana University Press, 1964), p. 59.

Artisans or small shopkeepers were likewise not free when their economic livelihood was threatened by imports and foreign-controlled local industries. Equality
might be a principle stated in the constitution, but it had little meaning in a
society where upper-class persons spoke rudely to members of the lower class and
treated them with contempt.

The imperial powers continued to control the Middle Eastern countries,
and their troops and officials were quite conspicuous. Their affluent life-style,
with the privileges they enjoyed, made the indigenous people resentful. The
nightclubs, brothels, and foreign movies insulted them. Furthermore, many
nominal Muslims began to adopt the mores and customs of the foreigners, and
to cease worshiping God.

Out of these conditions grew the Muslim Brotherhood, a movement that
began in 1928, became very strong in Egypt in the 1930s and 1940s, and was
suppressed by the revolutionary government in the 1950s. Although it originated,
prospered, and declined in Egypt, its strength and appeal were not restricted
solely to that country. It was an Islamic movement that started in Egypt, but its
message was to the whole Muslim world. It opened branches in other Arab
countries and inspired similar movements in Iran (the *Fedayan-i-Islam*) and
Pakistan (the *Jama^c at Islam*).

The Muslim Brotherhood gave the masses the opportunity to express
dissatisfaction with the existing state of affairs, and it offered them hope for the
future. They joined it in droves, went to its meetings and lectures, avidly read its
extensive literature, and participated in its rallies and demonstrations. While
liberal democracy trickled down from the top circles of society, this movement
welled up from the bottom.

The Brotherhood was a reaction against the Westernized life-style of
people in the top circles of Egyptian society, their extreme wealth and osten-
tatious display, and their get-rich-quick-through-any-means attitude. It expressed
anger at the economic and political domination of Egypt by the British and other
foreigners, and at the presence of British troops in the country. One of its targets
was the monarchy, pliable in the hands of the imperial powers and insufficiently
committed to the Islamic religion and social order. In speeches and sermons, its
leaders attacked the cinema because it disseminated Western ways, misguided
the young, and challenged the supremacy of the mosque as an institution teaching
morals and values.

The 1978-1979 Islamic Revolution in Iran manifested some of these same
emotions and beliefs. As with King Farouk in Egypt, who reigned from 1936 to
1952, the life-style of Muhammad Reza Shah and of the people close to him was
Western. Similarly, the Egyptian and Iranian monarchs used their position at the
apex of government and society to become very rich personally, and their
relatives and close associates did the same. Both the Egyptian king and the shah
were regarded by their people as being under foreign influence and control; in
the former case that of the British, and in the latter that of the Americans. In
both countries there was a considerable foreign presence; in Egypt from the

nineteenth century through the 1950s, there were French, British, Greeks, and Italians; and in Iran in the 1970s, Americans.

Because of these factors and others, opposition to the regimes of King Farouk and of Muhammad Reza Shah grew. The former was forced to leave his country on July 26, 1952, and the latter on January 16, 1979.

The symbol and catalyst of the Iranian revolution was the Ayatollah Ruhollah Khomeini, a septuagenarian white-bearded religious leader who wore a turban and robes and was supported by peasants, workers, merchants, students, civil servants, and professionals. In mass processions comprising hundreds of thousands and sometimes more than a million, people waved portraits of Khomeini and cried, "God is the greatest"—the fundamental religious creed of Islam, which members of the Muslim Brotherhood also shouted as they demonstrated in Egypt in the 1940s and early 1950s.

Hassan al-Banna (1906-1949)

The founder of the Muslim Brotherhood was Hassan al-Banna. He was born in the small town of Mahmudiyya, about ninety miles northwest of Cairo, where his father, a graduate of al-Azhar, was the *imam* (leader of prayer) in the mosque. He began his education at the age of eight, going to schools that taught the Koran and related religious subjects. In 1923, at the age of sixteen he entered the Dar al-ᶜUlum, a teacher-training college in Cairo founded in 1873 that was neither exclusively religious nor completely secular. A devout village youth, al-Banna was shocked by much that he saw in large, cosmopolitan Cairo. He was offended by the attacks on religious tradition by those who felt themselves emancipated, and he was disgusted with the endless debating and bickering among top political and governmental leaders. He saw books, newspapers, and magazines that he felt had as their goal the "weakening of the influence of religion."[4] He and his friends were very wrought up:

> No one but God knows how many nights we spent reviewing the state of the nation . . . analyzing the sickness, and thinking of the possible remedies. So disturbed were we that we reached the point of tears.[5]

In 1927, at the age of twenty-one, he graduated from the Dar al-ᶜUlum and became a teacher of Arabic in a state elementary school in Ismailiya, a major city on the Suez Canal. There he observed the luxurious office building of the foreign-owned canal company and the magnificent homes of the European employees. The roads and entrances of the city were controlled by the company,

---

[4]"The Autobiography of Hassan al-Banna," quoted in Richard Mitchell, *The Society of the Muslim Brothers* (London: Oxford University Press, 1969), p. 4.
[5]Ibid., p. 5.

and no one could enter or leave without its permission. Even in the Arab quarter, all street signs were written only in French, the "language of economic occupation."[6] Other people also were disturbed by the Western economic, military, and cultural domination of this city and of Egypt in general, and in March 1928, six Egyptian workers from the nearby British army base came to him, agitated and distressed. They said, according to al-Banna:

> We know not the practical way to reach the glory of Islam and to serve the welfare of Muslims. We are weary of this life of humiliation and restriction. Lo, we see that the Arabs and the Muslims have no status and no dignity. They are not more than mere hirelings belonging to the foreigners. We possess nothing but this book [the Koran] ... and these souls ... and these few coins ... All that we desire now is to present you with all that we possess, to be acquitted by God of the responsibility, and for you to be responsible before Him for us and for what we must do.[7]

Al-Banna was moved and accepted the burden imposed upon him to lead a new movement. Together they took an oath to be "troops for the message of Islam,"[8] under the name of the Muslim Brotherhood.

The movement grew rapidly, gained dues-paying members in the hundreds of thousands, and became highly organized, with branches in every principal town and city in the country. Affiliated with it were publishing houses to spread its message through newspapers, magazines, and books, and a variety of economic enterprises that employed members and made money. But most important, the Brotherhood was a way of life and an attitude towards the world.

The Brothers felt that they were part of a movement that would transform the Muslim world by a mass religious revival and by millions of individuals returning to the moral code and social practices of Islam. They condemned "partyism," the electoral process, and the whole parliamentary system, asserting that these were major causes of the rampant selfishness, moral decay, and vicious factionalism in Egypt. Pragmatically and on principle, they felt that they could not install their new political order through elections, yet they did not organize themselves into a conspiratorial party that aimed to seize power through force of arms.

Ideology

According to them, the Western world—strong in science, able to master the environment and subjugate the world—was permeated with materialism, overrun with greed and tyranny, and was in "bankruptcy and decline." Neither

---

[6] "The Autobiography of Hassan al-Banna," quoted in Christina Phelbs Harris, *Nationalism and Revolution in Egypt* (The Hague: Mouton, 1964), pp. 148-149.

[7] Quoted in Mitchell, *Society*, p. 8.

[8] Ibid., p. 8.

the liberal democracies of Western Europe nor the people's democracies of Eastern Europe were exempt.

In contrast, Islam was "one of the strongest, noblest, most merciful, virtuous, and blessed"[9] of social and political orders. All the virtues and none of the defects of other political ideologies and systems existed in it.

> If the French Revolution decreed the rights of man and declared for freedom, equality, and brotherhood, and if the Russian revolution brought closer the classes and social justice for people, the great Islamic revolution decreed all that 1,300 years before. It did not confine itself to philosophical theories but rather spread these principles through daily life, and added to them [the notions of] the perfectibility of man's virtues and the [fulfillment] of his spiritual tendencies.[10]

According to al-Banna, the problem with Egypt was that it had willingly adopted too much of the West and had not adhered sufficiently to Islam. Its leaders were not practicing Muslims, they were trained in Western ways and thinking, and they could not lead a Muslim country, because they "forgot their glory, their history and their past."[11]

The members of the Muslim Brotherhood were intent upon purifying and revitalizing Islamic society. They knew that they could not return to the conditions of the seventh century, but the principles that reigned then could be restored. To them the wonder of Islam was that its fundamentals were universal and ageless, but its specific economic, political, and social institutions "develop[ed] with every age and change[d] with the progress of sciences and the ways of life."[12] It was not the time to worry about restoring the caliphate or other institutions of the seventh century; it was the time to confront the modern age, to deal with the modern institutions that existed in Egypt, and to adapt them to Islam's principles.

Crucial was the return of the Sharia to a central role in Egyptian society. To rule by God's revelations was an injunction from the Koran, and for Egypt it was a social and cultural imperative, because the Sharia was rooted in its soil, while Western law was not. Without the Sharia as its central inspiration, Egypt would be a "society of cultural mongrels and spiritual halfcastes."[13]

For the members of the Brotherhood, Islam needed a state to enforce its precepts. The precise nature of the state was not a burning issue, but three basic rules were: (1) The Koran is the fundamental constitution; (2) the government operates on the principle of consultation with the people; (3) the executive is bound by the teachings of Islam and by the will of the people.

[9] Ibid., p. 233.
[10] Ibid., p. 233.
[11] Ibid., p. 219.
[12] Ibid., p. 250.
[13] Ibid., p. 236.

It did not matter what name was given to the chief executive—caliph, imam, king, governor, president were all fine—but he should be an adult, male, Muslim, healthy in body and mind, knowledgeable in Islamic jurisprudence, just, pious, virtuous, and capable of leadership. His tenure was for life, but if he failed to maintain Islam and its laws, he could be warned, guided, and even removed. The people were the source of his power, and "bowing to [their] will was a religious obligation."[14]

Since the Sharia already existed to order society, there was no need for a Western-style legislature with the power to make positive law. In its place was a consultative assembly, representing the people and commanding the obedience of ruler and ruled, in which lay the real power of the state. How people were to be chosen for it was a "secondary matter," but clearly political parties were not to be used. It was also clear that not everyone should sit in this assembly; the preference was to be given to experts in Islamic law, to the "natural" leaders of the people, such as heads of families, of villages, and of other groups, and maybe to scientists and technicians knowledgeable in the facts of the modern world. In it there would be free discussion, and decisions would be made by a majority vote, after which the minority would not oppose the majority. Two matters were excluded from its purview: (1) "the facts of the sciences," and (2) "the principles of religion."[15]

Suppression

From 1945 until the revolution in 1952, violence shook Egypt, with the Brotherhood involved in a lot of it. Assassinations and attempted assassinations were directed against members of the Egyptian cabinet, prominent judges, and British military and civilian officials. Hotels, clubs, and restaurants where Europeans congregated were bombed or set on fire, as were houses in the Jewish quarter of Cairo and theaters that showed Western movies. The Arab-Israeli conflict of 1948 added to the tension. The Brothers cached arms and trained some of their members in paramilitary tactics for the purpose, according to them, of aiding the Palestinians. However, some of these units engaged in violence against the Egyptian government. Unable to tolerate this increasing threat to its existence, the government, on December 8, 1948, ordered the dissolution of the Brotherhood because of its "terrorism" and intent to "overthrow the political order." The Brotherhood resisted and did not disappear, so on February 12, 1949, al-Banna was assassinated—an act that was planned, or at least condoned, by the prime minister and the king.

Immediately following the revolution of July 1952, there was a measure of cooperation between the Brotherhood and the revolutionary officers, but on October 26, 1954, a member of the Brotherhood attempted to assassinate Gamal

---

[14] Ibid., p. 246.
[15] Ibid., p. 248.

Abdel Nasser when he was giving a speech in Alexandria. The act was the work of a clique within the society and was not ordered by the leadership, but it was used by Nasser as a pretext to crush the whole organization. By December 9 of the same year, six members had been hanged and thousands imprisoned. Since then the Brotherhood has been outlawed and suppressed, continuing to operate underground; periodically, the government arrests members who have been participating secretly in its activities.

The Muslim Brotherhood was a strong and sometimes violent reaction against the incursions of the West into Egypt, particularly into its value system and way of life. It asserted that a new order rooted in faith, based on the Koran, and governed by the Sharia could be established that would give strength to Muslims and enable them to prosper in the modern world. Liberal democracy had failed to bring social justice to Egypt, and the Brotherhood maintained that it could only be brought about through Islam.

As this book goes to press, the full dimensions of the Islamic Revolution in Iran are not yet known, but we can see that it shares with the Brotherhood some of the same impulses, drives, and values. The turmoil in Iran demonstrates that throughout the Middle East Islam remains a powerful ideological system, molding the culture that undergirds the structures of the society and polity.

SOCIALISM

Socialism is a strikingly new phenomenon in the Middle East. Although the state of Israel was led from 1948 to 1977 by a democratic socialist party (the Israel Labor Party, formerly known as *Mapai*), in the other countries of the region, socialism was an ideology espoused only by a small number of intellectuals and a few weak political parties before the 1960s. These countries had been absorbed in a struggle for independence. Getting rid of the colonial master was the focus of people's energies, not the social and political order that would follow. Also, since these countries had few if any industries, there was no large working class, the traditional source of socialist strength.

All this changed in the 1960s. Socialism became the official ideology of several important states: Egypt, Syria, Iraq, Algeria, and Libya. In Turkey socialist parties increased in strength, and the party that Ataturk had founded, the Republican People's Party, moved toward the left.

Not to be discounted as a cause for the rise of socialism was the increasing influence of the Soviet Union in the Middle East. The USSR seized opportunities to support regimes that were willing to receive its aid, such as Egypt, Syria, Iraq, Algeria, Libya, and Democratic Yemen (South Yemen). On the grounds that these states were being led by "progressive" elements, and that they were "on the road to socialism," the Russians supported them, expecting that they would eventually establish a social and political order similar to their own.

Socialism was particularly attractive to the army officers, who began to seize power in the 1950s. These leaders came preponderantly from lower-middle-class families, whose needs political leaders had previously ignored. They were appalled by the corruption of liberal democracy in the Middle East and were repelled by the reaction and fanaticism of the Muslim Brotherhood. To these officers socialism was the answer, for it could bring real democracy and social justice and still be in harmony with the Arab and the Islamic spirit.

There are about as many forms of socialism in the Middle East as there are states and political parties, and only a few generalizations can be made concerning all of them. However, except for Israel, the following hold true: (1) Socialism is a symbol of real independence from the Western European imperial powers. Since European companies continued to dominate the economies of Middle Eastern countries after independence, nationalizing foreign-owned corporations and establishing socialist economies enabled Middle Eastern governments to declare their political and economic independence. (2) Socialism is an assertion of modernity. It is a way to show that a country is part of the modern world and is no longer backward or traditional. (3) Socialism is an affirmation of the values of equality, sharing, and cooperation, which are felt to be superior to the capitalist values of private property and individual competition.

Four forms of Middle Eastern socialism will now be examined: (1) Islamic socialism, (2) the Arab socialism of Egypt, (3) Arab Baath socialism, and (4) socialism in Turkey. The socialism of the Labor Party of Israel will be examined in Chapter 6.

Islamic Socialism

Islamic socialism integrates socialist ideals and Islamic precepts. It attempts to demonstrate that Islam is the equal of any other sociopolitical system with respect to equality and justice. It is not backed by a political movement, a revolutionary organization, or a political party, but several states such as Egypt, Libya, and Syria encourage its propagation in order to strengthen and legitimize the official doctrine, Arab socialism. Arab and Islamic socialism are not regarded as contradictory, but as mutually reinforcing.

Originally published in 1959, *Islamic Socialism*,[16] by Mustafa al-Siba'i, has been reprinted several times and has a semiofficial status in Egypt and other Arab countries. The author, a Syrian born in Homs in 1910, was the editor of one of the Muslim Brotherhood's publications. He was the head of its Syrian branch and was the Dean of the Faculty of Islamic Jurisprudence and School of Law at the University of Damascus.

His book argues that the underlying principles and basic practices of socialism can be found in the teachings of Islam and in the life of the Prophet

[16]Excerpts of this work are translated in Sami A. Hanna and George H. Gardner, *Arab Socialism* (Leiden, Netherlands: E. J. Brill, 1969), pp. 66-79.

Muhammad. A hundred or a thousand years ago the word "socialism" may not have existed, but there was the same concern to alleviate poverty, to bring about justice, to produce social harmony, and to utilize private property only for the common good.

For Siba'i socialism is not a passing fashion, and Islamic socialism represents a "human tendency which finds clear expression in the teaching of the prophets and in the work of reformers from earliest times." Siba'i says that prophets in various ages have preached that "we should be fair to the unfortunate ... show mercy to the poor, and ... sweep away injustice." He further says,

> What socialism really aims at, in all its various ideologies, is to put a stop to the individual who would exploit capital to become rich at the expense of the misery and wretchedness of the masses and to bring about social equality among all citizens so as to eliminate all manifestations of poverty and deprivation ...
>
> I do not believe that anyone who knows Islam and understands its spirit can properly deny that Islam clearly [has] these same goals in mind .... To refrain from advocating Islamic Socialism ... is to put a hindrance in the way of Islam ... [17]

The practical problems on which socialists usually focus, such as organization of the workers, nationalization of industries, and capital formation, are ignored by Siba'i. His book presents no step-by-step program on how to improve the condition of the Arabs, no plan for economic development, no scheme to organize the people. It is simply a statement that Islam is socialist and morally superior to capitalism or communism.

The Arab Socialism of Egypt

On July 23, 1952, twelve army officers carried out a coup in Egypt that overthrew the monarchy. As a group they advocated no political ideology, and together they belonged to no political party. They were simply against the incompetency of the government of King Farouk and the domination of the country by the British. From 1952 to 1961, they carried out a land reform program, secured the withdrawal of British troops from the country, started to build the Aswan High Dam, nationalized the Suez Canal Company, secured military arms and equipment from the Czechs and Russians, and faced the Ango-French-Israeli attack of 1956. These actions followed no predetermined program or plan.

In July 1961 the government, led by Gamal Abdel Nasser since 1954, placed all important economic enterprises that had not already been nationalized under state control. It gradually began to proclaim Arab socialism as the official

[17]Ibid., p. 68.

ideology. This ideology was not the theory of a revolutionary party or the magnum opus of a great thinker; it was basically a justification for the actions taken by the Nasser government.

Anwar al-Sadat, who acceded to the presidency upon Nasser's death on September 28, 1970, has modified this ideology in respect both to its Arab component and its socialist component. Under his leadership, the Egyptian (as opposed to the Arab) character of the society has been emphasized, and capitalism has been given more opportunities to develop within the predominantly socialist economy. During the summer of 1978 Sadat abolished the Arab Socialist Union, the single party that had propagated Arab socialism, and established in its place the National Democratic Party, which espouses democratic socialism. While socialism in some form continues in Egypt, Arab socialism is now mainly of historical importance and should be considered a product of the Nasser era.

The theory of Arab socialism, such as it is, must be gleaned from speeches and interviews by Nasser, from articles by his close colleague, Muhammad Hasanayn Haykal, editor of the newspaper *al-Ahram,* and from official documents such as the National Charter of 1962, the constitution of the Arab Socialist Union, and the constitution of the state.[18]

Arab socialists in Egypt deplored class divisions in feudal and capitalist societies and rejected the Marxist doctrine of class struggle. In the new Arab socialist society that they were attempting to create, "working powers," (defined as "farmers, workers, soldiers, intellectuals and national capital") took the place of classes.

A basic premise of Arab socialism was that social and political freedom were interrelated. The era prior to 1952, when the king, the British, and the big landlords oppressed the Egyptian people behind a facade of constitutional government, was offered as an example of the futility of political democracy without social democracy. During that period because of gross inequality and rampant destitution, people voted for those who guaranteed their livelihood or for those who threatened them with deprivation should they refrain from support. Political parties were squabbling selfish cliques. Parliament was controlled by the large landlords. The whole democratic system was a sham, because social democracy did not exist along with political democracy.

According to the advocates of Arab socialism, introducing social justice to Egypt would make possible real democracy in which all authority was in the hands of the people. Since power in the hands of the government was really power in the hands of the people, checks and balances or constitutional safeguards were unnecessary.

Arab socialism would not sacrifice the present generation for a future one. Nasser felt that Egyptians had suffered long enough and should not suffer any

---

[18] For excerpts from some of these documents, see Hanna and Gardner, *Arab Socialism,* pp. 335-408.

further. His goal was not blind pursuit of economic growth but a "society in which well-being prevails."

Arab socialists regarded religion as a positive good, and they supported and encouraged its development. They were nationalists and did not consider themselves members of an international movement of the working class. Finally, they did not regard private ownership of the means of production as an inherent evil; whenever it was socially useful, they felt it should be protected.

Arab socialism was almost completely the product of the thinking and policies of Gamal Abdel Nasser. He wanted the Arabs to establish their own identity as Arabs and socialists, and he demonstrated that they could establish an economic and social order that grew out of their own thinking and fulfilled their needs. His variety of socialism was popular because it was modern and in line with political trends throughout the world, especially in the Afro-Asian world. While Nasser's socialism was labeled "Arab," it was really Egyptian and arose out of the conditions in that country.

Arab Baath Socialism

Founded in the early 1940s in Syria, the Arab Socialist *Baath* (Renaissance) Party has espoused a pan-Arab ideology but has achieved only a measure of political success. It has repeatedly been torn apart by ideological arguments and power conflicts. Since 1963 it has been the controlling party in both Iraq and Syria in principle, but this has been more fiction than fact, for these countries are really controlled by groups of army officers who have some allegiance to Baathist ideology.

In contrast to Egypt, where a group of army officers seized power, nationalized businesses, developed the ideology of Arab socialism, and established a party (the Arab Socialist Union), in Syria the Baath began as a party, formulated an ideology, gained political power, and finally attempted to implement its ideology. Another difference is that in Egypt, army officers created the party and formulated the ideology, but in the Baath Party, civilians did both.

In Syria and Iraq, the party has civilian and military wings which have engaged in bitter struggles, and in both countries the military has won. The two civilian founders of the party, Michel Aflaq and Salah al-Din Bitar, have frequently been forced into exile.

Baathists have always been few, and their influence has been grossly out of proportion to their number. One of their principles is that they are an elitist vanguard leading the Arab masses. They have kept their membership rolls secret, but in 1964, when the party was enjoying considerable success, it was estimated to have only 8,000 members in Syria, 2,500 in Iraq, and 1,000 in Jordan.[19]

---

[19] Kamel Abu Jaber, *The Arab Ba'th Socialist Party: History, Ideology, and Organization* (Syracuse: Syracuse University Press, 1966), p. 144.

The Baathist army regimes in Syria and Iraq have been absorbed in many difficult practical problems. In particular, both countries have deep ethnic and religious cleavages, and the governments have been continually resolving conflicts or putting down rebellions. The ideology described in the following paragraphs is the system of belief of the Baath Party as formulated in its early years and does not necessarily represent the policies that the army regimes in Syria and Iraq have carried out. It does, however, give an indication of the thrust of their policies.

For the Baath, nationalism is more important than socialism. The party constitution deals first with the "unity and freedom," the "personality," and the "mission" of the Arab nation. Only after considering these issues does it speak about socialism, saying: "The Party of the Arab Baath is a Socialist party. It believes that socialism is a necessity which emanates from the depth of Arab nationalism itself." It constitutes the "ideal social order" for the Arabs and makes possible a "trustful brotherhood" among them.[20]

The symbols and slogans of the party also stress nationalism. The party emblem is a map of the Arab world over which is superimposed a torch. Across the top is written: "One Arab nation with an eternal mission," and at the bottom, "Unity, Freedom, Socialism."

One of the fundamental principles of the party is the "eternal mission of the Arab nation." Nowhere is this precisely spelled out, but the constitution states: "This mission reveals itself in ever new and related forms through the different stages of history. It aims at the renewal of human values, at the quickening of human progress, at increasing harmony and mutual help among the nations." One aspect of the mission is to fight colonialism, a "criminal enterprise." Another is to extend the "fraternal hand to other nations" in order to collaborate with them for the establishment of "just institutions" which will bring "prosperity and peace, as well as moral and spiritual advance."[21]

The Baath works towards a "complete change" in Arab society, which has far more social ramifications than a simple revolution. It will produce a new Arab consciousness and will bring indescribable vitality to the Arab world. It will be a total psychological transformation of every Arab individual, and not simply a change of governments and institutions.

The present and past leadership of the Arabs has been so bad, so self-serving, so ignorant of its Arab heritage, says the Baath Party, that it must be replaced. A vanguard of Arabs, conscious of their past and dedicated to bringing about a new day, is needed. It should be small in number and carefully screened to keep out the corruption of contemporary Arab society and to cleanse and refurbish this society. The Baath conceives of itself as being this vanguard, and sees this as one explanation for its small membership.

The Baath declares that all public utilities, extensive natural resources, big

---

[20]Ibid., p. 169.
[21]Ibid., p. 168.

industries, and means of transportation should be owned and managed by the state. No owner of agricultural land should possess more than he can farm, and all farming should be subject to the overall economic planning of the state. Civil liberties must not become a cover under which the age-old Arab concern for self thrives; such liberties should be provided, but "within the national interest."

As a party, the Baath is in decline. It has been mostly composed of intellectuals and army officers, of "generals without soldiers," of "leaders without followers." Its organization always has been top-heavy, well-established at a pan-Arab level, poorly established in the villages, towns, and small cities of the Arab world. It has been able to achieve some temporary phenomenal success by association with wielders of power such as Nasser, with whom it collaborated in establishing the United Arab Republic (the union of Syria and Egypt that lasted from 1958 to 1961), and with army officer groups in Syria and Iraq. But since it has had no base of power of its own, it has lost out to the leaders or groups that did.

Socialism in Turkey

From 1922 till his death in 1938, Turkey was ruled by Kemal Ataturk, a military hero who freed his country from foreign occupation and control and created the modern Turkish nation-state. He founded the Republican People's Party, which after his death continued to rule Turkey until 1950, when it lost out in free elections to the Democratic Party. During the 1950s the Democratic Party became more and more oppressive, and in 1960 the army carried out a coup that removed it from office. In 1961 a new constitution was ratified, free elections were held once again, and this time the Republican People's Party achieved a plurality. It established a coalition government, which was followed by successive coalitions led by either the Republican People's Party or the Justice Party, the successor of the Democratic Party.

Since 1961 the political process in Turkey has been quite free, and intellectuals, bureaucrats, army officers, medium-sized entrepreneurs, and town and village notables have engaged in a debate as to the path the country should take into the future. The reforms of Ataturk have been accepted by all as the foundation of the modern state, and the question Turks have asked themselves is how to complete the revolution he began. Many feel that it can only be done through socialism.

Members of these Turkish socialist parties do not fight the same battles as do socialists in the Arab states. Turkey has been a united nation-state for more than fifty years, and to Turkish socialists, nationalism is obsolete, a cause for persons who dream of the past and want to maintain the social status quo. Turkish socialists have a distinctly internationalist and pro-working-class outlook. They identify with democratic socialists, Marxists, progressives, and radicals of Western Europe. Their primary concern is the continuation of Turkey's economic growth, so that it can become equal to the European states in respect to industry, agriculture, intellectual life, government, and social welfare. They advocate increased state planning and more participation of the people in political life.

Turkish socialists do not accommodate themselves to religious sentiment. Under Ataturk, Islam had its official status taken away, and its practice was generally discouraged. Under the Democrats this trend was somewhat reversed, but, more than any other Islamic country, Turkey is a secular society in which religious allegiance is most often an attribute of the poor, the uneducated, and the rural people, while secularism is associated with the wealthy, the better-educated, the wielders of power, and the city dwellers. In Turkey, socialists are generally the most fervent secularists.

Many of the Turkish socialist leaders are Marxists. They have been heavily influenced by the ideology and action of the French Communist Party and of French leftism, and they do not try to distinguish their socialism from democratic socialism and communism in western Europe.

In summary, Turkish socialism is the product of a free multiparty political system. It is internationalist, working-class oriented, and secular; its objective is to make Turkey into an advanced industrial social welfare state similar to those that exist in western Europe.

Conclusion

Until the 1960s socialism was almost unheard of in the Middle East and was the theoretical concern of only a handful of intellectuals who studied its progress in the rest of the world and thought about how it could be applied in the Middle East. Since then it has become the official ideology of some Arab states and one ideological line in the multiparty democratic system of Turkey.

To its proponents socialism can give coherence, a sense of purpose, and a system of values to modern Middle Eastern society. Its advocates feel that it can bring social justice, individual liberty, true democracy, and material well-being. However, groups to its left, communists and Marxists, think that it cannot.

MARXISM

Practically everywhere in the Middle East, communist parties are banned, their newspapers proscribed, and their members watched by the police or jailed. Yet communist ideology touches the minds and emotions of many—whether they are called progressives, radicals, socialists, Marxists, Maoists, communists, or leftists. Publications emanating from the Soviet Union, China, and the eastern European countries, and leftist newspapers, magazines, and books published in the Middle East all make Marxism a subject of lively debate.

The fire of the Marxists is directed against the "reactionaries" and "feudal-ists," such as King Hassan of Morocco, King Hussein of Jordan, and the ruling family in Saudi Arabia, who rule absolutely and in collusion with "imperialism" and selfish internal interests. It is also aimed at the "bourgeois nationalists," such as Sadat of Egypt and President Hafiz al-Asad of Syria, who, according to the Marxists, are dictators who exclude the people from power and have carried out only partial social revolutions. They "promote anti-communism, anti-democracy, extreme chauvinistic nationalism; they isolate the people from the socialist camp, compromise with imperialism . . . and constantly maneuver between imperialism and socialism."[22]

The basic appeals of the Marxists are few and are restated over and over again in slightly different variations: (1) All change must have as its objective "the elimination of the exploitation of man by man and the building of a classless socialist society."[23] (2) "Imperialism" in its "old and new forms" on the eco-nomic, political, and ideological level, must be vigorously combated. To most Middle Eastern Marxists this means American and Western European imperialism. (3) Rather than simply being a slogan, democracy must become a reality. The government should rely on the masses, and their democratic organizations should participate directly and actively in the political and economic life of the country. The "single petty-bourgeois parties" must be set aside, because they cannot bring about the revolutionary remodeling of the social structures, and in their place must be established a "united front against imperialism and reaction" that includes communists.[24] (4) Radical social and economic reform must be carried out. Agricultural reform must go beyond that carried out by the current "revolutionary" regimes so that the wealthy peasant is eliminated and the methods of farming modernized. The state sector of the economy should be extended and reinforced, all for the purpose of raising the standard of living of the masses. (5) Finally, some Marxists call for reinforcement and enlargement of relations with the socialist camp, particularly with the USSR.

The "new class" of administrators in Egypt is criticized for its fear of the people and its high salaries, which enable its members to live above and apart from the people. This class "stops evolution, bleeds white the public sector for their own interests, speculates, engages in business and invests the surpluses in real estate and agricultural land."[25] The Marxists criticize a new class of entre-preneurs and businessmen that has arisen in Turkey, partially as the result of American economic aid, "which is fast becoming the representative of the new

---

[22] "Le Communisme et les problemes du monde arabe: un échange d'opinions de theoriciens marxistes de six pays arabes," *Orient* (Paris), no. 27 (3 Trimestre 1967), p. 198.

[23] Ibid., p. 197.

[24] *Yearbook on International Communist Affairs, 1971* (Stanford, Cal.: Hoover Institution Press, 1971), p. 277.

[25] Michel Kamel, "La Notion d'alliance nationale," in *La Pensée politique arabe contempo-raine*, ed. Anouar Abdel-Malek (Paris: Editions du Seuil, 1970), p. 296.

type of colonialism in the country."[26] They also condemn Turkey's alliances with the United States, a country "which seeks to subject Turkey to its domination" and has foisted on it "a horrid system of exploitation."[27]

In the Arab world the most radical thought comes from a number of young writers who might best be called radical intellectuals.[28] The stimulus for these intellectuals was the disastrous defeat for the Arabs in the war with Israel in June 1967. The Arab armies were well-equipped, and they knew that fighting was a distinct possibility and that they should be prepared for it; yet when the Israeli attack came, the armies crumbled. To the radical intellectuals, this humiliation was caused by serious inadequacies in the values and structures of Arab society, such as the "tribalist" state of mind, the traditional patriarchal society where all decisions are left to "father" or some other important person, and by misunderstanding of science and technology, which leads "to merely benefiting from the fruits of modern science without touching its roots or achieving a serious understanding of its motivating forces."[29]

But the overarching weakness of Arab society, according to these writers, is the supernaturalist concept of the universe, which sees everything as God-controlled and God-willed, and encourages the belief that change is hopeless, that duty is more important than happiness, and that it is better to obey arbitrary authority than to fight it. Under this philosophy, "Heaven has ordered, and the earth is bound to obey, the Creator has planned, and the creature has to be content with his lot . . . "[30] The liberal democrats feared to attack this theistic concept of the universe, the Muslim Brothers believed it, and the socialists have for the most part felt that it did not contradict their doctrine; but these young radicals have declared it to be a fundamental weakness of Arab society, and are launching an attack on the most "sacred cow" of all, Islam, which they believe has dominated Arab society for too long. Only when it is pushed aside can there be the change in beliefs, values, and customs that will enable modern social structures to thrive, they say.

The radical intellectuals call for revolt against the past and against the present-day values and structures of Arab society. To them Arab nationalism, Arab socialism, and liberal democracy have failed because they are semirevolutionary. Marxism best expresses their radical mood and promises a thorough and complete revolution.[31]

[26] Quoted in Aclan Sayilgan, *Rifts Within the Turkish Left (1927-1966)* (Washington, D.C.: Joint Publications Research Service, No. 14243, July 1967), p. 18.

[27] Ibid.

[28] Adel Daher, *Current Trends in Arab Intellectual Thought*, Rand Publication No. RM-5979-FF (December 1969).

[29] Quoted in Daher, *Current Trends*, pp. 22-3.

[30] Ibid., pp. 23-4.

[31] Ibid., p. 28.

CONCLUSION

By the year 1979, after a century and three quarters of Western influence, change in some form has come to all the countries of the Middle East. They have acquired advanced weapons, organized their armies along modern lines, and established modern ministries and government departments with staffs of educated persons. They have imported large quantities of consumer goods, and in some countries established industries of their own. Everywhere cement buildings, asphalt roads, and modern airports have been built. Likewise all governments of the Middle East except Lebanon provide social services such as free public education, public health service, and medical care.

The material change and modernization of the government and administration have been significant, but an overarching belief system to integrate all this and give meaning to society has not yet been found. While liberal democracy is now pretty much a historical phenomenon, socialism, Marxism, and Islamic fundamentalism are very much alive, and their proponents are competing for popular support and state power in just about every Middle Eastern country.

Part II

COUNTRY STUDIES

Chapter 6

Israel

In many respects Israel is unlike the other Middle Eastern countries. It is Jewish in a predominantly Islamic region, technologically advanced in an area that is only now entering the industrial age, Western in culture and life style in a region that is part of the East, and is a society of immigrants, or the children of immigrants, in a region where people have dwelt continuously in one village or town for millennia. Its people are formed into numerous and multifarious organizations (political parties, labor unions, corporations, professional associations, pressure groups, communal agricultural settlements, co-ops, a large governmental bureaucracy, and an army of reservists), whereas in the rest of the Middle East people live in communities (families, clans, villages, tribes, religious groups). Israel has the highest level of economic development, the greatest degree of social organization, and the most modern political system in the area.

The trauma of colonialism, the turmoil produced by the penetration of modern Western civilization, the shame of having armies routed in battle, and the weakness that comes from being economically backward have not been experienced by Israelis. However, they have had experiences unlike those of any other people in the Middle East or the world: almost 2,000 years of exile and persecution and, in the twentieth century, what Jews call the Holocaust, a trauma that has only one meaning to them—the Nazi extermination of six million Jews.

GEOGRAPHY AND ECONOMY

Israel lies on the shores of the eastern Mediterranean and is bordered on the north by Lebanon, the east by Syria and Jordan, and on the southwest by Egypt. Only the last country has signed a peace treaty with Israel, so the borders that it has with the other three are de facto and neither permanent nor legal.

In land area Israel is small, about half the size of the Netherlands. More than half of the country is desert, effectively reducing the area in which most people can live. Distances are short: from Tel Aviv to Jerusalem is only forty miles, and from Tel Aviv to Haifa or Beersheba, sixty miles.

Accentuating the smallness of the country is its intense urbanization. Of its total population of 3.7 million (1978 estimate), 84 percent live in urban areas and the rest in rural locales. There are about one million people in the Tel Aviv metropolitan area alone—about 30 percent of the country's total population. In the cities of Jerusalem, Tel Aviv, Haifa, and their surrounding districts dwell 55 percent of the country's inhabitants. A long-range forecast for the years 1980-1982 predicts that Israel's population will be four million, with 90 percent of it in urban areas and concentrated in the coastal plain between Nahariya in the north and Ashdod in the south, giving to this area one of the highest population densities in the world.

Urbanization is producing a certain tension between the country's ideals and reality. The founders of the state romanticized farming and believed that by touching and caring for the soil, one came to know and love one's country. Israel, however, is rapidly becoming a technologically advanced society like Holland, Sweden, or Switzerland, and the values of the frontier farmer will have to give way over time.

In agricultural output per farm worker, Israel is among the most advanced nations in the world. Technology, irrigation, and intensive use of the one-third of the land that is arable have made this possible. In the mid-1970s, 95 percent of the potential water resources were being used and 85 percent of the country's food needs met by local production. In the future, scarcity of water combined with population growth will necessitate the importing of more and more food products.

Israel's natural resources are minimal. It has no coal and no significant oil reserves. There are deposits of potash, bromide, and magnesium in the Dead Sea, of phosphates in the Negev (the desert in the South), and of copper ore of poor content at Timma, fifteen miles north of Eilat, the port on the Gulf of Aqaba. These minerals, except for magnesium, are being commercially exploited.

While poor in natural resources, Israel has been quite rich in capital. Throughout history, Jews in the Diaspora have sent funds to their coreligionists living in Eretz Israel. In the 1930s some European Jews fleeing Nazi persecution were able to bring with them much of their capital. In the twenty-year period from 1950 to 1970, $10 billion flowed into Israel, an unusually large amount for

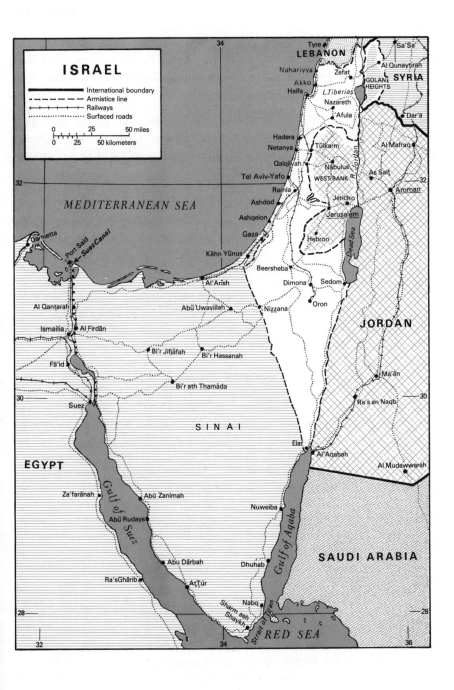

ISRAEL

— International boundary
– – Armistice line
+—+ Railways
········ Surfaced roads

0   25   50 miles
0   25   50 kilometers

MEDITERRANEAN SEA

LEBANON
Tyre
Sa'Sa
Nahariyya
Zefat
Al Qunaytirah
Akko
GOLAN
SYRIA
Haifa
L.Tiberias
HEIGHTS
Nazareth
Afula
Dar'a

Hadera
Netanya
Tulkarm
Al Mafraq
Qalqilyah
Nabulus
As Salt
Tel Aviv-Yafo
WEST BANK
Ramla
Amman
Ashdod
Jericho
Ashqelon
Jerusalem
Gaza
Hebron
Dead Sea
Kähn Yünus

Damietta
Port Said
Suez Canal
Al Qantarah
Beersheba
Al'Arish
Dimona
Sedom
Abū Uwayilah
Nizzana
Oron
Ismailia
Al Firdān
Fā'id
JORDAN
Bi'r Jifjafah
Bi'r Hassanah
Ma'ān
Bi'r ath Thamāda
Ra's an Naqb
Suez
SINAI
Elat
Al'Aqabah
Al Mudawwarah
EGYPT
Za'farānah
Abū Zanimah
Gulf of Suez
Nuweiba
Gulf of Aqaba
Abū Rudays
Abu Dārbah
Dhuhab
SAUDI ARABIA
Ra'sGhārib
AţŢūr
Nabq
Sharm ash Shaykh
RED SEA
Strait of Tiran

a country whose population was at the time only two to three million. The money came from reparations and restitutions paid by the government of West Germany, grants from the United States, and contributions from Jewish communities throughout the world. Since the founding of the state, government bonds have been offered for sale throughout the world. Taxation has been high, mostly to support the heavy defense expenditures, but also to discourage consumption and increase investment. Israel can absorb large amounts of capital because it has a population endowed with technical skills and an institutional framework oriented toward economic growth.

An unusually large number of persons with abilities vital to the economy live in Israel. Jews in Europe were forced to flee and leave all their possessions behind, but they brought with them the knowledge and skills that they had learned from their fathers and grandfathers. The result of this transplantation of skilled peoples has been the growth in Israel of such profitable industries as diamond cutting, making garments from fur pelts, and the manufacturing of precision instruments and tools.

The founders of the Jewish state laid great stress on economic self-sufficiency. Feeling that all other peoples, especially the Arabs, were hostile to them, they endeavored to build in Eretz Israel the economic structures that would make them self-sufficient and free from boycotts, strikes, or any other form of local or international economic sanction.

However, among the advanced industrial nations, economic interdependence is more the norm than self-sufficiency. Israeli leaders realize that if the standard of living of their people is to continue to rise, the country must produce exports that can sell in the industrialized world. While in the early years of statehood, investment was in industries that produced consumer goods for the home market, in the 1970s its focus has been changing in the direction of export industries, and Israel's economy is becoming increasingly integrated with the economies of western Europe and the United States.

One of Israel's potent economic assets is its educational system. Ninety-four percent of the adults are literate. There are seven universities or institutions of higher learning, several comparable with the best in the world, where the emphasis is on science, engineering, and technology. Israel has 1,388 university students per 100,000 inhabitants, the third highest proportion in the world after the United States and Canada.

In 1977, 85 percent of the people living in Israel were Jews and 15 percent non-Jews (Arabs of the Muslim, Christian, or Druze faith). Of the Jewish population, 52.1 percent were born in Israel, 21.5 percent in Asia or Africa, and 26.4 percent in Europe or the Americas.[1] Those born in Europe or descended from Europeans are called Western or Ashkenazi Jews, while those born in Africa or Asia or descended from them are called Oriental or Sephardi Jews. The Sephardim (the plural of Sephardi) have more children, their community is expanding more

---

[1] *Statistical Abstract of Israel,* no. 28 (1977), Table 21, p. 45.

rapidly than that of the Ashkenazim (the plural of Ashkenazi), and they now form more than half of the Jewish population. They decidedly predominate among the young. They are the new immigrants, the "ethnics," to apply an American analogy, while the Ashkenazim are the old immigrants, the equivalent of WASP.

Literacy is lower among the Sephardim than among the Ashkenazim. While the former comprise more than half of the population, they compose only 13 percent of the student body in universities and other institutions of higher education. The employment of Sephardim is less regular, their occupations are of lower status, their incomes smaller, and their housing less adequate. They tend to be more traditional and religious than the Ashkenazim. They have larger families, stronger kinship ties, and are generally more patriarchal.

POLITICAL CULTURE

Zionism

The Zionist movement began in the nineteenth century; its purpose was to encourage the settlement of the Jews in Palestine and to establish there a sovereign Jewish nation-state. Zionism is the Jewish nationalist movement, and its origins are multiple and ancient.

One of its roots is in religion. According to the Bible, the primordial father of the Jews, Abraham, entered into a covenant with God that was binding upon him and his successors. In it God promised his love and commitment; in return Abraham agreed to obey God and God alone; and to him and his descendants God pledged the land of Caanan. Divine love for the Jewish people, their obedience to God, and the promise of the land thus became fundamentals of the Jewish faith.

Abraham inaugurated the first period in Jewish history, that of the Patriarchs (seventeenth to sixteenth century B.C.). During this time the Jews traveled from the land of Abraham's birth, Ur in northern Mesopotamia, to Canaan, and later to Egypt, where they lived from the fifteenth century B.C. until the thirteenth century B.C., when they were led out under the leadership of Moses. They then wandered in the wilderness in Sinai and around 1200 B.C. entered Canaan under Joshua. At first they lived there in loosely associated tribes under leaders called Judges (1200-1020 B.C.). They formed a united nation (1020-928 B.C.) under Kings Saul, David, and Solomon. Upon the latter's death, the nation split into a northern kingdom, called Israel, which lasted from 928 to 721 B.C., when it was destroyed by the Assyrians; and a southern one, Judah, which lasted from 928 to 586 B.C., when it was captured by the Babylonians and its inhabitants forced into exile. In 539 B.C., Cyrus the Great, the ruler of Persia, conquered Babylon, and one year later allowed those Jews who so desired to return to their homeland, Eretz Israel. Except for a short period of independence in the second and third centuries B.C., under the Maccabees (also called the Hasmonians), the Jews lived there till A.D. 70 under a succession of foreign rulers: Persian, Greek, and Roman.

In A.D. 66 they began a rebellion against the oppression of the Romans. In 70 the latter destroyed their Temple and razed the city of Jerusalem, and in 73 crushed the last elements of Jewish resistance at Masada. Most Palestinian Jews left and settled in different parts of the Middle East and Europe. Only a handful remained in Palestine. Thus began the Galut ("exile"), frequently referred to as the Diaspora ("Dispersion").

Jews settled in countries that later adopted Christianity or Islam as the state religion. In both Christian and Islamic realms, the purpose of the state and society was the perpetuation and propagation of the faith. Since Jews did not believe in the faith of the majority, they separated themselves or were separated into distinct Jewish communities, living in special Jewish quarters of the cities or in all-Jewish villages. Restrictions were imposed upon them, differing in harshness according to the ruler or the circumstances. At best the Jews were tolerated; at worst they were persecuted. In Europe they suffered from one expulsion after another. Spain, France, England, Poland, Rumania, and Germany, at one time or another, exiled their entire Jewish populations. In the Muslim world the Jews did not suffer this fate. Jewish communities lived continuously from either the time of the Babylonian exile in 586 B.C. or from the destruction of the Temple in A.D. 70, until the late 1940s in Iraq, Yemen, Palestine, Egypt, North Africa, Turkey, and the Balkan countries.

The French Revolution of 1789 brought about the emancipation of the Jews of western Europe. It marked the end of the theocratic state and the beginning of the secular nation-state in which all citizens, whatever their religion, were equal. Gradually throughout the nineteenth century, in one country after another, Jews were given civil and political rights and became equal legally to everyone else. They were free to enter the public schools and universities and any profession or occupation they might desire, even the military. Jews left the ghetto, stopped wearing their distinctive dress, spoke the language of their fellow citizens, and became, except for private religious practices, indistinguishable from them. Emancipation meant increased security, enhanced social status, and greater prosperity, but it also brought with it the danger of assimilation. Jews could intermarry with non-Jews, renounce their faith, or simply stop thinking of themselves as Jews. Many did.

In eastern Europe, primarily the Czarist Empire, which encompassed Poland and in which the bulk of the European Jews lived, the effects of the French Revolution were very limited. The empire of the Czars was "Holy Mother Russia"; church and state were closely bound together, working to preserve the distinctive autocratic and theocratic Slavic Orthodox civilization.

Jews were regarded as heretics, aliens, and subversives bringing in dangerous ideas from the West. The restrictions on them became increasingly severe, and the social ostracism greater. Toward the end of the century pogroms (anti-Jewish riots) broke out, often abetted by priests or the secular authorities.

Multiple movements developed in eastern Europe concerned with how to "alleviate the Jewish condition." Millions of Jews emigrated to the United States. Large numbers became Marxists, abandoned their Jewish identity, joined radical international socialist movements, and worked for the overthrow of capitalism, which they believed to be the root of the Jewish plight. Some desired to reestablish the Jewish state in Eretz Israel, and a small number even emigrated there, thus beginning the process of its establishment.

Ironically it was from a western European assimilated Jew, Theodor Herzl (1860-1904), that Zionism received its greatest impetus. Born in Budapest, he had grown up and was educated in the German cultural milieu of the Austro-Hungarian Empire. As the Paris correspondent for a Viennese newspaper, he observed the Dreyfus trial in 1894. It convinced him that even in a liberal and advanced country like France, anti-Semitism was endemic and the Jews could only be free from persecution if they had their own sovereign state. In 1896 Herzl published a book called *Der Judenstaat* ("The Jewish State"). It was quickly translated into other languages, caught the imagination of Jews, especially those in eastern Europe, and became the chief political treatise of the Zionist movement.

Under Herzl's leadership, a Zionist Congress was assembled in Basel, Switzerland, in August 1897. Jews from all over the world and of all religious and political persuasions attended. The Congress founded the World Zionist Organization, which became the political instrument for the establishment of the Jewish state. It drew up a program advocating Jewish settlement in Palestine, the arousing of Jewish national consciousness, and the raising of funds for these ends.

Within the Zionist movement there were many differences as to goals, organization, and tactics. Some persons looked upon the return to the Jewish homeland as a religious act and felt that in establishing a new state Jews should abide by God's law as expressed in the Torah. Others were primarily committed to the preservation of the Jewish culture and "spirit" through the foundation in Palestine of Jewish educational institutions, museums, and libraries. Another group, the "politicals," wanted to give the Jews a place of physical safety and security, a refuge where they would be free from persecution.

Herzl died in 1904, and a new leader of the Zionist movement arose. Chaim Weizmann was born in Russia, but in 1904 settled in England. He was a chemist, and since his research made a significant contribution to the British war effort, he was able to establish contacts with the leaders of British society and politics. Gradually he convinced some key persons of the merits of the

Zionist cause. The Balfour Declaration of November 2, 1917, was the result. It was an official statement of the British Government issued by Lord Balfour, the Foreign Secretary:

> His Majesty's Government view with favor the establishment in Palestine of a national home for the Jewish people and will use their best endeavors to facilitate the achievement of this object, it being clearly understood that nothing shall be done which may prejudice the civil and religious rights of the existing non-Jewish communities in Palestine, or the rights and political status enjoyed by Jews in any other country.

This became official British policy, and while the British controlled Palestine between 1917 and 1948, Jews were permitted to immigrate there. By 1948 they numbered 650,000. Upon the British withdrawal on May 15, 1948, the Jews formed the state of Israel.

Zionism developed and continues to exist in response to two threats: (1) persecution or, in modern times, genocide; and (2) assimilation. Since both lead to the extinction of the Jewish people, it is the primary aim of the state of Israel to prevent this. The threat of extinction by assimilation has led to the creation in Israel of Jewish cultural institutions which will preserve the language, literature, history, and national consciousness of the Jews. The threat of extinction through persecution or genocide is countered by making Israel a place in which all Jews are welcomed simply because they are Jews. Upon arrival in Israel, if a Jew desires, he or she can immediately become an Israeli citizen.

The twenty-seventh World Zionist Congress meeting in Jerusalem in 1968 defined the contemporary aims of Zionism as:

> the unity of the Jewish people and the centrality of Israel in Jewish life; the ingathering of the Jewish people in its historic homeland, the land of Israel . . . the strengthening of the State of Israel . . . the preservation of the identity of the Jewish people through the fostering of Jewish and Hebrew education and of Jewish spiritual and cultural values; the protection of Jewish rights everywhere.[2]

Socialism

For the founders of the state, the men and women of the Second *Aliyah* (Hebrew, literally meaning "ascent"; more generally, "immigration" to Eretz Israel) who immigrated to Palestine between 1905 and 1914, Israel meant not simply a national rebirth, but also the establishment of a new commonwealth based on social justice. They firmly believed that the one could not take place without the other, and they called themselves Labor Zionists. These persons had

[2] "The New Jerusalem Program," *Middle East Record* (Jerusalem: Israel Universities Press), vol. 4 (1968), 571.

grown up in eastern Europe at the turn of the century and had become imbued with both the nationalism that was stirring the peoples in this area, such as the Poles and Hungarians, and the social revolutions that were arousing the oppressed classes.

Some Jews, such as Leon Trotsky, eschewed their Jewish identity and submerged themselves in the cause of the international proletariat. But others, such as David Ben-Gurion, Zalman Shazar, and Itzhak Ben Zwi, wanted to fight for the causes of both international socialism and Jewish nationalism. In the years before World War I they immigrated to Palestine and began to build a Jewish state in which there would be a Jewish class of workers and farmers who would be full participants in the international socialist revolution.

The first kibbutzim and moshavim ("communal agricultural settlements") were founded in the period during and shortly after World War I on these precepts of nationalsim and socialism. Land that had been fallow was bought, settled, and placed under cultivation, not by private farmers, but by communities of Jews. The kibbutzim and moshavim were located in areas of sparse Jewish settlement, often on the borders of Palestine, so that the Jews would later be able to claim all of Palestine as their sovereign territory. But the cooperative settlements also had a social thrust. Their founders shared the Marxist belief that the right of possession and management of land should go to those who make it bloom by the labor of their hands, so the kibbutzim and moshavim were owned by the toilers, and run according to the principles of direct democracy. Everyone was equal, and all leaders were elected by the membership and were responsible to it.

Today no more than 10 percent of the Israeli population live in cooperative settlements, but the values that they represent are widespread in the society. Kibbutzniks (members of a kibbutz) have a disproportionate share of the leadership positions in both politics and the military because Israelis regard them as ideal types. The values they represent and the lives they live—of self-reliance, courage, simplicity, equality—are the ideals of Israeli society.

Labor Zionists believed that in Europe the Jew was being crushed by the exclusive nationalism of the majority and by "exploiting capital." They were determined that in Eretz Israel neither would exist. They built a society that was Jewish as well as democratic, cooperative, and egalitarian. The Zionists stressed that Jews must work in the fields and factories and not exploit the easily available cheap Arab labor. They believed that labor led to a spiritual change in oneself, to self-renewal, to the creation of the "new Jew."

The generation of these socialist pioneers is now aged and passing from the scene. The socialism they created was a product of the conditions in which they had lived, both in Europe and in Palestine, before the creation of the state of Israel. Israel is now coming to resemble the small socialist nations of Europe, where socialism is pragmatic, diffuse, and nonideological, and is mostly a general attitude that stresses egalitarianism and social welfare.

Religion

Approximately 25 percent of the Jewish population of Israel is religiously observant. Fifteen percent vote for one of the religious parties. The religious differ among themselves on many issues, but their overriding concern is that Israel be a state where the government, through its policies and laws, supports the Halakah ("Jewish religious law").

There are several religious parties which have been successful in getting laws enacted enforcing the sabbath, prohibiting the raising of pigs and the sale of pork in Jewish neighborhoods and towns, and granting state aid to religious schools. They have worked for the continuation of the system whereby marriage, inheritance, and divorce are under the jurisdiction of rabbis functioning in religious courts. The most well-known and controversial matter is the question, "Who is a Jew?" The religious parties maintain that this must be determined according to the Halakah by Orthodox rabbis. Nonreligious parties argue that pragmatic and secular criteria should be used. Since Jews can gain automatic Israeli citizenship under the "Law of the Return" simply by expressing their desire to be citizens, while non-Jews have to wait for a period of time and go through a naturalization process, the matter of who is a Jew is quite important.

The religious issue has bedevilled the politics of Israel since the state's founding, yet although the differences have been sharp, they have not led to the disintegration of the society. The state does not have a constitution and operates instead under a series of basic laws. In 1948, agreement could not be reached over the issue of whether Israel was to be a secular or theocratic state, so the matter was "put over" or "delayed." This has become a political practice; when agreement cannot be reached between the religious and secular forces, rather than one side pushing its way through, a decision is made not to reach a decision.

Also, the major parties compete for the religious vote. They want to increase their strength at the polls, so they do nothing to antagonize the religious elements and make vague, general appeals to them. In most of the elections since 1948, Mapai (now called the Israel Labor Party) has had a plurality of the seats in the Knesset (the Israeli parliament, a unicameral body), but not a majority. In order to form a government it has therefore had to find a coalition partner, usually the National Religious Party. The basic deal between the two has been that the Labor Party will have free rein on most domestic, economic, and social matters, and the National Religious Party will get its way in some religious matters. In 1977 this same arrangement was made between the Likud Coalition, which had gained a plurality in the national elections of that year, and the National Religious Party.

Even though there are many militant secularists in Israel and a clear majority of the Jewish population is not religious, there has been no campaign to wipe out religion in the country such as occurred in France after the Revolution of 1789 or in Russia after 1917. Religious elements are tolerated because they contribute to making the country "Jewish." Most Jews recognize that Judaism has been the center of the Jewish nation in the past and has contributed to its culture, traditions, and history. They feel that such things as observing the Sabbath from sundown on Friday to sundown on Saturday give Israel its Jewish flavor, even though secularists may not use that time for worship but for outings and fun.

The Holocaust

A people who have been persecuted for millennia, exiled from many of the countries in which they have lived, and in this century been the object of a systematic campaign of total extermination, naturally are concerned with security. The Holocaust (the Nazi murder of six million Jews), followed closely by the Arab attempts in 1948 to overrun and destroy the state, deeply affect the national psyche and make defense a concern and a passion that override all other matters.

Israel spends $1,176 annually per person (1977) on defense, contrasted with $480 per person in the United States (1977). This represents 29.9 percent of Israel's gross national product, compared with 6 percent of the United States'.[3]

Young men at about the age of eighteen serve in the regular Israeli army for three years, and after discharge are in the reserves until age fifty-five. Unmarried women between eighteen and thirty-eight are also liable for military service. In times of emergency, persons not in the Defense Forces take over essential civilian positions that have been vacated by those who have been called up. Everyone is in some way a part of the defense effort.

Anti-Semitism, which has been endemic throughout history, and Arab hostility produce in Israelis a sense of being alone. Their gut feeling is that non-Jews cannot be depended upon to help Jews in their hour of need. The silence and inaction of the Western world while the Nazis were exterminating the Jews, the sudden turn in French foreign policy during the war of June 1967 from supporting Israel with military assistance to withdrawing assistance, and the failure of the Common Market nations, except for Holland, to assist Israel in the war of October 1973, confirm this feeling. Jews feel that together they must work and defend themselves, since their existence depends upon their own efforts, and theirs alone.

The Holocaust, the memory of which is kept alive in Israel through museums, memorials, special days of commemoration, and lessons and special projects in the schools, causes Israelis to feel that they are engaged in the "last stand" of the Jewish people. With the experience and the memory of Hitler so

---

[3] *The Military Balance, 1978-1979* (London: International Institute for Strategic Studies, 1978), pp. 88-89.

real and immediate, there is a determination not to allow anyone else to carry out a similar malevolent plan.

In southern Israel are found the ruins of Masada, an ancient fortress on a hilltop. Here, in A.D. 73, Jewish fighters made their last organized stand against the Romans. After a seven-month siege, the Romans finally reached the top of the hill and found that the defenders, except for two women and five children, had committed suicide rather than surrender. Today recruits for the Israel Armored Corps take an oath on its summit—"Masada shall not fall again"—and this sentence is learned by all Israeli children as soon as they are able to talk and comprehend it.

The "last-stand" feeling gives to Israeli society and politics a seriousness, determination, cohesion, and brusque efficiency that does not exist elsewhere in the Middle East. Ideological differences among Israelis are sharp, social differences are many, but all agree that nothing can come second to the defense of the state's territory and institutions.

The Old and the Young

Repeated reference has been made to the founders of Israel. These persons, who came to Eretz Israel shortly before and after World War I, were visionaries and utopians for whom ideas and principles were more important than reality. When they arrived in Palestine, the land was controlled by the Ottoman Turks or the British, no more than 10 percent of the population was Jewish, and the country was desiccated, primitively farmed, and unindustrialized. The Zionists' idea of creating a Jewish farming class and proletariat in these conditions seemed ridiculous, and the hope of establishing a Jewish state even more so. Yet they ignored the facts as they exercised their will.

Zionists regarded the Jew of the Diaspora as a caricature of the "real Jew," and having been born and reared in the Diaspora, they wanted to transform themselves into "new Jews." Traditional Jewish occupations, tailoring and peddling, they disdained; Yiddish, the German-Jewish language of the European ghetto, they refused to speak; the dress, mores, mannerisms, and habits of the Jews in Europe, they repudiated. Instead they became farmers or common laborers, spoke Hebrew, dressed simply, and behaved in an assertive, aggressive way. In the process of reviving the land, each individual was rebuilding himself and herself and engaging in self-renewal.

In the 1970s the first generation of pioneers was beginning to fade from the scene, but they still held positions of power. Golda Meir (born in Russia in 1898, died in Israel in 1978), who was prime minister from 1969 to 1974, is representative of this group. Yitzhak Rabin, born in Palestine in 1922 and prime minister from 1974 to 1977, was said to represent the new generation of younger native-born leaders, yet he was succeeded as prime minister in 1977 by Menahem Begin, born in 1913 in Poland and more representative of the older generation. The issue between the old and the young is not so much over who should rule the country as it is over the values and purpose Israel should have once its founders are dead.

The old were ideologues who loved to discuss Zionist and socialist theory; the young are more concerned with the here and now: how to survive the next Arab-Israeli war. The old experienced the persecution and degradation of Jewish life in eastern Europe prior to World War I, and many lived through the horrors of Nazi persecution; the young alternately want to remember and forget the old Jewish world in eastern Europe and the Holocaust. The old lived much of their lives in the small Jewish society of mandated Palestine under British rule, when the members of Jewish organizations were few, relations were personal, rules were self-imposed, and participation was voluntary. The young live in a Jewish society that is vastly larger and thoroughly bureaucratic. Legal sanction has replaced voluntarism, and bureaucracy has supplanted self-motivated cooperation. The old still preach the virtues of dedication, effort, and self-effacement, but the young question their relevancy in a bureaucratic and technocratic society.

The older generation felt itself to be master of the situation; the younger one feels that it is caught in a situation it did not create. The older persons are aggressive, self-righteous, and self-confident nationalists; the younger ones are tormented existentialists who act and then question their actions. The old always struggled to be Jewish; the young feel that simply being a Jew and living in Israel makes one Jewish.

The Arabs Living in Israel

Arabs comprise 15 percent of the population of Israel, a larger minority than the black community in the United States. Due to the Arabs' higher birth rate, this percentage is growing. The Arabs live separately in their own towns, villages, or city sectors, and the contact with Jews is minimal or nonexistent. Arabs enjoy full civil and political rights, but until 1966 many living in border regions were under military administration. All Arabs are exempt from service in the armed forces. Today those living in East Jerusalem have all the rights of permanent residents of Israel, yet may keep their Jordanian or other former citizenship. They have the opportunity to apply for Israeli citizenship, but only a very few have done so.

In the material sense, the Arabs living in Israel are clearly better off than before Israeli independence: their standard of living is higher because of the greater opportunity to secure jobs in the modern Israeli economy; their educational system has been improved, and literacy has advanced greatly; public health is much better, with the result that their mortality rate has gone down. Some social advances have also been made: women have an enhanced status, and young educated persons now have some influence and power in Arab communities, as opposed to the old traditional elites who used to run them.

But material advance for the Arabs living in Israel has been counteracted by the spiritual problems of being Arabs in a Jewish state. The symbols of the state—the star of David on the flag and the menorah on the state seal—do not excite Arabs. The fundamental policies of the Zionist movement—the ingathering of the exiles, the revival of the Hebrew language, the development of Jewish culture, the inculcation in the young of Jewish pride and a sense of Jewish history, the creation and defense of the state—do not stir them. The Israeli national passion for archeology, which centers on the excavation of ancient Jewish sites, does not interest them. The Arabs may learn Hebrew, but to them it is a foreign language. They can run for political office at the local level, and be elected representatives in parliament, but they know that becoming an important cabinet minister, prime minister, or president of the state is a distinct improbability.

The predicament of the Arab in Israel is similar to the one Zionists portray of the Jew in economically developed liberal democracies. In these states, Jews have complete civil, political, and religious equality, but, so the Zionist argues, are in danger of losing their souls. If Jews speak Hebrew at all, it will only be on very limited occasions. If they study Jewish history, it will be something they do over and beyond that of the history of the country in which they are living. Their friends and peers will be mostly non-Jews whose customs, habits, and mores will become their own. Under such conditions it is impossible to be a full Jew, Zionists argue. Arabs in Israel confront these same problems; their choices are to become a hyphenated Israeli (an Arab-Israeli), convert to Judaism (which is discouraged and very rarely done), or emigrate.

Israel is a Jewish state, not a binational one, and one of its reasons for being is to make the Jew feel at home. Arabs can only feel that they are outsiders. It is perfectly possible for them to become active citizens of the state, but they can never become Israeli patriots. Arabs may vote, serve in public capacities, and enjoy the freedom that the state gives them, but they cannot live in that organic relationship to the land that is so romanticized by Zionists; Arabs will not tread every nook and cranny of the country so that they and it become "one"; they will not commit to memory Jewish folklore, nor will they assiduously study Jewish history. An Arab's heroes will not be Jewish ones. One's loyalty will always be to the Arab *community* in which one lives and possibly, in a vague sense, to the greater Arab nation, but never to the *nation-state* of Israel.

Western and Oriental Jews

Jews comprise 85 percent of the Israeli population, and among them the Orientals (Sephardim) comprise a slight majority, while the Western Jews (Ashkenazim) are in a minority. The two groups are different in many ways, and a primary social question for Israel is the degree to which they are going to integrate.

Prior to independence (May 15, 1948), the Jewish community in Palestine was overwhelmingly Western. Between 1919 and 1948, 90 percent of the immigrants were from Europe or America, and only 10 percent from Africa or Asia. The immigrants of this period were imbued with secular nationalism, and many were ardent socialists. Their aspirations were to colonize the land and to establish a new independent and modern Jewish society. They had the skills and abilities characteristic of modern societies, and they created the country's major social and political institutions and established its most widely prevailing values and beliefs. Today they occupy almost all of the leadership positions in the country, and they are its "dominant social type."

Since independence, the Orientals have steadily increased in number. Between 1948 and 1964, 55 percent of the immigrants were Orientals. Quite often they came as entire communities: a village from Morocco, or the Jewish residents of Baghdad would immigrate together. In Israel they often settled as groups. They were drawn to Israel primarily by the Messianic call to return to the land of their forefathers. Most did not have even the elemental skills or education that go with being a part of a modern society. Today the Orientals have lower social status, poorer-paying jobs, and less political power.

The Oriental Jews in Israel have been subject to intense socializing forces. The government, dominated by Westerners, thinks of itself as a modernizing elite, and of the Orientals as traditional masses. It makes every effort to insure the absorption of the Orientals. The army, political parties, Histadrut (the country's giant labor union), and the mass media have taken over the role of primary socializers, which in the countries of former residence belonged to the family. Orientals are being taught the habits of good citizenship, inculcated with patriotic values, and pressured to have social solidarity with all other Israelis, whatever their previous country of residence.

In those Islamic countries in which most Oriental Jews formerly had lived, minorities were allowed little or no participation in the political process. The government was Muslim and authoritarian. Individuals were subjects, not citizens, and were given no opportunity to seek redress of grievances. Jews distrusted the authorities and had no common purpose with them. Relations with them were characterized by hostility, lack of cooperation, fear, and distrust.

In Israel, Oriental Jews learn that they have political rights, not just duties. They can vote in local and national elections and serve in political offices. They are guaranteed freedom of speech and of assembly, and have all the protections of due process in criminal and civil proceedings. Their primary duty is to support the right of the Jewish people to their own state in the land of Israel, and to fight for its continued existence in the armed forces.

Because of the identity of purpose between the Oriental Jew and the state, and as a result of the openness of the political process in Israel, the Sephardim have come to exercise their rights and to participate freely and fully in Israeli politics. They have no fear of expressing their grievances, and they vote, without inhibition, for those parties that support their interests and viewpoints.

Patriotism is a new emotion for the Oriental Jew in Israel. In their former country of residence, the Sephardim were sojourners unable to develop any permanent attachment to the land. Through Gadna (para-military battalions for youth ages fourteen to eighteen) and the army, they travel the length and breadth of Israel, visit the sites of ancient battles, hear retold the tales of heroism of Jews in the past, examine the remains of ancient Jewish fortifications, and see the evidence of the vibrant Jewish life in the Eretz Israel of the past. In the schools, history, geography, economics, and geology are used to instill myths about the land. Sephardim experience an identity and closeness to their country that they have never known before.

However, the "absorption process" pushed by the government has had more limited effectiveness in eliminating the differences between Oriental and Western Jews. The latter frequently stress that they came from the more advanced parts of the world, and that it was through their efforts that the state of Israel was created. They frequently make the point that the Western Jews of the Second *Aliyah* separated themselves from the already existing Oriental communities in Palestine in order not to be drawn into their passive and pious existence. An army textbook states that the settlers of the Second *Aliyah* were "proud to be as they were since they had come to support themselves by 'work' and not to take 'charity.' "[4] Because of these claims of superiority, Oriental Jews are tempted to depreciate and even deny their origins. For example, North African Jews frequently claim that they come from southern France.

In history books and the mass media, the Oriental Jewish culture is slighted. Great Jewish thinkers who lived in the East, such as Alfasi (1013-1103), who lived in Algeria, Morocco, and Spain, and Maimonides (1135-1204), who was born in Spain and lived in Morocco, Egypt, and Palestine, do not get the same attention as their counterparts in the West. The contributions of Moroccan, Tunisian, and Egyptian Jews to Hebrew literature and religious thought in the seventeenth, eighteenth, and nineteenth centuries is given scant attention by the Ashkenazim. The East is usually portrayed as an abode of backwardness, and the Jews who lived there as being the victims of the low cultural level of the Arabs. This picture, which is not quite accurate, does not give Oriental Jews pride in their past or confidence in their contemporary role in Israel, and it creates among the Western Jews a feeling of superiority and condescension towards their Oriental fellow-citizens.

The Ashkenazim and Sephardim are also differentiated by the fact that secularism predominates among the Westerners, and religion among the Orientals. For the most part the former give Judaism a secular and nationalistic emphasis, interpreting the religious law "liberally." The latter treat religion as divine revelation, regarding the religious law as immutable. The religious parties in Israel enjoy strong support by the Orientals.

[4] Quoted in Maurice Roumani, "Some Aspects of Socialization in the Israeli Army: The Case of Oriental Jews" (paper delivered at the Annual Meeting of the Middle East Studies Association, Milwaukee, Wisconsin, November 8-10, 1973).

When these subjective differences are added to the objective ones of income, education, and status, the gap between the two groups is great. The feelings of solidarity that do exist relate not to one another but to common institutions such as the state, the army, or a political party. Orientals are good citizens and Israeli patriots, but they and their Western Jewish compatriots have not yet come together to form a unified society.

POLITICAL GROUPS

Nonassociational Groups

The early Zionists and the founders of the state of Israel moved in the social milieu of Western Jews. They envisioned in Eretz Israel a homogeneous Western Jewish society, highly developed economically and egalitarian socially. However, today Israel is heterogeneous and composed of four distinct nonassociational ethnic groups: (1) Western Jews, (2) Oriental Jews, (3) Arabs living in Israel, and (4) Arabs living in East Jerusalem and the Administered Territories (area conquered by Israel in the war of June 1967 and administered by the Ministry of Defense). It is beginning to have the problems of other multiethnic societies such as Belgium, Canada, and Cyprus.

The grievances of the Oriental Jews and of the Arabs are expressed in diffuse, anomic, and incoherent ways, and not through interest groups in a continuous, organized, and specific fashion. Oriental Jews have held protests to publicize their low wages and poor housing. The Arabs in East Jerusalem have not voted in the municipal elections as the authorities have urged them to do, and along with Arabs in the Administered Territories, have demonstrated at frequent but sporadic intervals.

Oriental Jews and Arabs have some local associations, such as the Sephardi Council of Jerusalem, yet nothing exists on a national level. Political parties, particularly Likud, the Israel Labor Party, and the National Religious Party, have appealed to one or another of the concerns of the Orientals, with the former making a special effort to mobilize the Arabs. Because of the policies of the government and of the major parties, the demands of these ethnic minorities have been diffused and compromised with those of other groups.

The Arabs, both in Israel and in the Administered Territories, are encouraged to be politically passive. For a long time they have been ruled by someone other than themselves: the Turks, the British, the Hashemite Dynasty of Jordan, and now the Israelis. The authorities do not allow the Arab schools to become a source of anti-Israel protest; they deport persons from East Jerusalem and the Administered Territories who have become too outspoken, and they keep the Arabic newspapers within definite boundaries, while still giving them a high degree of freedom. The Arabs living within Israel vote for members of the Knesset, but those who are elected on the Arab list of the Israel Labor Party are the old, traditional leaders who follow the dictates of the Labor leaders, even when it comes to matters affecting the Arab community. However, those elected from both of the two communist parties are anti-Zionist and outspoken in their defense of the Arab community, but since independence these parties have together never held more than six seats in the 120-member Knesset.

Heretofore the government has operated on the assumption that a "melting-pot" or "pressure-cooker" society existed, but indications are that not all Israeli citizens and those subject to its administration have been "melted down." A major policy question for the future is whether to continue on this assumption, or to operate on the supposition that Israel is a multiethnic society. The latter would require major changes in the political system. The answer to this question will depend upon the astuteness and perspicacity of present-day Arab-Israeli and Jewish-Israeli leaders, and upon the outcome of the peace negotiations between the state of Israel, the neighboring Arab states, and representatives of the Palestinians.

Associational Groups

Interest groups, also called associational groups, proliferate in Israel. Some, such as Histadrut and the various kibbutz federations, are economic in their orientation. Others are protest movements that rise and fall on the basis of one issue. They include the Black Panthers, which articulated the grievances of the Oriental Jews in the late 1960s; the Young Couples, which protested inadequate housing for young married couples in the early 1970s; the Land of Israel movement, which arose after the 1967 war and maintained that Israel should keep all of the land it had captured; and the Peace Movement, which grew up after the same war and advocated surrender of the captured lands in exchange for peace with the Arabs.

Through strikes, demonstrations, lectures, pamphlets, newspapers, and letters to editors, these interest groups put pressure on the government. Many are affiliated with a political party, and it is hard to tell where the interest association leaves off and the party begins. Religious groups have close ties with the religious political parties. Kibbutz federations are affiliated with the Labor Zionist parties.

The most conspicuous example of this marriage of interest group and party is the relation between Histadrut and the Israel Labor Party (ILP). Histadrut was established in 1920 by some Labor Zionist parties, including Mapai, the predecessor of ILP. It was intended to be the labor union for the Jewish workers in Palestine, but since the country was underdeveloped and without much economic activity, it also became a business enterprise. It established and ran bus lines, factories, a bank, a construction company, a supermarket chain, water networks, electricity grids, a health insurance plan, hospitals and medical clinics, and schools. Thus it now represents both labor and management.

Partisan elections are held for the leadership of Histadrut, and since the founding of the organization, they have been won by Mapai or, later, the ILP. From 1948 to 1977, this party also gained the largest share of the votes in the general elections in the state of Israel, in part because of its firm hold over Histadrut. Between 1948 and 1977 the Labor Party controlled the Cabinet, the Knesset, and Histadrut. Decisions made in the former's Central Committee later became those of the Cabinet and of Histadrut. Leaders of Histadrut became leaders in the government, and vice versa. In 1977 ILP lost the general elections, but it maintained control over Histadrut and used it to attack the policies of the Likud government and to try to regain political power.

The conclusion to be drawn from this brief sketch is that in Israel, interest groups and political parties are often not functionally distinct. At their founding, political parties are closely affiliated with interest groups, or after their establishment they penetrate the latter and capture their supporters.

POLITICAL STRUCTURES

Jewish Self-Government in the Mandate Period

The British Mandate (1920-1948) was the formative period for the Israeli political system. During this time, Israel's major political structures were established and its predominant political practices developed. The Jewish settlers adhered to many different ideologies and could not be coerced into a common mold. Custom, precedent, and the practices in Western democracies restrained their leaders, guiding them in establishing institutions that in reality performed the functions of government.

The major structures of the mandate period were: (1) the British Mandate Government, (2) the Chief Rabbinate, (3) the Elected Assembly and the National Council, (4) the Jewish Agency, (5) Histadrut, and (6) the political parties. At the time of independence, the Mandate Government was replaced by the State of Israel, and the Elected Assembly and the National Council by the Knesset and the Cabinet, while the other bodies continued to exist and function as before. The leaders of the Jewish community during the mandate became the officials of the sovereign state of Israel, and the political practices of the former were carried over to the latter.

The British Mandate Government. Beginning in 1918, when their armed forces defeated those of the Turks, until 1948, when they withdrew all forces, the British were the sovereign rulers of Palestine. From 1920 to 1948, they operated under a formal document called a mandate given to them by the League of Nations, later succeeded by the United Nations. Their major interests in Palestine were to insure that oil flowed through the pipeline from Iraq to Haifa, and that the Suez Canal was protected from all potential enemies. To guard these interests, British troops were stationed in Palestine, forming the country's only defense force. The Palestine Police Force was controlled and administered by the British; in addition, the civil and criminal courts came under their jurisdiction, as did the telegraph and postal service, the railways, and the ports.

The Chief Rabbinate. Continuing the Turkish practice, the British considered the country to be composed of different religious traditions, and recognized a leader for each: two Chief Rabbis for the Jews, one Ashkenazi and one Sephardi, a Patriarch for the Greek Orthodox, a Grand Mufti for the Sunni Muslims, and corresponding leaders for the other religious groups. To each of these, who was advised by an appointed council, the British delegated responsibility over ecclesiastical affairs and matters of personal status, such as marriage, divorce, child custody, and inheritance. The Chief Rabbi, Patriarch, or Grand Mufti was the head of an extensive system of courts that dealt with these issues in accordance with the religious law of each group. The Chief Rabbinate in contemporary Israel is an office directly carried over from this system, and enjoys the same high degree of autonomy that it had under the Turks and the British.

The Elected Assembly and the National Council. Under the system of delegated authority, the Jews chose an Elected Assembly, which in turn selected an executive body, the National Council. All Jews in Palestine could participate in the elections for the Assembly under the system of proportional representation. Elections were held every three years, with all parties competing in one electoral district. To the British the National Council was the sole representative of the Jews in Palestine, overseeing the economy and the social, educational, and medical services of the *Yishuv* (the Jewish community in Palestine prior to independence). Subject to the approval of the British High Commissioner, the Elected Assembly had the power to tax and to formulate a budget.

The Elected Assembly and the National Council functioned until the end of the British Mandate, when they were replaced by a Provisional Council of State and a provisional government, which in turn were replaced in 1949 by the Knesset and the Government of the State of Israel.

The Jewish Agency. Article 4 of the mandate document provided for a "Jewish Agency," which was to advise and cooperate with the Administration of Palestine in such "economic, social, and other matters as may affect the establishment of the Jewish National Home and the interests of the Jewish population in Palestine." A branch of the World Zionist Organization, the Jewish Agency had its headquarters in Jerusalem. At first it had an identity of its own, but by 1947 it was the same as the Executive Committee of the World Zionist Organization. It represented the Zionist Movement and world Jewry before the mandatory government, the British government in London, the League of Nations, and later the United Nations. In Palestine it was in charge of facilitating Jewish immigration, buying land on which Jews could settle, promoting Jewish settlement in agricultural cooperatives, fostering the Hebrew language and culture, and providing for the meeting of Jewish religious needs.

Side by side with the British mandatory government and the National Council, the Jewish Agency was a dominant force. It was the body tying the Jews in Palestine to Diaspora Jewry, and it represented all Jews in the world. It had considerable economic resources and was deeply involved in urban and rural settlement and in other activities that built up the state. Today it has been given official status under a law passed by the state of Israel in 1952, and is still the body most responsible for immigration, settlement, and relations with Diaspora Jewry.

Histadrut. Another important organization of the *Yishuv* period, and one that continues to play a dominant role in Israeli society, was Histadrut. Founded in 1920 by a number of Zionist socialist political parties, it had as its purpose the creation of a Jewish workers' state in Eretz Israel, a utopian goal that appeared to have no possibility of being achieved. At that time the Jews in Palestine were few, the number of Jewish workers was even smaller, the country was underdeveloped, bereft of modern industry and agriculture, and lacking the organizations that make a modern state. Histadrut resolved that it was going to be the "state on the way" and rather than simply carrying out the functions typical of a labor union, it did everything necessary to develop a Jewish workers' society. It became the core of the *Yishuv.*

Histadrut's activities have been multifarious. It has been involved in everything that promoted the establishment of a secular labor-Zionist Jewish society and nation. It aided immigration, led Jewish defense efforts, pushed the revival of the Hebrew language and culture, brought abandoned and ruined land under cultivation; established industries, banks, and insurance companies; ran a newspaper, theater, and sports association; aided the needy and the aged; and organized a system of clinics, hospitals, and medical insurance. Shortly after its founding it became both the largest labor union and the largest employer in the country. In its many economic enterprises were employed the vast majority of Jewish workers. Because of its size, it determined wage policies and labor conditions for the entire *Yishuv.*

Histadrut has always been run according to democratic principles. At regular intervals its members elect on a partisan basis, through the system of proportional representation, delegates to a General Conference, the highest authority in the organization, which in turn chooses a Council, and this, an Executive Committee. During the period of the *Yishuv,* most Jews participated in the elections for the General Conference of Histadrut and the Elected Assembly, the former being the plenary body for the labor organization and the latter for the Jewish community at large. The electoral system in both was proportional representation by party list.

Political Parties. Political parties were the most powerful of all the major institutions of the *Yishuv.* Each had its origins in a small Zionist club that was first created in Poland, Russia, or some other European nation. Each had a world view to which it was trying to win converts, and each competed vigorously for the loyalty of every new immigrant. Many ran cooperative agricultural settlements, urban housing projects, labor exchanges, soup kitchens, loan funds, and newspapers that promoted the party's principles. Each had a youth division, a women's division, an education section, and a public relations bureau. Since the institutions of the Jewish state were still being formed and there was no singular authority in the Jewish community, the parties could be very ideological and uncompromising. Splits and mergers were generally followed by more splits and remergers.

The political parties were represented in three of the major institutions of the *Yishuv* (Histadrut, the Elected Assembly, and the Jewish Agency), and provided a connecting link among them. The same persons would often appear in leadership positions in two or more of these institutions. For example, Ben Gurion was Secretary General of Histadrut from 1920 to 1935, the leader of Mapai from 1920 to 1965, and the chairman of the Executive Committee of the Jewish Agency from 1935 to 1948.

Mapai predominated over all other parties. It had majority control of Histadrut and a plurality in the other institutions of the *Yishuv*. It held the community together and brought about an important degree of coordination and unity. It was not backed up by the force of law, and it had to mobilize and motivate the community to cooperate voluntarily with it.

Voluntarism and cooperation characterized the political process of the *Yishuv*. Although the differences among the various parties were enormous, they all shared in some general way the objective of the establishment of a Jewish state. Proportional representation enabled all parties to compete and to have some share in the decision-making process. The hostility of the Arabs and the inability of the British to protect the Jewish community from Arab attack were negative forces pushing the various parties together.

During the *Yishuv*, the major political parties and their leaders exercised power in constructive administrative and political situations. All parties realized the necessity of tolerance and learned the art of compromise. They shared power with other groups within Palestinian Jewry, with the British, and with the Diaspora Jews who worked in the World Zionist Organization.

Independence has brought changes, but they have been less important than the carry-over from the *Yishuv*. The whole political process is now less voluntaristic since there is a state. Decision making is more centralized, and there is now a bureaucracy with formal standardized procedures. Decision making tends to be more practical and oriented toward the present, rather than ideological and futuristic.

One of the basic struggles between parties has been the expansion of state authority. Groups long used to exercising power in an autonomous fashion are not eager to give it up. Some have been successfully absorbed into the state or made subordinate to it, but others have not. In the former category lie *Haganah* and *Irgun Zvai Leumi* (Jewish defense organizations of the *Yishuv*) and the Jewish Agency. In the latter one are the Rabbinate, the political parties, and Histadrut.

Israel continues to exist without a constitution. In part this reflects the fact that prior to independence there was an ongoing political process that functioned without one, and in part it indicates that there are still some basic unresolved questions that have been indefinitely postponed.

The Political System Since Independence

Political Parties. The oldest, strongest, and most enduring political structures in Israel are the political parties. Although their names have changed, and divisions and mergers occurred, each can trace its origins back over half a century or more to some Zionist organization in Europe. Except for the Communists, all have agreed on the establishment of a Jewish state or national home, and the differences among them have been over the social, political, and economic order that should be established in that state.

Each party has been intensely ideological and has insisted upon total commitment from its members to its principles and policies. Political parties have not simply competed for votes, but have also been actively engaged in the upbuilding of Jewish society in the Eretz Israel through agricultural settlements, industries, housing projects, youth groups, and any organization that would bring about the society they envisioned for Israel. Their devotion to cause and principle, their all-encompassing nature, their total outlook on life, give them many of the qualities of religious sects.

The Labor Parties: The labor parties are advocates of Labor Zionism, a hybrid of Jewish nationalism and socialism. As nationalist parties they have fostered the rebirth of the Hebrew language and encouraged Jewish literature, poetry, and all of the arts. They feel that religion can contribute to the Jewish national identity and historical consciousness, but are strongly opposed to a union of religion and state. As socialist parties they have aimed to create in Eretz Israel a society in which the means of production are owned by the workers, few social distinctions exist, and the welfare of all is promoted. During the approximately seventy years of their existence, they have established kibbutzim and moshavim, since they believed them to be miniatures of the social ideal they wanted for the whole country. They also founded Histadrut in 1920 so that it might become the core of the new Jewish society.

The Israel Labor Party is the largest and most powerful labor party. Since 1930, the year it was created, it has had majority control of Histadrut and this has been its major base of support. It is preeminently the party of the country's establishment, and from 1948 to 1977 all of the country's prime ministers were members of ILP.

It is the most open, the most aggregative, and the most pluralistic of Israel's parties. Its platforms and policies have been designed to attract as wide a cross-section of the electorate as possible. It has drawn to its side Oriental Jews, Israeli Arabs, and many of the new class of professionals and administrators. The constant percentages of the vote that it has received attest to the fact that it is adaptable, for since independence, Israeli society has changed enormously, from one comprised mostly of Western Jews to one with a majority of Oriental Jews; from a small, frontier "pioneering" society to a technocratic-bureaucratic one.

Another labor party is Mapam, which is to the left of the ILP and is, in effect, the political arm of one of the three major kibbutz movements, Kibbutz Artizi. It has tried to be an internationalist Marxist party but has encountered difficulties in this respect because of the anti-Zionist and anti-Israeli policies of the Soviet Union. In respect to domestic matters it takes a militant Marxist stance, but in foreign affairs it is noted for its moderate policy concerning Israel's Arabs and Arab-Israeli relations. It is the party of Israel's "doves," and has attracted a considerable number of Arab voters.

The Religious Parties: All of Israel's religious parties are in some degree committed to the creation of a theocratic state. Their major concerns have been state enforcement of religious law, protection of the independence of the Rabbinate, and the securing of government subsidies for the religious schools.

The most prominent is the National Religious Party (NRP), which regularly secures about 9 percent of the vote. It has always worked within the Zionist movement and has directed its efforts towards the establishment of a state, but one to be governed by the religious law. It has been successful in maintaining and strengthening Sabbath laws, in securing the passage of an act drastically limiting the breeding of pigs and the sale of pork, in preserving the autonomy of the Rabbinate, and in protecting state subsidies for religious schools. It has opposed the adoption of any constitution that provides for the separation of religion and state. In respect to economic and social issues, it advocates a non-Marxist socialism similar to that of the Labor Party, with which it has frequently formed a coalition. In these governments, a member of the NRP is Minister of Religious Affairs, while Labor party members are Ministers of Foreign Affairs, Defense, Finance, and Prime Minister. Thus the National Religious Party is very much a part of the ruling establishment. This is a major reason why religion has an entrenched position in Israel.

The two *Aguda* ("association") parties, Aguda Israel and Poalei Aguda Israel ("Workers of the Association of Israel") have as their goal the preparation and bringing together of the Jewish people in Eretz Israel in order to create in it a kingdom under the rule of God. They believe that a truly religious state can only be established upon the coming of the Messiah. Therefore they have been ambivalent toward the founding of the contemporary Jewish state, which they affirm is too much the work of man. During the British Mandate they separated themselves from the mainstream of the *Yishuv* and generally opposed the efforts of the Zionist leaders. However, the Nazi Holocaust altered their viewpoint somewhat, and in an agreement worked out with Ben Gurion, their representatives signed the Declaration of Independence and became members of the Provisional Council of State on the condition that the religious status quo be maintained. They have participated in subsequent coalition governments.

The *Aguda* parties are most insistent that Israel be a state guided by the Torah and governed by the religious law. They have opposed women's suffrage and the drafting of women into the defense forces, since they believe both violate God's law. Their support mainly comes from old Jewish districts in Jerusalem and Tel Aviv, and they secure 3 to 5 percent of the vote.

They are Israel's true believers and its most uncompromising political faction. They are effective in organizing demonstrations and at playing the role of martyr. Every government has respected their power and treated them with respect for fear of being accused of religious persecution.

The Center and Right Parties: The Center has never posed any threat to Labor predominance in Israel politics, because Labor established the nascent institutions of the state such as the kibbutzim, moshavim, and Histadrut, controlled them from their inception, and through them came to dominate the politics of the *Yishuv* and of the state.

With the rise to power of the Nazis in the 1930s, German Jews began to migrate to Israel. When the war began, these immigrants were followed by any Jew in Europe who could escape the Nazis and evade the British in order to get into Palestine. Most of these persons were well educated and had been prosperous citizens in Europe, so a middle class was introduced into the *Yishuv*. Its members strengthened the Center in Israeli politics, but because they came late, were not cohesively organized, and were Zionists more out of necessity than out of conviction, they never challenged or overthrew Labor supremacy.

Since the 1930s the Right has been the only significant opposition to the ILP. Its consistent line of attack has been that Labor is too conciliatory towards the British and/or the Arabs, is not sufficiently prepared militarily to defend the Jewish people, is unwilling to take decisive military action, and has created a gargantuan bureaucratic state that stifles free enterprise and initiative. Since 1973 the Center and the Right have been represented by Likud, a coalition of the Herut ("Freedom") and Liberal parties. In 1973 Likud won thirty-nine seats in the elections to the Knesset. This resulted in its becoming Israel's second largest party, and in 1977 it won forty-three seats, which made it the largest. It formed a government under the leadership of Menachem Begin as prime minister.

The Liberal Party has championed causes that appeal to the upper middle class. It has fought against the dominance of Labor and of Labor-controlled business enterprises, which means that it has fought the power of Histadrut. It has argued for tax relief for the middle class. It has championed civil liberties and has urged the adoption of a constitution for the state. When it ran by itself in the 1961 election, it secured 14 percent of the vote. Its place and power in the Israeli political system have always been ambiguous. One certainty about the Liberal Party is that it has stood to the right of Mapai and to the left of Herut.

Herut has been the arch enemy of Mapai. Except for a Government of National Unity formed at the time of the war of June 1967, it was not a part of the government until 1977. Its origins go back to 1925, when Vladimir Jabotinsky formed the Revisionist Movement within the World Zionist Organization. He and his followers objected to Chaim Weizmann's moderate policies towards the British and the Arabs. They urged the use of underground military tactics to achieve Zionist objectives. They were incensed that the British had separated Trans-Jordan from Palestine and prohibited Jewish immigration into it, for they regarded it as part of the Jewish homeland. In 1935 the Revisionists left the World Zionist Organization and formed their own group. In the 1930s some of their leaders formed Irgun Zvai Leumi ("National Defense Organization") an underground terrorist organization that operated independently of Haganah, the regular defense force of the *Yishuv*. In 1948 Irgun was dissolved, its members became the nucleus of the Herut Party, and its leader, Menachem Begin, became the party leader.

Begin and Ben Gurion hated each other, and their verbal attacks upon one another were vicious. The animosity between the two parties that each led was just as great. Mapai charged Herut with being irresponsible in bolting from the World Zionist Organization and in carrying out terrorist activities on its own, while Herut accused Mapai of being too weak in confronting the enemies of the Jews.

Herut advocates the retention of East Jerusalem, the West Bank, and Gaza, territories gained in the 1967 war. In domestic affairs it urges an end to Histadrut power, more free enterprise, and a reduction of governmental economic controls and regulations.

POLITICAL LEADERSHIP

Israeli political leaders are arch rivals and antagonists. Each has a firmly held system of political values and a domineering personality. They mince no words in denouncing the person and the policies of their adversaries, and the language of politics is sharp and often vitriolic. In the past two decades, public disputes have erupted between the executive secretary of Histadrut and the prime minister, the chairman of the Mapai Party and the prime minister, the two chief rabbis and all the secular leaders, and the head of the World Zionist Organization and the prime minister.

The Zionist socialist pioneers had utopian expectations that the new society they were creating would be a confederation of self-governing autonomous communities in which the people would govern themselves, and leaders would be superfluous. These beliefs were institutionalized in the kibbutzim, where all roles were interchangeable and all governing was done by the community as a whole. These same pioneers also wanted the society to be egalitarian.

Today the same democratic spirit pervades Israeli society. Cabinet ministers live in modest official apartments, dress simply, drive their own official cars, and have small salaries. Unlike other heads of government, the Israeli prime minister rides in a plain sedan, not a limousine, lives in an apartment and not in a pretentious official residence, and appears at concerts and theatrical productions without a panoply of assistants and retainers. Israeli prime ministers, male and female, have been noted for their casual dress. In short, they have not created around themselves a monarchial air of mystery, but have projected the image of simplicity and modesty.

Living for thousands of years under non-Jewish rulers has produced among Israelis an intense and deep-seated suspicion of authority. In eastern Europe and the Middle East, when Jews were often the subject of persecution by the authorities, the most that they could hope for from these governments was neutrality. The British, during the period of the Palestine Mandate, tried to reconcile their own interests and those of the Jews and the Arabs. Often they took measures that the Jews did not like, and the latter responded with acts that defied British authority. For example, they smuggled immigrants and arms into the country, and operated clandestine defense organizations. In contemporary Israel the centuries-old feeling that "the government is against you" continues, and the belief is strong that it is not to be trusted and must be checked.

While leaders in Israel are never allowed to become mythical figures and authority is divided and checked by many competing elites, there is nonetheless an Establishment. It is a constant subject of analysis and debate in the press. Basically it consists of a few hundred persons who have firm holds on the institutions and instruments of power. They control the assignment of jobs in the top positions of the state and other important institutions, and they preside over the distribution of the wealth that is produced in Israel and that comes from sources overseas. The Establishment is based neither on wealth nor on aristocratic lineage. Its roots are in the Second *Aliyah,* and most of its members are persons who came as young people to Eretz Israel from eastern Europe in the period 1904-1930. They created the institutions of the new Jewish society and state and became the leaders of institutions which they formed. They have known each other for decades, have worked together in several different institutions, and have tenaciously held onto power until they were well into their seventies, and many even until they were in their eighties.

The election of 1977, in which Labor, preeminently the party of the Establishment, failed to gain a plurality for the first time in the history of modern Israel, can be interpreted as an electoral slap at the Establishment.

POLITICAL POLICIES

Three major unresolved policies are the subject of intense debate in Israel: (1) the nature of the peace settlement with the Arabs, (2) the role of socialism and of free enterprise in the economy, and (3) the meaning of the Jewish character of the society.

The Peace Settlement

On March 26, 1979, Menachem Begin, prime minister of Israel, and Anwar al-Sadat, president of Egypt, signed a peace treaty in Washington in the presence of Jimmy Carter, president of the United States. The first such agreement to be signed by an Arab state with Israel, it is hopefully a model to be followed by others. It provides for the return to full Egyptian sovereignty of the territory in the Sinai conquered by Israel in 1967, the establishment of the old boundary between the British mandate of Palestine and Egypt as the permanent legal border of Israel and Egypt, the termination of the state of war between the two countries, and the establishment of full diplomatic, economic, and cultural relations.

While this treaty settled the conflict between Egypt and Israel, it left unresolved the issues of East Jerusalem, the West Bank, and the Gaza Strip. These are territories that were also conquered by Israel in the war of 1967 and were part of British-mandated Palestine. From 1948 to 1967, Egypt administered the Gaza Strip and Jordan controlled East Jerusalem and the West Bank. The people who live in these areas are Arabs who identify themselves as Palestinians, and since 1948 they have been ruled by the Egyptians, Jordanians, and the Israelis. Several Palestinian organizations claim to speak for them, the largest and most widely recognized being the Palestine Liberation Organization (PLO).

The Camp David accords worked out by Sadat, Begin, and Carter in September 1978 provided for a negotiation process among Egypt, Israel, Jordan and representatives of the Palestinian people to resolve the question of the West Bank and Gaza only. East Jerusalem was not mentioned. The objectives stated in the accords were the establishment on the West Bank and in Gaza of a "self-governing authority" [also called an "administrative council"] . . . "freely elected by the inhabitants" that would not harm the "legitimate security concerns of the parties involved." After this "authority" is established and inaugurated, there is to be, according to the accords, a five-year transitional period during which negotiations are to take place to determine the final status of the territory and its relations with its neighbors, and to conclude a peace treaty between Israel and Jordan. "The negotiations will resolve, among other matters, the location of the boundaries and the nature of the security arrangements." "The solution from the negotiations must also recognize the legitimate rights of the Palestinian people and their just requirements."

An overwhelming majority of Israelis consider Jerusalem to have been "reunited" in 1967, and to be "eternally" a part of Israel. Most political factions consider the West Bank and Gaza (sometimes referred to by their ancient Jewish names of Judea, Samaria, and Gaza) as a part of "historic Israel." The fate of these areas is hotly debated by Israelis, with some groups arguing that Israel should be concerned only for security in them, and others saying that Jews have a historic claim to these areas and should be allowed to settle in them.

Peace has been arrived at between Egypt and Israel, but the territorial claims of these two states were not sharply in conflict. The truly difficult negotiations are in respect to East Jerusalem, the West Bank, and Gaza, where both Jews and Palestinians have historic claims. With a background of a half century of conflict between Arabs and Israelis, deep hostility between Palestinians and Israelis, memories of the Holocaust ever present for Jews, and the humiliations of imperialism still fixed in the minds of Arabs, total peace is not going to be arrived at quickly or easily. All parties will have to agree to something each finds less than desirable.

The Economy

The Zionist pioneers envisioned a classless egalitarian society based on cooperative farming and communally owned small industries. "Capital" was a bad word that was always associated with "exploitation." While these socialist objectives have left an imprint on the values of contemporary Israel, the economy is not purely socialist and might better be labeled as mixed. An upper middle class of entrepreneurs, professionals, and technocrats now exists, and it contributes significantly to the economy. Many persons have high incomes and enjoy the rewards of affluence: villas, luxury automobiles, pleasure boats. At the other end of the economic ladder are Oriental Jews and Israeli Arabs, who are caught in low-paying, marginal jobs. The existence of both violate the Zionist-socialist values, and the question is how much and to what extent the government should attempt, through its investment and taxation policies, to equalize economically all citizens of Israel.

The Jewish Character of the Society

All the major political parties in Israel are pledged to the "preservation of the Jewish character of the state." Yet exactly what this means is a subject of debate. Should the memory of the Holocaust be preserved, and if so, how? Should Ashkenazi or Sephardi Jewishness be preserved? What contribution does religion make to the character of the individual Jew? Can a Jewish state exist if that state is secular? What is Israel's relation to Diaspora Jews? Can the Jewish character be maintained if Israel has a large Arab minority? And finally, "Who is a Jew"?

CONCLUSION

Since it is a society created by settlers, not as the part of a world-wide empire of some mother nation but as a culturally distinct nation-state, Israel resembles Australia, New Zealand, and the United States more than the other Middle Eastern nations. A majority of its population is literate, trained in the skills of an industrial technological economy, and possessed of the attitudes and values that lead to effective social organization. Its rural areas are as modern and as intensely organized as those of the cities as a result of the strenuous promotion of rural settlement and development by the Zionist movement and the Israeli state. Its society is egalitarian, with minimal economic and social differences.

Jewish Israelis have the civic sense that is essential to a well-functioning political system. They are loyal to the state and support the existing political order; they are tolerant of religious and social differences and respect the strongly held opinions of others; and even though political rhetoric is often bombastic and full of threats, they are willing to bargain and compromise. The government knows that there are certain limits beyond which it cannot go in trying to suppress political opposition or heterodox and obstructive Jewish minorities, because every Jew is needed for national defense and the strengthening of the economy.

Although Jewish Israelis come from vastly different societies and cultures, although they have many different mother tongues and conflicting values and customs, they are all Jews with parallel experiences of discrimination and persecution and a common memory of once having been an independent nation in Eretz Israel. In present-day Israel they experience a personal security and a freedom they have never felt before, in addition to the exhilaration of knowing that, for the first time in their lives, the government is Jewish and is on their side. This produces intense loyalty to the state, and Jewish Israelis are convinced that if the state is weakened or destroyed, their freedom and personal security will disappear.

REVIEW OF THE MAJOR EVENTS IN THE MODERN HISTORY OF ISRAEL

1881	Outbreak of new pogroms in Russia.
1882	Beginning of the First Aliyah, composed mainly of Jews from Russia; ends in 1904.
1896	Publication of *Der Judenstaat* ("The Jewish State"), written by Theodor Herzl.
1897	First Zionist Congress meets in Basel, Switzerland.

1905	Beginning of the Second Aliyah, from which came the founders of the state; ends in 1914.
1917	Balfour Declaration issued by the British Cabinet.
1918	British and Arab troops complete the conquest of Palestine from the Turks.
1920	Founding of Histadrut. Beginning of the British Mandate over Palestine.
1939	British White Paper limiting Jewish immigration into Palestine.
1939-1945	World War II; six million Jews die in Nazi death camps; illegal immigration of Jews from Nazi-occupied Europe into Palestine.

1947

April	Britain requests a special session of the United Nations General Assembly to consider the problem of Palestine.
May	General Assembly establishes a United Nations Special Committee on Palestine (UNSCOP).
Nov.	General Assembly favors the plan of the majority of UNSCOP recommending the partition of Palestine into a Jewish state and an Arab state, with Jerusalem under international administration.

1948

Jan.	Beginning of hostilities between Jewish and Arab militias and of the flight of Palestinians out of the country.
May	Final withdrawal of British troops; declaration of independence by the state of Israel; armies from Lebanon, Syria, Jordan, Egypt, and Iraq attack Jewish forces in Palestine; beginning of a massive immigration of Jews, a majority of whom are Orientals.

1949	Egypt, Lebanon, Jordan, and Syria conclude armistice agreements with Israel.
1956	After Gamal Abdel Nasser nationalizes the Suez Canal Company, Britain, France, and Israel attack Egypt.
1957	Territory conquered by Israel in the Sinai Peninsula in 1956 is returned to Egypt.
1967	In the Six-Day War, June 5-10, Israel conquers the Sinai Peninsula, Gaza, East Jerusalem, the West Bank, and the Golan Heights.
1973	Egypt launches a surprise attack in October across the Suez Canal, conquering some land on its east side; Israel counterattacks and conquers some land on its west side; fighting lasts about three weeks.

1974   Egypt and Israel sign an agreement disengaging their forces in the Sinai Peninsula and establishing a United Nations buffer zone between them.

1977   General elections; *Likud* Coalition defeats the Israel Labor Party.

1978   Camp David accords worked out between Menachem Begin and Anwar al-Sadat with the assistance of Jimmy Carter.

1979   Signing and ratification of a peace treaty between Israel and Egypt.

Chapter 7

Lebanon

On April 13, 1975, a civil war began in Lebanon. It has shattered the country's economic, social, and political systems. The Lebanese, the most urbane, educated, and Westernized of the Arabs, have committed mindless acts of murder, senselessly destroyed the commercial heart of their capital city, Beirut, and have expelled entire populations from villages and refugee camps. Vindictiveness, impulse, blind hatred, uncontrollable rage, sadism, and a dehumanization of the enemy have been the war's primary characteristics. The hostilities in Lebanon have confirmed the frequently made observation that civil wars are the most horrible of wars.

In January 1976 a Syrian meditation team began to negotiate between the various parties; that April, Syrian troops entered the country in order to try to restore a semblance of order. Their numbers rapidly increased, and in October the Syrian presence in Lebanon was legitimized by the foreign ministers of the Arab League states, who officially created a 30,000-man multinational Arab peacekeeping force for Lebanon, of which the Syrian troops already present formed the overwhelming majority. This force became the dominant military organization in the country. The Syrians could not resolve the major issues dividing the Lebanese factions, but they did return the country to a more normal state.

In the middle of 1979, the civil war was still going on, and its major causes had not been resolved. No one knew when real peace would come to this troubled and beleaguered country.

Ironically, this war began in a country that had been characterized as an island of political stability and economic prosperity in the turbulent Middle East. Some people even called Lebanon the "Switzerland of the Middle East"; because of this reputation, Lebanon was a political and monetary haven. Politicians out of favor in other Arab countries sought exile there. Arab intellectuals who found the atmosphere too stifling elsewhere came to Lebanon, where they could freely express their ideas and could write without having to worry about censorship. Oil-rich sheiks from the Arab states of the Persian Gulf invested their money in Lebanese banks, bought Lebanese real estate, and used the Lebanese as their agents in world-wide financial transactions. European and American companies established Middle East headquarters in Beirut because it had good transportation and communications connections with the rest of the world, many of its citizens were bilingual, and had been biculturally educated, and most of the material goods and comforts available in the West could be found there.

Prior to the civil war, scholars held two opinions as to the nature of the country's social and political systems. The first was that of the optimists. They praised Lebanon as a country in which different religious groups had worked out a system of "balanced confessionalism" that apportioned political power fairly, protected freedom of the press, speech, and assembly, and provided Lebanese with a high standard of living through a free enterprise economy. A book published in 1973 by Elie Salem, a professor at the American University of Beirut, expressed this viewpoint:

> Lebanon is among the most modernized countries in the Arab world.[1] [It] has developed successful institutions to ensure continuing modernization with a minimum of social and political strain and without resort to a radical ideology. The diversity of beliefs and attitudes in Lebanese society has furthered rather than hindered modernization. The slow gains accomplished, step by step, in cultural, economic and political spheres are the result of stable political institutions and of a formula for government based on conciliation and consensus.[2]

The second position regarding Lebanon was held by the pessimists. They described Lebanon as a "precarious republic,"[3] an "improbable nation,"[4] and a "mosaic society"[5] that was sorely fragmented by religious divisions and social

[1] Elie Salem, *Modernization Without Revolution: Lebanon's Experience* (Bloomington: Indiana University Press, 1973), p. 1.

[2] Ibid., pp. 3-4.

[3] Michael C. Hudson, *The Precarious Republic: Political Modernization in Lebanon* (New York: Random House, Inc., 1968).

[4] Leila M. Meo, *Lebanon: Improbable Nation: A Study in Political Development* (Bloomington: Indiana University Press, 1965).

[5] Halim Barakat, "Social and Political Integration in Lebanon: A Case of Social Mosaic," *Middle East Journal,* 27 (Summer 1973), 301-18.

classes. In their view, the political system did little to alleviate these cleavages, could not accommodate itself to change, and was unable to establish social justice. At best it was simply a mechanism for maintaining truces among mutually hostile groups. Michael Hudson, director of Georgetown University's Center for Contemporary Arab Studies, best expressed this viewpoint:

> The Lebanese Republic . . . is a conglomeration of paradoxes and contradictions. Since it became independent of France in 1943, it has struggled from one crisis to another, avoiding disaster by the narrowest of margins. Lebanon as a polity is archaic, inefficient, and divided; it is also liberal, democratic, and—in general—orderly. It is Arab and Western, Christian and Muslim, traditional and modern. Its precarious survival is a fascinating subject for the student of politics.[6]

The civil war has demonstrated that the pessimists were correct.

GEOGRAPHY AND ECONOMY

Lebanon is the shape of a rectangle one hundred and fifty miles long and twenty to fifty miles wide. Running its length and paralleling the Mediterranean coast are two mountain ranges: the Lebanon and Anti-Lebanon. The first rises sharply from a narrow coastal plain to heights of about 10,000 feet and then drops sharply to form a valley, the Beqa. Out of the Beqa arises the Anti-Lebanon, which is about 7,000 feet high. Its ridge forms the border with Syria. The Lebanon Mountains are well populated, while the Anti-Lebanon are only sparsely inhabited.

From mid-November to mid-March rain falls across the mountains and valleys, enabling the people to grow fruits, vegetables, and grains. Planting is in the fall and harvesting in the spring, after the rain has watered the land and the sun has caused the plants to grow. Fruit and olive trees commonly grow on terraced hillsides. Springs frequently break out from linestone outcrops, and around them villages have been located for millennia. The springs from rivulets, which in turn become rivers that tumble down the mountainside, often through gorges, and flow into the Mediterranean Sea.

Because of its high and low elevations, Lebanon has an extremely varied climate, and consequently a wide variety of agricultural products can be grown. The coastal plain has fertile soil, wet winters, and vast possibilities for irrigation because of the many rivers that flow through it. On it vegetables, citrus fruits, and bananas are grown. But the plain is narrow, and sometimes interrupted by mountains which come right down to the sea. The coastal cities also are steadily encroaching on the agricultural land. The plain of Akkar along the coast north of Tripoli is wide and is traversed by four rivers. In the past its farmers were

[6] Hudson, *Precarious Republic,* p. 3.

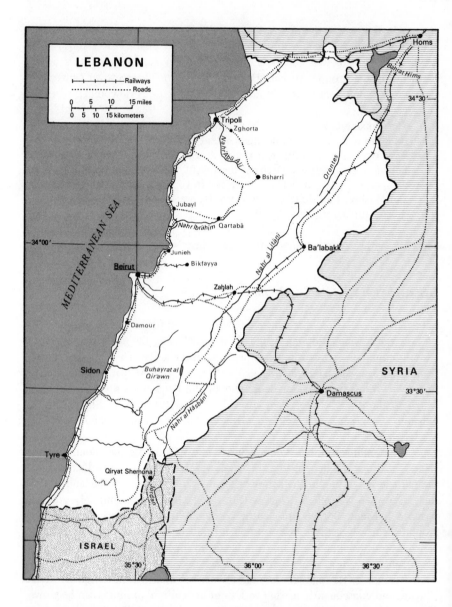

LEBANON

├─┼─┼─┼─┤ Railways
·········· Roads

0   5   10   15 miles
0   5   10   15 kilometers

Homs

Bahrat Hims

34°30′

Tripoli
Zghorta

Nahr Abū ʿAlī

Bsharrī

Orontes

Jubayl

Nahr Ibrāhīm Qartabā

34°00′

Junieh

Beirut

Bikfayya

Nahr al Līṭānī

Baʿlabakk

Zaḥlah

MEDITERRANEAN SEA

Damour

Sidon

Buhayrat al
Qirʿawn

SYRIA

Nahr al Hāsbānī

Damascus

33°30′

Tyre

Qiryat Shemona

Jordan

ISRAEL

35°30′

36°00′

36°30′

involved only in the production of cereals, but increasingly vegetables, citrus fruits, and peanuts are being grown there. On the slopes of the mountains at elevations between 300 and 3,000 feet, olives, figs, almonds, grapes, and tobacco are produced. In the regions varying in height from 3,000 to 4,800 feet, apples, vegetables, grapes, and cereals are cultivated. In summer the nights are cool, and in winter there is snow. The region is filled with hotels; in the summer, Arabs from the Persian Gulf, Saudi Arabia, Jordan, Syria, and the Lebanese coast have come here to escape the heat. In the winter, ski resorts cater to young upper-class and upper-middle-class Lebanese and foreigners. In the Beqa Valley cereals predominate, but cane sugar, beets, apples, and grapes are also grown. Modern dairy farming and chicken and egg production have also grown in importance there.

Cities

Beirut is Lebanon's largest city, with an estimated population of 800,000 (1977) inhabitants. Since World War II Beirut has grown in size and importance, so that now it dominates the country economically, socially, and politically. In it are located all important government offices, all major businesses, and all of the country's universities. Persons with wealth or education live in Beirut because it has luxury apartments, fancy grocery stores, fine clothing shops, night clubs, cinemas, and two TV stations. Since it is no more than a two-hour drive from any spot in the country, Beirut residents can still maintain ties with the villages from which they and their families came.

Tripoli, the second largest city in Lebanon, has an estimated population of 175,000 (1977). Since it is only seventy-five miles, or an hour and a half drive from Beirut, it is very much overshadowed by the latter. The citizens of Tripoli feel that they live in a provincial city and frequently go to Beirut on one-day visits to shop or to secure permits or licenses from the government.

Population

Population statistics for Lebanon are rather inaccurate, since a census has not been taken since 1932. Births, marriages, and, above all, deaths are not always registered with the authorities, and registration is done at the place of origin of the family, not at that of residence. Furthermore, emigrants who have maintained their Lebanese citizenship are included among the registered inhabitants of the country. Despite all this, the estimated population of Lebanon is 3.165 million (1978).

The Overseas Connection

Bordering on the sea, Lebanon has for thousands of years had connections with peoples and lands overseas. The ancient Phoenicians sailed all over the Mediterranean from the ports of Tyre and Sidon in the south of present-day Lebanon. During the Crusader period in the twelfth and thirteenth centuries, the Maronites (the largest Christian community in Lebanon) established close contact with the French and affiliated themselves with the Papacy in Rome. From the mid-nineteenth century until World War I, Christian Lebanese, mostly poor and with little education, emigrated to North and South America, West

Africa, and Australia. After World War I this emigration resumed, but involved smaller numbers. Since World War II it has not been significant. The emigrants have prospered overseas, and many send money back to relatives in the "old country," invest in private businesses there, and frequently return for vacations and visits. Those who keep their Lebanese citizenship have the privilege of voting in Lebanese elections even though they may hold dual citizenship.

Not only have many Lebanese gone overseas, but peoples from other countries have come to Lebanon. In the twelfth and thirteenth centuries, the Crusaders ruled over Lebanon and adjacent lands. In the nineteenth century Russia, Britain, and France intervened politically and militarily on different occasions to protect Christians and Druze (a religious sect that is neither Christian nor Muslim). French Catholic and American Protestant missionaries established schools, colleges, universities, hospitals, and printing presses in Lebanon. From 1920 to 1943 France controlled the country under a mandate from the League of Nations. In 1958 the United States landed troops in the midst of a civil war, fearing that the country might be taken over by communists.

This connection with peoples and cultures across the seas, however, has been almost exclusively a Christian one. Lebanese Muslims have developed ties in the opposite direction, overland to the peoples and cities of the Middle East.

The Overland Connection

In addition to bordering on the Mediterranean, Lebanon opens into the heart of the Arab world. The port of Beirut serves Damascus and Jordan. Tripoli is connected by a good road and railroad to Homs, Hama, and Aleppo, major cities in Syria. Its citizens are Sunni Muslims, as are most of the Syrians. It is easier to drive from the towns of the Beqa Valley to Damascus or Homs than to go over the high mountains to Beirut. Finally, the low mountains and hills of southern Lebanon roll imperceptibly into the hills of northern Galilee in Israel.

These factors mean that Lebanon is also connected to the Arab Muslim world, a relationship that Lebanese Muslims have maintained and developed. The intellectual and political movements in the Arab world, the struggle for independence from the British and the French, the opposition to Zionism and the state of Israel, the attempts at Arab nationalism and unification, have interested Lebanese Muslims more than Lebanese Christians. The former have also been less loyal to an independent Lebanon and more likely to urge a merger with Syria.

Since World War II a new overland connection with the interior has developed, this one with the oil-rich states of the Persian Gulf and Saudi Arabia. Lebanese Muslim and Christian technicians, engineers, physicians, teachers, professors, and businessmen have emigrated to these regions because jobs were available and the pay was high. Like those who went overseas to America, West Africa, and Australia, these Lebanese maintain ties with the homeland, travel there frequently, and send money back to their relatives. Lebanon has also developed an extensive trade with these neighboring states. It ships to them fresh fruits, vegetables, chickens, and eggs, and receives, in return, money and oil, which it transships elsewhere and for which it gets a commission.

Thus in respect to geography, religion, culture, and economics, Lebanon has ties to the West and to the Arab East. It is linked with both Christian Europe and the Arab Muslim world.

Mount Lebanon

From 1861 to 1914, the Lebanon Mountains comprised an autonomous territory within the Ottoman Empire. Called Mount Lebanon, the area was the homeland of the Maronites and the Druze. Its existence and autonomy were the result of European intervention in the internal affairs of the Ottoman Empire. In 1920 the French formed *Grand Liban* ("Greater Lebanon") by adding to Mount Lebanon the regions of Tripoli, the Beqa, Beirut, Sidon, and Tyre. In the old Mount Lebanon there had been an overwhelming Christian majority, but in the new Greater Lebanon there was a closer balance between Christians and Muslims.

In the civil war that has been going on since 1975, the Christian-rightist stronghold has been in the territory of Mount Lebanon, and their "capital" has been Junieh, a port town just to the north of Beirut. The Muslim-leftist alliance has controlled territory south of Beirut and in the Beqa Valley. The two sides have fought over Beirut. Some persons from the camp of the rightists have advocated the partition of Lebanon so that the Christians could at least continue to control Mount Lebanon. Persons from the leftist alliance have argued that the territorial integrity of Lebanon should be maintained, with its political system changed so that the majority Muslims can rule.

Religious Communities

Religious communities are all-important in Lebanon, yet little solid information is available on the size of any, since the subject is politically sensitive. The country has operated on the political fiction that the 1932 census, taken by the French, accurately reflected the distribution of the sects (see Table 7-1). This census established that the Christians comprised 52 percent of the population and the Muslims, 45.5 percent. On this basis, political and administrative positions were divided between Christians and Muslims on a 6:5 ratio. Seats in the unicameral parliament, positions in the civil service, and posts in the cabinet have been apportioned according to this ratio.

Leaders of the Christian-rightist alliance in the civil war have defended this system and have been willing to modify it only slightly. They have consented to change the ratio from 6:5 to 5:5, with seats in the parliament and

	Number of people	Percentage of population
Maronite	261,043	30
Greek Orthodox	90,275	10
Greek Catholic	52,602	6
Armenian	34,296	4
Other Christians	14,065	2
All Christians	**452,281**	**52**
Sunni	182,842	21
Shiite	158,425	18
Druze	56,812	6.5
All Muslims	**398,079**	**45.5**
Jews	10,469	1
Total	**860,829**	

SOURCE: Wilhelm Kewenig, *Die Koexistenz der Religions-gemeinschaften im Libanon* (Berlin: De Gruyter, 1965), p. 57.

cabinet distributed on the basis of this new formula. They have also agreed to abolish the sectarian distribution of positions in the civil service except at the highest level, and to have persons selected for such jobs solely on merit. Leaders of the Muslim-leftist alliance have argued that the sectarian ratio should be abolished altogether, and that religious community should cease to be the foundation on which the Lebanese political system is structured.

Homelands of the Communities

Each community has a homeland, a section of the country where its people are concentrated and where they have been living for centuries. The Sunnis predominate in the smaller coastal towns, in Tripoli, and in the Akkar region to the north of Tripoli. The Maronites live in Mount Lebanon. The Druze inhabit the mountains to the east of Beirut. The Shiites live in southern Lebanon and in the Beqa Valley. Members of all communities are found in Beirut, but segregate themselves into different quarters, with the exception of upper-middle- and upper-class persons, who tend to live together in the nicest part of the city.

The residential segregation of the sects is not absolute. As can be seen on Map 2, each major sect predominates in an area, but does not live there to the exclusion of others. While the majority sect controls a town or district, the minority sect has considerable political power, since it has coreligionists in other areas who can defend it. Political alliances are formed in order to protect two or three groups and to work for a common advantage. These alliances, however, are continually shifting.

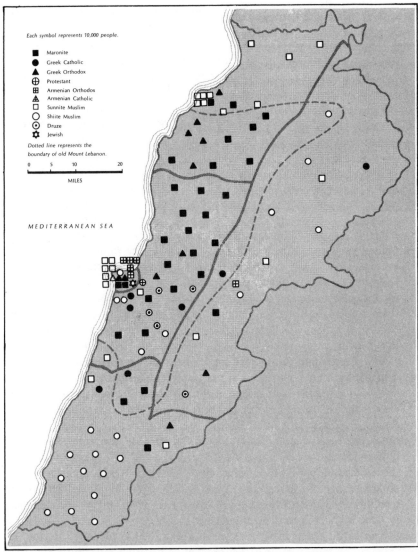

MAP 2. DISTRIBUTION OF MAJOR RELIGIOUS SECTS IN LEBANON (Reprinted by permission of Michael C. Hudson, *The Precarious Republic: Political Modernization in Lebanon,* New York: Random House, 1968)

Economy

Lebanon has an economy that is closely interwoven with those of its neighboring Arab countries and with the world, and its prosperity is dependent upon regional and world economic conditions. Services such as banking, trade, and tourism, which produce the bulk of the national income, are related to the oil industry in the Arabian Peninsula. Lebanon has little industry of its own; most of the manufactured products consumed there are imported. Large quantities of manufactured goods pass through to Syria, Jordan, and Iraq, bringing considerable revenue to the government and to middlemen. Agriculture employs about half of the labor force, yet produces only about a tenth of the national income.

Two-thirds of the Lebanese gross national product is derived from services. The country's location, its people's knowledge of French, English, and Arabic, and their extensive personal contacts in the West and in the Arab World make it the region's most important banking and trading center, and one of the most important in the world. Banking has been furthered by the stability of the Lebanese pound and by a law similar to Switzerland's that allows a depositor to conceal his identity. Imports have been encouraged by low tariffs, and the transit trade has been stimulated by a free port in Beirut, where goods can be stored and processed without payment of duties before shipment to their final destination. Tourists from Arab countries and Europe are attracted to Lebanon by the coolness of the mountains in summer and by the hotels, nightclubs, bistros, discothèques, cinemas, cafés, and restaurants in Beirut.

Twenty-two percent of the country's national product comes from industry and construction. Traditionally the former has been concentrated in crafts and food processing. Modern industry is severely hampered by a shortage of skilled workers and experienced managers, the absence of protective tariffs, the small market in Lebanon, and the unwillingness of banks and investors, domestic and foreign, to put their money into it. The strong ties of family and the communal nature of Lebanese society do not produce the atmosphere of trust that is necessary for the growth of public corporations. Except for a few foreign-owned oil refineries and cement factories, industries are small and family-owned.

Construction has been considerably stimulated by the influx of oil money from the Arabian Peninsula, and Beirut is filled with luxury apartments and modern office buildings owned by oil-rich sheiks. Many of them are partially empty, but their owners regard them as investments that will appreciate in value, rather than as a source of current income.

Eleven percent of the national product comes from agriculture. Farms are generally small and fragmented, which lowers their efficiency of operation. Over four-fifths of the farm land is owned by its cultivators. The cost of land and of its improvement are high, and the small farmer can only secure loans from local money lenders at exorbitant rates. Therefore the major part of new investment has been made by wealthy merchants and professional men. The country is self-sufficient in terms of fruits and vegetables, but it must import cereals and meat.

Between the Arab-Israeli war of 1948, which secured Israel's independence, and the Arab-Israeli war of 1967, which ended with Israel occupying the West

Bank of the Jordan River and the Sinai Peninsula, Lebanon experienced an economic boom. Because of the Arab economic boycott of Israel, the concomitant severing of telephone, telegraph, and mail service, and the cutting of all transportation routes between Israel and the Arab world, international business moved its base of operations from Palestine/Israel to Lebanon. This coincided with the oil boom in the Arabian Peninsula which began in the early 1950s. The pipeline of the Iraq Petroleum Company, which had terminated in Haifa, was diverted to Tripoli in northern Lebanon. Trans-Arabian Pipeline (TAPLINE), constructed by the Arabian American Oil Company (ARAMCO), went from Dhahran in Saudi Arabia to Sidon in southern Lebanon. Service industries for the oil industry, such as advertising, accounting, architecture, technical design, construction, printing, banking, and legal services, all flourished in Beirut. The hotels in Beirut and the resorts in the mountains grew in number and prospered from the legions of European and American oil technicians and rich Arabs seeking fun or doing business in Lebanon. This activity did not move to Egypt, which prior to the revolution of 1952 had been the communications, transportation, and commercial center of the Middle East, because of that country's socialist and anti-imperialist policies. In Lebanon there were no restraints on local or international businesses.

The closing of the port of Haifa to trade with the Arab world also contributed to Lebanon's economic growth. Physically Haifa is a better port than Beirut and is less closed off by mountains from Jordan, Syria, and Iraq, but the Arab boycott of Israel meant that trade was henceforth diverted to Beirut, whatever the physical inconveniences. Also, between 1948 and 1967 Jordan controlled the West Bank, which included most of the major sites (Jerusalem, Bethlehem, Jericho) in the Holy Land. Western tourists desiring to see them usually came in through Lebanon, Syria, and Jordan, and went out by passing from East Jerusalem in Jordan to West Jerusalem in Israel. From there they went back to Europe or the United States.

Though Lebanon experienced an economic boom between 1948 and 1967, the wealth was distributed most unevenly. According to a report commissioned by the government and issued in 1960, 4 percent of the population were rich, 14 percent well-to-do, 32 percent had a moderate income, and 50 percent were poor and miserable.[7] The top 4 percent garnered 32 percent of the country's income, and the bottom half, only 18 percent.[8] The Lebanese government's statistical office reported in 1969 that 50 percent of the labor force worked in agriculture and earned only 11 percent of the GNP, but 30 percent were engaged in services and earned 67 percent of it. Twenty percent were employed in

[7]Government of Lebanon, Ministère du Plan, *Besoins et Possibilités de Développement du Liban* (Beirut: Mission IRFED, 1960), p. 93.

[8]U.S. Government, *Area Handbook for Lebanon* (Washington, D.C.: U.S. Government Printing Office, 1969), p. 213.

industry and construction, and earned 22 percent of the GNP.[9] "Despite the sizable growth of a services-based middle class, the main social trend . . . was toward polarization into a few rich and vast numbers of poor. . . ."[10]

In 1966 and 1967, Lebanon's economic boom came to a halt. In October 1966 Intra Bank, a major Lebanese institution, declared bankruptcy. It had engaged in speculative undertakings, and rumors of its unsteady position brought a rush of depositors to withdraw funds. The government shored it up, enabling it to reopen, but a severe blow had been dealt to national and international confidence in Lebanese financial institutions. In June 1967 Egypt, Jordan, and Syria were soundly defeated in the third Arab-Israeli war. Israel captured the West Bank of the Jordan River, and the tourist trade that had gone through Lebanon to it was now terminated. In September 1970 the Jordanian army, under orders from King Hussein, suppressed Palestinian guerilla operations in Jordan, so the guerillas moved their bases to southern Lebanon and carried out raids into Israel from it. Israel retaliated by bombing and attacking Palestinian bases and refugee camps. This brought a migration of Palestinians and Lebanese Shiites from southern Lebanon to a string of settlements around Beirut. They were joined by peasants from other parts of Lebanon, mostly Sunnis, who had to leave their land because of the commercialization of agriculture. They lived in shacks and makeshift dwellings, and the area became known as the "belt of misery."

After 1967, growth in the service sector of the Lebanese economy leveled off, real estate fluctuated wildly in value, banks could not find opportunities for investment in Lebanon and exported capital overseas, and tourism did not increase dramatically. Unemployment went up, and labor disturbances and strikes multiplied. The conflict between the well-off and the poor grew more bitter. Since Maronites tended to predominate among the former and Sunnis, Shiites, and Palestinians among the latter, the class conflict was also one between religious communities.

POLITICAL CULTURE

Family

In Lebanon, family loyalty is a dominant social value. Individuals owe their first allegiance to their nearest kin. One is expected to preserve the family's honor, reputation, and status by not bringing any scandal upon the family name and by maintaining its traditional economic and educational levels. An

[9] Government of Lebanon, Ministère du Plan, Direction Centrale de la Statistique, *Recueil de Statistiques Libanaises, Année 1969*, p. 319.
[10] Samih Farsoun and Walter Carroll, "The Civil War in Lebanon: Sect, Class, and Imperialism," *Monthly Review*, 28, no. 2 (June 1976), 20.

individual's achievement bestows enhanced prestige upon the whole family. Likewise, one's failure tends to degrade its name.

The primacy of the family is manifest in politics and business. There are many prominent political families who support one another in the quest for local or national leadership, jobs in the administration, subsidies, exemptions from taxation, and other forms of government favors. In the business world, family members own common enterprises or interlocking companies, hire only their own relatives, and make loans to each other.

Traditionally families provide for the maintenance of all members who cannot support themselves. A son who upon graduation from the university cannot secure a job, will be given free room and board by his parents or an uncle. A woman who has lost her husband will receive support from her father-in-law or from her husband's brothers. A man whose business has fallen upon hard times will receive loans from his relatives.

In the extended family, Lebanese find relationships of unquestioned trust and a sure defense against outside persons or organizations, whatever the issue or cause. It is the one sure refuge from all the vicissitudes of life.

Sect

All Lebanese carry an identity card which identifies, among other things, their sect. It is very difficult for them legally to change this designation, even though they may have converted to another faith. Many Lebanese have ceased to believe in religion, but this has not caused them to lose their sectarian identity, which assumes a cultural more than a religious form.

The sectarian structure of Lebanese society is a legacy from the Ottoman Empire. At that time, each major non-Muslim religious community (Greek Orthodox, Armenian Gregorian, Catholic, and Jewish) was recognized by the sultan as a millet ("nation"). The Sunni Muslim community was the governing millet. Each non-Muslim millet was allowed to practice its own religion, teach its young the precepts of its faith, speak its own language, develop and maintain its culture. Each was granted wide autonomy to govern its internal affairs under its own legal system, especially in respect to matters of personal status (marriage, divorce, and inheritance). The religious head of the community, the patriarch, bishop, or rabbi, was also the temporal head, and was so recognized by the Ottoman authorities. He was an intermediary who brought to the government's attention individual grievances and community concerns. Members of non-Muslim millets were exempt from military service, but they had to pay a special tax, the *jizyah*, which Muslims did not have to pay.

The Lebanese educational system reinforces sectarianism. Private schools predominate, and parents tend to send their children to schools of their own religion, where they learn the attitudes, values, and prejudices of the community. In 1970-71, the most recent year for which information is available, there were

464,319 students in private primary and secondary schools and 268,422 in public schools.[11] The former usually have a foreign as well as a religious affiliation (French Catholic, American Protestant, Armenian Orthodox, Arab Muslim), and use the language and textbooks of the foreign country as the media of instruction.

In the private schools children are socialized in a narrow sectarian culture and way of looking at others and at the world. The Maronites tend to go to French Catholic schools, where from an early age they use the French language, read books popular with their counterparts in France, and study French and European history, thus developing pride in Western civilization. Armenians go to schools that teach in the Armenian language and develop Armenian national consciousness. Greek Orthodox and Protestants generally attend American Protestant schools, which instruct in English and use American books. Sunni Muslims attend schools that teach in Arabic and are similar to schools in Syria and Egypt. Only those who cannot afford the tuition of the private schools send their children to public school, and since the Shiites are the poorest community in Lebanon, they are heavily represented there.

Social welfare needs are largely met by family and sect. The usual practice is for the family to take care of its own, though often it cannot do enough and then must turn to benevolent societies that are maintained by both Muslims and Christians. These give cash, food, clothing, and free medical care to the needy, pay educational expenses of deserving students, support the aged and infirm, care for orphans, and provide recreational activities for the young. In addition there are Muslim and Christian charitable foundations (*waqfs*), which derive their income from agricultural land or urban real estate. They are used to build and maintain mosques, churches, hospitals, schools, and cemetries, and to pay for the personnel needed to run them.

The "general welfare" and the "good of the country" are not operating principles in Lebanon, and generally each sect thinks of its own interests only. This produces a society that is fragmented and discordant, and it prevents the development of a modern, social-welfare state. However, the disadvantages of such a state—impersonalism, the omnipresence of bureaucratic rules, a standardized mass society—do not exist in Lebanon. Rather all Lebanese live within a network of family and sectarian relationships that provide them with a home base where they are unconditionally accepted.

In the modern European sense of the word, Lebanon is not a nation. Lebanese do not regard each other as "brothers" or "sisters," fellow citizens, or compatriots; they do not feel that they live in a "sacred fatherland," and they are not acculturated to the same national values through the schools, the army, and the communication media. Rather than being a nation, Lebanon is a state in which different communities simply coexist.

[11] Government of Lebanon, *Recueil de Statistiques, Année 1971*, pp. 451, 447.

Social and Civic Immorality

In their private relations, Lebanese are very polite. They defer to each other as to who should go through a door first, and they fight for the honor of paying a restaurant check. Yet in public, with persons whom they do not know, they are rude, arrogant, and bossy. They drive wildly, switching lanes, honking horns, disobeying traffic signs, and generally showing no concern for their own safety or for that of others. When a bus stops, everyone who is waiting for it pushes and shoves in order to get on. Even when their seats have been assigned on an airplane, Lebanese stampede to get on the plane once the gate has opened.

Businessmen refuse to give information about the financial assets of their company—or worse, they give false information. The owners and constructors of buildings routinely ignore zoning codes, making Beirut a concrete jungle with narrow streets upon which the sun never shines, full of structures that abut each other. Births and deaths are not always registered with the appropriate government office, and personal income is routinely distorted on tax returns. Cash is preferred to checks in order to conceal transactions. Child labor laws, health and sanitation regulations are everywhere ignored. Laws and rules in general are not regarded as promoting the public welfare, and are disobeyed whenever possible.

The feeling exists that one can and should get rich quickly by any means— fair or foul. Real estate speculation, hoarding, using political position to enrich oneself, and quick deals that turn a high profit are considered normal.

As noted earlier, Lebanese lack a civic sense or public spirit. "I," "me," or "my group" is always primary over society or country. The government, laws, and police are regarded as unnecessary and oppressive, to be ignored whenever possible.

POLITICAL GROUPS

Lebanon is a social mosaic rather than a pluralistic society. In the latter, groups compete with one another in order to secure the benefits that government can grant and to avoid the penalties it can impose. Such groups share a common system of values and are in agreement concerning the constitutional order and the fundamental laws. They interact competitively yet harmoniously in a unified social and political order.

In a social mosaic, each group looks upon itself as a separate entity, living next to but not with other groups. Together they have no common loyalty to a nation or a state, and share no common political or social culture. They disagree on how the political system should be structured and what should be the basic policies of the government in respect to foreign affairs, defense, economic development, and welfare needs. The groups tend to check and stifle each other so that fundamental reform cannot take place.

The dominant group cleavage in Lebanon is religious, between Christians and Muslims. Social class, ideology, and foreign orientation tend to reinforce it. Christians usually are better educated, more affluent, and in more prominent positions in the capitalist economy, while Muslims tend to be more poorly educated, less affluent workers and peasants. Christians are generally right-wing, even fascist; Muslims are generally left-wing, and sympathetic to socialism and Marxism. Christians are inclined to identify with Europe and the West, finding their allies there, while Muslims feel themselves to be a part of the Arab and Muslim worlds, affiliating with persons, organizations, and countries within them.

The Armenians and the Palestinians are two major groups that have entered Lebanon in the present century. Significantly the former, who are Christian but not Arab, have been granted citizenship and are well integrated into the political and economic systems though they preserve their own language and culture. The Palestinians, who are Arab and not Christian (the overwhelming majority are Muslim) have not been granted citizenship, have been kept out of the political system, and have not been integrated into the national economy, even though they speak Arabic and share the Arab culture common to almost all Lebanese.

Palestinians

No one knows precisely how many Palestinians live in Lebanon, but the estimates vary from 150,000 to 300,000. They fled to Lebanon after the 1948 and 1967 Arab-Israeli wars. Almost all are Sunni Muslims, and about 90 percent reside in refugee camps scattered along the coast, supported by the United Nations Relief and Works Agency (UNRWA) and other bodies. The remaining 10 percent, generally the more educated persons, are integrated into the Lebanese population but do not hold Lebanese citizenship.

All maintain their Palestinian identity, refuse to consider themselves Lebanese, and wait for the day when they can return to their homeland. They do not want to become Lebanese citizens, since they feel this would mean abandoning hope for the return to Palestine. The Christian Lebanese do not want to grant them citizenship, since the population balance would then be tipped in favor of the Muslims. While Israel continues to exist, Palestinians remain residents of Lebanon, living outside its society and polity.

The refugee camps possess de facto extraterritoriality. The Lebanese police and army do not enter them; rather, armed Palestinian guerrillas maintain order. In them recruitment, training, and the solicitation of money for the guerrilla organizations takes place, and the schools teach Palestinian history, literature, poetry, and art—all that is deemed necessary to maintain a Palestinian national consciousness. Anti-Zionism and hatred of the "Zionist imperialist settler-state" are universal attitudes.

The presence of the Palestinians in Lebanon contributes to its internal fragmentation and policy dilemmas. Since 1970 Palestinian guerrillas based in Lebanon have been making raids into Israel, resulting in reprisals from the Israeli armed forces. After each such incident, demands are made on the Lebanese government to increase its military budget, build up its army, and protect the country from Israeli attack. Lebanese Muslims support these calls, but the Christians do not.

Deprived of formal legal participation in national politics, and as a sub-proletarian class living a marginal existence, the Palestinians have allied with the Muslims who, though better off politically and economically than they, have also been underprivileged. Together Palestinians and Muslims have demanded radical changes in the Lebanese economic and political systems.

Because they suffer from national and economic deprivation, the Palestinians have come to be regarded by progressives, Marxists, and radicals throughout the Arab world as the spearhead of revolution in the Middle East. These Arabs feel that in the Palestinians the national and the social revolutions have been joined, and that in the process of "liberating Palestine," the Palestinians will also carry out the revolution against the "feudalist" and "state-capitalist" regimes in the Arab world that are supported by American and Western European "imperialism." This social revolutionary aspect further accentuates the differences between Palestinians and Maronites, the dominant group in the Lebanese Christian community, which tends to be right-wing and conservative.

The Maronites in Lebanon call the Palestinians "foreigners." The Israelis do not want them to live in Israel. As long as they are homeless and without a state of their own, they will be a destabilizing factor in Lebanon and the region.

Maronites

Comprising about 30 percent of the population according to the 1932 census, the Maronites are the single largest community in Lebanon, and the one with which the state is most closely identified. They made up a comfortable majority in old Mount Lebanon, and in essence the French created the present state for them.

They trace their origins back to a fifth-century Christian monk, Saint Maron, who started a religious movement in the Homs, Hama, and Aleppo regions of Syria. After the Muslim-Arab conquest of the seventh century, the Maronites left this fertile area for the harsh and inhospitable mountains of Lebanon, where they were able to fend off Muslim attempts at conquest and could develop a nearly independent society and state. During the period of Crusader rule, from about 1098 to 1291, they established close contact with the French. They entered into communion with Rome, a relationship that was broken but then reestablished in the sixteenth century, when the Maronites became one of the Eastern Rites, which recognize the Pope as the Supreme Head of the Church but maintain their own non-Latin liturgy.

The Maronites have been small mountain farmers, yet today a large number are businessmen and professionals. Prior to the 1860s they were ruled by a feudal aristocracy and by the clergy. Today many prominent families play an active role in politics, and the Maronite patriarch is one of the most important persons in Lebanon.

The Maronites are one of the most literate communities in the country, with an educated elite that has received a thorough French education, knows French better than Arabic, and has highly assimilated French culture. The Maronite community has emigrated more than any other in Lebanon and it has a world-wide network of ecclesiastical and social relations with the center in Lebanon.

Greek Orthodox

With 10 percent of the population, according to the 1932 census, the Greek Orthodox is the second largest Christian sect in Lebanon and the fourth largest of any in the country. Living throughout the eastern Mediterranean and Russia, the Greek Orthodox have formed separate but related national churches, each with its own patriarch and autonomous religious jurisdiction. Those who live in Lebanon are under the Patriarch of Antioch, who now resides in Damascus. They are not concentrated in Lebanon alone and have no special or historic attachment to the Lebanese state.

The Greek Orthodox Church has long considered itself the true inheritor and preserver of Christianity, and has taken pride in its Eastern traditions. In Syria and Lebanon the clergy are all Arab, and the liturgical language is Arabic; "Greek" is merely a historical designation. When the Muslim Arabs conquered the Middle East, Greek Orthodox believers did not flee to the mountains, but became the largest Christian community in the Islamic empires and the one which had the best relations with the caliph or sultan.

They are one of the world's major faiths, not a schismatic and persecuted sect, and are Arab and Eastern. Among the Christian communities of Lebanon, they are the most favorable to pan-Arabism and the best able to cooperate with the Sunnis. Frequently they act as mediator between them and the Maronites. They are unhappy with Maronite domination of the Lebanese political system. Many have sided with the Muslims in the civil war.

The Greek Orthodox are urbanized and well educated, and in Beirut many are rich bankers. In the past there has been a wide gulf between the rich and the poor, but a middle class is now developing. Since the seat of the Patriarch is in Damascus, and because of a long tradition of influential lay councils in dioceses and parishes, leadership of the Greek Orthodox community has been more in the hands of upper-class laymen than of the clergy.

Greek Catholic

In 1709 some members of the Greek Orthodox Church broke away and joined the church in Rome, thereby forming the Greek Catholic community, which accepts all Roman Catholic dogma but maintains some of the ancient rituals of the Greek Orthodox Church. Greek Catholics live in Lebanon, Syria, Israel, and Egypt, and their Patriarch alternates his residence between Cairo and Damascus.

These Christians form 6 percent of the population of Lebanon and comprise one of its best educated communities. Their communal spirit is not as strongly developed as that of the Maronites and Greek Orthodox, and they are less prominent in politics. Like the Greek Orthodox, they are culturally a part of the Arab world, and the leadership of their community is mostly in the hands of lay people rather than clergy.

Armenians

Except for the Palestinians, the Armenians are the most recent arrivals in Lebanon, and are the only group that has not assimilated itself into the Arabic culture. At the end of the nineteenth and in the early part of the twentieth century they suffered a great deal in domains ruled by the Turks, so they fled them and settled all over the world. In 1929 Ataturk carried out a Turkification policy, and still more Armenians left. Those who came to Lebanon were given citizenship by the French mandatory government in 1924. They form about 4 percent of the population and live mostly in Beirut, its suburbs, and in one town in the Beqa Valley. They are mostly an urban middle class consisting of crafts-people, merchants, lawyers, and doctors.

They are still cultural foreigners temporarily resident in Lebanon, maintaining their own school system in which Armenian history, culture, and language are given primary emphasis. Armenians always speak their own language among themselves, and most have a limited knowledge of Arabic. The Turkish atrocities are still very much alive in their minds, and have the same effect on their outlook as does the Holocaust on Jews. They share with Lebanese Christians a religious bond that transcends national differences, and for this reason they have been welcomed into the country, given citizenship, and are full participants in the political process.

The Armenians are divided into three religious denominations: Orthodox, Catholic, and Protestant, with the first comprising the overwhelming majority. They are well organized into two political parties: the Hunchak Party, which is

Marxist and sympathetic to the Soviet Union; and the Dashnak, which is nationalist, anti-Communist, and anti-Soviet. The infighting between the two is fierce, weakening the political power of the community as a whole. The Armenians are important in Lebanese politics because they have a common interest with the Maronites in maintaining the independence of Lebanon and its political and economic systems. These give both communities the freedom to preserve their distinct national and religious identities and dominant economic positions.

Sunni Muslims

The Sunni Muslims, who comprise about 21 percent of the population, are the second largest community in Lebanon and the one least devoted to the state and its institutions. They are adherents to the major branch of Islam, whose believers live in the area from Morocco to Indonesia.

The Sunnis very much resented the creation of Grand Liban by the French because it accompanied the demise of an independent Arab kingdom in Arabia, Iraq, and greater Syria in which they were the overwhelming majority. Furthermore they were cut off from their coreligionists in Syria and the rest of the Arab world, thereby becoming a minority group in the new Lebanese state. Also they were ruled by the French and the Maronites, both Christians, which violated the Islamic precept that government should be in the hands of Muslims. Even today the Sunnis have not unequivocally decided whether they belong in Lebanon or in some greater Arab political entity, and they are the most "un-Lebanese" of the Lebanese.

They live on the coastal plain of Lebanon and in some parts of the Beqa and South Lebanon. In the cities of Tripoli, Sidon, and Tyre they are a clear majority, and in Beirut they are about even in number with the Christians.

They occupy all professions and trades. There is a large stratum of peasants and workers, a small middle class of merchants and professionals, and a small upper class composed of the owners of large tracts of agricultural land and of urban real estate and businesses. As a rule Sunnis are not as well educated as Christians. They are more resistant to change and more zealous in defending Arab culture and civilization against Western inroads.

Shiite Muslims

The Shiite Muslim sect formed as the result of a schism that took place in Islam in the decades after the death of Muhammad. Throughout Islamic history the Shiites have constantly been at odds with the Sunnis and have generally been on the losing side. Today Shiites live in communities that have only the loosest of ties with each other in Yemen, southern Iraq, Iran, and southern Lebanon.

In Lebanon they are the poorest, least educated, and least modernized of the major groups. They equal 18 percent of the population, according to the 1932 census, but their power is not commensurate with their numbers. When crises occur they tend to join hands with the Sunnis, which produces a Muslim-Christian confrontation.

Druze

The Druze are an eleventh century offshoot of Shiism, and their beliefs are kept a secret from outsiders. They live almost exclusively in two areas: the Shouf region, which forms the southern part of Mount Lebanon and is to the southeast of Beirut, and Jabal Druze (the "Mountain of the Druze") in southwestern Syria near Mount Hermon. In Lebanon they act as a buffer between the Maronites in the north and the Shiites in the south. They are organized into tightly-knit villages and clans, and have several leading families. Two of the most famous are Jumblat and Arslan, both of which have been prominent in Lebanese politics for a century or more. There are Druzes in every parliament and cabinet, where they occupy a crucial middle position between the Maronites and Sunnis, making alliances with one side or the other and extracting concessions favorable to their interests.

Most of the Druze are small farmers. Their literacy rate is about the same as the Sunnis, and a moderately large number of them are engineers, doctors, and lawyers.

POLITICAL STRUCTURES

One of Lebanon's most severe problems has been the inability of the Lebanese to transform their political system. The current one is based on formulas and compromises agreed upon in the 1930s and early 1940s. Fundamental issues such as the taking of a new census; the writing of new laws on immigration, naturalization, and the rights of citizens; the changing or abolition of the confessional system in assigning seats in parliament; the modification of the custom that the president of the Republic is always a Maronite, the prime minister a Sunni, and the president of the Chamber of Deputies (the one-house parliament) a Shiite, have all gone unresolved for decades.

More significantly, not only has it been impossible to bring about fundamental political change, it has also not been possible to introduce new programs or policies—what one might call "simple" reforms—into the government. In the early 1970s some liberal technocrats were appointed to the cabinet. They tried to introduce reforms such as imposing higher taxes on luxury items, reducing the soaring cost of medications, enforcing tax laws already in existence, improving public education, and reforming the school curriculum to help create national unity. All these attempts failed, and all the ministers involved had to resign.[12]

The description that follows is of the political structures as they have existed to date. At the time of the writing of this book, the various factions have not yet agreed upon ways of modifying them.

The National Pact

During World War II, when it became obvious that at the cessation of hostilities France would give Lebanon its freedom, the leader of the Maronites, Bishara al-Khuri, and of the Sunnis, Riyad al-Sulh, came together to discuss the general outlines of a broad governing formula after independence. The agreement they arrived at became known as the National Pact, and though it was never written down or formally signed, it has been the basis of the Lebanese constitutional order.

The pact was based on the assumption that Christians and Muslims were divided over the issue of Lebanon's identity and destiny. It assumed that the Muslims wanted a total identification with the Arab world and that the Christians desired foreign protection to prevent this from taking place. Therefore the compromise was reached that independent Lebanon would identify with, but not become a part of, the Arab world.

In the pact it was agreed that the three highest offices in the country (the president of the Republic, the prime minister, and the president of the Chamber of Deputies) would be given to a Maronite, a Sunni, and a Shiite, in that order. The offices of deputy prime minister and vice-president of the Chamber of Deputies would go to the fourth largest sect, the Greek Orthodox. The seats in the one-house legislature would likewise be apportioned among the sects, as would all positions in the bureaucracy from cabinet permanent secretary down to postal clerk.

The Maronites, confident that they controlled the most important position in the new government, and secure in the knowledge that the country was not going to be merged into a greater Arab state, could forego their dependence upon France and actively seek independence. The Sunnis could join in because they were in a position of power and knew they were not going to be cut off from their brethren in Syria and the rest of the Arab world.

The leaders of the communities set the tone for the new state in several ways. They determined that the purpose of the state was to maintain harmony among the sects, this to be achieved through the preservation of the status quo. Radical social disruption, rapid economic development, and governmental efficiency were sacrificed, and all change was to be gradual, evolutionary, and

---

[12]Halim Barakat, *Lebanon in Strife: Student Preludes to the Civil War* (Austin: University of Texas Press, 1977), p. 192.

incremental in order not to upset the delicate balance that the founders had established.

The President of the Republic

The president of the republic is the most powerful person in the country. He is elected by the Chamber of Deputies for a six-year term, and can only be reelected after an interval of six years.

The president appoints all ministers, including the prime minister, and can dismiss them. He proposes laws to the Chamber, promulgates those passed by it, and issues supplementary regulations to insure their execution. He has the right to grant pardons and to negotiate and ratify treaties.

The president is the head of state. He symbolizes Lebanon, its unity, its purpose, and its mission. Through speeches and public ceremonies he furthers toleration and cooperation among the sects and common efforts for the good of all Lebanese.

While decisive, the president's power is not absolute. He must be able to work with the prime minister, who is always a Sunni of great standing, and he must secure the cooperation of at least some of the various blocs in the Chamber of Deputies, each of which is headed by a powerful leader.

The president rules through a cabinet composed of a prime minister and other ministers. The signatures of the president, the prime minister, and of the minister concerned, appear at the bottom of all presidential decrees.

The Cabinet

The Government (president and cabinet) has the right to initiate laws, and can declare as urgent a proposed bill it has submitted to the Chamber of Deputies. If the Chamber does not act on the bill within forty days, it can become law through decree of the president and the cabinet.

The ministers supervise and direct the departments and sections of which they are the heads. They assure, each in his jurisdiction, the application of laws and regulations.

The Chamber of Deputies

The single-house legislature shares with the president and cabinet together the right to initiate laws. It alone possesses the power to enact them, and it has a significant role in financial affairs. Taxes cannot be levied, modified, or abolished except by law, nor can a public loan or any other obligation imposing a charge on the budget be contracted except by law.

Every six years, sitting as an electoral college, the Chamber chooses a new president. Election is by secret ballot, and a two-thirds majority is required. However, after the first ballot a majority is sufficient.

Parliamentary blocs based on confessional loyalties, regional interests, or personal allegiance, function in the Chamber in lieu of political parties. They are usually named after their leader, have little internal discipline, and lack an ideological viewpoint. The alliances within and among the blocs are constantly shifting, and deputies associate with one or the other, depending upon the issues debated and the personal interest involved.

The Electoral System

The Chamber of Deputies is currently composed of ninety-nine deputies. Since independence its size has varied from fifty-five to the present figure, but the number has always been a multiple of eleven so that a ratio of six Christian to five Muslim seats can be maintained.

Elections take place over a two- to three-week period, with different parts of the country voting at different times. Since most Lebanese cast ballots at their place of birth rather than their residence, these staggered elections alleviate transportation problems and enable the security forces to move from region to region to maintain order.

By law the country is divided into electoral districts, and to each a certain number of sectarian seats is allocated. For example, in the district of Shouf there are three Maronite seats, two Druze, two Sunni, and one Greek Catholic. The voters choose candidates for all seats in their district, and though they may be Maronites, for instance, they participate in the selection of persons for the Druze, Sunni, and Greek Catholic seats.

This system has brought about the development of electoral lists. In each district, candidates of different faiths competing for the different sectarian seats, form lists. The usual pattern is that the most powerful person of the major sect recruits members of the other sects to be on his list. Thus in the district of Shouf, a Maronite would consult with a Druze, Sunni, and Greek Catholic, desiring to have on his list popular persons from other sects to enhance his chances of winning. The colisters from the less numerous sects want to be associated with the most popular person from the most numerous sect. This achieves a "mutual coattail" effect.

At the polls voters insert into an official envelope their choice of candidates. The lists from which the voter chooses are formed by personal alliances that shift from election to election, and have neither an ideological nor a partisan basis. Voters make their selections on the basis of general promises, proven ability of the candidates to provide government benefits to the districts, family connections, and frequently, vote-buying.

This system has inhibited the organization of political parties, but the necessity of forming lists has forced the leaders of different sects to cooperate, and so sectarian moderation has been promoted.

Political Parties

Parties are not as important in Lebanon as in some other countries. The most powerful person in the country is the president, and by custom he is above party politics. He chooses and leads the cabinet, in which care is taken that the various sects, not the political parties, are equitably represented. Of the ninety-nine people in the Chamber of Deputies, no more than one-third have ever been party representatives, and no party or combination of parties has ever formed a government and led the nation. The deputies are for the most part powerful communal leaders, prominent businessmen, and large landowners who form loosely organized and continually shifting blocs.

However, parties do exist, and they have a great deal of visibility. They espouse ideologies, put forward political programs, praise and criticize the government, and inform and misinform the public. Generally they appeal to the members of one sect, their political ideology harmonizing with its dominant values. Their name ("national," "liberal," "progressive") may indicate an ideological stance common to persons of all sects, but inevitably their following is very homogeneous. The *Katā'ib* ("Phalanges"), the Liberal National Party, and the National Bloc are Christian; *al-Najjāda* (the "Helpers") is Muslim; the Progressive Socialist Party is Druze; the Dashnak and Hunchak parties are Armenian, and the Baath is Muslim and Greek Orthodox.

The parties publish their own newspapers, or at least have access to ones that are sympathetic to their point of view. Several operate their own youth organizations, which sponsor sports and recreation programs and inculcate in the young the ideology of the party. Many run private militias, the ranks of which are filled with young men who are well-trained, disciplined, and equipped with small arms and some heavy weapons. In times of civil disorder the militias protect the villages, regions, and urban quarters where the party is strong. They are beyond the control of the government, and the Lebanese army and national police have traditionally refrained from interfering in fights among them.

POLITICAL LEADERSHIP

The Za'ims

For decades and even centuries, persons from the same political families have controlled Lebanese national politics. They have been constantly in the public eye, continually involved in political debates, appearing and reappearing in parliaments and cabinets. Most have inherited their political position, and they work frenetically to promote their sons in politics so that the family tradition will be carried out.

Called *za'ims* (the Arabic plural is *zu'amā'*), they are the Lebanese version of the political boss. Their support comes from a town, region, or sect, the interests of which they advance, and their national power results from having a local political base. They are the heads of the Lebanese political parties, the commanders of the militias, the leaders of the parliamentary blocs, and generally they are also prominent in the professions and business.

Sulaiman Franjieh, President of Lebanon from 1970 to 1976, is the *za'im* of the Maronite town of Zghorta, near Tripoli. Kamal Jumblat, who was assassinated in 1977, was a member of the Chamber of Deputies from 1943 to 1977, a participant in many cabinets, the head of the Progressive Socialist Party, and the leader of the Muslim-leftist alliance in the civil war. He was the *za'im* of the Druze in the Shouf area to the southeast of Beirut.

Three well-known Maronite *za'ims* involved in an intense personal rivalry are Pierre Jumayyil, leader of the *Katā'ib* Party, who hails from the town of Bikfayya in the Matn area immediately northeast of Beirut; Raymond Iddi, leader of the National Bloc, whose father was president of Lebanon from 1936 to 1941 and who comes from the district of Jubayl between Beirut and Tripoli; and Kamil Shamoun, president of Lebanon from 1952 to 1958, leader of the Liberal National Party, who prior to the civil war came from the area around the town of Damour, a short distance south of Beirut.

Private wealth and high political office are indispensable to the maintenance of the position of *za'im*. Wealth enables him to provide to his constituents loans, small monetary gifts, and jobs. Most *za'ims* have a number of businesses. He uses his political position to speed up the granting of a license, get someone out of jail, or improve a road in a particular area. Ideology and party affiliation are largely irrelevant to his followers, who support him because of his established position and past services.

The *za'im* system survives since Lebanese would rather associate with a small local group than with a wider one. *Za'ims* comprise the overwhelming majority of the deputies in Parliament, and they determine the election of presidents, the formation of cabinets, and the adoption of policies. The compromises reached among them are those basic to Lebanese politics, and their quarrels reflect the fissures in Lebanese society.

The Higher Clergy

The Lebanese Maronite community is led by a patriarch, the Sunni community by a mufti, the Shiites by an imam, the Druzes by a sheik, and the Greek Orthodox and Greek Catholics by patriarchs. These religious leaders are concerned as much with the material welfare and political power of their communities as with strictly religious matters. They frequently defend the rights of their followers in public pronouncements and represent them before the president of the republic and the prime minister, usually in coordination with the leading *za'ims* of their communities. When a new cabinet is being formed or a vacancy in the bureaucracy is being filled, they are consulted as to who should be chosen.

As a group the high-ranking clergy are committed to the preservation of the rights of each community and to the maintenance of religious values against the forces of secularism. They make frequent statements condemning narrow confessionalism and religious bigotry, and in order to promote this tolerance they visit each other on religious holy days and appear together at public ceremonies on state holidays. Muslim leaders socialize with Christian leaders on Easter and similar occasions, and the latter do the same on Muslim holy days. However, in the civil war that began in 1975, the high-ranking clergy have had no appreciable effect in dampening religious passions.

Business Leaders

The free enterprise economy of Lebanon has produced a plutocracy based on banking, real estate, insurance, hotels, commerce, and industry. Most of the people are closely associated with the *za'ims* or are *za'ims* themselves. Many hold seats in parliament or give financial support to someone who does. They make the acquaintance of cabinet members, prime ministers, presidents, and top bureaucrats. Because of their position and connections, they can have a law or regulation evaded or bent to serve their interests.

They are cautious investors who favor enterprises which will bring a quick, high return, and they generally shun industry since it does not furnish these possibilities. They oppose protective tariffs because these would reduce imports, which are a source of their income. They frequently invest overseas when it is safer and the returns are higher than investing locally, and they look with skepticism upon economic development initiated by state investments and enterprises.

Intellectuals

Intellectuals hold a somewhat paradoxical position in Lebanon. A university or a secondary-school degree is highly prized, and *za'ims*, businessmen, and bureaucrats find that their status is enhanced if they are involved in the university and intellectual communities. It is quite common for bureaucrats also to hold part-time teaching positions in one of Beirut's universities. There are many associations of professionals or intellectuals, such as the *Cénacle Libanais* ("Lebanese Literary Circle"), the Institute of Developmental Studies, the Lebanese Association of University Professors, the Lawyers Syndicate, and the Doctors Syndicate. Many such organizations maintain buildings or rent a floor or two where they have a bar, meeting rooms, and facilities for parties. Membership in these societies provides many opportunities for socializing.

However, as a class, intellectuals have only a marginal influence on the political process. They earnestly and brilliantly debate the crucial issues of the day and put forth many proposals for social and political reform. Yet usually the politicians applaud their proposals while they continue the old practices. Since most intellectuals do not hold positions of power, they tend to be a counter-elite critical of the existing regime. From them have come many proposals for social reform, modernization, restructuring of the bureaucracy, and an end to confessionalism, which, combined with pressure from the bottom of Lebanese society, have produced a small measure of change in the past ten to fifteen years.

Army Officers

The Lebanese armed forces have been quite small. Prior to the civil war that began in 1975 they numbered only about 15,000 men. Their budget was low and their weapons were old. Most of the officers were Christian, while the majority of enlisted men were Muslim. The armed forces did not become involved in the Arab-Israeli wars, and their primary mission was internal security.

During the civil war of 1958, the restraint and judiciousness of the army commander General Fuad Shihab, helped to dampen the conflict. Because of his skillful leadership during that tense and delicate time, a majority of the Chamber of Deputies chose him to be president of the republic for the term 1958-64. His successor from 1964 to 1970, Charles Helou, was also the choice of a coalition of top army officers and members of parliament. The general thrust of the policies initiated by President Shihab and continued by Helou was to modernize the bureaucracy, expand its capabilities to perform services, and introduce a measure of planning into the economy.

While in the civil war of 1958 the army did not lean to one side or the other and so gained a reputation for fairness, in the war that began in 1975, many people have felt that it has favored business interests and the Christian-rightist alliance. In 1976 the army split into several factions. One of the tasks of the president who assumed office in September 1976, Elias Sarkis, has been to reconstitute the Lebanese army into a body free from factionalism and favoritism.

POLITICAL POLICIES

As of the middle of 1979, Lebanon is still occupied by a 30,000-man Arab peacekeeping force from which all but the Syrian forces have withdrawn. The numerous private militias still exist, are well armed, are in good fighting spirit, and rule over pieces of territory. Israel has de facto military control over the area of Lebanon south of the Litani River. Elias Sarkis is president, and parliament has granted him authority to rule by decree, but he can do little more than mediate among the different factions. The cabinet is composed of technocrats who have drawn up plans for Beirut's reconstruction and the economic revival of the country, but the *za'ims* stand on the side, do not participate in government, continue to wield enormous political power, and make it questionable whether these plans can be realized when basic political issues have not been resolved.

The war has brought out all the fissures in Lebanese society. It has been a class conflict between the rich and the poor, and it has been a religious conflict between Christians and Muslims. It has been an ideological struggle between those who want Lebanon to remain a conservative laissez-faire state run by an elite of *za'ims* and businessmen, and those who want to change it into a secular, socialist, democratic state led by the popular majority. Finally, it has been an international conflict, since each faction has found allies outside the country.

The mindless destruction of property and the horrible atrocities against people continue, and they leave a legacy of bitterness that will be extremely difficult to overcome. The underlying social, economic, and political problems that brought on the war have not been resolved, and for many *za'ims* they have not even been recognized as existing.

REVIEW OF THE MAJOR EVENTS IN THE MODERN HISTORY OF LEBANON

1858	Beginning of a peasant revolt in Mount Lebanon.
1860	Strife between communities of Maronites and Druze; the French intervene on the side of the Maronites.
1861	Establishment by the Ottoman government of the autonomous territory of Mount Lebanon.
1914	World War I begins; the Ottoman Empire sides with Germany and Austria; Ottoman authorities end the autonomy of Mount Lebanon and rule it directly.
1916	In the secret Sykes-Picot Agreement, France, Britain, and Russia assign control over Syria and Lebanon to France following the defeat of the Ottoman Empire.
1918	British and Arab troops capture Damascus from the Turks; Arabs under the leadership of Faisal (later to become king of Iraq) attempt to establish an independent nation-state in Syria, Lebanon, Palestine, and Jordan with its capital at Damascus.
1919	The British begin to evacuate the coastal plain of Lebanon, and French forces move in.
1920 April	At the San Remo conference in Italy, the Allies place Syria and Lebanon under French mandate.

July	French troops defeat Arab forces near Damascus, capture it, and end the efforts to create an independent Arab nation-state.
Sept.	The French form *Grand Liban* ("Greater Lebanon").
1924	The mandatory government gives Lebanese citizenship to the resident Armenians.
1926	The mandatory government promulgates a constitution that formally is still in effect.
1932	The French authorities take a census, which has not been followed by another one.
1940	The Nazis conquer France; the Vichy French government attempts to maintain its authority over Lebanon.
1941 June July	The British defeat the Vichy French forces in Syria and Lebanon.
Nov.	The Free French government proclaims the independence of Lebanon.
1943 Aug.	General elections are held.
Sept.	The Chamber of Deputies elects Bishara al-Khuri president of the republic; he then appoints Riyad al-Sulh prime minister. The two men announce their agreement to the National Pact.
Nov.	The Chamber of Deputies amends the constitution, eliminating the articles referring to the mandatory power.
1948	Establishment of the state of Israel; some Palestinians flee to Lebanon.
1958	Civil war breaks out; the United States lands troops at the request of the Lebanese president.
1967	In the June war, Israel captures East Jerusalem, the West Bank, and Gaza, causing more Palestinians to flee to Lebanon.
1970	Under orders from King Hussein, the Jordanian army suppresses Palestinian guerilla activity in the country; they then move their bases to southern Lebanon.
1975	Civil war begins.
1976 Jan.	Syrian mediation team begins negotiations among the various Lebanese factions.
April	Syrian troops enter Lebanon.

Oct.   Foreign ministers of the League of Arab States create a peace-keeping force for Lebanon, which includes the Syrian troops already there.

1978

March   After an attack by Palestinian guerillas, Israeli troops cross into Lebanon and take control of most of the region south of the Litani River.

June   Israeli troops complete their withdrawal from southern Lebanon and turn over control of some areas to Christian militias.

Chapter 8

Egypt

Strategically located at the nexus of Africa and Asia and situated in the middle of the Arab world, Egypt has unusual importance in the region and in the world at large. When European imperialism flourished in the Middle East, Egypt bore the brunt of its attack. In every Arab-Israeli war (1948, 1956, 1973), Egypt was the major adversary of Israel and the chief concern of the latter's military planners. Although neither the United States nor the Soviet Union has launched a physical attack against Egypt, both have wooed, cajoled, and pressured it to be a member of either the "Free World" or the "Socialist Camp."

Egypt has always been a power in the Arab world because of its large population, military strength, advanced bureaucracy, charismatic leadership, and relatively developed economy. On the continent of Africa it has been a champion of those exploited by imperialism and oppressed by racism. In Cairo is located al-Azhar, a thousand-year-old Islamic seminary and university, which has on its faculty many well-known and learned theologians and attracts students from every Islamic country. It makes Egypt a center of the Islamic world.

In his widely-read book, *Egypt's Liberation: the Philosophy of the Revolution*,[1] Gamal Abdel Nasser stated that Egypt was a part of three circles: (1) the Arab circle "that is a part of us," and of which "we are a part." (2) the African

[1] Gamal Abdel Nasser, *Egypt's Liberation: The Philosophy of the Revolution* (Washington, D.C.: Public Affairs Press, 1955).

continent "which Fate decreed us to be a part of," and (3) the Islamic world "with which we are united by bonds created not only by religious belief, but also reinforced by historic reality."[2]

Among Middle Eastern nations, Egypt has been in the forefront of social, economic, cultural, and political change—all that goes under the rubric of modernization. The Western impact came early, with the Napoleonic invasion of 1798-1801. Following this period, Muhammad Ali (1805-1848) attempted through drastic and draconian means to develop the economy and modernize the army and navy. From 1882 to 1952 the British controlled Egypt and instituted changes in agriculture, communication, transportation, and administration. Since 1952 socialism has been instituted, and the bureaucratic polity has grown much stronger.

Liberal democracy had numerous supporters in Egypt, and it was tried in various forms between 1866 and 1952. The Muslim Brotherhood was founded and flourished in Egypt, and though it is now suppressed, its ideals and values exist in a diffuse fashion. Arab socialism was the creation of Gamal Abdel Nasser, who popularized it throughout the Arab world. Finally, Marxism has been quite strong in Egypt, spawning several different communist parties, now all suppressed, but manifesting itself in leftist circles and periodicals.

In summary, Egypt has been a prize that has been fought over, a forerunner for the Middle East of social and political change, and a vortex in which all the modern Arab and Islamic social, political, and intellectual currents have swirled.

GEOGRAPHY AND ECONOMY

Importance of Location

Egypt's position on the map gives it maximum exposure to the world. It fronts on the Mediterranean, which gives it easy access to Europe; borders on Israel, which formerly made it one of the "confrontation states" with Israel; contains the Suez Canal, through which passes traffic from all over the world; shares a common frontier with the Sudan, tying it to black Africa; and has as its western neighbor Libya, the connecting link between Egypt and the Arab West, called the Maghreb.

In Hellenic times and in the days of the Roman empire, Egypt was a part of the world that had the Mediterranean as its center. For most of the nineteenth century and much of the twentieth, this sea was dominated by the British. Today the fleets of the United States and the Soviet Union maneuver in the eastern Mediterranean and exert influence on Egypt.

Through the Sinai Peninsula during its five millennia, Egypt has from time to time expanded its control into Asia, particularly the regions that are today

[2]Ibid., pp. 85-86.

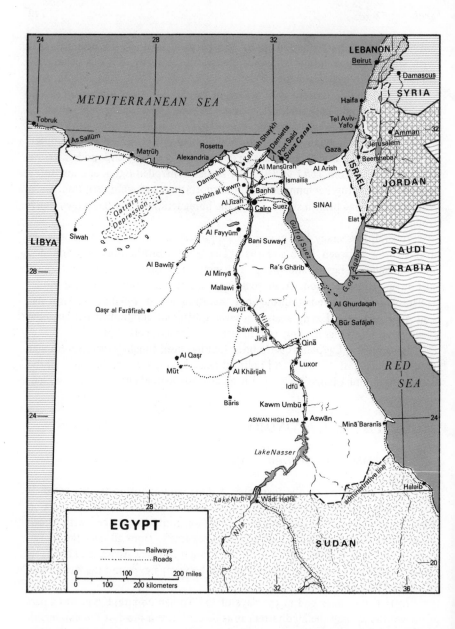

Africa. The port of Suez on the Gulf of Suez, an extension of the Red Sea, was, controlled by Israel, Jordan, Syria, and Lebanon. The Sinai has been a two-way street through which have come numerous armies, the most important being those of the Arab-Muslims of the seventh century, the Turks in the fifteenth century, and the Israelis in the twentieth.

The Red Sea has been Egypt's avenue of transportation to Asia and east before the building of the Suez Canal, a location from which ships went down the coast of east Africa, around the Arabian Peninsula into the Persian Gulf, and across the Indian Ocean into India. The construction of the Suez Canal has simply made the port all the more important in this respect.

Through the Nile Valley, Egypt has had extensive contact with sub-Saharan Africa. Traders have gone up and down the Nile, and the peoples and cultures of Egypt and Africa have fruitfully mixed and interchanged. Many Egyptians are very dark-skinned, and the Islamic religion and Arabic language are today predominant in the northern Sudan.

The western part of Egypt, called the Western Desert, is part of the Sahara which stretches across all of North Africa. Throughout history conquerors have come through it, or the Egyptians in turn have gone out to conquer the regions of North Africa.

The Nile

Egypt has been called by Herodotus "the gift of the Nile," for without this long, sinuous, slow-moving body of water, there would be neither vegetation nor people in the region. In Cairo, rainfall averages only a little over one inch a year. Traditionally the rich soil along the river banks, the water from the river itself, and the labor of the peasants have in combination brought an abundance of food. For all practical purposes, Egypt is the Nile Valley, and 99 percent of its people live within a few miles of the river or one of its branches, on about 4 percent of the total land area. In this river valley the density of population is about 2,000 people per square mile. The populated area about equals the total land area of Holland, one of the world's most densely populated countries, but in Holland there are about 15 million people, whereas Egypt's population is now approaching 40 million![3]

Upper and Lower Egypt

Cairo is the dividing point between Upper and Lower Egypt. The former is the region to the south of Cairo, "up the Nile." It is a thread of villages and towns about 650 miles long that cluster on the banks of the river and terminates in Aswan. Here the people have been more isolated from the outside world and thus today are still traditional.

Lower Egypt is the region to the north of Cairo: triangular in shape, flat, extremely fertile, interconnected with numerous branches and sub-branches of the Nile, and woven together with man-made canals and irrigation ditches, it is packed with people who live in villages which are never more than about a mile

[3]*Arabia and the Gulf* (London: Portico Publications Ltd., April 18, 1977), p. 8.

apart. Lower Egypt has had more contact with the outside world and the cosmopolitan metropolises of Cairo and Alexandria. Here, more than a hundred years ago, the change was made from annual to perennial irrigation, the latter involving the construction of dams and canals to control the flow of the Nile's waters so that they can be directed into fields year round. Thus Lower Egyptians learned rather early how to manage and exploit nature, a key aspect of modernity.[4]

Population

In 1882 the first census using modern techniques was carried out, and the figure arrived at for the total population of the country was 6.7 million. In 1897 the first of a decennial census was conducted. These have continued up to the present, with delays for war and revolution. Table 8-1 summarizes their results. In 1976 the population was 36.656 million, and estimates for the year 2000 vary from a low of 54.771 million to a high of 70.759 million.[5]

When these figures are placed side by side with those for the amount of cultivated land and the per capita acreage (see Table 8-2), the dimensions of the ever-increasing population pressure become sharply defined.

TABLE 8-1. EGYPTIAN POPULATION GROWTH, 1897-1976

Year	Population in millions
1897	9.365
1907	11.190
1917	12.718
1927	14.178
1937	15.921
1947	18.967
1960	26.085
1966	30.075
1970	33.329
1976	36.656

SOURCE: John Waterbury, "Manpower and Population Planning in the Arab Republic of Egypt," *American Universities Field Staff Reports*, Northeast Africa Series, 17, no. 2 (1972), p. 7; figure for 1976 from *United Nations Statistical Yearbook, 1977* (New York: 1978), Table 18, p. 68.

[4] Richard Critchfield, "Egypt's Fellahin," *American Universities Field Staff Reports*, Northeast Africa Series, 21, no. 7 (1976), pp. 1-2.
[5] John Waterbury, "Manpower and Population Planning in the Arab Republic of Egypt," *American Universities Field Staff Reports*, Northeast Africa Series, 17, no. 2 (1972), p. 8.

TABLE 8-2. PER CAPITA LAND RESOURCES IN EGYPT, 1897-1966

Year	Population in millions	Cultivated land, in millions of acres	Per capita acreage
1897	9.7	5.1	0.53
1907	11.2	5.4	0.48
1917	12.8	5.3	0.41
1927	14.2	5.5	0.39
1937	15.9	5.3	0.33
1947	19.0	5.8	0.31
1960	26.0	5.9	0.23
1966	30.1	6.0	0.20

SOURCE: John Waterbury, "Manpower and Population Planning in the Arab Republic of Egypt," *American Universities Field Staff Reports,* Northeast Africa Series, 17, no. 2 (1972), p. 3.

Almost all members of Egypt's elite recognize that this is their country's most critical socioeconomic problem. Over the past two decades, family planning clinics and birth control educational programs have been instituted, but these massive efforts have not yet had a measurable effect. The simple availability of contraceptives is not sufficient since people must desire to use them, and that involves changes in attitudes. Increasing numbers of Egyptians are coming to believe that in order to be successful, family planning programs must be linked with social reform, especially with regard to the status and role of women. When the respect accorded a woman by her husband is no longer determined by the number of male sons she gives him, and when education and employment replace this source of respect, she and her husband will desire to limit the number of their offspring.[6]

Cities, Towns, and Villages

With a population of 6,133,000 (1976 estimate), Cairo is the largest city on the continent of Africa and in the Middle East. Cairo or another city in the general area has been the capital of the country throughout five thousand years of Egyptian history. In the capital today are concentrated all the major institutions of government, the headquarters of the major manufacturing and commercial enterprises, much industry, and the country's most important religious, educational, and cultural institutions. In modern times, middle- and upper-class Egyptians have wanted to live there because "everything" is to be found there. It has also been a lodestone attracting lower-class persons because of the availability of jobs and the glitter of modern urban life.

[6] See the excellent series on this subject: John Waterbury, "Manpower and Population Planning in the Arab Republic of Egypt," *American Universities Field Staff Reports,* Northeast Africa Series, 17, nos. 2-5 (1972), and "Egyptian Elite Perceptions of the Population Problems," 18, no. 3.

Alexandria (population 2,259,000; 1974 estimate) is a thin strip of land fronting on the Mediterranean, backing on a large brackish lake, and connected to the rest of the country by a narrow neck of land. It has always been physically and psychologically somewhat separate from the rest of the country, and is both Mediterranean and Egyptian. The three cities of the Suez Canal area (Port Said, Ismailiya, and Suez), all with population under half a million, are only a little more than a century old. Rather than looking to the Nile, they turn to the canal and the international traffic that plies it. They tend to be more oriented to the outside world than is the rest of the country.

The differences between Egypt's large cities and its towns and villages are sharp. In the former are wide avenues, paved streets, and multistory cement buildings; cars, buses, taxis, and animal-drawn carts are locked in huge traffic jams. In the villages are one or two paved streets, dirt alleys, houses made of sun-dried brick (with only an occasional cement abode), and animals, carts, bicycles, and a few motorized vehicles all in a chaotic mess. The cities have modern water, sewage, electrical, and telephone systems. In the villages people get their drinking water from the irrigation canals, where they also dispose of wastes; only a very few homes or buildings are likely to have electricity, and probably the only telephone is in the local police station. Large numbers of people are likely to be wearing Western dress in the cities: trousers and an open shirt for the men, sometimes a suit with a tie; dresses, pants, or latest Western style for the women. But in the villages, the galabia, a long robe that drops straight from the shoulders and extends to the ankles, is the norm for men; women wear voluminous, opaque figure-hiding black dresses and cloaks, but no veils. Though it is easy to overdraw the contrasts, it can be said that the city and the village are two different worlds.

For more than a century the cities have been subject to the influences of the West. Their architecture bears the imprint of European styles from the 1860s to the present. In the cities lived both the Europeans who were permanent residents of Egypt and the Westernized Egyptians. The ruling class of Egypt, both before and after the revolution of 1952, has come from the cities. Prior to 1952 the rulers were from the land-owning and commercial class; since 1952, they have been part of a new middle class composed of persons whose parents or grandparents most likely came from the villages, but who themselves have lived in the cities their entire lives, received a modern education, and been employed in the army, a commercial enterprise, or a government bureau.

The towns and villages have been the abode of the fellah (plural, fellaheen), the Egyptian peasant. The fellaheen have functioned in a world of tradition: local religious cults and sects, folk customs and mores, strong bonds of family and kin—a circle of consciousness that did not go much beyond their own villages. For them the West has been something alien, distant, unknown, and hostile. To integrate these two worlds has been one of the tasks of the leaders of the revolution of 1952.

Natural and Human Resources

Egypt's most valuable natural resources are the water of the Nile and the land adjacent to it. Exploiting them has made possible the creation of a large and intensive agricultural system which provides about one-third of the national product and employs 50 percent of the economically active population. In recent years oil production has increased rapidly, and in the very near future Egypt will be an oil-exporting state. Major fields exist in the Western Desert, the Gulf of Suez, the Red Sea shore area, and in the Sinai Peninsula. Iron ore mined near Aswan is sufficient to support the steel factory at Helwan, just south of Cairo.

Egypt's human resources are probably its major asset. With a large population it can maintain a large standing army. Today these soldiers are mostly literate and knowledgeable in technology, a result of the enormous increase in the number of schools since the revolution of 1952. The country's large pool of university graduates, trained in Egypt and abroad, is put to use the country's own multifarious economic enterprises, government bureaus, research institutes, and in the officer corps of the armed forces. Many of these highly skilled persons have secured employment in the schools, bureaucracies, and economic enterprises of other Arab countries such as Libya, Algeria, and the states of the Arabian Peninsula. Thus the sheer number of Egyptians, in addition to Egypt's large pool of educated persons, give it power regionally and internationally.

Ethnic and Religious Characteristics

The Egyptians are an unusually homogeneous people. The physical traits that originated with the earliest dwellers of the Nile valley still predominate and give them common physical features. The Arabic language is spoken by 98 percent of the people. This ethnic and linguistic solidarity, uncommon in many other countries of the Arab world, has been a major factor reinforcing Egyptian national identity.

About 90 percent of the population are Sunni Muslims. The Islamic faith was adopted by the Egyptians after the Arab conquest of the seventh century. Except for a period in the tenth to the twelfth centuries when it was ruled by a Shiite dynasty, Egypt has always been a Sunni country. Seven percent of the Egyptian people are Coptic Christians. Prior to the Arab conquest of the seventh century, Egypt was a part of Eastern Christendom and of the Byzantine Empire centered in Constantinople. The conversion of persons to Islam was slow and gradual, and not all Egyptians accepted the new faith. The Copts are those persons who remained true to Christianity. Because they have been a minority and have intermarried much less than the Muslims, they claim to be more purely Egyptian, and the direct descendants of the people who lived in the Nile Valley in Pharaonic times.

Economic History, 1805-1952

Today Egypt has one of the more developed economies in the region, and this can be attributed to the fact that economic modernization, while undertaken in fits and spurts and never totally comprehensive, was begun in the nineteenth century.

Prior to the nineteenth century, the Nile Valley was irrigated exclusively by the basin method. This involved building low dikes around fields; these dikes caught the water when the river flooded. Canals were also dug connecting the basins to the Nile, and they brought in more water from higher levels upstream. When the river receded from its flood stage, seeds were sown on the wet soil, and quickly grew in the warm sun. Since the Nile flooded only once a year, only one crop could be cultivated in a year's time.

Under Muhammad Ali, ruler of Egypt from 1805 to 1848, and his grandson Ismail, who ruled from 1863 to 1879, the change was made to perennial irrigation. Since the termperature in Egypt rarely drops below freezing, the advantage of this system is that two or three crops can be grown on the same land in a year's time.

In 1882 the British took control of the country, rebuilding and enormously expanding the already existing irrigation system. One of their greatest accomplishments was the construction of the first Aswan Dam, completed in 1902 and made taller in 1906 and 1934.

Though cotton was grown by the ancient Egyptians in small quantities, perennial irrigation made possible its large-scale cultivation, and it has long been Egypt's dominant export. Production of cotton on a commercial scale was begun in 1821. During the American Civil War, Britain could no longer get cotton from the southern United States, so it secured the product from other sources, including Egypt. Output there rose from 501,000 cantars[7] in 1860 to 2,140,000 in 1865, reaching 7,664,000 in 1913.[8]

Cotton brought in the overwhelming majority of the country's export revenue, 77 percent for 1878-82, and 89 percent for 1908-12.[9] It was the main beneficiary of the government's investment in public works and was the magnet drawing foreign capital into the country.

In the nineteenth century, great advances were also made in transportation and communication, primarily to support the production and export of cotton. Docks and port facilities were built, especially at Alexandria. Railways were constructed, telegraph lines laid out, and by 1914 Egypt had an internal system

[7] A measurement for cotton corresponding to about 95 pounds.
[8] Charles Issawi, *Egypt in Revolution: An Economic Analysis* (London: Oxford University Press, 1963), p. 27.
[9] Ibid., p. 28.

of transportation and communication comparable to that of many European countries.[10]

At the outbreak of World War I the economy had become export-oriented and integrated as a supplier of raw materials into the world-wide economic system. Financially it has become to all intents and purposes an extension of the London money market, with large movements of funds to and from London each year.

In the period 1920-1952, problems developed in the Egyptian economy, and its underlying weaknesses became evident. During World War I the rapid expansion of land under cultivation came to an end. In the 1920s and 1930s the price of cotton fell drastically on world markets, and since it produced a high percentage of the country's national income, the economy stagnated. World War II and its after-effects brought sharp rises and drops in prosperity.

The Egyptian economy immediately prior to the revolution of July 23, 1952, was a dependent colonial free enterprise system. Agriculture accounted for 90 percent of the GNP, and cotton was the biggest money earner, with almost all of it exported. The largest single economic enterprise was the Suez Canal Co., which was owned and run by British and French interests. Large banks, insurance and trading companies were invariably owned by foreigners, and much of Egypt's agricultural land was tied up in huge estates owned by several hundred families. The king was the largest landowner of all. The masses of fellaheen subsisted on around sixty dollars a year, while rich landowners, businessmen, and many foreigners spent frivolously and engaged in conspicuous consumption.

Economic History, 1952 to the Present

Between 1952 and 1970, Gamal Abdel Nasser more radically transformed the Egyptian economy than in any other period of the country's history, with the possible exception of the Muhammad Ali era. In 1956 Nasser nationalized foreign enterprises, the principal one being the Suez Canal Company, in order to end European control over the economy. Between 1961 and 1966, Nasser nationalized many large privately-owned Egyptian firms in order to end exploitation and bring about Arab socialism. The capital thereby redirected was used to finance development and social welfare.

Nasser's objective was to bring about economic development without undue social pain—he repeatedly said that one generation should not be sacrificed for the welfare of the next—and while investment was made in industry and in expanding the agriculturally productive land, the rudiments of social welfare

[10]Ibid., p. 26.

(free universal education, medical care, pensions, subsidies on basic goods) for all were instituted. Also, enormous numbers of new state-sector jobs were created many of which were superfluous.

The attempt to build a social welfare state before a modern diversified economy was created produced strains, and from 1966 on the economy declined. Money was lacking for plant maintenance and modernization; some new factories were not completed; others could not import the necessary raw materials in order to be able to manufacture their products; and often the final assemblers of a product could not get parts from suppliers. The result was that Egyptian industries manufactured products, when they did at all, that were high in price, low in quality, and could not be sold in hard-currency markets. The government could not curb imports (food grains, capital equipment, foreign expertise, arms), and the result was that the balance of payments deficit grew until it became very severe.

Anwar al-Sadat inherited these problems when he became president upon the death of Nasser in 1970. Since Egypt was selling about 60 percent of its cotton and buying all of its arms from the Communist bloc, one alternative was to rely totally on these nations. Sadat rejected this course of action because it would stifle Egypt's independence and because the technology and equipment which would come from the Eastern bloc would be inferior. Nasser had tried to combine development, military preparedness, and welfare socialism all at once. Sadat realized that this was impossible.

Beginning in 1971 he encouraged the discussion in private of an economic movement called the "Opening." During the spring and summer of 1973, the discussion moved into the public sphere, and the basic formula was declared to be:

$$\text{Arab capital} + \text{Western technology} + \text{Egyptian labor and markets}$$
$$- \text{ the population explosion}$$
$$= \text{economic growth.}[11]$$

By Arab capital was meant money from the oil-rich Arab states. Of course, capital and technology would not flow into Egypt as long as the east bank of the Suez Canal was occupied by the Israelis, the canal itself was nonfunctional, the canal cities of Port Said, Ismailiya, and Suez were uninhabited, and there was the ever-present possibility of the outbreak of war.

Thus the October 1973 Arab-Israeli war had both a political and an economic rationale. Politically its objective was to remove occupying armies from Egyptian soil. Economically it stimulated the oil-rich Arab states to support Egypt with some of their money, it shook up the West through the dramatic increases in the price of oil, and it lit a fire under the United States so that it started to work actively for an agreement between Egypt and Israel. It enabled

---

[11] See John Waterbury, "The Opening," *American Universities Field Staff Reports,* Northeast Africa Series, 20, no. 3 (1975), p. 1.

the Suez Canal to be reopened, modernized, and enlarged and allowed the inhabitants of the cities along it to return to their homes.

Similarly, economic factors were behind the signing of the peace treaty with Israel in 1979. Of the Arab states involved in the struggle with Israel, Egypt had borne the heaviest burden in men killed and disabled, in disruption of its economy, and in hardship on its people. The ever-present possibility of another war was discouraging American, European, and oil-rich Arab investors from putting their money into Egypt. The high levels of defense expenditures plus the heavy expenses for social welfare were taking too much out of the economy, and it was gradually sinking. The standard of living of the masses could not be raised above the bare subsistence level, and the desire of the very large middle class for more of the material goods common in Europe, America, and Japan could not be satisfied as long as Egypt was legally at war with Israel and a real war occurred about every decade.

Nevertheless, the economy of Egypt is still in a very precarious state. The infrastructure is decrepit, government red tape boggles the mind, the telephone system within the country and to points outside is antiquated, and the port facilities are inadequate. As an economic reprisal against Egypt for signing a peace treaty with Israel, Saudi Arabia has stopped its monetary support of Egypt. Furthermore, the public will not give up the welfare socialism that was begun in the Nasser era, and when one considers that the minimum wage in Egypt is £ E 12.00 (about $24.00) a month, one can understand their point of view. In January 1977 some of the subsidies on basic goods (food, cloth, clothing, fertilizers, pesticides) were removed, resulting in price increases and causing massive riots that forced the government to reinstate the subsidies.

At present foreign capital is not flowing into the country, the economy is not attaining the levels of sustained growth desired, population growth still moves inexorably upward, unrest and dissatisfaction are widespread among all social classes, and expensive armaments are still being bought. All the economic calculations and gambles of President Sadat have not yet paid off.

POLITICAL CULTURE

Since 1798 Egypt has undergone far more social and cultural change than most other Middle Eastern countries. The short but influential sojourn of Napoleon and his soldiers and savants (1798-1801), the reforms of the modernizing autocrat Muhammad Ali (1805-1848), the efforts at Westernization under Khedive Ismail (1863-1879), the influx of several hundred thousand Europeans throughout the nineteenth century, the building of the Suez Canal (completed in 1869), and the British occupation from 1882 to 1956, had long-lasting effects on Egyptian society and on the way of thinking of Egyptian leaders. In Chapters 4 and 5 we have already examined some of the resulting social and ideological changes.

Prior to the revolution of 1952, the intellectual and social change affected only the Egyptian upper-middle and upper classes. These persons, all city dwellers, were educated in the numerous Western schools in Egypt. In most of them the language of instruction was French or English, and the curriculum was the same as in European schools. The graduates possessed the values and skills necessary to function in the modern world, but their education encouraged them to scorn Egyptian and Arabic culture.

At the same time, the middle and lower classes were either unschooled or educated in traditional Islamic schools which taught only the Koran and subjects related to religion. They learned no foreign languages and came to know little about the West and the modern world. They felt that persons with a Western education were un-Egyptian, un-Arab, irreligious, and foreign. The result of this social and educational bifurcation was the creation in Egypt of two cultures and social mileus, each disturbing the other.

One of the primary objectives of the revolutionary regime has been to end this split. The land reforms and nationalizations of the 1950s were designed to destroy the economic and political power of the old upper class, the resident foreigners, and European interests in Egypt. The nationalization of the private foreign schools, expansion of the public educational system, enlargment of the state radio, encouragement of the manufacture and sale of transistor radios, installation of a state television network, establishment of Higher Institutes of Socialist Studies, and the institution of troupes of actors and lecturers to go from village to village, were all intended to be cultural unifiers spreading knowl-edge about science and technology, enhancing the sense of identity with the state, inculcating the spirit of Arab nationalism and of Arab socialism, reinforce-ing the values of modernized Islam, and raising consciousness of the world at large. The hope was that the divisions among social classes would be lessened and that all Egyptians would come to share a common culture that is modern, Arab, egalitarian, and based on the values of Islam.

The reality in Egypt today is that traditional and modern values coexist, sometimes contradicting and sometimes supporting each other. The strongest are those that have permeated the society for centuries, such as the attitudes of the peasant, the bonds of family and kin, Egyptian national consciousness, and Islam. The newer ones, such as Arab nationalism, democracy, and socialism, are not as strong, but are increasing in acceptance.

Peasant Values

About 60 percent of the Egyptian people are peasants, or fellaheen. They are the tillers of the soil, tied to a never-ending routine of labor, living in villages in abject poverty and privation. For centuries they have been exploited by all who ruled the country.

One of the most trenchant observers of the fellah has been Henry Habib Ayrout, S. J., who was born and raised in Cairo, but has been living in upper

Egypt for forty years, where he is the director of a system of free village schools. He says that the fellaheen are changeless. "They have changed their masters, their religion, their language, and their crops, but not their way of life.... Although they dwell at the crossroads of international traffic, in a country which has been the scene of some of history's most decisive events, they remain as tranquil and stable as the bottom of a deep sea whose surface waves are lashed with storms."[12]

Another observer of Egyptian rural life, James B. Mayfield, says that fellaheen feel that circumstances are uncontrollable, no matter how great their efforts, and that the physical and social environments are filled with dreadful and unknowable forces. Because of their insecurity, the fellaheen hesitate to use their own initiative, doubt their judgment, and tend to let others make decisions for them. In the villages in which they live, the social structure is hierarchical, with men above women, elders above youth, educated persons above the illiterate, and the wealthy above the poor. One's social position is usually the result of inheritance, not of achievement, and everyone accepts what God has ordained, whether it be one's position in society, an attack of insects on the crops, a drastic decline in the price of cotton, or death.[13]

However, the fellaheen have adapted themselves to some new circumstances. They changed their religion from that of ancient Egypt to that of Greece and Rome, then to Christianity, and finally to Islam. The fellaheen have lived under a succession of rulers. They have grown new crops such as cotton, sugar cane, and corn, and have changed from basin to perennial irrigation.

Today the revolutionary regime is making the most massive attempt in Egyptian history to change the way of life of the fellaheen. In addition to trying to raise their standard of living, it is attempting to inculcate in them new beliefs and values such as Arabism, modernized Islam, popular sovereignty, and socialism. In order to increase the probability that the peasants will accept these ideas, the government argues that they are natural twentieth-century developments growing out of the Egyptian, Arab, and Islamic heritage. Many books and tracts have been published declaring that the goals of Islam are the same as those of socialism. The government hopes that when the peasants feel that the new values are really a modern manifestation of those which they have been practicing and believing all along, they will come to accept them.

Family

Among the three countries studied thus far, Egypt occupies a middle position in respect to the political role of the family. In Lebanon family and religious community are all-important, in Israel family has a minor position, and

---

[12]Henry Habib Ayrout, *The Egyptian Peasant,* trans. John Alden Williams (Boston: Beacon Press, 1963), pp. 1-3, passim.

[13]James B. Mayfield, *Rural Politics in Nasser's Egypt: A Quest for Legitimacy* (Austin: University of Texas Press, 1971), pp. 58-66, passim.

in Egypt it plays a very important social and political role but is not the over-riding social and political institution.

Today in Egypt the family is the basic social unit for the majority of the population. The individual's duties and obligations to it take precedence over commitments to one's place of employment, a political party, or in many cases, to the state. The extended family is still the most common form of family organization, but the nuclear family is on the increase, especially in the cities and towns.[14]

Under the old regime, families that owned large amounts of land controlled the top levels of Egypt's politics. The king's family and about five hundred others continuously held positions in the cabinet. The men who have led the country since 1952 represent a different social class and family background. Most have come from peasant families that owned small pieces of land which the members themselves farmed. They have a modern education, usually through the university level, and while their fathers may have been farmers, they hold positions in the civil bureaucracy or the armed forces.

At the local level the family is still the critical institution. A young man, though married, stays with his father, helps him in the fields, and generally does not buy land of his own. Small shops, handicraft enterprises, restaurants, and cafés are all family businesses. Though there is an element of democracy in the selection of village mayors and village leaders, the richer and more prominent families are still deferred to, and tend to control the political process.

The new state economic enterprises have made family businesses a less important part of the economy, the state schools and the pervasive government-controlled media are decreasing the family's importance as a socializing institution, and the state social welfare agencies preempt it as the sole provider for the needs of its members.

However, in the new democratic socialist state the family is still important, and is the strongest and most viable institution for maintaining social order.[15]

Egyptian and Arab Consciousness

Five thousand years of recorded history, with far more than half having taken place prior to the arrival of the Arabs and of Islam in A.D. 640, give the Egyptians a historical awareness that is far greater than that of other Arab peoples. The monuments of ancient Egyptian civilization, such as the Pyramids and the Sphinx, are unmistakable reminders to all Egyptians that they have

---

[14]U.S. Goverment, *Area Handbook for the United Arab Republic (Egypt)* (Washington, D.C.: U.S. Government Printing Office, 1970), p. 103.

[15]Mayfield, *Politics,* pp. 84-6.

existed as a people and a nation for a very long time. Egyptians, however, speak Arabic, and the Arabic culture has been predominant in Egypt for at least a thousand years. Cairo has been a religious and cultural center for the Arab East equally as long. So the question has frequently arisen in both this century and the last: "Are the people who live in the Nile Valley Egyptians or Arabs?"

Prior to 1958 and the union of Egypt and Syria, both the Nasser regime and the governments of the monarchy emphasized the Egyptian identity, and in particular the emancipation of Egypt from British control. The other countries of the Middle East were also under European control and involved in their own anti-imperialist struggle, and for Egypt to become involved in them was difficult and a diversion of its energies.

The triumphs of Nasser in the 1950s in asserting Egyptian independence, however, made him a hero in the Arab world. In 1954 he negotiated an agreement with the British concerning the evacuation of British troops from Egypt. In 1955 he refused to succumb to American pressure to join in the Baghdad Pact; in the same year he concluded an arms deal with the Russians that broke the Western monopoly on supplying arms to his country. In 1956 he nationalized the Suez Canal Company in retaliation for the United States' denying Egypt aid in the building of the Aswan High Dam, and he emerged from the Anglo-French-Israeli invasion as a liberator and victor in the eyes of the Arab people. From then till his death in 1970, he played an activist role in the Arab world, attempting to unify it and to fight against its enemies: Israel, Britain, France, and the United States. He also attacked, in speeches and through the Egyptian radio and press, Arab leaders whom he regarded as "reactionaries," "feudalists," or "lackeys of the imperialists."

In the Nasser era, the government stressed the Arab character of the Egyptian people. From 1962 to 1978, the sole political party was called the Arab Socialist Union, and from 1958 to 1971 the state was known as the United Arab Republic, even though the actual union of Syria and Egypt lasted only from 1958 to 1961.

Under the leadership of Anwar al-Sadat, there has been a gradual shift away from the Arab emphasis of the Nasser era. In 1971 the name of the country was changed to the Arab Republic of Egypt, and in 1978 the Arab Socialist Union was abolished and replaced with the National Democratic Party. The program of the new party emphasizes the suffering, struggle, and victories of the Egyptian people and puts Egyptian national and social unity above Arab unity.[16] In 1979 President Sadat signed a peace treaty with Israel, a decision that brought upon him the strong condemnation of other Arab leaders and indicated that he put the national interests of Egypt, as he perceived them, above the interests or desires of the Arab world.

---

[16] *Al-Ahram al-Iqtisadi* (Cairo), no. 553, Sept. 1, 1978.

The Islamic Religion

In Egypt, religion is more than simply formal observance; it is a powerful social force affecting the ways in which people think about social issues, political matters, personal morality, and family relations.

Most persons are observant of religion in some way. The fellaheen feel that religious forces are ever present. They constantly invoke the name of God and frequently say verses from the Koran which they memorized in childhood. They go to a mosque frequently, sometimes to pray one of the five daily prayers, or just to sit and think, and occasionally to listen to a homily given by one of the mosque officials. The middle-class person who wears Western clothing and works behind a desk attends the Friday worship service regularly, observes Ramadan, and may go to the great expense of making the pilgrimage to Mecca. The President of the Republic and the other high officials regularly attend the Friday noon worship service and pray in village and town mosques when traveling around the country. When they get together with the representatives of other Arab states, a standard ritual is for all to attend a mosque service.

The 1971 constitution states that "Islam is the religion of the state" and that the "principles of the Islamic Sharia are a major source of legislation" (Article 2). Furthermore it says that the "family forms the basis of society," and "it is built on religion, morals and patriotism" (Article 9). After declaring that education is a right guaranteed by the state, the constitution affirms that "religious education is a primary subject in the general education curriculum" (Article 19).

During the late 1950s and early 1960s, the revolutionary government absorbed into the state educational system the schools that trained religious functionaries such as preachers, religion teachers, and specialists in Islamic law. The government furthermore reformed the curriculum of these schools so that the students now learn in them both the traditional religious and the modern secular subjects such as mathematics, science, and modern history. The overall result has been to inculcate in the students a modern, reformed Islam that is in harmony with and reinforces the values of socialism, Arabism, and democracy.

At the summit of the hierarchy of all the religious educational institutions is al-Azhar. The Egyptian government, through scholarships and travel allowances, encourages students to study there as they have done in the past. The foreign students at al-Azhar gain respect for the type of Islam practiced in Egypt and for the democratic socialist society that is being built there. When they return to their home countries, the Egyptian influence on them continues, and, through them affects others.

In respect to a formal religious policy, the contemporary Egyptian government has adopted a middle course between the ideology of the Muslim Brotherhood and Marxism. The former advocated structuring society exclusively along religious lines, and the latter actively combats religion, including its social role. Both movements have been very strong in Egypt and there continue to be adherents of both viewpoints, though they now express their ideas in indirect and diffuse ways. The government attacks both through the state-controlled radio, television, newspapers, and the whole publishing industry, and it clearly feels that neither is suitable for contemporary Egypt. Rather it is trying to create a society that in all respects is modern, yet in which religion is a vital force.

The government regularly uses Islam as a medium to legitimize its policies. For example, the sermons preached every Friday at noon in every mosque in the country—Muslims worship together on Fridays at noon as Christians do on Sunday mornings—are almost all the same, because the Ministry of Religious Affairs directs what their subject and general line of argument shall be. Socialism, the struggle against Western imperialism, the malevolent influence of atheistic communism, the conflict with Israel, the new social order in Egypt, are topics that are touched upon along with more typical religious subjects. The rector of al-Azhar, revered as a religious authority and leader, occasionally justifies certain government programs by issuing a statement saying that they are in harmony with the Koran and other Islamic scriptures. For example, birth control has been sanctioned by him in this manner.

In a country where Islamic values and beliefs influence the attitudes of every one, the union of Islam with the political ideology of the state gives a deeper justification and emotional impetus to the new social, political, and economic order. It also serves to distinguish and differentiate Egyptians from Americans and Russians alike, for in the United States and the Soviet Union, a high degree of secularization has taken place, and the state either openly attacks religion or is neutral to it. Egyptians feel that neither system is suitable for them, and that the union of religion and state which they have produces a better social order and a higher quality of life.

Socialism and Democracy

In Chapter 5 the fundamentals of Arab socialism were reviewed extensively. Suffice it to say here that it was a system of beliefs that was the product of the thoughts and actions of Gamal Abdel Nasser; its fundamentals were stated in his speeches and proclamations; it developed in an ad hoc fashion in the 1950s and early 1960s; and it eschews the political ideologies of the communist East and of the liberal-democratic West. Stress was placed on the uniqueness of Arab socialism and on the fact that it was Egyptian, Arab, and Islamic in origin.

Since the abolition of the Arab Socialist Union in 1978 and its replacement with the National Democratic Party, the official ideology of the state has been democratic socialism, which, according to Sadat, rests on four principles: (1) religious and spiritual values, (2) balance between the welfare of the individual and that of society, (3) national unity and social peace, and (4) realization of Arab unity, with due regard for the differences in the Arab world.[17]

Democracy in Egypt is said by the government to be neither the kind that exists in the communist states, nor that of the Western liberal-democratic states, nor the pseudodemocracy that Egypt had under the monarchy. What the government means by democracy is basically mass participation in the political process under the aegis of the sole political party. The concept of democracy as envisioned by the Egyptian government can perhaps best be summarized by a statement that Nasser often made and that is also in the Charter of National Action: "Democracy is political liberty, socialism is social liberty; the two cannot be separated."

Pamphlets and booklets on socialism and democracy abound in Egypt. Lecturers travel to every village, town, and city in the country to speak on these subjects. Students in the public schools receive extensive indoctrination in them. But the question remains: "To what extent are socialism and democracy truly operating principles for all Egyptian citizens, and to what degree have they superseded older values and principles?" This is a vital question and, unfortunately, one that cannot be adequately answered. What can be said is that socialism represents a certain thrust and direction in Egyptian society. It serves to identify Egypt with the nonaligned Afro-Asian world. It establishes that Egypt is not a part of either of the superpower blocs. It indicates that the Egyptian state is committed to state direction of economic benefits to all elements of the society. It also shows that a national effort is needed to raise the standard of living of the Egyptians, and that this must be brought about by unified national action, hard work, and sacrifice.

POLITICAL GROUPS

With a high degree of ethnic and religious homogeneity and a long and well-developed sense of national identity, Egypt is one Middle Eastern state that is not fraught with divisions along ethnic or religious lines. The one significant minority, the Copts, is well integrated into the society and has not, in the history of Muslim Egypt, engaged in a separatist revolt. During the nineteenth and the first half of the twentieth century, numerous Europeans moved into Egypt, but since the 1952 revolution they have left in large numbers, and now are so small in number as to have no social, economic, or political power.

Since 1952, interest groups, philanthropic societies, autonomous religious organizations, and labor unions have been coopted by the state. Mosques and the clergy who conduct religious activities in these groups are under its close supervision. Christian churches and their clergy are likewise regulated and

[17]Ibid.

watched. Religious societies that give charity to the poor or engage in educational activities must be licensed by the government. Private schools have lost their autonomy. There is only one labor union in the country, and it was founded and is controlled by the government. All the major economic enterprises have been nationalized, so there are no corporate associations or chambers of commerce with significant power.

This is the culumination of a long social process, as explained in Chapter 4, that began with Muhammad Ali and culminated under Gamal Abdel Nasser when Egypt became a bureaucratic polity. The main characteristic of this kind of state is that the bureaucracy has expanded to such a degree that it controls all the key institutions of society, and technocrats manage all significant economic and political activity. There is not very much that is outside the scope of the government and its administration.

When it comes then to analyzing the groups in Egypt today that are autonomous and do play a role in politics, one concludes that there are only three: the army, the civil bureaucracy, and anomic groups (demonstrations, strikes, riots, and the like).

The Army: A Historical Sketch

From 525 B.C. to A.D. 1952, Egypt was dominated by a succession of foreign conquerors: Persians, Greeks, Romans, Arabs, Turks, the French, and the British. Each controlled the Egyptian army by staffing the officer corps with its nationals while filling the ranks of the enlisted men with fellaheen. The supreme commander was always someone appointed by the foreign ruler. The army was then used in wars in which the foreign power became involved, but in which the Egyptian interests were not necessarily served. With such a history, the army came to be viewed by the Egyptian people for the most part as an instrument of oppression and of foreign domination.

The most recent of these foreign conquerors were the British. In 1882 they occupied the country and soon thereafter disbanded the old Egyptian army, reconstituted a new one, staffed the upper ranks with British officers and filled the lower echelons of the officer corps and the enlisted ranks with Egyptians. However, while some of these "Egyptians" had been living in Egypt for some time, they were of Turkish ancestry, and only the lowest ranks were filled with true Egyptians. From 1882 until the British departure in 1956, the size and social composition of the army was a continuing source of friction between British officials and Egyptian leaders.

In 1936 an event took place which was then of little significance but was later shown to be of great historical importance: the rules of admission to the Egyptian Military Academy in Cairo were changed so that they did not exclude all but the upper class. This made possible the inclusion of sons of middle-class families in the classes of 1938, 1939, and 1940, and they formed the cadre of officers called the Free Officers, which in 1952 carried out the revolution.

These officers' dissatisfaction had begun in 1948, when Egyptian troops along with the armed forces of other Arab states were unable to defeat the Israelis and destroy the newly born state of Israel. The Egyptian officers at the front attributed this failure not to their men's lack of bravery or to their own failure as military leaders, but to ineptitude, corruption, and inadequate support from King Farouk and his government in Cairo. Matters came to a head in 1952, when the Free Officers Group challenged the king's appointment as chief of staff of an officer in whom they had no confidence, and the appointment of the King's brother-in-law, a man with no military experience, as minister of war. They launched a rebellion, and by the morning of July 23, most important military bases, airports, communications centers, and radio transmitters were in their hands. The old regime collapsed, unable to muster a glimmer of popular support.

The revolution was an event of sociological as well as political significance, for it brought to the pinnacle of power a new type of ruling elite. Whereas formerly the country had been controlled by the king, a class of very wealthy Egyptians, and the British, now it was ruled by twelve young men who came from families of humble origins. Their fathers and grandfathers had been peasant farmers, small landowners, or minor government employees. For example, Nasser's father was born into a peasant family in Upper Egypt, but spent most of his life in Alexandria and Cairo as an assistant postmaster.

Prior to 1952 most Egyptians had a low opinion of the armed forces, and to be an officer did not bring much social status or political power. After the revolution, favoritism and nepotism were eliminated, and the selection, training, and promotion of officers were systematized so that merit became the primary criterion of advancement. Young men from middle-class families now engaged in an intense competition to get into the armed forces, and to be an officer meant gaining recognition in the new society.

In addition, prior to 1952 the armed forces were not a source of national pride. They were subservient to the overall strategy of the British, and won no battles that the government and the Egyptian people could glorify. All this changed with what the Egyptians call the "Tripartite Aggression," the attack by the British, French, and Israelis against the Suez Canal Zone in 1956. The hostilities lasted only about a week, the Egyptian army did not engage in much combat, and owing to American and Soviet pressure, the invading armies withdrew. The conflict was proclaimed by the government as a victory for the Egyptian people and their army. For the first time in the modern history of the Middle East, the will of the British and of the French had been thwarted, and Nasser became an instant hero throughout the Arab world.

Between 1962 and 1967 the army became involved in an attempt to shore up the Republican forces in Yemen. This war was protracted and inconclusive and did not win much credit for either the Egyptian army or its government. A greater debacle was the June war of 1967. After Nasser closed the Straits of

Tiran to Israeli shipping and massed troops in the Sinai Peninsula, the Israelis launched a surprise attack which routed the Egyptian forces in the Sinai and enabled Israel to occupy the entire peninsula up to the Suez Canal. The minister of war and some high-ranking officers were tried and found guilty of malfeasance and negligence, and the commander-in-chief committed suicide. Generally the civilian leaders blamed the disaster on incompetence in the officer ranks, and thereby absolved themselves of any responsibility for the defeat.

This humiliation for the army and the nation was overcome by "The Crossing." On October 6, 1973, the Egyptian army launched a surprise attack across the Suez Canal and reconquered the east bank. The hostilities lasted three weeks, longer than any other Arab-Israeli war; some of the tank battles were as large and as ferocious as those of World War II, and the losses in personnel and equipment on both sides were enormous. The war ended as a stand-off, since the Israelis had been able to penetrate through Egyptian lines and almost encircle one Egyptian army. Yet it clearly demonstrated to the world that Egyptians could now plan and launch a large and coordinated attack using advanced and highly technological weapons. Sadat and the army became heroes glorified in song and popular literature, and an immeasurable boost was given to Egyptian honor and self-respect.

The Army: Its Social and Political Role

Since 1952 Egypt has been governed by a regime of military origins. The coup that overthrew the monarchy was led by eleven army officers who in the ensuing years donned civilian dress and became presidents, vice presidents, cabinet ministers, and speakers in the parliament of the new regime. Other officers in the armed forces assumed positions as ambassadors, provincial governors, under-secretaries, and directors of state corporations. The military budget grew, and in spite of national economic adversity was not reduced. Characteristics often associated with the military, such as discipline, hierarchy, and patriotism, came to be the traits of the new society and were manifested in the one-party political system and in the large and powerful civil bureaucracy.

Former army officers are found throughout the administration of the state and of the economy. Ex-officers in the upper reaches of the civil bureaucracy—they do not accept lower-level jobs—number well into the hundreds, and one scholar asserts that the figure is as high as 1,500. Nasser and Sadat have been the primary examples of soldiers who donned mufti and then took government jobs. Military officers are pampered in terms of pay, pensions, and perquisites in comparison with the civilian bureaucrats, and because of this and their sense of national mission, they have something of an elite status. The more their numbers have grown in the civilian administration, the more military assumptions about national priorities have been taken for granted, and the harder it has been for the regime to legitimize itself as a duly-constituted civil authority based on a popularly-mandated constitution and supported by a mass political party.

Most observers of Egyptian politics in the late 1970s agree that the army is the only potential adversary to the Nasser-Sadat regime, which has now been in power for more than twenty-five years. Intrigues have been plotted against both rulers, but so far all have been discovered and suppressed. Nasser and Sadat were both conspirators, and they know the tricks of the trade and have used them against their enemies.

The Civil Bureaucracy

Since the revolution of 1952, Egypt has been run by a small elite of army officers, in or out of uniform. Under them is an elite of upper-grade civil servants. Working for both has been a massive bureaucracy with about one million members. While avowedly created for the purposes of external and internal security, economic development, and the dispensing of social services, this bureaucracy has also been used in multifarious ways to maintain social stability and to siphon off political unrest. The Egyptian government is an archetype of a bureaucratic polity.

The military men who took control of the country in 1952 have from the beginning of their rule been scornful of politicians, and have repeatedly dwelt upon the vices (cronyism, nepotism, graft, separation from the people) of the political leaders of the previous regime. One of their early acts was to outlaw political parties and popular organizations such as the Muslim Brotherhood and the Communist Party, and to arrest or exile their leaders. Thus they effectively eliminated all those who, in one way or another, might be able to generate a mass following in opposition to themselves.

Rather than working with politicians, the army elite has preferred to rule through administrators. Just below it in the pyramid of power have been numerous civilian ministers, advisors, diplomats, and technocrats chosen from a variety of sources. Some were senior public servants before 1952; others were recruited from university faculties. Most have been selected for their technical expertise and administrative skill, especially in the fields of finance, economic planning, and foreign affairs. They have had considerable social status and public respect, but no political base. When they did not perform according to the president's expectation, they have been dismissed with no public outcry, to be replaced with others of the same type.

Through the nationalization of economic enterprises and the establishment of numerous new state social services, the army elite has greatly expanded the administrative sector, and the persons who hold jobs in it owe their careers to the revolution and its programs. Along with the military, they are a powerful deterrent to any changes in the policies of the state.

A government decree issued in 1962 guarantees employment to all university graduates, whether qualified or needed,[18] and in a state where almost every enterprise above the small shop is nationalized, this means government employment. The bureaucracy is already overstaffed, and is encountering increasing difficulty in absorbing the aspirants to white-collar jobs. Estimates indicate that between 1975 and 1981, the government will have vacancies for under 120,000 holders of new degrees in nontechnical fields; yet by law, it will be required to absorb more than 700,000 graduates in these fields.[19]

Another problem is the oversupply of persons with the kinds of degrees (liberal arts, commerce, law) that lead to white-collar jobs, and the undersupply of those with the technical and mechanical training that leads to blue-collar jobs. Repeated government efforts to encourage the latter have been blocked by social mores that assign low status to those who work with their hands.

The current regime is dependent upon the support of middle-class persons who are widely employed in the state administration and who owe their improved life style to the revolution. These citizens live in close psychological proximity to the way of life they left behind, and are very much aware of how precarious is their new, improved status. To protect this base of support, the regime keeps expanding educational facilities which turn out graduates with a useless theoretical education, employs them even when they are not needed, and continues to provide the minimal social services to which people in the middle-class have become accustomed. If the government did not do this, it could expect the ennui, alienation, and dissatisfaction already present among government workers to increase, and riots and demonstrations, especially among students, to become more numerous.

Egyptian novelists and playwrights have for a long time attacked the inefficiency and self-serving quality of the bureaucracy. Cartoonists love to lampoon the fat bureaucrat, coffee cup in one hand, newspaper in the other, and piles of paper on his desk, who continually frustrates the simple requests of the common citizen. A contemporary playwright, Ali Salem, is just one of a long line of literary men who have dealt with this theme. He himself was a bureaucrat in the Ministry of Health, and his experiences there led him to conclude that he had but two options: suicide or writing plays. In one first performed in Cairo in 1968, *The Well of Wheat,* he develops the theme that the best-intentioned leaders and the most compassionate and noble programs will be distorted and sabotaged by the self-serving nature of the bureaucracy. For the person employed in that bureaucracy, hard work, skill, and noble vision count for nothing, while careerism, opportunism, and adeptness in bureaucratic intrigue lead to advancement. The people are always the ultimate victims.[20]

---

[18]*Area Handbook for Egypt,* p. 174.

[19]Ibid., p. 92.

[20]For a translation of this play, see *American Universities Field Staff Reports,* Northeast Africa Series, 19, no. 2 (1974).

Bureaucracies can produce wealth, but they can also consume it, and in Egypt today bureaucratic waste is a national economic drain. As a result of the present regime's social composition and weak political organization, it has great difficulty attacking it.

Demonstrations and Riots

Living in densely populated cities and in a countryside swarming with people, Egyptians are never far from one another. Crowds are the norm, and it does not take much provocation or stimulus to turn a peaceful one into a chanting demonstration or an angry mob. On numerous occasions, spontaneous mass protests and riots have broken out which either led to significant change in government policy or the downfall of a regime. On rare occasions, the regime in power and its policies have been given support. The occurrences of these demonstrations have been sufficiently frequent to have become an established, but not legitimate, part of the political process.

The prevalence of demonstrations and riots is partially a function of Egyptians living in a bureaucratic polity in which important policies are made by experts in the bureaucracy rather than by the people or their representatives. Those in government are always well educated, frequently with M.A. and Ph.D. degrees, while the masses for whom the decisions are being made are lower class and uneducated. A communications gap exists between the two, and in Egypt one way by which this is bridged is through demonstrations and riots.

These have frequently been instigated by workers or students. At one of Egypt's industrial centers, such as Helwan or al-Mahallah al-Kubra, a new regulation or an increase in prices can be the spark that sets off a demonstration. At the major universities such as Cairo, Ayn Shams, and Alexandria, all of which have too many students, inadequate buildings, and too few professors, and where politics is talked about all the time, a few students can start protest marches which move off the campus and into the city streets. Professionals and intellectuals such as professors, writers, engineers, and administrators often support both the workers and the students by circulating and signing petitions. Sometimes the urban poor will be drawn into the demonstration, and frequently those of the small communities will be excited to anger along with city dwellers. The close proximity of village to village means that word can spread fast, even without radio and television coverage.

In this century there have been five instances of demonstrations and riots that have been not simply local, and which have had some immediate or long-range political effect. They are described in Table 8-3.

The British in 1919 and Nasser in 1968 got the political message from the riots and responded with sufficient quickness and thoroughness to suppress them and then institute reforms which were sufficient to alleviate the tension in the country. A demand of the rioters in 1952 was the expulsion of the British from the country, which the Farouk government could not achieve—a major

TABLE 8-3. DEMONSTRATIONS AND RIOTS IN EGYPT

Date	Description of demonstration	Targets of demonstrators	Cause	Political Effect
March 1919	Riots and demonstrations by peasants and city dwellers all over Egypt.	Europeans, European property, railroad stations, telegraph lines.	Arrest and exile by the British of Saad Zaghlul, a popular nationalist leader.	The British released Zaghlul from prison and began to negotiate with him. Partial independence was achieved for Egypt.
Jan. 1952	Guerrila activity in the Canal Zone against the British. Riots, burning, and looting in Cairo.	European institutions, such as the Shepeard's Hotel, restaurants frequented by Europeans, and movie theaters.	British troops attacking Egyptian police in a government compound in Ismailiya.	Weakening and discrediting of the King and his government. On Feb. 10, the free officers decided to overthrow the government, which they finally did on July 23.
June 1967	Demonstrations calling upon Nasser to return to office.	None.	Nasser's resignation after the Arab defeat in the June war.	Nasser withdraws his resignation on June 10.
Feb. and Nov. 1968	Student and worker demonstrations in Cairo, Alexandria, Ayn Shams, and Mansura.	None.	A general malaise after the defeat in the June war: dissatisfaction with the country's leaders except for Nasser, unhappiness about nonfunctioning political institutions, a desire to implement the ideals of Nasser and to renew the struggle against Israel.	Nasser accepts some demands and rejects others. He institutes "a program for change" called the "30 March Program."
Jan. 1977	Riots in Alexandria and Cairo.	Posters of Sadat, large American and European cars, the American University, nightclubs frequented by rich Arabs.	Government announcement of the end of price subsidies on staple foods and other basic consumer goods resulting in higher prices.	Revocation of the government decree.

factor in its downfall. The rioters of January 1977 demanded an end to the straitened economic circumstances in which the lower and the lower-middle classes were being forced to live; as of the middle 1979 it is not yet known whether Sadat has responded with sufficient vigor to these demands.

POLITICAL STRUCTURES

Constitutions of Revolutionary Egypt

To legitimize itself and sustain itself in power, the regime that has ruled Egypt since 1952 has relied more on military force, popular enthusiasm, and a revolutionary spirit than on constitutions and laws. It has ruled under six constitutions (see Table 8-4), all of which—except for that of 1923, which it inherited from the previous regime, and the provisional constitution of 1953, which was a broad statement of guiding principles—have had the common characteristics of providing for a powerful president, a cabinet subordinate to him, and a unicameral legislature with very limited powers. The other major political institution has been a mass-mobilization single party controlled by the president. The most recent constitution (1971) officially sanctions this party, but in the

TABLE 8-4. CONSTITUTIONS OF TWENTIETH-CENTURY EGYPT

Date promulgated	Name
April 19, 1923	Royal Order No. 42, of 1923, establishing a constitutional regime for Egypt
Jan. 16, 1953	Proclamation establishing a three-year transitional government
Feb. 10, 1953	Constitutional proclamation establishing government during the three-year transitional period
July 18, 1953	Constitutional proclamation by the Revolution Command Council establishing a republic in Egypt
Jan. 16, 1956	Constitution of the Republic of Egypt
March 5, 1958	Provisional constitution of the United Arab Republic
March 25, 1964	Constitution of the United Arab Republic
Sept. 11, 1971	Constitution of the Arab Republic of Egypt

SOURCES: Muhammad Khalil, *The Arab States and the Arab League: A Documentary Record* (Beirut: Khayat's, 1962); and Abid al-Marayati, *Middle Eastern Constitutions and Electoral Laws.* Copyright © 1968 by Frederick A. Praeger, Inc. Reprinted and adapted by permission of Holt, Rhinehart, and Winston.

previous constitutional eras, the party was extraconstitutional. Thus the multiplicity of constitutions should not be allowed to hide the fact that there has been permanence in the ruling elite and a high degree of continuity in the methods of governance.

In the years just after the revolution of 1952, the officers did not know what form of government to establish and they proceeded to make critical decisions in response to events. They introduced institutions almost in an experimental fashion, first testing them, then changing them, and then trying them out again in a slightly altered form. Always the initiative was from the top, and the final sanction was from there also, even though there was a formal process of popular discussion, review, and approval.

The constitution of 1923, providing for a monarchy with extensive powers, a cabinet, and a parliament, remained in effect until December 10, 1952, when the Revolutionary Command Council (RCC) abrogated it. On January 16, 1953, the RCC abolished all political parties and announced that the following three years were to be a period of political transition during which the Council would rule. On February 10, 1953, the Council decreed a provisional constitution setting out the general principles to guide it during the transition. This was endorsed by a popular referendum on June 23. On June 18, 1953, Egypt was proclaimed a republic, and thus the legal fiction that it was still a monarchy ended. On January 16, 1956, the three-year transition period came to an end, and on that same day a new constitution, including a representative national assembly, was promulgated. One week later it was accepted in a popular referendum.

In February and March 1958, however, upon the initiative of the Syrian leaders, Nasser agreed to join his country with Syria in a new, unified state. On March 5 the provisional constitution of the United Arab Republic was promulgated and ratified in a popular referendum in both countries. On September 28, 1961, the Northern Region (Syria) broke away and declared its independence. Many of the institutions intended for this unified state were never set up, and Nasser and his advisors ruled for the most part through decree. After the break this constitution remained in effect for Egypt only. In March 1964 Nasser published the draft of a document, "The Constitution of the United Arab Republic." Despite its name, it pertained to Egypt only and was valid until September 11, 1971, when the people, in a national referendum, approved a new constitution, that of the Arab Republic of Egypt, which is still in effect.

The Constitution of 1971[21]

The Constitution of 1971 proclaims that Egypt is a "democratic socialist state based on an alliance of the People's working forces . . . namely, peasants, workers, soldiers, the intelligentsia and national capital." It says that the Egyp-

[21] For the complete text, see *The Middle East Journal,* 26 (Winter 1972), 55-68.

tian people are "part of the Arab nation seeking to realize total unity," and that "Islam is the religion of the state." The economic basis of the state is declared to be the "socialist system which is based on adequacy and justice in a manner preventing exploitation and aiming at removing class distinction." "The Arab Socialist Union is the political organization which . . . represents the alliance of the people's working forces," and it "is the tool of this alliance in entrenching the values of democracy and socialism, following up national action in its various domains, and propelling this national action toward its chartered objectives."

The President

The most important office in Egypt is that of the President of the Republic. This office has extensive powers and dominates the other branches of the government. Its holder is head of state, head of government, and supreme commander of the armed forces. The president is nominated by the People's Assembly and is approved by an absolute majority of the people in a referendum; should a nominee fail to achieve an absolute majority, then the Assembly nominates another candidate. The president serves for a six-year term. He "lays down, in collaboration with the cabinet, the general policy of the state and supervises its execution. . . ." He may appoint one or more vice presidents, has the authority to determine their powers, and can dismiss them. He appoints and dismisses the prime minister, deputy prime ministers, and deputy ministers. He has the right to propose, veto, and promulgate legislation. When the Assembly is not in session, he may issue decrees that have the force of law and are subject to ratification by the Assembly when it next meets. Under unusual circumstances and by investiture by the Assembly, he may issue decree laws that are not subject to Assembly ratification. This was the case from the time of the October War in 1973 until late in 1975. The president may declare war, subject to Assembly approval or a state of emergency, and may call for national referenda on important matters.

The Cabinet

The cabinet, called officially in the constitution "the government," is the "higher executive and administrative body of the state." It participates with the president in preparing the state's general policy and overseeing its implementation. Among its main tasks are supervising and controlling the ministries and the other official agencies, drafting legislative and decree proposals, implementing the economic development program, and preparing the national budget.

The People's Assembly

The unicameral People's Assembly is the highest legislative body in the country. It consists of 350 popularly elected members and 10 additional ones who may be, and so far have been, appointed by the president. The constitution prescribes that half of the members must be workers or peasants, and defines in very specific terms who so qualifies. This is to insure that the Assembly represents all of the Egyptian people and not just a middle- or upper-class elite, as in the past. The Assembly approves the state's general policy, plan for social and economic development, and budget. It passes laws and resolutions and has the right to question all ministers, censure the prime minister, and withdraw confidence from the other ones. It has an extensive committee system through which all legislation passes.

The Party System

Since the revolution of 1952, Egypt has functioned under several different party systems, all of which have been established by the national leader, Nasser or Sadat, in an attempt to avoid the cliquishness and bickering of parties in prerevolutionary Egypt and the repressiveness of totalitarian single parties. They sought to establish an institution that could mobilize the nation behind new programs and policies, be a forum in which political issues are debated, and be a channel of communication upwards from the people to the leaders. The fact that Nasser and Sadat each tried two or three different systems indicates the difficulty they have had in trying to put these different objectives into effect.

On January 16, 1953, the Revolutionary Command Council (RCC) banned all existing political parties. It felt that their leaders were self-serving, that they lacked contact with the peasantry and working class, that they were prone to feuding with each other, and that they were not advancing the country's interests. In their place, on January 23, 1953, the RCC created the National Liberation Rally, a mass organization to "organize the people . . . foster their unity and coordinate the efforts of the workers."[22] It was headed by Nasser, and its slogan was "unity, discipline, and work." Not much of a success, it was allowed to fade away by 1956.

In May 1957 a new party, the National Union, was formally established. In 1958, after the unification of Syria and Egypt, elections for its basic organizational units were held in both regions, and Nasser expended considerable effort to try to make the party operational. However, the secession of Syria from the United Arab Republic in September 1961 was a death blow to his second attempt at establishing a mass-based political organization, and in November 1961, he formally dissolved it. Nasser said that it failed because "Reaction managed to infiltrate into [it] and to paralyze its revolutionary potentialities and turn it into a mere organizational facade unstirred by the forces of the masses and their genuine demands."[23]

---

[22] From a speech by Gamal Abdel Nasser, quoted in Don Peretz, "Democracy and the Revolution in Egypt," *Middle East Journal,* 13 (Winter 1959), 30.

[23] Quoted in Peter Mansfield, *Nasser's Egypt* (Baltimore: Penguin Books, 1965), p. 197.

The quandary that Nasser confronted in these two attempts was that he wanted the party to be both an instrument of mass mobilization and of control. Although he desired to organize the masses, he also wished to exclude from the ranks of his political organization Muslim Brothers and Communists, many of whom would have been good organizers.

In October 1962 a new party of mass mobilization and national unity was established, the Arab Socialist Union (ASU). According to the implementing statute of December 7, 1962, its objectives were to attain sound democracy and to realize the socialist revolution of the working people.[24] In practice, an American scholar found its primary function to be to mobilize the people behind the socialist ideology and revolutionary programs of the leaders of the state. Also, it served as a channel of communication upward to the leaders and downward to the masses, recruiting persons into the leadership structure, supervising and evaluating the performance of the administration at all levels, and acting as a sounding board for ideological positions and policies from the country's leaders.[25]

Criticism of the ASU centered on its close link with the state and its centralized bureaucratic character. Nasser created it and watched its development and operation very closely. In 1971 Sadat faced a threat from within ASU but moved quickly and arrested the leaders; then he closely controlled the party. It had had only two chairmen, Nasser and Sadat, and the secretary-general was always a close associate of one of these men. The central committee and the higher executive committee included many cabinet ministers, governors, and other high state officials. Its structure followed the administrative divisions of state, and most of the full-time party leaders were former government or professional people.

The ASU was a mass organization, the purpose of which was to encompass a wide spectrum of the Egyptian people and move them toward common goals. Although Muslim Brothers and Communists were excluded, their followers who reformed themselves and expressed allegiance to the Nasser-Sadat revolution could join. ASU incorporated people of different social classes. Sadat allowed three different political-ideological sections—Right, Center, and Left—to form within it, and they discussed and argued with considerable freedom and vehemence about programs and policies for the nation.

However, Sadat felt that the Arab Socialist Union was not serving national needs, so in 1978 he asked the People's Assembly to abolish it, and he formed a new political organization, the National Democratic Party. It has not been in existence long enough to analyze its operation, but if past practice prevails, it

[24] *Area Handbook for Egypt,* p. 190.
[25] Mayfield, *Politics,* p. 139.

will be firmly led by the President of the Republic and will be closely linked wth the bureaucracy.

POLITICAL LEADERSHIP

Rise of the New Middle Class

Prior to 1952 most of the political elite of Egypt (leaders of the major parties, cabinet ministers, and high-level civil servants) came from among the class of landowners of large estates which were farmed by peasants and administered by bailiffs. These landowners numbered about 11,000 and possessed the great bulk of the country's agricultural land. In contast to them were about 70 percent of all the property-holders in the country who owned an acre or less, but who had only about one-eighth of the cultivated land.[26]

The eleven men who led the coup in 1952 ranged in age from 29 to 34 and were either majors or lieutenant colonels. All were graduates of the classes of 1938, 1939, and 1940 of the Egyptian Military Academy in Cairo. Some owned land, but not large amounts, and all owed their modest position in society to their military-scientific education and position in the army officer corps. They clearly represented the "new middle class."

This is a new class in Middle Eastern society that has only arisen in recent times with the building up of modern armies and with the creation of new state economic enterprises, ministries, and governmental agencies to promote economic development. It is composed of persons employed in the middle and upper levels of these organizations. They have a modern education (usually in the fields of science, engineering, business administration, or economics), are salaried, and work in an office building five days a week. Since military might and economic expansion are objectives of practically all the regimes in the region, the number of persons in this class is rapidly expanding.

Because of this new character to the ruling elite, Egypt is a much changed country. The old elite was tied in with the imperialist economic structure through its ownership of land, on which cotton was grown and then sold to textile mills in England. Many of its members had studied law or the humanities in France or England, and they tended to favor a liberal-democratic form of government. Most were wealthy and had no real contact with the daily concerns of the Egyptian peasantry.

The new elite, having no ties to the imperialist economic structure, shattered that structure through its policies of nationalization. Its members are technocrats and have created a Third World form of the modern technocratic

[26]*Area Handbook for Egypt,* pp. 277-78.

state with a very powerful chief executive, a weak legislature, and a large and powerful bureaucracy. The new elite speaks to the masses, striving to better their existence and to involve them in the political process.

Alliance of Civilian and Military Technocrats

Nasser respected the patriotism, technical knowledge, and administrative skills of military officers. In the 1950s and 1960s, he appointed numerous army officers to cabinet positions and agency heads, once they had resigned their military commission. This resulted in a meshing at the top of the Egyptian bureaucracy of officers in mufti and civilian technocrats.

R. Hrair Dekmejian has studied the background of the 131 persons who held cabinet positions between September 1952 and September 1962 and has discovered that 33.6 percent were military officers and 66.4 percent were civilians. Although he studied only the members of the cabinet, the military also occupied key positions in the several layers of government just below the cabinet. Many were officer-technocrats, persons who, in addition to their training in military science, had received degrees in nonmilitary fields such as engineering, physics, political science, law, history, and journalism.[27]

It is only natural that Nasser, himself an army officer, should have turned to fellow officers to lead the country. He inserted in the top ranks of the government those who he felt had the requisite skills, commitment, and energy to carry out the new revolutionary policies he had instituted. These people worked with civilian technocrats, who often had training similar to theirs and were committed to economic development and military strength, but the officers were the dominant force in this alliance, since behind them was the might of the army.

Nasser: The Charismatic Leader

From the revolution of July 1952 until his death on September 28, 1970, Gamal Abdel Nasser was the dominant force in Egyptian politics, standing above the cabinet, the bureaucracy, and the army, controlling and guiding them, and locked into a mystical relation with the Egyptian masses. He embodied their will and was their voice. When he spoke, it was not Nasser speaking, but the Egyptian people.

He was undoubtedly a charismatic leader. The most widely used definition of charisma is that by Max Weber: "a certain quality of an individual personality by virtue of which he is set apart from ordinary men and treated as endowed with supernatural, superhuman, or at least, specifically exceptional qualities."[28]

[27]R. Hrair Dekmejian, *Egypt Under Nasser: A Study in Political Dynamics* (Albany: State University of New York Press, 1971), p. 173.
[28]Quoted in Dekmejian, *Egypt Under Nasser*, p. 4.

The charismatic leader received a "gift of grace," but society must be prepared to accept the charismatic leader. Egyptian society circa 1952 was certainly ready for one. The army had been disgraced in the Arab-Israeli war of 1948. The country's political leaders could not get the British occupying forces out. A social chasm existed between the elite at the top, living in opulence, and the masses at the bottom, living in dire poverty. The ruling house lacked legitimacy because of its foreign origins; it was founded in 1805 by Muhammad Ali, an Albanian. No coherent ideology undergirded the society and polity, and the Muslim Brothers, with their romanticism and conservatism, vied with the liberal democrats for popular acceptance.

Nasser came on the scene and was acclaimed as the savior of the Egyptian nation and the leader of all the Arabs. Throughout the Arab world his speeches and actions were followed closely. He could arouse the masses to frenzies of adulation as no other Arab leader could.

He possessed this charisma, first, because of some of his personal qualities. He was ethnically Egyptian—Egypt had been ruled for at least 2,000 years by a succession of foreigners and foreign dynasties—and he came from the middle class with ancestral roots among the fellaheen. Also he was a soldier who had served his country well.

But more important than who he was, was what he did, and in the years 1955 and 1956 he had some spectacular achievements in the international arena. He refused to join the American-sponsored Baghdad Pact, which was directed against the Soviet Union and included two former imperial powers that had ruled over Egypt (Britain and Turkey). He attended the first summit meeting of Afro-Asian excolonial states at Bandung, Indonesia in April, 1955, where he associated with such figures of the Third World as Nehru, Chou En-lai, and Tito. He emerged as a leader of the conference, with Egypt recognized as one of the leading states in the Third World. Since 1948 Egypt had been trying unsuccessfully to get arms from the West, and in September 1955, Nasser stunned the world by announcing that he had concluded an arms deal with the Soviet bloc. In July 1956, after John Foster Dulles cancelled an American commitment to aid in the construction of the Aswan High Dam, Nasser nationalized the Suez Canal Company, which was owned by British and French interests and had long been a symbol of foreign economic domination of Egypt. Then in October 1956 the Israelis, the British, and the French attacked Egypt, with Nasser becoming a hero-martyr desperately fighting two major European powers in addition to Israel. With the subsequent withdrawal of the invading forces, followed by nationalization of British and French holdings in Egypt, a military defeat was turned into a resounding political and moral victory. The capstone of Nasser's spectacular achievements was the union with Syria in February 1958, which fulfilled a long-felt desire of the Arabs for political unity. Nasser became the supreme hero of Arab history, "sent by destiny" as a "messenger."

Though Syria seceded from the United Arab Republic in 1961, and though

Egyptian armed forces were bogged down in a protracted war in Yemen from 1962 to 1967, Nasser had already received the "gift of grace" that endows charismatic leaders. He and the Egyptian people were one; his actions and his voice were theirs. They would not let him resign in June 1967, and when he died suddenly on September 28, 1970, the masses poured out their emotions for him in a frenzy of grief.

While Sadat has two great achievements to his name—the 1973 assault across the Suez Canal (called in Egypt simply "the Crossing,") and the Egyptian-Israeli peace treaty of 1979—he is not the charismatic leader that Nasser was. Nasser showed to the world that Arab armed forces could successfully launch a well-coordinated surprise attack using modern technological weapons, and it gave a tremendous boost to Egyptian and Arab morale. Sadat regained possession of territory in the Sinai Peninsula that Egypt had lost in the 1967 war, which enhanced his stature in the Western world but at the same time caused him to be regarded as a traitor in most of the Arab world. Sadat has not received the divine "gift of grace" characteristic of charismatic leaders.

POLITICAL POLICIES

Egypt is confronted with two major policy questions, one external and the other internal. The first is its role in the Arab world, now that it has signed a peace treaty with Israel; the second is alleviation of the country's very pressing economic problems.

In November 1977, President Sadat stunned the world by paying a visit to Jerusalem, Israel, where he and Prime Minister Menachem Begin of Israel pledged not to engage in war any more. In Washington in September 1978 the two signed the Camp David framework for peace in the Middle East and followed it up with a peace treaty signed March 16, 1979, again in Washington. These actions brought a wave of condemnation from Arab leaders and from the Palestine Liberation Organization. At a meeting in Baghdad in March 1979, ministers of the League of Arab States voted to move the headquarters of the League from Cairo to Tunis and to urge member states to sever diplomatic and economic relations with Egypt.

Egypt has the largest population of any Arab state, the most diversified economy, and the biggest standing army, but since it is not rich in oil, withstanding pressure of this sort is difficult. It has been a leader in the Arab world, and the peace treaty represents either boldness and initiative on its part, or else loneliness and isolation.

The riots in Cairo in January 1977 revealed the depth of Egypt's economic problems. Too many people are competing for too few resources, and the country is now living beyond its means. Nasser tried to carry out rapid economic development and at the same time provide some minimal state services to the lower and middle classes. A large new middle class also appeared, and since its members are educated and in contact with the developed world, they desire the standard of living prevalent there. So the problem of the nation is that consumption is too high, and investment is too low. Through the economic policy called the "Opening," Sadat is trying to attract foreign investment, but so far not much has come in. Economics remain the country's number one problem and public policy issue.

REVIEW OF THE MAJOR EVENTS IN THE MODERN HISTORY OF EGYPT

1798-1801	Occupation of Egypt by French military forces under the command of Napoleon Bonaparte.
1805-1848	Rule of Muhammad Ali.
1869	Opening of the Suez Canal.
1882	Beginning of British military occupation.
1948	First Arab-Israeli war.
1952	The Free Officers led by Gamal Abdel Nasser carry out a revolution.
1954	Britain and Egypt conclude an agreement concerning the evacuation of British troops.
1955	Nasser concludes an arms deal with the Soviet bloc.
1956	
July	The United States withdraws its offer to aid in the construction of the Aswan High Dam; in response, Nasser nationalizes the Suez Canal Company.
June	Evacuation of the last British troops.
Oct., Nov.	Israel, Britain, and France attack Egypt.
Dec.	British and French troops withdraw.
1957	Israel withdraws its troops from the Sinai Peninsula.
1958	Unification of Syria and Egypt to form the United Arab Republic.
1961	Syria secedes from the union; Egypt retains the name United Arab Republic.
1967	
May	Egypt closes the Straits of Tiran to Israel shipping at the entrance to the Gulf of Aqaba.

June	Israel launches an attack and routs the Egyptian army in the Sinai Peninsula.
	Nasser resigns from the presidency but then withdraws his resignation after a public outcry.
1970	Nasser dies, and Anwar al-Sadat succeeds him.
1971	New constitution promulgated; official name of the country becomes Arab Republic of Egypt.
1973	Egypt and Syria launch a surprise attack against Israel; Egyptian troops cross to the east bank of the Suez Canal, but Israeli troops break through to the west bank.
1974	Egypt and Israel sign a disengagement agreement.
1975	
June	Sadat reopens the Suez Canal on the eighth anniversary of its closing.
Sept.	Egypt and Israel conclude another disengagement agreement.
1977	
Jan.	The government issues a decree ending subsidies on staple foods and basic consumer goods; after massive demonstrations, it revokes the decree.
Nov.	Sadat visits Jerusalem.
1978	Sadat and Menachem Begin sign the Camp David agreement establishing a framework for peace in the Middle East.
1979	Sadat and Begin sign a peace treaty ending the state of war between Egypt and Israel.

Chapter 9

Iran

With an area of 636,296 square miles (more than twice the size of Texas), a population of 34.2 million (1977), very extensive oil reserves (9 percent of the world's total) and the world's second largest reserves of natural gas, Iran is an important country in the Middle East and in the world. It is strategically located adjacent to the Soviet Union, to the great plain of central Asia which stretches into western China, and to the plain of western Pakistan which leads into the Indian subcontinent. Also it has a long coast on the Persian Gulf, with its colossal oil wealth, and it borders on the great plain of the Tigris and Euphrates valley.

From the middle of the nineteenth until the middle of the twentieth century, Russia and Britain struggled over Iran. Russia was expanding southward, and Britain was fearful that this would threaten India. The two countries met in Iran, and in various ways each tried to control it to their advantage.

Since the midpoint of the twentieth century, this struggle has been replaced by an American-Soviet one, with the critical difference that Iran is no longer weak and helpless and can fend off the superpowers. The men who have led Iran since the Islamic Revolution of 1978-1979 are determined to have neither the United States nor the Soviet Union dominate the country.

The ruler of Iran from 1941 to 1979 was Muhammad Reza Shah Pahlavi.

He frequently stated that it was his desire to transform Iran into a medium-sized power, such as France or West Germany. Through investment of oil capital in industry and agriculture, expansion of the educational system, procurement of arms, and the training and development of the armed forces, he attempted to achieve this objective. He frequently evoked the symbols and memory of Cyrus the Great (who died in 529 B.C.), and it was the glory and power of this ancient Iran that he had hoped to reestablish in the twentieth century.

GEOGRAPHY AND ECONOMY

Until the 1930s Iran was known to the West as Persia, the name given to it by the ancient Greeks. Although Iran is now the country's official name, the government allows both to be used interchangeably in Western-language documents.

Plateau, Mountains, and Desert

Iran is on a high plateau dotted with even higher mountains. The tallest of these is Mount Demavand near Tehran; it is about 19,000 feet high. Ranges with peaks rising above 10,000 feet are not unusual. These form a V lying sideways, the point of which is located in the northwest near the borders of Turkey and the Soviet Union. The top part of the V is formed by the Elburz Mountains, which stretch from the northwest along the southern edge of the Caspian Sea until they join other ranges that are along the southern side of the Soviet border and continue into Afghanistan and Soviet Turkmenistan. The bottom part of the V is formed by the Zagros Mountains, which run southeastward along the border with Iraq and east of the Persian Gulf. The plateau inside the V is at its highest in the northwest, and gradually declines toward the southwest to become the empty desert of eastern Iran, western Pakistan, and western Afghanistan. Water is available in the valleys of the mountains and on their slopes, and it is here that the Persian people have clustered since the beginning of their history. The desert in the middle of the V is mostly uninhabited.

Transportation between the different regions has in the past been hazardous, since the country is divided by mountains and separated in some places by wide expanses of desert; but today it is being made easier with airplanes, roads, and railroads. Up until the reign of Reza Shah Pahlavi (1925-1941), Iranian roads were no more than tracks in the desert, and its railroads were practically nonexistent. Reza Shah built a railroad 895 miles long, from Bandar Shahpur on the Persian Gulf through Tehran to Bandar Shah on the Caspian Sea, for the

express purpose of knitting the country together. His son, Muhammad Reza, carried out an extensive program of railroad, road, and airport construction, giving Iran a good transportation network in spite of its rugged terrain.

There are two exceptions to this picture of Iran as a land of mountain fastness. The first is the province of Khuzistan in the southwest, which is a continuation of the low-lying plain of Iraq. It once was the country's most important agricultural region, but because of changing rivers and the neglect of its irrigation works, it declined. Now modern dams and canals are being built in an attempt to revive agriculture. Khuzistan is also where the country's oil is concentrated.

The second exception is the Caspian seacoast, which is wet, humid, and tropical. It is densely populated and produces a wide vaeriety of crops such as rice, sugar cane, flax, cotton, tobacco, and tea.

The mountains have served to guard Iran throughout its history and to enable Iranians to preserve their national identity. The western frontier and the country inland from the Persian Gulf are protected by lofty ramparts of rock. The Caspian littoral is separated from the plateau by the highest mountains in the land. A range uniformly over 10,000 feet high protects Iran from Turkey, and vast empty deserts serve the same function in the east, along the Afghan and Pakistan borders. The sole gap in this system of natural defense is to the east of Tehran, where the Elburz Mountains diminish and the Iranian plateau opens into the great plain of central Asia. Through this break came the Mongols in the thirteenth and fourteenth centuries.

Most of the inside of the *V* is desert which starts near Tehran and stretches for a distance of nearly eight hundred miles toward the southeast. The two largest deserts are Dasht-i-Lut and Dasht-i-Kavir (*dasht* meaning "plain," *lut* meaning "barren," and *kavir* meaning "salt"). In the past, caravans were able to pass through these deserts, but they presented a formidable barrier of distance, emptiness, aridity, heat in summer, and cold in winter. Today roads are making passage easier.

The Cities

The cities of Iran are usually located on gentle mountain slopes near streams and rivers or in high mountain valleys. Tehran, the capital, is on the southern slope of the Elburz Mountains. Its water comes from the mountains nearby, and the desert begins where the last city street ends. According to the 1976 census, Tehran's population was 4,496,000. Until World War II it was a city of modest size (500,000), but since then it has grown by leaps and bounds, so that now one out of every eight Iranians lives there. In it are located all the government ministries and the central offices of all banks and of most economic institutions. Governmental and economic decisions, even for remote provinces, are invariably made in Tehran, and this has encouraged both individuals and firms to locate there, and has created much overcrowding. As Paris dominates and controls France, so Tehran does Iran.

With a population of 672,000 (1976), Esfahan is Iran's second largest city. It is located in a valley whose rich soil and abundant water produce many agricultural products. From 1036 to 1796 Esfahan was the capital of Persia, during which time mosques, palaces, and other beautiful buildings were erected. Because of their exquisite design and ornamentation, they are architectural masterpieces. Today Esfahan is the center of Iran's textile and steel industries.

The third largest city, Mashad, located in the far northeast, is an important shrine for Shiite Muslims. It has a population of 670,000 (1976).

Tabriz, Iran's fourth city, is at a high elevation in the northwest, one hundred miles from the Turkish border and sixty miles from the Soviet Union.

It has a population of 599,000 (1976) and is the country's coldest city, with temperatures sometimes dropping to −18°F. For centuries it has been famous for its beautiful hand-woven carpets, which are still manufactured there. It is the capital of the Turkish-speaking East Azerbaijan province.

Two other large Irianian cities are Abadan and Shiraz. Abadan (population 296,000 in 1976) is in the southwest on the Shatt al-Arab (the river formed by the Tigris, Euphrates, and other rivers flowing together). It possesses one of the world's largest oil refineries. Shiraz (population 416,000 in 1976), a former capital of Iran, is located in a 5,000-foot-high valley in the southwest.

Since World War II there has been a heavy migration from the rural areas to the cities. The poor have moved to urban areas in search of manual labor, and the middle and upper classes, who have always tended to live in the cities, have stayed there because of white-collar employment, the proximity to the decision-makers, and the social life.

This has created very serious social problems. Poor families are living in one- and two-room slum dwellings; many are either unemployed or semiemployed. Traffic congestion and pollution are severe, particularly in Tehran. Finally, people in towns and villages have little autonomy, since they must consult with a governmental official in the provincial or national capital about many questions.

Ethnic Groups

About two-thirds of the people living in Iran are Persians. Ethnically these are Persian-speaking people who migrated in ancient times into the Iranian plateau from the area north of the Caspian Sea. They predominate in central Iran, and for centuries the cities of this area such as Tehran, Qom, Esfahan, Shiraz, Yazd, and Kerman have been their stronghold. Persians are quite conscious of the powerful empires they founded and led in the past and of their great contributions to the world in the fields of philosophy, art, architecture, and poetry. Today Persians lead the country in almost every way: in politics, the military, the arts, business, and commerce.

The Turks comprise Iran's second major group. Originating in Central Asia, they migrated into the Middle East at various times from the ninth century onward. In the eleventh century A.D. they were united under the Seljuq dynasty, which established an empire over much of the Middle East. From the fourteenth through the early twentieth centuries, the Turkish Ottoman empire ruled over much of the Middle East and Europe from its capital at Istanbul, and the rivalry between it and the Persian empires of the same time was intense. Numerous battles were fought in attempts by each to subdue the other, or at least to gain some territory.

The Turks of Iran are concentrated in the northwestern province of Azerbaijan, living as nomads or seminomads, and as urban dwellers in cities such as Tabriz. While most have learned to speak and understand Persian, they have not been assimilated to the point of giving up their language and customs.

The third major non-Persian group is the Arabs. They are concentrated in the southwest in the province of Khuzistan and along the coastal plain bordering the Persian Gulf. Most are nomadic herders, but some are farmers living in isolated villages.

The Kurds comprise the fourth largest ethnic group. Dwelling in the Zagros Mountains from northern Khuzistan to the Soviet border, they speak a language of their own and are Sunni Muslims. About half are herders, moving their flocks from place to place, and the other half are farmers and city dwellers. Since they also live in northern Iraq, eastern Turkey, and the Caucasus region of the Soviet Union, they have been denied a unified national existence and have been a minority problem in each of these areas. They have been a pawn in the power politics of the region, used by one or the other of the states to weaken its adversary. For example, from 1945 to 1946 the Soviet Union guided and directed the establishment of the independent Kurdish Republic of Mahabad completely within Iranian territory, and in the early 1970s the shah of Iran and the American CIA supported a Kurdish revolt in northern Iraq. In 1975 both gave up their support of the rebellion and it collapsed.

Armenians and Jews form small communities in Iran and have had a long relationship with Persia. Historic Armenia was in present-day northwestern Iran, eastern Turkey and southern Russia. Today Iran borders on the Soviet Republic of Armenia. The Armenians in Iran live mostly in cities, have their own schools, are literate in both Armenian and Persian, and are predominantly middle class. The Jews have been in Persia since ancient times, for it was the Persian King Cyrus who defeated their conquerors, the Babylonians, thus making possible their return to Jerusalem. Some did not return, and today about 60,000 live in Iran, with half of them in Tehran. Since the establishment of the state of Israel, some have started to speak Hebrew, and some have emigrated to Israel.

Important nomadic groups in Iran are the Bakhtiari, Qashqai, and Baluchi. The Bakhtiari live in the Zagros Mountains and have in the past provided military forces for Persian rulers. In contemporary Iran, persons from leading Bakhtiari families have held high government posts, and it is common for Bakhtiari *khans* ("rulers") to spend a lot of time in the capital as well as with the tribe. The Qashqai live in the vicinity of Shiraz and speak a dialect of Turkish. Reza Shah tried in vain to force them to settle and become farmers. The Baluchi live in the blisteringly hot and inhospitable region bordering Pakistan. Because of poor communications between Tehran and this area, the government has had difficulty controlling them. The Baluchi are probably the poorest nomadic group in the country.

Natural Resources

The most important of Iran's natural resources is oil. Since earliest times, oil and gas seeps were known, and the ancient Persians, in whose Zoroastrian religion fire played an important part, erected fire altars fueled by seeping oil deposits. The first major oil field discovered in modern times was at Masjid-i-Sulaiman (125 miles northeast of Abadan) near the site of an ancient fire temple. In 1979 the country contained 9 percent of the world's proven oil reserves, fourth in the world behind Saudi Arabia, the USSR, and Kuwait (Table 2.1). By comparison, the United States had only 4 percent.

Iran's reserves of natural gas are the second highest in the world, preceded only by the Soviet Union. Found in the same reservoirs with petroleum, natural gas was formerly flared off as a waste product of oil production. Now it has become an important commercial asset and is exported to the Soviet Union through a pipeline from the oil fields in Khuzistan province to the Soviet border at Astara. It is also liquified and shipped overseas. Finally, it is used domestically to generate electricity and to manufacture petrochemicals such as fertilizers, plastics, and synthetic fibers.

In the mid-1970s one of the world's largest deposits of copper was discovered near Kerman. Exploitation of this resource is only now beginning.

Economy

No adjective such as socialist, communist, or free enterprise can be attached to the Iranian economy; public and private enterprise are mixed, with the public sector very dominant.

Iran is a late-comer to the development process. Prior to 1900 the country was almost totally devoid of modern industry, communications, and transportation. Oil was first exploited on a commercial basis in 1908, and the Abadan refinery started production in 1909. During the rule of Reza Shah, textile and food-processing factories were established, and the Trans-Iranian railroad from the Persian Gulf to the Caspian Sea was completed. World War II and the political turmoil in Iran of the post-war years brought a halt to economic development, and not until 1953 could Mohammad Reza Shah and his government start building the economy of the country on a very limited base. He repeatedly said that he wanted to turn his country into "one of the five industrial powers before the end of the century" and that it would become a model not only for the Third World, but also for the West, whose "decadence" he deplored.[1]

[1] Quoted in Eric Rouleau, "Iran: The Myth and the Reality," *Manchester Guardian Weekly*, October 24, 1976, p. 12.

The biggest income earner, the oil industry, is in government hands. The exploitation of all minerals is reserved for the government, with the result that the nascent steel, copper, and lead industries are state-run. Railways, roads, telegraphs, telephones, electric power companies, dams for irrigation and power, and large irrigation canals are state-owned. In addition the state provides many social services in the fields of education, low-cost housing, and medical care.

The government either fully owns or holds a majority interest in the most important industrial enterprises and financial institutions in the country. Among these are the National Iranian Oil Co., the National Iranian Gas Co., the National Iranian Petrochemical Co., the Central Bank of Iran, and since 1979, banks that were formerly privately owned.

Both state and private economic activities are subject to government control and licensing for the purposes of economic planning. An important government agency, the Plan Organization, under the direct supervision of the prime minister, establishes five-, six-, or seven-year development plans to direct the growth of the economy. The Fifth Five-Year Plan was in effect from 1973 till 1978.

By the late 1970s, after about twenty-five years of intensive economic development, agriculture was still important, though its share of the gross national product had declined as a result of industrialization and the expansion of oil production. In 1959, along with forestry and fishery it contributed 30.4 percent of the GNP, while in 1970 the figure was 18.1 percent. Iranian agriculture is not entirely of a subsistence nature, and much of the country's industry, such as textiles, carpets, and sugar, depend on it for raw materials. About 62 percent of the population lives in rural areas and relies primarily on agriculture. Compared to the rest of the economy, agricultural production has been increasing relatively slowly; the growth rate has not exceeded 2.5 percent since 1960, which is less than the rate of increase of the population. In the 1970s Iran was forced to import some foodstuffs.

Oil is the biggest single industry in the country. No major new field has been discovered in recent years, so in order to maintain its high level of production, Iran will have to rely increasingly on better techniques to get more oil out of the ground. At present about 20 percent of the oil can be removed, but with more advanced techniques the percentage can be increased to about 40. It was the policy of the shah to keep production at peak levels, and it was expected that, at the rates he had decreed, the fields would begin to face depletion in the 1980s. The government that came to power in the revolution of 1978-1979 decided to cut production in order to keep supplies tight throughout the world, maintain high prices, and stave off depletion of the nation's oil resources.

Beginning in the 1960s, the government of the shah started investing large amounts of capital in mining and manufacturing, with the objective of developing industries that could provide substitutes for imported items or produce goods for export from Iranian raw materials. In the first category were consumer products such as autos and refrigerators, and in the second, steel and petrochemicals.

The shah was optimistic about the country's economic future. He felt that almost anything was possible with money, and that Iran would have increasing affluence as the years went by and the industrial nations paid more for imported oil. But critics outside Iranian government circles argued that economic development was not dependent solely on capital, but was also affected by the efficiency and degree of cooperation in the society, by the customs and habits of the people, and by politics. They argued that too much was being spent on imported consumer products, and that many of the import-substitute industries really did not decrease the amount of foreign products entering the country, but simply brought in parts and assembled them in Iran. Furthermore, the export industries that Iran was trying to develop were entering a very competitive international market in which the quality of Iranian products would probably not measure up to that of products already in existence. These critics also said that the oil would dwindle around 2000 and that Iran was borrowing heavily in foreign money markets and incurring some serious debts. They further criticized the relatively slow development of the agricultural sector of the economy and the failure of the educational system to provide the country with enough skilled laborers, technicians, foremen, and lower-level managers.[2]

Iran's heavy expenditures for arms were also questioned. The shah had declared that he wanted to make Iran into the "world's fifth-ranking military power in the next five to six years."[3] To achieve this objective he spared no expense. Approximately half of the nation's 1976-77 budget was devoted to the armed forces, $9.4 billion, or eleven times that spent in 1970. Most of the weapons, chiefly aircraft, were coming from the United States, which sold Iran $10 billion worth from 1972 through 1976. These weapons were the best that America could produce. A U.S. Senate report on the subject stated that Iran did not have the industrial plant, the economic infrastructure, or the skilled technicians to handle the more advanced weaponry.[4]

POLITICAL CULTURE

Up until about 1900 Iran was largely unaffected by the social and cultural changes described in Chapters 4 and 5. While Cairo, Tunis, and Istanbul were cities in which Western social and political ideas were studied, critically analyzed, and experimented with, this was not happening to the same degree in

[2] Ibid.
[3] Quoted in Eric Rouleau, "Illusion of Grandeur," *Manchester Guardian Weekly*, October 31, 1976, p. 12.
[4] Ibid

the cities of Iran. More isolated by geography, inhabited by comparatively few Europeans, off the main trade routes of the time, and subject to conquest by autocratic, repressive Czarist Russia as well as by Britain, Iran was not affected by outsiders from other areas of the Middle East.

However, since 1900 Iran was been affected by social and cultural movements, and the issues have been largely the same: What social and political changes need to be introduced to make Iran strong enough to resist foreign encroachment? What role shall religion play in the modern Iranian society? What individual liberties shall be permitted? Which cultural and social values and institutions should Iranians adopt and adapt from the West, and which should they reject? These problems have all been confronted under conditions of very rapid change, very extensive foreign influence and, for most of this century, under an oppressive system of censorship that has not permitted a free exchange of ideas.

Iranian Nationalism

Among educated Iranians nationalism is a commonly shared value. Different versions are vigorously debated, and it is asked: Which person has done or is doing the most to further it? What form should nationalism take?

By the standards that historians and political scientists usually apply, Iran is definitely a nation. Since around 1500 B.C. the Iranians have lived together in the plateau between the Elburz and the Zagros Mountains, have shared many common historical experiences, have spoken the same language, practiced the same faiths (first Zoroastrianism, then Shiite Islam) and developed an illustrious culture. They have been the founders of powerful empires, have given birth to poets and philosophers, have built magnificent architectural edifices, and have created beautiful paintings, miniatures, tiles, mosaics, and carpets. However, in this century and the last, Iran has suffered severe physical and psychological blows, and Iranians of all political persuasions have struggled to maintain their country's independence and cultural integrity.

In the nineteenth century Russia moved steadily southward and, piece by piece, seized territories to which Iran lay claim. In 1828 Russia fought the Persians, defeated them, and took the Caucasus area to the west of the Caspian Sea. In the second half of the nineteenth century it conquered, one by one, the city-states of central Asia, some of which Iran claimed; and by 1884 it was able to impose upon Iran the contemporary border to the east of the Caspian Sea.

From the 1850s through the 1880s the British took an interest in the Iranian territory in the east and south. They had the predominant voice in the delimitation of the border between Iran and Afghanistan and between Iran and Baluchistan, then a part of India and now a part of Pakistan.

Apprehensive about the growing influence of Germany in Iranian affairs, Britain and Russia in 1907 signed a convention dividing Iran into three commercial zones of interest. Russia received the northern part of the country, Britain the southeastern part, and a neutral zone between them was established. All this was done without consulting the Iranian government. In 1914 Russian and British troops occupied Tehran to prevent the country from falling under German or Turkish influence during World War I. The revolution in Russia in 1917 led to the withdrawal of the Russian troops, and the Bolshevik government renounced the extraterritorial privileges that the Czarist government had obtained in Iran, but it did not return any territory to it.

In 1919 Britain pressured Iran into accepting a proposed treaty which, in effect, would have put it under complete British domination. Although the shah and cabinet appeared ready to acquiesce, popular feeling was against it, and the agreement was never ratified. In 1920 communist Russian troops, in collaboration with a local separatist group, established the Soviet Socialist Repubic of Gilan, a province of Iran on the Caspian Sea. In 1921 the troops were withdrawn, the "republic" collapsed, and Iranian troops took over.

In the early years of World War II, Iran tried to maintain its neutrality. The British and the Russians, however, felt that Iran was favoring the Germans, and in 1941 invaded the country. The Iranian army collapsed in a few days, and Reza Shah Pahlavi was forced to abdicate and leave the country. For the duration of the war, British and Russian troops occupied the country and transported war materiel over the Trans-Iranian Railroad from the Persian Gulf to the Soviet border west of the Caspian Sea.

As the war came to an end, the old Anglo-Russian rivalry came to the surface again, but with a new dimension: the struggle was now between the communist and noncommunist world, the latter being led by the United States. The Soviets did not evacuate their occupation zone but instead aided in the establishment of two republics: the Autonomous Republic of Azerbaijan with its capital at Tabriz, and the Kurdish Republic of Mahabad near Azerbaijan. Under American and British pressure and with the help of some astute Persian statesmanship, the Russian troops left in May 1946, with the result that the two "republics" collapsed.

Economic concessions given to foreigners in the nineteenth and twentieth centuries also aroused nationalist sentiments. In 1890 the shah granted an English company a fifty-year exclusive concession to cure and sell all of Iran's tobacco. This aroused so much protest that the shah had to cancel the agreement in 1892. From 1908 to 1954 the Anglo-Iranian Oil Company, owned by the British government and British private interests, had the exclusive right to explore for and export the oil of southern Iran. This company was the object of intense nationalist attack, particularly from 1945 to 1953, because it, in effect, had political control over some tribes and regions of southeastern Iran, did not promote Iranians to important positions, and gave more money in taxes to the British treasury than royalties to the Iranian one.

Opposition to this foreign encroachment has been a major aspect of Iranian politics in the twentieth century. In 1906 and 1907 a constitutional revolution took place against the autocracy of the shah and his weakness in the face of foreign pressure and penetration. In the early 1920s the dynasty that had been so inept and autocratic, the Qajars, was overthrown by Reza Khan, a colonel in an Iranian military unit. In 1925 he had himself designated shah by the parliament and founded a new dynasty, the Phalavis.

Reza Khan was a nationalist who was deeply ashamed of the sorrowful condition of his country: the foreign manipulation of the court, foreign control of important sectors of the economy and of several military units, brigands on the roads, and tribes that were not subject to the central authorities in Tehran. Reza Shah embarked upon a vigorous program of nation-building that involved the development of a unified national army, the bringing of the rebellious tribes under central government control, and the arousal of national consciousness by "purifying" the language by ridding it of foreign words, reviving pre-Islamic architectural motifs, and glorifying the nation's history.

However, Reza's abdication and exile in 1941—forced upon him by the Russians and the British, who had routed his armed forces and occupied the country—brought his reign to an ignominious end. After his downfall a barrage of criticism was loosed against him, and he was accused of neglect of the nation's needs and of blind autocratic rule. His twenty-one-year-old son, Muhammad Reza, assumed the throne but did not really have control of things until after 1953.

The period of 1945 to 1953 was one of comparative freedom, and also of intense nationalist activity. It was dominated by the personality of Muhammad Mossadegh, leader of a coalition of parties called the National Front. Mossadegh was prime minister from 1951 to 1953; he had a deep-seated and emotional hatred of the Anglo-Iranian Oil Company, which he felt was exploiting Iran. Under his leadership the company was nationalized, yet because of a boycott by Western governments and international oil companies, Iran lost large amounts of money. In August 1953 a coup took place that was secretly encouraged and supported by the United States Central Intelligence Agency. Mossadegh was removed from office and the shah was returned to a position of power.

Born in 1919, Muhammad Reza Shah directly experienced the many infringements on Iranian sovereignty, and they burned into his psyche a determination not to see Iran pushed around again. However, he compromised himself, for in 1953 he was reestablished in power with the aid and assistance of the United States, and he removed from office the very nationalistic prime minister, Muhammad Mossadegh. Claiming that his nationalism was "positive" while that of Mossadegh was "negative" apparently did not help him in the eyes of the Iranian people. His ties to the United States were too close, and he came to be called in Iran the "American shah."

In 1968 the British announced that they would withdraw their naval forces from the Persian Gulf by 1971. Operating on the assumption that Iran was an "island of stability in the turbulent Middle East," American leaders decided to encourage it to assume the British role of defending the West's interests in the Gulf and the Arabian Peninsula. The United States government permitted Iran to buy planes, helicopters, and destroyers from American companies, and the British sold it hovercraft, giving the Iranian armed forces the mobility to intervene where the United States and Iran felt necessary.

Whereas the shah perceived this policy as that of two strong allies working to further common interests, many Iranians saw it as subservience to a foreign power, simply another example in modern Iranian history of the country being exploited. Up until the early 1950s it was the Russians and the British who were the exploiters, but from that point on, it was the Americans. One of the most frequent cries of the Ayatollah Ruhollah Khomeini during the first months of the 1979 Islamic Revolution was, "Stop interfering in our affairs!"

Constitutionalism and the Anti-Shah Tradition

Since the beginning of this century, constitutionalism and democracy have been a part of the Iranian political rhetoric. In principle Iran was a constitutional monarchy from 1906 to 1979, but in reality it had only a few brief periods of freedom, having been ruled by autocratic monarchs. Arrayed against them have been constitutionalists, who have had strong disagreements among themselves, and many of whom have been decidedly undemocratic in their thinking. What has united them has been opposition to a shah who was inefficient, venal, subservient to foreign interests, or a violator of civil liberties and human rights. Thus "constitutionalism" might more correctly be called the anti-shah tradition in Iranian politics.

In 1906, as the result of a movement led by intellectuals, merchants, and mujtahids (Muslim Shiite religious leaders), the ailing shah, Muzaffar, and his son, Muhammad Ali, the crown prince, reluctantly accepted a constitution. Along with some amendments added in 1907, it provided for an elected assembly (the Majlis); and reaffirmed that Shiism was the state religion. It defined the civil liberties of all citizens, and prescribed the rights of the monarch. Because the Majlis elected under the new constitution challenged Muhammad Ali Shah's authority, he dissolved it in 1909 and ruled absolutely until he was overthrown. Ahmad Shah, son and successor of Muhammad Ali Shah, continued on the throne until 1925, but only as a figurehead. In this period Iran was ruled in a confusing and chaotic fashion by a divided Majlis and the representatives of Britain and Russia.

In 1921 Reza Khan carried out a virtually bloodless coup and from then until 1941 was the real ruler of the nation. He had a limited education, had spent his life in the army since the age of fourteen, and neither understood nor respected constitutional government.

In 1941, after the ascension to the throne of his son Muhammad Reza Shah, political prisoners were released, political parties were allowed to flourish, and genuinely free elections to the Majlis were permitted. One of those who had been imprisoned by Reza Shah was Muhammad Mossadegh, and from 1944 to 1953 he was more dominant in Iranian politics than the young shah. From 1951 to 1953, as prime minister, Mossadegh engaged in a struggle with the shah over the power of their respective offices, asserting that he was responsible to the Majlis and that he, not the shah, should control the armed forces. These were challenges that the shah could not tolerate, so he asserted his royal authority, and with the army staged a coup that removed Mossadegh from office.

From 1953 to 1979 the shah ruled absolutely. Prime ministers and cabinets were totally subservient to him, elections were rigged, only political parties that support the shah were allowed to function, the press was strictly controlled, the educational system was so constructed that it tolerated no dissent and glorified the shah, and writers and artists were forced to write encomiums to him or else vegetate in bitter silence. Especially in the last years of his rule, arbitrary arrest, torture, and inhuman treatment of prisoners were common. Mysterious deaths, most likely perpetrated by the shah's secret police, were not unusual. From time to time he opened the door a little to democracy, but discovered that there were too many forces behind it wanting to get in, and then slammed it shut. Through appeals to patriotism and the imperial tradition of Iran through the ages, he tried to channel national energies into the multifarious tasks of economic development and social reform in order to make it an efficient, orderly, technocratic state.

The revolution that swept over Iran in 1978 and 1979 came from all social classes and from all ideological persuasions. It united students, intellectuals, civil servants, clergymen, workers, peasants, and the middle and lower ranks of the armed forces: it brought together Marxists, social democrats, and Islamic fundamentalists.

On April 1, 1979, after a nation-wide referendum, the Ayatollah Ruhollah Khomeini announced that Iran was an Islamic republic, thus formally ending over 2,500 years of monarchy. However, he was not able to present a constitution for the republic, and this subject was one of great debate that showed the sharp ideological differences in the revolutionary movement.

In Iranian history, a tyrant has sometimes been removed, yet constitutionalism has not emerged triumphant. Although the forces have been united in their opposition and have found a common rallying cry in "constitution" or "human rights," once having removed the tyrant from office, they have been unable to agree on what kind of new political system to establish in place of the old one.

Monarchy

Monarchy had a long and illustrious history in Iran. From Cyrus the Great, who ruled from 559 to 529 B.C. to Muhammad Reza Shah Pahlavi, Iran had an almost uninterrupted succession of kings, with kingship becoming a part of the national and religious culture. In pre-Islamic Zoroastrian times, the king was considered to be the leader of the forces of light against those of darkness. In Islamic times he tried to associate himself with the Imam of All Time, who according to Shiites is the direct descendant of Muhammad and bearer of mystical knowledge. The greatest masterpiece of Persian literature, the epic poem, *Shah Nameh* ("The Chronicle of Kings"), written by Ferdosi (who died sometime between A.D. 1020 and 1026), celebrates the heroic achievements and illustrious deeds of Persian kings, and is familiar to all Iranians, literate and illiterate. The mystique and reverence that surrounded these kings led one scholar to state that the institution of monarchy "lies at the heart of Persian culture and tradition," and that it formed a part of the "historical and cultural tradition to which the majority of Iranians . . . subscribe."[5]

In this century, however, the person and institution of the shah have had a very checkered history. The constitutional movement of the first two decades was against the extravagance, reaction, and incompetence of the shahs of the time, with its objective to limit their power. The coup of Reza Khan in 1921 took place in a power vacuum created by the ineffective rule of Ahmad Shah. Reza Khan considered establishing a republic and probably would have done so, had it not been for the opposition of the Islamic religious leaders, who feared that secularism on the model of Ataturk's in Turkey would infiltrate Iran. In 1925, he chose the option of monarchy.

In 1941, his son, Muhammad Reza, ascended to the throne. During his reign of a little more than thirty-seven years, he faced opposition from a variety of people and groups. In order to reaffirm monarchy as an institution, he staged an elaborate coronation ceremony in 1967, with paeans of praise about him before and after it. In 1971 he celebrated 2,500 years of Persian kingship at Shiraz, capital of the Achaemenid Empire, during which the mighty Persian kings and powerful Persian armies of the past were glorified in speech and pageant.

The revolution of 1978-1979 revealed that the allegiance of contemporary Iranians to monarchy was not deep. Neither secularists nor believing Muslims desired to continue it.

Shiite Islam

The overwhelming majority of Iranians adhere to Shiite Islam, which has been called "the distinctive adaptation of Arab Islam to Iranian culture."[6] Shah Ismail (1501-1524 A.D.), the first of the Safavid rulers, established it as the

---

[5] Roger M. Savory, "Iran: A 2,500-Year Historical and Cultural Tradition," in *Iranian Civilization and Culture,* ed. Charles J. Adams (Montreal: McGill University, Institute of Islamic Studies, 1972), p. 78.

[6] Leonard Binder, *Iran: Political Development in a Changing Society* (Berkeley: University of California Press, 1962), p. 77.

religion of the state, a position it held under subsequent dynasties. In 1979 Iran became an Islamic republic, and Shiite Islam continued to enjoy official recognition.

Islam was brought to Persia by the Arabs who conquered the country in the seventh century. The Persians eventually adhered to a heterodox form of Islam (Twelver Shiism), which they used to distinguish themselves from the Arabs and the Turks, who became predominantly Sunni. By adopting and adapting it, the Persians forged a political weapon of immense strength which has enabled them, through centuries of effort, to preserve their cultural and national traditions.[7]

In origin, Shiism was a political movement, the *shi'at'Ali* (party of Ali"), being the supporters of the claim of Ali, son-in-law of the Prophet, to the caliphate. The Persians created the legend that Zayn al-'Abidin, son of Hussein, who was the younger son of Ali, married the daughter of Yazdigird III, the last of the Persian Sassanid kings. They thereby fused their own national and religious traditions.

Persian kings also tried to tap the charismatic appeal of the imam. For Shiites, imams are the descendants of Muhammad through his daughter Fatima and his son-in-law, Ali. This line culminated in the twelfth imam, the Lord of the Age, who disappeared from the face of the earth in 939 A.D., but who Shiites believe will reappear some day when God wills. He is also called the Hidden Imam. The Safavid kings (1500-1736) tried to establish themselves as representatives of the Lord of the Age, but subsequent dynasties did not attempt this. Rather, the mujtahids are regarded by devout Shiites as representing the Hidden Imam on earth. In principle, the king was subordinate to them.

The relationship between Shiite mujtahids and Persian kings was not unlike that between the Pope and the kings in Europe in the Middle Ages. The Pope was regarded by Catholics as the Vicar of God, and the kings were, in principle, subordinate to him. In both cases, there was often tension between the spiritual and temporal leaders.

Reza Shah had equated traditional Shiite Islam with backwardness and criticized it severely. He did not disestablish it, as was done in Turkey, but rather allowed it to continue within a sphere that he carefully delineated.

Muhammad Reza Shah also tried to control and contain religion but was unsuccessful, and it developed into the force that in the end overcame him. Though he rebuilt and refurbished numerous mosques, distributed charity through religious institutions, said that he had religious visions, and felt that his survival of two assassination attempts was the result of divine intervention, he was religious only in the formal sense, and his support of Islam was ritualistic. He did not stress the fact that Iran was Islamic, nor that he was an Islamic ruler. Rather, he emphasized the Persian imperial tradition and his role as a modernizing monarch.

[7]Savory, "*Iran*," p. 84.

In the 1960s and 1970s, the shah's government harassed, restricted, and arrested religious leaders. It attempted to portray them as reactionary or under foreign influence, but they became stronger and stronger as the oppression of the shah's regime increased. Mullahs (lower clergy), mujtahids, and ayatollahs (mujtahids who achieve special eminence) emphasized that Shiite Islam has historically been a religion opposed to tyranny. In the first century of Islam, the mortal enemies of the Shiites were Mu'awiyah and his son, Yazid, the Umayyad rulers in Damascus, who tried to put an end to the followers of Ali. Hassan and Hussein, sons of Ali, both died martyrs' deaths—the former by poisoning, which Shiites believe was the result of an intrigue by Mu'awiyah, and the latter in battle against the forces of Yazid.

In the revolution of 1978-79, the clergy skillfully employed allegory in speeches and sermons; the shah was portrayed as the modern equivalent of Yazid, and those who fought against his regime, suffered in prison, and died were seen as acting out the same historic roles as Hassan and Hussein. The word *mujahid* (one who fights in a jihad) came to designate persons fighting against the shah. Opponents of the shah who died in prison or in some mysterious fashion were eulogized by the clergy with allegorical references to the early Shiite martyrs who also died through poisoning or through mysterious means. Unarmed young people stood before the troops and dared them to shoot; if they did, the youths died martyrs' deaths and were mourned and praised by their peers. The holy month of Muharram, in which Shiites memorialize the death of Hussein and stage religious processions, became the month in which political protest often reached a peak. It coincided approximately with December 1978, and the massive religious-political demonstrations during it were one factor that led to the shah's departure from the country on January 16, 1979.

Khomeini portrayed the shah as Taghout, an ancient idol at Mecca who was worshipped by the people of the region prior to the adoption of Islam. The prophet Muhammad condemned idol worship and had numerous idols destroyed. Statues of the shah abounded in modern Iran, and during the recent revolution they were smashed with the same frenzy that the early Muslims displayed against the idols of Arabia. The clergy preached against the officially sponsored glorification and near deification of the shah, comparing it to the idol worship Muhammad had condemned. A slogan on banners carried in demonstrations was, "Long live Khomeini, the idol smasher; death to this Yazid [Muhammad Reza Shah], the law breaker."

During the 1960s and 1970s, mosques served as a channel of communication and a source of revolutionary discontent beyond the control of the authorities. While the state-controlled radio, television, and press reported only laundered versions of what was going on and derided critics of the shah, the thousand of mosques, shrines, and religious schools in the country became a network of revolutionary organization and propaganda. Speeches and sermons of the Ayatollah Ruhollah Khomeini were tape-recorded at his place of exile, taken to Iran or sent over international direct-dial telephone, made into duplicate recordings in Iran, and then passed from hand to hand and listened to in homes and mosques. Copying machines turned out statements, directives, and the texts of speeches and lectures. Khomeini made statements in Paris, and the next day they were posted on walls all over Iran. The BBC Persian-language news broadcasts received in Iran daily at 8:15 P.M. were listened to by millions because they carried statements by Khomeini not reported on the Iranian state-controlled radio and television. Using both traditional methods of oral communication and modern technology, the mullahs and mujtahids developed an elaborate and sophisticated network of communication rivaling the official radio, television, and press.

The simple life-style of the Shiite clergy contributed to their popularity and strength. In contrast to the imperial splendor in which the shah lived and the luxurious life-style of his close associates, the Muslim clergy, even the revered ayatollahs, live plainly and simply. They dress in robes and turban, eat simple unadorned food, and live and work in modest, unpretentious buildings. They are accessible to the common people, who feel comfortable in their presence.

While the social and political elite of the country had cut themselves off from the common people by their wealth, frequent trips outside the country, close association with foreigners, and their feeling of superiority brought on by their urbanity and education, the mujtahids and ayatollahs were unmistakably Muslim and Persian. While the close associates of the shah were able to make money through business enterprises by virtue of their connections and inside knowledge, the clergy were living mostly on the gifts of the faithful and were dispensing religious donations to the poor and needy. During the revolution, they established banks that gave loans without interest and cooperative stores that sold basic food at wholesale prices or less. Khomeini repeatedly said that he was the champion of the weak and the oppressed.

The clergy also gained the support of the middle class. As will be seen later in this chapter, the middle class had supported Mossadegh and never gave more than grudging support to the shah. As the cruelty, corruption, and oppression of the shah's regime increased, significant numbers of young educated men and women found in Islam the ideological foundations for their struggle against the regime and for their identification with the people. One man who had enormous influence on them was Ali Shariati.[8]

Born in 1933 in a village on the edge of the desert, Shariati was first educated by his father, a prolific writer on religious subjects and a prominent mujtahid well known for his efforts to bring modern-educated youth back to the faith. He studied in the eastern Iranian city of Mashad, and during the years of repression after the overthrow of Mossadegh in 1953, he was imprisoned for a number of months. He gained mastery of Arabic and French and translated

[8] For a brief biography of Shariati along with a translation of some of his writings, see *On the Sociology of Islam: Lectures by Ali Shari'ati,* trabs. Hamid Algar (Berkeley: Cal.: Mizan Press, 1979).

books from these languages into his native Persian. In 1959 he went to Paris to further his studies in sociology, earned a doctoral degree, and participated there in Islamically oriented organizations opposed to the shah. Upon his return to Iran in 1964, he was arrested at the border crossing between Turkey and Iran and was not released until six months later. Despite his doctorate, he was allowed to teach only in secondary schools and a college of agriculture, but after a number of years he was appointed to the University of Mashad. Students there flocked to the young professor, but the authorities disliked the content and methods of his teaching and forced him to resign. He then began a brief but very creative period during which he lectured at religious centers and universities, gave free classes, and wrote books and articles on religious and social subjects. He was imprisoned again, this time for eighteen months, under conditions of severe hardship. He was released, went to England, and died there on June 19, 1977 under mysterious circumstances—a deed that Iranians feel was the work of the shah's secret police.

Dr. Ali Shariati integrated traditional Islamic belief and modern learning. His lectures contained references to religious personages such as Moses, Muhammad, Ali, and Hussein, as well as to modern thinkers such as Herbert Marcuse, Albert Camus, Franz Fanon, and Karl Marx. He fought against both the religious traditionalists, who regarded the modern world as threatening and were against all change, and the rootless modern-educated intellectuals, who blindly imitated the West and were removed from their culture and society. He argued that Islam was not unique to one time and place but was like an ever-flowing stream that received new currents of inspiration and thinking from prophets and interpreters of the faith as it moved through history.

Shariati viewed history as a struggle between truth and falsehood, between oppressors and oppressed, between the usurper and the deprived; he set this forth symbolically in the story of Cain and Abel, sons of Adam and Eve, which appears in both the Koran and the Bible. Cain, in a fit of anger, killed his brother Abel. To Shariati, Cain represented the forces of evil in history—that is, the rulers who dominate and bring suffering upon the people, the rich who exploit them, and the official priesthood who deceive them. Confronting them are the forces of good, symbolized by Abel; to Shariati these forces were God and the people, who he said were virtually synonymous in the Koran. Through his interpretation, Islam became populist and revolutionary.

A dynamic and progressive religious leader, Shariati had a profound influence on the thinking of Iranian youth. He argued persuasively for them to stay close to their religious and cultural heritage and to the society in which they were reared. He urged them not to be mesmerized by the West and its ideologies. He demonstrated that one could integrate modern learning with faith and traditional Islamic studies, that one could be Western-educated and still be devout.

The Islamic revolution of 1978-79 showed that Shiite Islam is still a dominant force in Iranian society. A religion with a heritage of persecution and martyrdom, it became the catalyst for those oppressed by the shah, offended by corruption, insulted by American political influence, and angered by social injustice. The shah had crushed the secular political opposition, but the Shiite clergy survived; and in alliance with other groups, they brought about his downfall.

POLITICAL GROUPS

Because there are both important similarities and differences, it is useful to introduce the subject of political groups in Iran by making a comparison with Egypt. In both countries, events in the early 1950s determined which persons and groups would be dominant in the society and have power in the political system.

As noted in Chapter 8, during the evening of July 21-22, 1952, a clique of young, middle-class army majors and colonels staged a coup in Egypt that resulted in the elimination of the monarchy and the destruction of the political and economic power of the land-holding aristocracy that had been allied with it. The regime that developed in the two decades thereafter was led by Gamal Abdel Nasser, and astute, charismatic nationalist leader; he was succeeded upon his death in 1970 by a close associate, Anwar al-Sadat. Both had origins in the middle class and received support from those whose backgrounds were similar: officers, educated technocrats, and hosts of less important people whose position in society had been improved by the revolutionary government.

In Iran, from April 1951 to August 1953, Prime Minister Mossadegh led a loose coalition that included a very significant middle-class element that unsuccessfully challenged the monarchy and the aristocracy. It sought an end to the influence and control that the British-owned Anglo-Iranian Oil Company exercised over the Iranian society, economy, and government. It desired more power for the Majlis and the prime minister, and less for the monarch. The military coup, the return of the shah from a brief forced exile, and the imprisonment of Mossadegh in August 1953 were a defeat for the new middle class and a victory for the monarchy, the aristocracy allied with it, and the more senior promonarchical elements in the army.

After surviving this crisis, the shah banned all political parties, the communist Tudeh ("Masses") Party in particular. He purged the armed forces, the Bar Association, the Chamber of Commerce, the craft guilds, the teacher's association, the police, and the gendarmerie. The shah realized that, in addition to crushing his opposition, he needed to build up support. He reached a partial rapproachement with the religious leaders, who had been one element in the Mossadeh coalition, and secured a settlement with a consortium of Western oil companies that was beneficial to Iran, discontinuing many of the privileges accorded the old Anglo-Iranian Oil Company. He thus satisfied some of the nationalist feelings that had sparked the Mossadegh movement. He launched several economic development plans that opened up thousands of new positions which could be filled by middle-class persons, and in 1963 he launched his "White Revolution," called a "Revolution of the Shah and the People," which was aimed mostly at gaining support from the peasantry, traditional supporters of the monarchy.

Through adroit political leadership and a combination of suppression, reforms, and cooption, the shah was able, in the decade following the near-toppling of his regime, to neutralize the opposition and build up a precarious base of support. Unlike Egypt, this base was not founded on the new middle class. Rather, it was a precarious coalition of persons from leading families, the army, the internal security forces, and some individuals coopted from the new middle class.

The Army

The army was the institution most responsible for the continuity and stability of the Pahlavi regime. Through it Reza Shah gained power in the 1920s, and Muhammad Reza Shah returned to power in 1953.

The Iranian army has a tradition that goes back continuously in history for about 2,500 years. The shah and his government pointed particularly to the Achaemenid (550-330 B.C.) and Sassanid (A.D. 226-651) periods, when the nation's armies conquered and controlled expanses of territory far beyond the borders of present-day Iran.

The history of the Iranian army in the nineteenth and the first half of the twentieth century was not so glorious, however. In the early nineteenth century there was no regular army except for the palace guard, and the shah had to rely in times of national emergency on tribal levies led by the nobility; these were poorly trained, equipped, and disciplined. In periods of conquest they fought courageously because there was an opportunity to collect booty, but when retreat and defeat became a reality, they tended to break up and become marauding bands. Some nineteenth-century leaders attempted to establish a regular army, but their efforts never got very far, in spite of the steady stream of French, British, Italian, Austrian, Russian, and Swedish officers who came to the country to give advice or to command units. In 1879 the Czarist government organized a Persian Cossack Brigade led by Russian officers, and used it to control northern Iran. In October 1920, the Russian officers were dismissed and Reza Khan, who had joined the unit in 1894 and had risen through the ranks, took command. On February 21, 1921, he used the unit to carry out a coup that resulted in his becoming minister of war, then prime minister, and finally shah.

Reza Shah inherited a motley assortment of units, some of which had been under the leadership of foreigners, and others under tribal khans. They were equipped with weapons from many different nations, were all trained differently, and employed various military tactics. Some units had been formed to serve the national interest of a foreign nation, and some to provide protection and enhancement of a tribe's power. Reza Shah's great achievement was to mold this disparate assortment of soldiers and officers into a national army under the direction of the central government. He used it in instance after instance to bring unruly tribes under the authority of the government in Tehran and to bring peace to the provinces. In order to cement the allegiance of the officers of the Crown, he gave them unusual privileges and to many, title to large tracts of land.

But by 1941 Muhammad Reza Shah inherited a decimated and demoralized army. The army upon which his father had expended so much effort had fallen apart when it was attacked by the British and Russians. The young shah found a new ally, the United States, which supported and assisted him in rebuilding the army. American military aid began in 1942 and continued throughout his reign.

The struggle of the early 1950s between Muhammad Mossadegh and the shah was in large part over who was to control the armed forces. By 1952 the Majlis, dominated by the antishah forces, had gained control over the budget and the appointment and dismissal of all ministers except the minister of war. In July of that year the shah agreed that the prime minister and the Majlis could also control the war ministry. Mossadegh discharged scores of officers loyal to the shah, reduced the military budget, and decreased the size and activities of the American military mission in Iran. In the spring of 1953 a committee of the Majlis determined that the shah was to be only the ceremonial commander-in-chief of the armed forces, with the minister of defense directing the army and controlling appointments and promotions of officers. The coup of August 1953 brought an end to these developments and resulted in the shah once again becoming the real, as well as the titular, commander-in-chief.

With American monetary and political support, the shah purged the armed forces of communists and opponents of his rule. In 1956, with American administrative advice and assistance, he established the State Organization for Intelligence and Security, better known according to its Persian acronym, SAVAK, to watch over civilians and find who was against the government in either thought or deed.

After ridding the army, navy, and air force of opponents, the shah began an expansion and modernization program that increased the size of the military from 135,000 in 1955 to 300,000 in 1976, and added to their arsenal billions of dollars' worth of new weapons, most of which were purchased from the United States, although some came from Britain and France. The increase in oil prices in 1973 boosted by six times the oil revenue to Iran and added another spurt to weapon-buying.

Muhammad Reza Shah built up a formidable armed force that gave power to the state in the region and in the world. Considering the colossal strength of the Soviet army, Iran could do little to stop an attack by it, but the Iranian army could probably have been effective against one from Iraq or Pakistan. More important, the military forces were regarded by American leaders and the shah as an "instrument of stability" in the Persian Gulf. From 1973 to 1975 Iranian troops helped the pro-Western Sultan Qabus of Oman crush a rebellion in Dhofar Province led by the Popular Front for the Liberation of Oman and the Arabian Gulf, which was supported by the leftist-radical government in South Yemen. It was a part of American and Iranian strategy to have Iranian troops available to support the regimes in Saudi Arabia, Kuwait, and the other states of the Persian Gulf, should they be threatened by leftist revolutionary movements.

The armed forces were also an instrument of internal security and were meshed with the other security organizations. The director of SAVAK and much of its senior staff were former army officers. The commanders of the gendarmerie and of the national police were former generals, with many of their subordinate officers borrowed from the army. If these security forces could not quell urban riots or tribal rebellions, then the army was brought in. This was the case numerous times until the end of the shah's regime in 1979.

The shah paid close attention to the armed forces, making all senior promotions and appointments, selecting the commanders of all major units and of the military schools. He reviewed appointments to the military academies, attended their graduation ceremonies, and passed on promotions in the lower ranks. He played an active role in determining which major weapons systems Iran would buy. He treated the top commanders as his personal friends and pampered them with high salaries, free housing, lavish officers' clubs, and imported luxury goods. He gave to lower-ranked officers benefits commensurate with their rank, which enabled them to enjoy a life-style much higher than that of other classes in the society.

The Civilian Bureaucracy[9]

Beginning in the mid 1950s, the shah and his governments committed themselves to massive programs of economic development and social modernization using the country's abundant oil revenues. As a result government ministries, organizations, agencies, and companies have become almost too numerous to count. There are ministries typical of all governments, such as the Plan Organization, and the Red Lion and Sun Organization (the Iranian Red

---

[9] Little has been written about the Iranian bureaucracy per se, but quite a bit about the new middle class that staffs it. Most helpful in this regard are: James A. Bill, *The Politics of Iran: Groups, Classes and Modernization* (Columbus, Oh.: Charles E.Merrill Publishing Company, 1972), and James A. Bill, "The Patterns of Elite Politics in Iran," in *Political Elites in the Middle East,* ed. George Lenczowski (Washington, D.C.: American Enterprise Institute, 1975).

Cross); and government companies such as the National Iranian Oil and the National Steel Company. They supervise, own, or control the most important sectors of the Iranian society and economy, and dispense the gamut of social services which modern states provide.

These governmental and quasigovernmental institutions are staffed with hundreds of thousands of persons from the new middle class. They are people who have a modern secondary or university education and possess the special skills necessary for the nation's economic development and social moderniza-tion, yet they are the class that was most disaffected with the monarchy and the social system centering on it. They wanted to be able truly to participate in important political decisions, which was not possible. They wished to be free from being pressured to heap lavish praise upon the shah, ascribing every major political and social advance to his genius. They desired an end to the gross inequities in Iranian society, in which playboys and jet-setters lived lavishly while millions were in dire poverty. They sought quality education, not just the rote learning that took place in overcrowded facilities. They demanded the opportunity to think freely, speak openly, and write criticially. They wanted an end to the favoritism and cronyism that went on in the government, the administration, and high circles.

Under the old order many members of the new middle class felt that they could not bring about change, that their talents, education, and skills were not being utilized for the betterment of society. They fall into four categories: (1) the uprooters, who were angered at the social injustice in Iran, were totally dissatisfied with the existing social and political system, and wanted to bring about radical change; (2) the technocrats, who learned advanced and sophisti-cated skills at a university, often abroad, who were dissatisfied with the inefficiency and wastefulness of Iranian society, and wanted opportunities to put their abilities to work; (3) the maneuverers, who were unconcerned with the social injustice that angered the uprooters and the inefficiency that frustrated the technocrats, and who exploited the system for their own personal benefit; and (4) the followers, who floated in the safest and easiest direction, gravitating toward the persons, groups, and classes who hold the most power.[10]

Economic development, to which the shah was committed, required the growth of bureaucracy, which brought about the expansion of the new middle class. Some of its members could be coopted or bought off with soft, lucrative positions in the government, but others could not. They became immensely dis-satisfied with the hierarchical, stratified social and political system centered in the monarchy, which the shah was determined to preserve. The dilemma, of course, was that he wanted to bring about reform without revolution and economic development without major changes in the structure of the society.

[10]Bill, *Politics,* pp. 71-2.

The Aristocracy

A common cliché about Iran was that it was a country ruled by a "thousand families." While this was an oversimplification, it was true that a social, political, and economic elite existed that supported the institution of monarchy and was perpetuated by it. The number of families in this group was probably closer to three hundred than a thousand. Many of them were members of it continuously since before the middle of the last century.[11]

In everyday social intercourse Iranians are quite conscious of who has high status, and they commonly put their hand on their heart, bow, and repeat flowery phrases to show deference. Prime ministers did not disdain saying in public that they were "slaves of the shah," and important officials bowed low and kissed his hand. Peasants were even more deferential, kissing the hand, knee, and the feet of important persons, and sometimes slaughtering an animal in his presence. The more educated and urbane are ambivalent about these practices, alternately condemning and performing them.

The primary source of affluence, political power, and social status for the Iranian aristocracy was agricultural land. After World War II, and especially after the beginning of the shah's White Revolution in 1963, members of the aristocracy shifted their investments from agriculture to urban real estate, commerce, industry, banking, and overseas investments. The shah himself owned large tracts of crown lands and sold some of them in the 1950s, but he still controlled huge land areas as well as important banks and businesses and was undoubtedly one of the wealthiest men in the world.

In Iran wealth and social position were influenced by one's relation to the ruler. Shahs confiscated the properties of enemies and rewarded friends with grants of land. Many of the ancestors of the contemporary aristocracy rendered meritorious service for Reza Shah or for a Qajar monarch and were enriched accordingly. Muhammad Reza Shah did not grant land, but he did encourage his close associates to make lucrative investments in Iran or abroad. Generally the result was that those who were politically powerful were rich and those who were rich were politically powerful. Wealth was not a guarantee of security, however, and many affluent people in Iranian history were reduced to penury by an angry shah. Muhammad Reza was no exception; he rewarded and punished, balancing off personal and family rivalries, all for the purpose of making sure that no one was totally secure, and no one could challenge him.

The top three hundred families fell into two groups: (1) national elite families that rose above their original local bases of power to positions of national importance; and (2) provincial elite families that were clustered in a particular province, city, or town, with influence in only a relatively small

[11] Bill, "Patterns," p. 32.

region. The former had relatives in the provinces, but their headquarters was Tehran. Persons from this group held important positions in civil administration, the armed forces, the cabinet or parliament, the judiciary, commerce, industry, medicine, education, and the arts. They were represented in all the major areas of Iranian national life.[12]

There were forty national elite families, with an inner core of ten who had direct access to the shah. All forty together occupied a total of 410 Majlis seats and 66 Senate seats from 1906 to 1967. With the exception of the ruling Pahlavi family, not a single national elite family failed to enjoy parliamentary representation. From 1955 to 1975, twelve different men served as prime minister, six of them from the top forty families. Three others belonged to the second level of major families, and only two had their origins outside the top forty. The final prime minister, Amir Abbas Hoveida, who held that office longer than any other person since World War II, had a father whose background was modest, but his mother had impeccable aristocratic credentials.[13]

The elite families were closely linked by marriage. The shah is married to Farah from the Diba family, and his previous wife, Soraya, was from the Esfandiari family. Both are in the top forty. The long-time ambassador to the United States, Ardashir Zahedi, was formerly married to the shah's daughter, Shahnaz. While the Zahedi family was not in the national elite, Ardashir's father was the general who led the coup of August 1953 that restored the shah to power. Meritorious service was rewarded by a well-placed marriage. A former minister of culture, Mihrdad Pahlbud, is the husband of Princess Shams, the sister of the shah. These are only a few examples, all involving the royal family, but they were common throughout the top ranks of Iranian society among members of the cabinet, parliament, the top levels of the armed forces, and the administration.

The aristocracy of the previous regime was well educated and highly sophisticated. Many studied at the best universities in Germany, France, Britain, and the United States. They knew French, German, or English well, and traveled frequently outside the country. A 1970 study of persons holding the title of Director General showed that 51.4 percent had a baccalaureate degree, 17.9 percent a master's, and 20.5 percent a doctorate. Other studies revealed that one-third of the deputies in the twenty-first Majlis (1963-1967) and over 90 percent of the members of the cabinets from 1965 to 1974 had been educated abroad.[14]

In other countries of the world, aristocracies survived by absorbing into their ranks members of the middle class. In Iran under the shah, men of education and talent but of humble social origin did make it to the top, but as was

[12] Ibid., pp. 32-6.
[13] Ibid., p. 33.
[14] Ibid., p. 28.

observed previously, most members of the new middle class were hostile to the social and political order he established.

POLITICAL STRUCTURES

With documents dating from 1906 and 1907, Iran had the oldest continually functioning constitution in the Middle East until 1979 and was frequently called a constitutional monarchy. Yet during most of the twentieth century the government was a royal dictatorship.

From the time of the 1953 coup until his forced departure from the country in 1979, the shah was at the center of power, ruling through the army, national police, the gendarmerie, and SAVAK. The prime minister, cabinet, and Majlis simply followed his lead. The only political parties permitted were those that he created, and no one whom he disfavored was allowed to run for a Majlis seat.

Educated in Iran by Iranian and French tutors, a student for four years at a school in Lausanne, Switzerland, fluent in English and French, Muhammad Reza Shah is a man of considerable urbanity, sophistication, and worldly knowledge. He knows how democracy works in the West, and from time to time allowed a small measure of it to function in Iran. His primary objective, however, was the maintenance of the monarchy and his personal power, and when he introduced some degree of freedom, it was with the intention of building a wider base of support for himself and the monarchy. When this did not happen, he reasserted his absolute authority. Although he is a modern-educated person who intellectually comprehends democracy, instinctively he was a Persian monarch who commanded and demanded obedience.

The Constitution Under the Monarchy

The Fundamental Laws of 1906 and the Supplementary Fundamental Laws of 1907 were regarded together as the constitution of Iran until the proclamation of the Islamic Republic on April 1, 1979.[15] At the time of the writing of this book, a new constitution has not been made public, so I will summarize some of the provisions of the old one.

The 1906 document contained fifty-one articles and dealt mainly with the organization, powers, procedures, and rights of the Majlis, the lower house and the principal lawmaking body. The 1907 document contained an opening section of "General Dispositions," the two most important of which were that

---

[15]Two English translations are available: Helen Miller Davis, ed., *Constitutions, Electoral Laws, Treaties of States in the Near and Middle East* (New York: ANS Press, 1970), pp. 106-28; and Abid A.Al-Marayati, ed., *Middle Eastern Constitutions and Electoral Laws* (New York: Praeger, 1968), pp. 4-43. The first translation is used here.

the official religion of Iran was Shiite Islam and that no enactment of the Majlis could be at variance with the "sacred rules of Islam." This last provision was to be implemented by a committee of "not less than five mujtahids or other devout theologians" who had the power to veto a law passed by the Majlis. While it existed in the constitution, it was never carried out in practice.

The supplement of 1907 had a section that was the equivalent of a bill of rights; article 26 said that "the powers of the realm are all derived from the people; . . . ." article 27 declared that the powers of the realm were divided into three categories: legislative, judicial, and executive. The first was shared by His Imperial Majesty, the Majlis, and the Senate. The second belonged to religious courts in matters connected with religious law, and to civil tribunals in respect to ordinary law. The executive power, "which appertains to the King," according to the constitution, was "carried out by the Ministers and State officials in the august name of His Imperial Majesty in such manner as the Law defines."

Other provisions of the 1907 supplement concern relations between the Majlis and the Senate, the prerogatives of the Throne, the powers and responsibilities of the ministers and of the courts, and the definition of taxation authority.

Political Parties[16]

In the first quarter of this century, political associations (in Persian, *anjomans*) played a major role in the struggle against absolutism. Located mostly in the cities and composed of merchants, artisans, intellectuals, and clerics, they devoted themselves to the discussion of political topics and to organizing for action. They spawned some parties that showed signs of being able to draw together different ethnic groups and social classes and to formulate political platforms and policies. Foreign interference and the shallowness of the support for these parties prevented them from growing, however.

From 1925 to 1941 Reza Shah experimented with parties, but he was not enthusiastic and never allowed them to develop. In 1927 he ordered government officials to promote the development of four political groups, but all soon disappeared. In January 1939 he formed the Organization for the Development of Thought to inform the people about government programs, guide public opinion, and promote national pride. This came to an end with his abdication in 1941. Unsuccessful at developing either a multiparty or a one-party system, the shah governed without parties. The suppression of political debate and activity during his rule resulted in its explosion after his abdication.

A host of political parties emerged, many staying on the scene for only a short period of time, and a few having a lasting effect. On the left was the largest

[16]The source for most of this section is: G. Hossein Razi, "Genesis of Party in Iran: A Case Study of the Interaction Between the Political System and Political Parties," *Iranian Studies*, 3 (Spring 1970), 58-90.

and best organized of all, the *Tudeh* ("Masses") Party. The core of its leadership was composed of forty-nine intellectuals who had been imprisoned by Reza Shah in 1937 on charges of communist activity. They were released after his abdication and in 1942 founded the *Tudeh* Party, formulating a party platform and program that were liberal, moderate, and addressed primarily to workers, peasants, and intellectuals. Their program called for legalization of trade unions, progressive labor legislation, equality of minorities, bureaucratic reform, free health services, tax-supported public education, and friendly relations with all of Iran's neighbors, particularly the Soviet Union. Only later did its program become Marxist and revolutionary.

The *Tudeh* was the only mass-based "branch" (as opposed to "cadre") party to exist in Iranian history. Its members paid fees, were issued cards, and were organized into cells. It translated and published books, owned a number of newspapers, had unions affiliated with it, and controlled a majority of the country's organized laborers, even though its leadership was mostly middle class. It elected eight deputies to the fourteenth Majlis in the late 1940s. Outlawed in 1949, it continued to exist throughout the Mossadegh era and was not repressed until the shah returned to power in 1953. Since then it has only been able to operate underground and from communist East European countries.

On the right were conservative pro-British, extreme nationalist, and reactionary religious parties. None became very large or was able to establish a nation-wide organization or mass base. In the center were a number of parties that formed a coalition called the National Front led by Muhammad Mossadegh.

The fall of Mossadegh brought an end to this period of political party efflorescence. In the years immediately after his return, the shah banned all parties. In 1957 he tried to establish from above a system in which there would be a government party and a loyal opposition, both supporting the Crown. *The Melliun* ("Nationalists") Party—the followers of Mossadegh had been called Nationalists, so this was an overt attempt to capture the spirit and the following of that movement—was placed under the leadership of Dr. Manuchehr Egbal, the prime minister; the *Mardom* ("People") Party was headed by Asadollah Alam, a boyhood friend and one of the most loyal and servile supporters of the shah. The *Melliun* was supposed to be the "conservative" majority party, with the *Mardom* representing the "liberal" minority. Asadollah Alam came from one of Iran's great landowning families notorious for being pro-British. A less likely candidate to rally "liberal" forces and lead the "people" could hardly have been found. Few Iranians were fooled by this charade, and the shah's credibility suffered a great deal from attempting to bring it off. By 1960 he had allowed the *Melliun* to disappear and the *Mardom* to become insignificant.

After the dismal experience with these parties, the government operated without them, keeping the Majlis suspended for about two and a half years, despite a constitutional prohibition. During this time the shah launched the White Revolution, which was approved by a 99.9 percent majority in a popular referendum on January 26, 1963. To nominate candidates for the Majlis election in September 1963, the government formed a "congress of the delegates of the peasants, workers, women, intelligentsia, and other classes of the people." Because of the aversion of the shah and his security organizations to any institution that might act as a point of countervailing power, it did not develop into a single-party system along the lines of those in communist countries and some Afro-Asian ones.

In 1964 a number of high-level officials formed the *Iran-i-Novin* ("New Iran") Party. Though most ministers and deputies were members, it never had a popular base. In 1975 it was dissolved along with the *Mardom* Party, which had continued to exist in a subdued way throughout the 1960s and 1970s. The Secretary-General of *Mardom,* Nasser Ameri, was allegedly forced to resign by SAVAK.[17] He died in an auto accident a few weeks later.

On March 2, 1975, the shah established by imperial decree the *Rastakhiz* ("Resurgence") Party as the only legal one. In a speech announcing his decision, he bluntly stated his viewpoint toward those who took it lightly:

A person who does not enter the new political party and does not believe in the three cardinal principles which I referred to [the Monarchy, the Constitution, and the White Revolution] will have only two choices. He is either an individual who belongs to an illegal organization, or is related to the outlawed *Tudeh* Party, or in other words is a traitor. Such an individual belongs in an Iranian prison, or if he desires he can leave the country tomorrow, without even paying exit fees and can go anywhere he likes, because he is not an Iranian, he has no nation, and his activities are illegal and punishable according to the law.[18]

At a national congress on May 2, 1975 attended by 4,500 delegates, a constitution for the party was adopted. Amir Abbas Hoveida, the prime minister, became the party's secretary-general.

The shah was notably unsuccessful in trying to organize "loyal" parties, and the *Rastakhiz* Party was no exception. In the last year of his reign it fell apart and he abolished it. As in the case of the other parties he founded, it was established from above, was led by government officials and close associates of the shah, was more or less an arm of the bureaucracy, and had no mass support or plausible ideology. In principle it united those who believed in and supported the shah's White Revolution, but in reality many joined because it was necessary in order to remain or advance in their job.

[17] Arthur S. Banks, ed., *Political Handbook of the World: 1977* (New York: McGraw-Hill Book Company, 1977), p. 184.

[18] *Kayhan* International Edition, Tehran, March 3, 1975, p. 2.

POLITICAL LEADERSHIP

The Shah

His Imperial Majesty, Muhammad Reza Shah Pahlavi, Shah of Shahs, Light of the Aryans, as his titles indicate and the frequent references in this chapter imply, was the hub of the Iranian political system. One of the few remaining absolute monarchs in the world, he was on the throne from 1941 to 1979, longer than any of the other dominant political figures of the twentieth century, including Churchill, Roosevelt, Stalin, de Gaulle, Tito, or Brezhnev. His political longevity was a testimony to his diligence, astuteness, and acumen. He worked hard at being shah and personally performed the many actions that permitted the government to function. "From the appointment or promotion of officers in the army to the decisions as to whether or not to pave the main street of Tabas, His Imperial Majesty [was] the arbiter."[19]

Born on October 26, 1919, he was the eldest son of Reza Khan. As is the case with crown princes, he had an unusual childhood. He was surrounded by servants and flatterers who made it possible for him always to be at the head of his class, the leader of his group of boys, or even the commander of military units of grown men. When the young prince was six years old his father separated him from his mother and sisters so that he could have a more "manly education," and put him under the care of a French governess, educating him in a specially organized school on the palace grounds with a group of carefully selected boys. From 1932 to 1936 he studied at Le Rosey secondary school near Lausanne, Switzerland. This experience expanded his horizons considerably, but not as much as would have been the case for a more "normal" child. With him to Switzerland went a personal physician, a Persian-language tutor, and two Iranian boys selected by his father to be his companions. While other boys at the school could go to parties in the nearby cities, he had to stay in his room. In 1936 he returned to Iran, entered the Military Academy, and graduated two years later as a second lieutenant at the head of his class. In 1939 his father married him to Princess Fawzia, sister of King Farouk of Egypt. The two were not compatible and were later divorced.

In 1941, at twenty-one years of age, he suddenly became king. His powerful and domineering father had abdicated under pressure from the British and Russian governments. The Imperial Iranian Army was utterly disorganized and the bureaucracy a collection of corrupt and nepotistic cliques. His father, who had been the center of power and adulation for about twenty years, was now reviled and castigated in public conversation and in the press. The young king

[19]Marvin Zonis, *The Political Elite of Iran* (Princeton: Princeton University Press, 1971), p. 18.

who had always been overshadowed by his father, felt insecure. He had not expected the duties of kingship to be thrust upon him so quickly, nor had he the time to come to appreciate the nuances of political leadership and administration. In addition the servility and sycophancy of the people at the court isolated him from many of the pervasive problems of Iran.

To the amazement of most inside Iran and out, the young shah overcame these handicaps of self and position, preserved his throne, consolidated and fortified his power so that it could not be challenged, carried out massive programs of social change and economic development, and raised Iran to heights of international power never before achieved in modern times. Despite his ignominious fall from power, he left his mark on Iranian history.

Muhammad Reza is a complex personality. He is intelligent, well-educated (to a large extent self-taught), and enormously self-disciplined. He is a man of the East who gloried in the ceremony and trappings of power that surrounded Persian monarchs, yet he is also a man of the West who is fascinated by all forms of advanced technology—he can pilot his own plane, for instance. He allowed peasants in simple clothes and aristocrats in formal morning coats to bow low before him and kiss his hand. He discussed highly technical subjects concerning the oil industry and international economics with ministers and directors who held advanced degrees from European and American universities. He is a soldier with a strong devotion to duty, to his country, to discipline, and to order, and a handsome, urbane, sophisticated gentleman who can transfix newspaper reporters from Western Europe or the United States by his charm and his excellent French and English. While many of his citizens considered him a torturer because of what went on in his prisons, many in the West regarded him as a storybook monarch with a beautiful, elegantly-dressed wife and four attractive and delightful children.

In an age when few monarchies were left, Muhammad Reza was a king who was convinced that monarchy was the best form of government for his people. He wanted to preserve it, while transforming his country into a militarily powerful, modern industrialized state. He was a reformer who launched a revolution to better the lot of his people, particularly the peasants, and an autocrat who was brutal to those who opposed him or fell from his favor. He was scornful of the "permissiveness" in Western societies and did not want it to penetrate Iran.

The Shah's Methods of Rule

During his thirty-seven years on the throne, Muhammad Reza Shah employed a number of different methods to maintain his authority. Probably the most effective was cooption. Representatives of the shah sought out and recruited well-educated, intelligent young people, offering them jobs that gave them status, power, money, and the opportunity for foreign travel. With enormous revenues from oil at his disposal, many social and economic programs to develop, a large administration to command, the shah, or those who spoke for him, had a lot to offer eager aspirants. Though a young person might have had a distaste for the regime, it was easy for him or her to rationalize the support implied in accepting a position in its government.[20]

In respect to the governing elite, the shah carried out a policy of divide and rule. One technique was to appoint personally antagonistic individuals to cabinet positions and to the directorship of major government organizations. The mutual hostilities of the persons involved, in addition to the rivalry and conflicting interests of the institutions they headed, prevented a coalescing of power that might have threatened the shah.

Another technique was to juggle appointments, appointing to high positions persons of low status and to low ones those of high status. All these were at the pleasure of the shah, keeping officials in a state of suspense.

A further method was to have overlapping bureaucracies. No single important task was assigned to one agency, so it and its head could not gain a monopoly on a vital governmental service. For example, three institutions supplied intelligence to the shah: (1) SAVAK, (2) the Special Intelligence Bureau within SAVAK, physically separate and financially independent from it, assigned the task of duplicating the work of SAVAK with respect to major threats to the regime, and (3) the J-2 branch of the Imperial Iranian Armed Forces.

Just as institutions were given duplicate responsibilities, individuals were assigned tasks that duplicated those of others. The shah asked these individuals to watch over a particular organization and its head. He was thus given information on the finances, policies, and personnel of the organization, learning through an independent source how effectively it was operating.

Another technique of divide and rule was to cut down anyone who became more popular, better-known, or was perceived by the public as being more capable than the shah. Individuals who gained such recognition were quickly reduced in stature, assigned to lowly positions, and sometimes banished entirely from the political elite. Their misstep was their failure to remain in the shadow of His Imperial Majesty. Muhammad Mossadegh was the prime example, but there are others as well.[21]

The shah also forced communications within the government and administration into vertical channels, so that important decisions were dealt with at the top, where the shah had a voice. Finally, in a society where "it ... [was] generally accepted that many officials enjoy[ed] the cream from the top of government expenditures,"[22] the shah tolerated corruption on the part of his

[20] Ibid., pp. 23-5.

[21] Ibid., pp. 91-5.

[22] Ibid., p. 102.

supporters and used allegations of malfeasance to dismiss and prosecute officials suspected of disloyalty to him.[23]

POLITICAL POLICIES

Between his return to power in 1953 and his fall from it in 1979, Muhammad Reza Shah had three overarching policies. The first was the preservation and strengthening of his own personal power, which he achieved to such a degree that he became the most powerful monarch in Iranian history. As with other contemporary dictators, modern communications, transportation, and methods of surveillance made it possible for him to penetrate almost all communities and organizations and to monitor all significant decisions. Truly the country was centered around the person of the shah.

The shah's second primary policy was to consolidate the monarchy in order to assure its continuance after his death. By divorcing Soraya Esfandiari, who bore him no children, and marrying Farah Diba, who in 1960 gave birth to a son, Reza Cyrus, he was assured of a successor to the throne. By staging a formal coronation in 1967 and celebrating 2,500 years of Iranian monarchy in 1971, he attempted to establish in the mind of the Iranian and world public the permanence of the Persian Crown.

The final policy was to enhance the power of the Iranian state in international affairs. To this end, the shah and his government glorified powerful Persian empires in the past, purchased large quantities of sophisticated weapons, paid close attention to the development of the armed forces, and established new industries such as petrochemicals and steel, which contributed to the economic power of Iran in world markets.[24]

Subordinate to these objectives was the "White Revolution." Called by the government a "Revolution of the Shah and the People," it was initiated in 1963 and originally had six points:

1. Land reform
2. Nationalization of forests and pastures
3. Public sale of state-owned factories to finance land reform
4. Profit-sharing in industry
5. Expansion of the franchise to include women
6. Establishment of the literacy corps

[23] Ibid.

[24] Marvin Zonis, "The Political Elite of Iran: A Second Stratum?" in *Political Elites and Political Development in the Middle East,* ed. Frank Tachau (New York: John Wiley & Sons, Inc., 1975), p. 195.

Thirteen other points were later added. The greatest emphasis was on land reform and the literacy corps, both of which achieved considerable success. Most of the other points remained largely on paper.[25]

The major problem was that, although the reforms were successful to some degree in alleviating the physical misery of some of the lower classes, they did not change the power relationships in Iran. For example, the literacy program was run by the most powerful members of the elite, including the shah's sister and his faithful friend Asadollah Alam.[26] The land reform program was part of the bureaucracy and was administered by the ministries of Agriculture, Interior, Finance, and the Department of Land Reform, along with agriculture, credit banks, cooperative organizations, the bureaucracy of provinces, and the gendarmerie. The first minister of agriculture to be charged with carrying out this program was Hasan Arsanjani. He was a tough crusader who believed in the program and pushed it hard, but the shah fired him in March 1963 and replaced him with a military general.[27]

By means of the "White Revolution," the shah introduced change from above in an attempt to preserve his rule and the traditional power relations in the country. Through it he made the aristocracy more dependent on him by severing them from their base of power in the countryside and integrating them into the national administration and economy, which he controlled. By gaining the allegiance of the peasantry, the majority of the Iranian people, he hoped to counterbalance his lack of support among the middle class.[28]

In order to carry out the different programs of the "White Revolution," however, the shah needed the technical, managerial, and organizational manpower that only the middle class could provide. For the most part it refused to dedicate itself to the programs of reform since it saw them more as ways of preserving the existing social and political systems than as reform. When the middle class did participate in them, it did so without zeal, enthusiasm, or commitment.[29]

The members of the middle class felt that they had been bypassed by the "White Revolution." They pointed to the list of reforms and argued that not one was directed toward them. They desired some improvement in the ridiculously inadequate and chaotic hospital and medical-care system. They craved an end to the overcrowded conditions in the schools and universities, and liberation from the stultifying intellectual atmosphere in which free inquiry on social and

---

[25] Bill, "Patterns", p. 30.
[26] Bill, *Politics*, p. 142.
[27] Ibid., pp. 142-43.
[28] Ibid., pp. 144-45.
[29] Ibid., pp. 147-48.

political topics was suppressed. They wanted a fair judiciary, independent of the will of the executive.[30]

With jobs and money the government lured the dissatisfied and alienated middle class into the agencies carrying out the "White Revolution." Such persons then became career-oriented and security-conscious, and their objections to the government faded away. Some Iranian professors, teachers, and scholars described the whole program as "bribery of the intellectuals."[31]

Intrinsic to the "White Revolution" were certain dilemmas the government could not resolve. In order to carry it out, the government needed the participation and commitment of the new middle class, which possessed technical and managerial skills. This, however, was the group least enthusiastic about the "White Revolution." Furthermore, as the revolution proceeded peasants upgraded their skills, becoming part of the middle class. The "White Revolution" did not resolve the regime's problem with this group, and probably made it worse.

More important than the "White Revolution" in determining the social, political, and economic order of post-World War II Iran was the counterrevolution of 1953. It reversed the movement in which the prime minister and the Majlis were gaining power and the shah was losing it. It was a defeat for the middle class, who backed Mossadegh, and a victory for the aristocracy, who supported the shah. It initiated the trend whereby Muhammad Reza Shah increasingly acquired more power until he became one of the world's most absolute rulers. It continued to permit foreign influence in Iranian affairs, with the British replaced by the Americans. It determined which persons would hold power in postwar Iran, who would have the most wealth, and who the most social prestige.

However, all of this came to an end with the Islamic Revolution of 1978-79.

REVIEW OF THE MAJOR EVENTS IN THE MODERN HISTORY OF IRAN

1890   The shah grants a fifty-year exclusive concession to an English company to cure and sell all of Iran's tobacco; agreement is cancelled in 1892 because of public protest.

1906-1907   The Constitutional Revolution is waged against the autocracy of the shah and foreign influence; a constitution is promulgated limiting in principle the powers of the shah.

1907   Anglo-Russian Convention dividing Iran into three commercial zones of interest.

---

[30]Ibid., pp. 149-50.
[31]Ibid., p. 152.

1908	Oil discovered at Masjid-i-Sulaiman.
1909	Formation of the Anglo-Persian Oil Company, owned by the British government and British private interests; name changed to Anglo-Iranian Oil Company in 1935 and to British Petroleum in 1954. Abadan refinery begins production.
1919	Great Britain pressures the shah and his government to accept a treaty giving it a paramount position in Iran; the Iranian parliament (Majlis) refuses to ratify it.
1920	Russian communist troops establish the Soviet Socialist Republic of Gilan in a province of Iran on the Caspian Sea; it collapses one year later.
1921	Reza Khan, commander of the Persian Cossack Brigade, assumes power through a coup d'etat.
1925	The Majlis vests the crown in Reza Khan and his heirs; he takes the name Reza Shah Pahlavi.
1926	Formal coronation ceremonies for Reza Shah Pahlavi.
1941	British and Soviet troops invade Iran and rout its army; British and Soviet authorities force Reza to abdicate and go into exile; his son, Muhammad Reza, ascends the throne.
1946	
March	Last British troops are withdrawn.
May	Last Soviet troops are withdrawn, bringing about the collapse of the Autonomous Republic of Azerbaijan and the Kurdish Republic of Mahabad.
1951	
March	The Majlis nationalizes the National Iranian Oil Company.
April	Muhammad Mossadegh, leader of a coalition of parties called the United Front, is appointed prime minister by the shah under pressure from the Majlis.
1953	The shah leaves the country for four days; an army-led coup d'etat, assisted by the American CIA, arrests Mossadegh and his principal supporters; the shah returns to Tehran and assumes absolute power.
1957	SAVAK (State Organization for Intelligence and Security) is established.
1963	The shah launches his "White Revolution." The Ayatollah Ruhollah Khomeini is sent into exile.
1967	Coronation ceremonies are held for Muhammad Reza Shah Pahlavi.

1971	Celebrations at Shiraz commemorate 2,500 years of Persian kingship.
1973	OPEC members quadruple the price of oil, vastly increasing revenues to the Iranian state; the shah uses much of this income to buy arms.
1978	Riots, demonstrations, and strikes commence in January and assume massive proportions by the end of the year.

1979

Jan.	The shah goes into exile.
Feb.	The Ayatollah Ruhollah Khomeini returns from exile. The army's Supreme Council orders troops to return to their garrisons and announces the army's neutrality in the political crisis.
April	After a nationwide referendum, the Ayatollah Ruhollah Khomeini proclaims the Islamic Republic of Iran.

Chapter 10

Turkey

Turkey is the only Middle Eastern country with territory in both Europe and Asia. A small segment, Istanbul and eastern Thrace, lies in Europe; and a much larger segment, called Anatolia or Asia Minor, is in Asia. Turkey is a member of several institutions centered in Europe: the North Atlantic Treaty Organization, the Organization of Economic Cooperation and Development, and the Council of Europe. It is an associate member of the European Economic Community and expects to become a full one after 1995. About 713,000 Turks live and work in western Europe, 526,000 in West Germany alone.[1]

The overwhelming portion of Turkish territory lies in Asia and forms a peninsula surrounded by the Black Sea, Sea of Marmara, Aegean Sea, and the Mediterranean Sea. It is bordered on the south by Syria and on the east by Iran and the Soviet Union. The Turks originated in the steppes of central Asia to the east of the Caspian Sea, and only in the eleventh century did they penetrate and settle Asia Minor, and in the fourteenth century cross over into Europe. They have been Muslims since the eighth century, and in times past were some of its most militant defenders. From 1923 to 1950 the Turkish government engaged in a program of vigorous secularism, but since 1950 this has been relaxed and the religious feelings, beliefs, and emotions of the Turkish people have come to

---

[1] *The Europa Year Book, 1978* (London: Europa Publications, 1978), p. 1,209.

the surface. In the United Nations, Turkey at times serves both on committees of Asian states and of European ones.

Turkey differs from other African and Asian states in that it became free of European economic, military, and political control in the decade after World War I. For most African and Asian states this was not the case until after World War II. Turkey has consequently had a twenty- to thirty-year head start over them in creating a sense of national identity, developing its economy, and building political structures which can maintain internal order, provide for the defense of the homeland, and allow for social transformation.

The founder of modern Turkey and the initiator of this extensive social and political change was Kemal Ataturk, who led Turkey from 1919 to 1938. Under his leadership the nation freed itself from the imperial control of the Western powers and divorced itself from its multinational Ottoman imperial past. It became a secular nation-state in which the Turkish language, history, and sense of peoplehood were paramount, and started developing its economy according to its own criteria of national needs. The other heroes and leaders of social change in the Middle East such as Gamal Abdel Nasser and David Ben Gurion did not come to power until after World War II.

The European and Asiatic, Western and Eastern, secular and Islamic characteristics of Turkey make it different from other Middle Eastern and Muslim countries. The start which it has had on social, economic, and political development and on the process of creating national consciousness and unity, also differentiate it. Turkey can be considered a less-developed European state and a more-developed Asian one.

GEOGRAPHY AND ECONOMY

Plateau, Rimland, and Highland

A quick glance at a topographic map of Turkey reveals three distinct regions: (1) the central plateau, (2) the coastal rimland, and (3) the eastern highlands.

Located between the Pontic Mountains in the north and the Taurus Mountains in the south, between a cluster of low mountains in the west and some high ones in the east, the plateau varies in height from 2,000 to 4,000 feet. For the most part it is bare and monotonous. Winters are cold, with freezing temperatures the norm, and many villages are snowed in for days on end. Summers are warm, and often hot, with temperatures above 90°F not uncommon. Between 10 and 17 inches of rain fall annually, enough to grow grain in some areas. There are extensive grasslands on which sheep and goats are grazed. Major cities in the plateau are Ankara, Sivas, Kayseri, and Konya.

The plateau is the heartland of Turkey. Beginning in the eleventh century, Turkish warrior-nomads from the east settled in it and intermarried with the

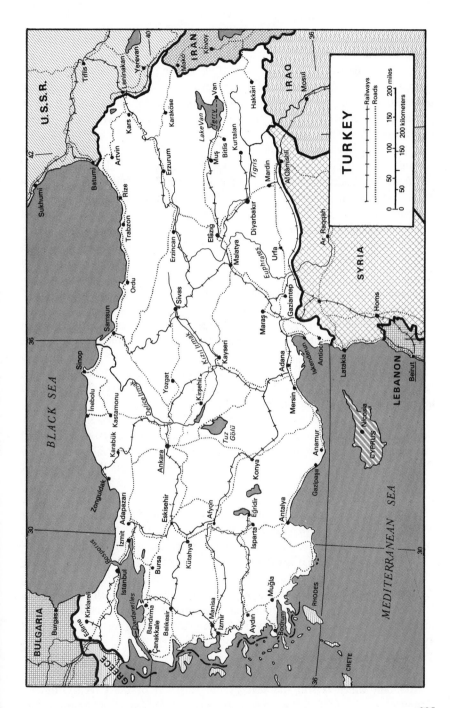

225

local people so that today there is no ethnic difference between the two groups. The plateau is poorer than the rimland, yet because grain can be grown there and livestock can be raised, it is self-supporting. In the past, overland trade routes from Europe to Mesopotamia and to central Asia passed through it, yet it remained isolated from the outside world, enabling the Turks living there to preserve their language and customs unadulterated by contact with other peoples and civilizations.

In 1923 the capital of Turkey was moved from Istanbul, a cosmopolitan city inhabited by a variety of people and heavily influenced by the Mediterranean world and the Balkans, to Ankara, at the time a small city located in the middle of the plateau and overwhelmingly Turkish in ethnic composition. Here in the heartland the new republic began its life free from the cosmopolitan influences which were so strong in Istanbul.

Surrounding the plateau on three sides is a coastal rimland which itself is composed of distinct regions. In the south is the Mediterranean area. It has a fertile soil and a warm climate and is ideal for growing citrus fruits and cotton. The land around the city of Adana in the southeast is flat and contains some of the country's best agricultural land.

The second region in the rimland is the Black Sea coast. It stretches from the Soviet border to near Istanbul. Rain falls year round and the winters are mild. Despite the narrow coastal plain, where in some places the mountains drop directly into the sea, this is a very productive agricultural area where hazelnuts, tea, tobacco, and corn are grown. It is also the region in which Turkey's steel industry is located, at Karabuk and Eregli.

The third part of the rimland is the section around the Aegean Sea and the Sea of Marmara. The European segment, Thrace, contains the cities of Istanbul and Edirne and is densely populated. About 25 inches of rain fall annually and the area is well suited to agriculture. The Asiatic portion, along the Aegean coast and the Sea of Marmara, has a fertile soil, rainy winters, and hot, dry summers. Farming is done in broad cultivated valleys, the most important of which are the Izmit Valley, the Bursa Plain, and the plain of Troy. Figs, grapes, and other warm-weather crops thrive here. The area is densely populated, especially around Bursa and Izmir. Rich chrome and tungsten deposits are also found there.

Characteristic of the entire rimland is an orientation toward the sea. Along the Aegean and Mediterranean coasts were the famous ancient cities of Troy, Antioch, and Tarsus, which were a part of the Mediterranean world in Greek and Roman times. In the coastal cities on the Aegean coast, especially in Izmir, hundreds of thousands of Greeks lived continuously from ancient times until 1923, when there was an exchange of populations between Greece and Turkey. Turks who had lived in Greece moved eastward across the Aegean, and Greeks who had lived in Turkey moved westward. A large Greek community remained in Istanbul, which is still the seat of the Patriarch of the Greek Orthodox Church. The Greeks felt that they were part of a civilization and culture that existed on both sides of the Aegean and did not feel a sense of kinship with the Turkish Muslims living next to them.

In Ottoman and modern Turkish history the plateau and rimland areas existed in a dialectical relation. Outside influences have been strongest in the coastal areas, and Turkish influences have been greatest on the plateau. Istanbul was the capital when Turkish territory stretched far north and south and included an incredible diversity of peoples and religions. Ankara has been the capital since Turkey turned away from Ottoman cosmopolitanism and opted for Turkish nationalism. The rimland has tended to be more productive and linked by trade with the outside world, while the plateau has been poorer yet self-supporting. Today the seat of government is in the plateau, but economic wealth is derived to a large degree from the rimland.

The third of the major geographic regions of Turkey is the eastern high-lands. Here many of the peaks rise above 10,000 feet, and the highest, Mount Ararat (Agri Dagi), is 16,946 feet high. The northeast is an extremely rugged region with high elevations, considerable precipitation, and a generally severe and cold climate. At Kars temperatures have been known to fall as low as –40°F. From the highest regions in the northeast to the lower ones in the southeast, the region is wild, sparsely inhabited, barren, and punctuated only by a few fertile river valleys. It is here that both the Tigris and the Euphrates rivers originate. Major cities are Erzincan, Erzurum, Elazig, Malatya, and Diyarbakir.

In the southeast live the Kurds, for the most part a nomadic people who graze their goats and sheep on high mountain slopes in summer and in lower regions in winter. They go where they need and ignore the international borders between Turkey and Iran, Iraq, and Syria. They have resisted the Turkish government's policy of encouraging minorities to leave or assimilate, and have continued to adhere to their distinctive language and culture. The government considers them to be Turks just like every one else and does not keep separate statistical records on them. Nevertheless their place in the Turkish nation-state is still an issue, and a call for autonomy for the Kurds has been raised in recent decades.

In summary the plateau is the heartland of the Turkish nation and the political center of the modern Turkish state; the rimland is the zone of industry and agriculture and contributes the most to the national economy; and the eastern highlands have been the homeland of the Kurds, who have fiercely pro-tected their own national identity and have refused total assimilation into the Turkish nation.

Ethnic Groups

Ninty-one percent of the people who live in Turkey speak Turkish as their primary language, live in accordance with Turkish customs, are at least nominally Muslim, and think of themselves as Turks. Around them the nation-state is formed. They are divided into two groups: The Anatolian Turks, who comprise about two-thirds of the Turkish population and who have been living in the borders of the present-day state for centuries, and the Balkan Turks, the other third, who emigrated from Rumania, Bulgaria, Yugoslavia, and Greece to present-day Turkey after World War I. Kemal Ataturk looked upon the Anatolian Turks, especially those who lived on the plateau, as the "real Turks," declaring that the future of the republic rested upon their shoulders. He romanticized and glorified their vigor, bravery, pure Turkish speech, and direct connection with the Turkish culture which originated in central Asia.

The Balkan Turks are the descendants of settlers in the European Ottoman domains. With the demise of the Ottoman Empire after World War I and the rise of new nation-states in the Balkans, these people found themselves unwanted, and many immigrated over the next two decades to Turkey. Since they had originally been chosen to go to the new lands of the Ottoman Empire because of their special skill in agriculture, the crafts, and the military arts, they looked upon themselves as an elite. After repatriation to Turkey they have become literate faster, been more willing to work in new industries, and have adapted to the modern society more readily than their Anatolian cousins. They hold leadership positions in the civil administration, political parties, the army, and the economy. They have intermarried with local people, and in time the distinction between Anatolian and Balkan Turk will disappear.

About 6 percent of the total Turkish population is Kurdish. Living mostly in the Zagros chain of mountains that run in an arc through Turkey, Iraq, and Iran, the Kurds number altogether about three million. It is estimated that about half of these people live in Turkey. They are mostly nomads, but increasingly are becoming settled as farmers and city dwellers, with many going to schools and universities and learning Turkish. A modern middle class is emerging, and it has established a Kurdish press and literature. In 1925 there was a Kurdish rebellion which Kemal Ataturk crushed, but since then there have been no uprisings. The government has encouraged them to assimilate, though most maintain some separate identity.

Smaller minority groups, numbering 1 percent of the population or less, are the Arabs, Armenians, Greeks, and Jews. The Arabs live in the provinces bordering Syria, where they are farmers, shopkeepers, and businessmen. The Armenians today are almost exclusively residents of Istanbul, where they maintain their language, Christian religion, customs, and historical consciousness through their own schools, newspapers, communal organizations, and the Armenian Orthodox (Gregorian) Church. Because of persecutions in the past, many do not feel a sense of loyalty to the Turkish state. Rather they identify with Armenians throughout the world. They have a high level of literacy, are usually fluent in two or more languages, and are hard-working. Because of these qualities they have prospered as merchants and bankers.

The Greeks are a remnant of the once-large population that lived in Thrace and along the Aegean coast. Today they are almost exclusively in Istanbul, formerly Constantinople, a city which in many ways they still consider to be rightfully theirs. They are the wealthiest minority in the city, play a leading role in banking and commerce, and publish two Greek newspapers. Their loyalty to Turkey is ambiguous, and when Greece and Turkey are involved in a dispute, such as the one over Cyprus, they usually keep quiet.

The Jews also are concentrated in Istanbul. Most are Sephardim, descendants of refugees from Spain expelled in 1492. They own small businesses and shops, and some are prominent in the intellectual community. Immediately after the establishment of the state of Israel in 1948, thousands migrated to that country, but by the 1970s this had tapered off and the Turkish Jewish community has stabilized at about 30,000 members.

Land Area and Population

Comprising 301,380 square miles of territory, Turkey is fourth in the Middle East in land area, after Saudi Arabia (829,995 square miles), Iran (636,296), and Egypt (386 661). It is still a big country by world standards, three times larger than the United Kingdom and two and a half times the size of Italy. Its population in 1978 was estimated at 43.120 million, making it the most populous state in the Middle East.

Cities

Istanbul, the capital of Turkey prior to 1923, contains many mosques, palaces, public buildings, and monuments that recall the Ottoman era. It is the country's largest city, with a population, according to the 1975 census, of 2,547,364 (excluding suburbs). Situated on both sides of the Bosporus and linked by a giant suspension bridge, it is a center of commerce, shipping, industry, the arts, and education. Located at one of the most important crossroads in the world, it has been cosmopolitan and outward-looking, but since World War II there has been a massive migration to it of people from the villages and towns of Anatolia, and the population has become more homogeneous—Turkish and Turkey-oriented, rather than Mediterranean- or Balkan-oriented.

Ankara, Turkey's second largest city, is situated in the middle of the Anatolian plateau. Since being designated the capital of the country in 1923, it has grown by leaps and bounds. In 1975 its population was 1,701,004. It was chosen by Kemal Ataturk as the Turkish capital because it was in the Turkish heartland away from the coast, where the European powers could exercise control through "gunboat diplomacy," and was distant from the seat of government of the Ottoman sultan against whom Ataturk was revolting. Ankara is a center of administration, commerce, culture, and education. While Istanbul symbolizes the Turkey of the empire, Ankara represents the Turkey of the republic. The difference is evident in the buildings and urban design of the two cities: Istanbul has twisting narrow streets; quaint, covered arcades; and many large and sumptuous mosques; but Ankara has broad avenues; stark, modern buildings; and a noticeable absence of mosques.

The third largest Turkish city is Izmir, a port on the Aegean Sea and the second most important in the country after Istanbul. Excluding the suburbs, its population according to the 1975 census was 636,834. In addition to being a transshipment center, it has a number of factories which process agricultural products from the fertile region in which it lies, and manufacture paper, metal goods, dyes, and textiles.

Another important city, and Turkey's fourth largest, is Adana (1975 population, 475,384), which lies in the large, fertile Cukurova Plain in the south center where the coast makes a ninety-degree turn. It processes and markets agricultural goods, principally cotton.

Cities as the "Center" of Turkish Society and Politics

Istanbul, Ankara, and to a lesser extent Izmir, have dominated Turkish political life. They have been the primary meeting grounds of those individuals whose words and actions have determined national policy, and they have been the dwelling place of the Turkish elite or what has also been called the "center" of Turkish politics.[2]

In Ottoman times society was divided into two classes: the *askeri,* the top civil, religious, and military leaders, and the *reaya,* Muslim and non-Muslim subjects who paid taxes and had no part in the government. *Askeri* meant literally the "military," and *reaya*, the "herd." The sultan and the *askeri* were responsible for maintaining the divinely-ordained hierarchical social order in which everyone had a place and function. They were the political "ins," and their center was the capital city of Istanbul.

At the very end of the eighteenth century and throughout the nineteenth, some sultans and members of the *askeri* introduced into Turkey Western military technology, administrative practices, legal codes, and schools. These were opposed by other people at the "center," but the modernizers won, and by the end of the century the top military and bureaucratic officials were almost all in the camp that advocated change. Istanbul, the "center" of the empire, became identified with modernism, secularism, and reform.

Upper-class persons at the "center" went to Western schools and universities, dressed in the Western manner, and tried to live according to the life style of the European upper class. They emulated Europe, and considered the peasants in their own society uncivilized. The gulf that had always existed between the *askeri* and the *reaya* had become a chasm.

---

[2] Ergun Özbudun, *Social Change and Political Participation in Turkey* (Princeton: Princeton University Press, 1976), pp. 25-59.

Kemal Ataturk, who became the leader of Turkey in the 1920s, continued this modernizing and secularizing trend. He, a general in the army, and his close associates came from the class of officials that had controlled the empire from Istanbul. They increased the power of the "center" in Turkish politics and expanded the reforms started in the nineteenth century. To them the peasants and the lower-class urban dwellers were people who needed to be educated and brought into "civilization." They preached and exhorted them to change into the "new Turk."

Ankara, Istanbul, and Izmir have been the dwelling places of the educated, Westernized, and secular persons who have controlled Turkish politics in the nineteenth and twentieth centuries. These are the places where modern Turkey first came into being, and from them modernity has spread to the smaller cities, towns, and villages.

Villages

Numbering over 30,000, scattered across a large and geographically diverse country, experiencing different rates and kinds of change, the villages of Turkey vary in their social structure, means of earning a living, and customs.

In the villages of the plateau the grazing of sheep and goats and the growing of grains constitute the typical means of livelihood. The family is the primary element of the society, with its members together plowing, planting, harvesting, and tending the livestock. In times of economic want, natural disasters, sickness, and death, they support each other, and when there are disputes or feuds with other villages, commonly over land and grazing rights, all join together in the common defense.

Villages in eastern Thrace and along the coast of the Black, Aegean, and the Mediterranean seas were, in ancient times, a part of the civilization of the Mediterranean world. Since the late nineteenth century, they have been heavily influenced by modern cultural and social patterns that have emanated from the big Turkish cities and from Europe. They are the most modern of Turkey's villages, and in them commercial farming and small-scale industries are common. They are usually connected by roads to larger towns and cities, with which they are economically interdependent. The family is still strong in these villages, but is not as dominant or all-inclusive as in the plateau. The commercial nature of these villages has resulted in the substitution for family relations of nonkinship roles such as employer and employee, buyer and seller, landlord and tenant.

In the southeast, villages show the heritage of nomadic life. The governments of the empire and of the republic have encouraged the nomads in this region to settle and become farmers. When this takes place the hierarchy of the tribal group usually continues. Those who were vassals as nomads remain so as tenant farmers, and those families which provided the hereditary chiefs continue to hold the positions of wealth, prestige, and power as large landowners. These villagers identify only nominally with the Turkish state and prefer to settle their internal disputes without the aid or intervention of government officials.

Villages as the "Periphery" of Turkish Society and Politics

While Istanbul, Ankara, and to a lesser extent Izmir have been the "center" of Turkish society and politics, the thousands of villages and towns have been the "periphery."[3]

Until fairly recently the people who lived in them have been overwhelmingly illiterate, and if they had any education, it was only in the Koran and related subjects. Villagers were taxed and conscripted but never allowed to have a voice in the making of major government policy. The modernizers at the "center" of the Ottoman Empire and of the Turkish Republic felt that they had a mission to educate and inform the villagers so they could enter the modern world. Protests, objections, and sullenness were categorized as "reaction."

Since World War II Turkish society has undergone very significant transformation, and the villages are no longer out of touch or out of step with the modern world. The Turkish economy is now above the "underdeveloped" level, though it has not yet reached the "developed" stage. Hundreds of thousands of villagers have migrated to the towns near their villages and from there to the big cities, where they can make more money in new businesses and industries. Others have gone to work temporarily in western Europe, returning with skills learned in an industrial society, a small nest egg, and the desire to live a better life. The construction of highways, which began on a significant scale in the 1950s, is ending the isolation of many villages. Radios are now a common possession, and they link the villager with the national culture which emanates from the cities. Regular television broadcasting began in 1968 in Ankara, and since then has been expanded to other large cities and provincial capitals. Finally, more and more villages are switching from a self-sufficient subsistence to a cash-crop market economy, which brings them greater prosperity and integrates them into the national economy. The "periphery" in Turkish society has changed and is no longer a dependent, passive, malleable group.

These social changes have been reflected in the changing programs and platforms of Turkey's two principal parties. The Democratic Party (DP), which governed from 1950 to 1960, drew its strength from the more prosperous villages and towns of western Turkey. Its policies appealed to the recently modernized people living in them. It respected the Islamic religion while still adhering to the official state policy of secularism. It built mosques with government funds and opened schools to train prayer leaders and preachers. It also advocated a somewhat free enterprise economic policy that benefited the new class of modern farmers and small businessmen.

The party founded by Ataturk, the Republican People's Party (RPP),

---

[3] In what follows, I have summarized the thesis of the rest of Özbudun's book, *Social Change*.

governed from 1923 to 1950, and was treated with deference and respect by villagers, especially in eastern Turkey. Realizing that Turkish society was changing and that it could no longer depend upon traditional obeisance for those in authority as a base of support, the RPP in 1965 adopted a left-of-center program that stressed economic and social issues. It is now attempting to attract the more advanced villagers and the urban industrial workers, social groups that are growing in size.

Both parties have come to realize that Turkish society is no longer merely composed of a small, educated, Westernized military-bureaucratic elite at the "center" and an enormous, uneducated, traditional mass at the "periphery." New elites and social classes have arisen, and the two principal parties have responded with innovative electoral tactics and programs. Turkish politics now resembles that of developed nations, where class and economic issues are emphasized.

Natural Resources

A variety of soils and climates makes possible the cultivation of a wide assortment of crops in Turkey. More than thirty rivers, each at least one hundred miles long, have the potential to be dammed and used for irrigation and the generation of electricity. In the eastern mountains and along the Black Sea coast are extensive forests.

In the past Turkey has been one of the world's major producers of chrome, but by the mid-1970s the supply of the ore was nearly exhausted. The mining of copper began in the 1930s and continues today. Iron ore, coal, and lignite are found in sufficient quantities that Turkey can support its own steel manufacturing complex. The weak spot in the country's list of natural resources is petroleum; Turkey has only small scattered fields which do not produce enough to satisfy the local market.

Wheat and barley are grown on the plateau where the summers are hot and the rainfall low yet sufficient for these crops. Sugar beets are raised over large areas, chiefly away from the coast. Cotton, the most important agricultural export, is concentrated in the Aegean and Mediterranean coastal regions. Tobacco, the second most important agricultural export, is grown in the Aegean region. Hazelnuts, the third most important agricultural export, are produced in the provinces fronting on the Black Sea. Olives, citrus fruits, figs, and grapes are also grown in significant quantities.

Economy

Although the Turkish economy is still characterized as underdeveloped, it is rapidly advancing toward that of a developed nation. Government policy aims to achieve by the mid-1990s the standard of living prevalent in Italy in 1973.[4]

[4] International Bank for Reconstruction and Development, *Turkey: Prospects and Problems of an Expanding Economy* (Washington, D.C.: World Bank, 1975), p. 24.

Since the beginning of the Turkish republic in 1923, economic development has been stressed. Kemal Ataturk established *devletçilik* (usually translated as étatism, "state socialism") as the economic policy of the country. In a manifesto issued in 1931, he said that private enterprise was useful and necessary for the economic health of the nation but that "it is one of our main principles to interest the State actively in matters where the general and vital interests of the nation are in question, especially in the economic field, in order to lead the nation and the country to prosperity in as short a time as possible."[5]

Ataturk and his associates pointed out that they were not socialists. They emphasized national unity, not class struggle, and said that they had no intention of collectivizing agriculture or of eliminating private enterprise in industry and commerce.

In 1934 the first five-year plan was instituted. Inspired by Russian precedent and helped by loans and advice from the Russians—Turkey at this time was wary of Western advice and assistance for fear that it might lead to domination— its aim was the simultaneous development of consumer (textiles, paper, glass, ceramics) and heavy (iron, steel, chemicals) industries.[6] World War II prevented the commencement of a second five-year plan. A new series was not begun until 1963. Its objective is to raise the Turkish standard of living to the level of some of the member nations of the European Economic Community in order that Turkey may join it in about 1995. Policy has been for the state to invest in projects that are capital-intensive, require advanced technology, are necessary for national defense, and benefit economically-depressed regions.

The public and private sphere contribute about evenly to the gross national product. Forests are protected and exploited exclusively by the state, and telephone, telegraph, railways, airports, and most shipping lines are government enterprises. The greater part of the banking system is under direct government control, and almost the entire output of steel, refined petroleum, paper, petrochemicals, and fertilizers is produced in state enterprises. Mining is heavily dominated by government companies. Private enterprise prevails in agriculture, small-scale manufacturing, construction, and wholesale and retail trade.

While the public enterprises have been the primary stimulus to Turkey's rapid economic growth over the past four decades, they have not been without their inefficiencies. In the late 1960s and early 1970s they had deficits as a group. These enterprises have lacked good management, efficient planning, and coordination with each other and private-sector industries. Prices of their products have been set by the government more on the basis of political than economic criteria. Many have had real freedom from state control, but have expected the government to cover their losses. Because the state enterprises contributed to about half of the gross national product, their inefficiency and

---

[5] Bernard Lewis, *The Emergence of Modern Turkey* (London: Oxford University Press, 1961), p. 280.
[6] Ibid., p. 281.

uncoordinated decision making have had widespread ramifications in the economy.[7]

Since 1970 inflation has been one of Turkey's most severe economic problems. Between 1970 and 1974, the annual rise in consumer prices ranged between a low of 12 percent and a high of 22 percent. In 1977 it was 40 percent, and in 1978 60 percent. Turkey thus has one of the highest inflation rates among the Western industrialized nations.[8] Caused by increased public expenditures, rapidly rising remittances from Turks working temporarily in Germany and other European countries, greater costs of imported goods, increased income in the world market for Turkish exports, higher state-guaranteed prices to farmers, and salary raises for civil servants, the government has been caught in a familiar predicament: if it pushes anti-inflationary policies too much, growth will be slowed; if it does not do enough, inflation will continue unabated.

A long-term economic problem is unemployment. Both in rural and urban areas it is acute and often hidden. Shantytowns are a part of every Turkish city, and unemployed people loitering on street corners and in shops are a common sight. With the continued rapid population growth, this problem is unlikely to be alleviated unless the development policies of the government can produce jobs in greater quantity than the number of people entering the labor market.[9]

POLITICAL CULTURE

Nationalism

A sentiment shared by almost all of the people living in Turkey is nationalism. This is a somewhat new feeling, for prior to the time of Ataturk, Turks were the leaders of the multinational Ottoman Empire and protectors and defenders of the Islamic religion. Ataturk largely succeeded in having them shift their loyalties to the Turkish nation.

The Turks originated in central Asia. As early as the ninth century, under different leaders and in different tribal groups, they started to migrate westward, adopting the faith of Islam and serving different Muslim rulers as elite soldiers. In 1071 a Turkish army under the leadership of Alp Arslan of the Seljuq dynasty defeated the Christian Byzantines at the battle of Manzikert (Malazgirt) north of Lake Van in the eastern part of present-day Turkey. This victory opened the door of Anatolia to the Turks, and they quickly moved across the plateau, settling in it and intermarrying with the local people. They squeezed Byzantium

[7]U.S. Government, *Area Handbook for the Republic of Turkey*, 2nd ed. (Washington, D.C.: U.S. Government Printing Office, 1973), pp. 263-4.

[8]Organization for Economic Co-operation and Development, *OECD Economic Surveys: Turkey* (Paris: OECD, 1974), pp. 43-5.

[9]Ibid., p. 50.

into a small area surrounding Constantinople, and in 1453 wiped the Christian empire off the map through the conquest of the capital city, which they renamed Istanbul.

Under the leadership of the Ottoman dynasty of sultans, the Turks forged an empire which at its height in the sixteenth century stretched from Hungary in the north to the Arabian Peninsula (except for Yemen) in the south, and from the borders of Persia in the east to Algeria in the West, it was composed of peoples of diverse races, nationalities, and religions.

Ataturk caused his people to turn their attention away from this empire, which they had been losing piece by piece from the late seventeenth century onward, to the Turkish nation centered in the Anatolian plateau. He caused them to realize that the imperial glories of the past were gone forever, and that they should focus on the defense of the Turkish heartland. Since Turkey was on the losing side in World War I, the victorious allies attempted to disember it and sanctioned a Greek invasion of Turkey's Aegean region. From 1919 to 1923, Ataturk rallied Turks from the interior in the defense of the fatherland. Under his leadership they defeated the Greek armies and negotiated the Lausanne peace treaty with the allies that respected Turkey's territorial integrity and sovereignty.

Today the Turkish people display strong nationalist attitudes and beliefs. Nationalism is the foundation of the republic, a basic tenet in the program of all political parties, and the supreme force dominating all activities in the society.[10] When young people in secondary schools are asked, "As a parent, what two specific things will you try hardest to teach your children?" answers such as "love of country" and "usefulness to the nation" are frequently given.[11]

Nationalist feeling, which prior to World War I was a sentiment experienced only among small groups of intellectuals, is today common to all social classes from the highly educated to the illiterate. It is a fundamental principle of the state and is described lyrically and with feeling in the constitution.

Secularism and Religion

Since the 1930s one of the fundamental principles of the Turkish republic has been secularism. It has been promoted by the Republican People's Party, the party of Ataturk, and is a basic characteristic of the state according to the constitution (1961). The model many Turks desire to emulate is that of some European states where politics is conducted without reference to religion.

While secularism has been the official policy of the state and of the RPP, religion has been strong among the common people, especially in the villages and

[10] Kemal Karpat, *Turkey's Politics: The Transition to a Multi-Party System* (Princeton: Princeton University Press, 1959), p. 251.

[11] Andreas M. Kazamias, *Education and the Quest for Modernity in Turkey* (London: George Allen & Unwin, 1966), pp. 222-23.

towns. This is one area in Turkish society where the "center-periphery" conflict has been strongest. Generally the secularists have come from the big cities and the centers of authority, and the religious people from the towns and villages. The public school system, the training which most Turkish men receive in the army, the laws of the state, and the police authority have been used by the "center" to propagate its viewpoint, one that the "periphery" has resisted. The secularists have not totally won out, and the believers have not been completely successful in resisting the inroads of secularism; each realizes now that it must respect the viewpoints and feelings of the other.

During the 1920s and 1930s Ataturk tried to alter the religious basis of society and the state. He abolished the caliphate, the office of *seyhülislam* (a high religious position), and the system of religious endowments and foundations (*vakf* in Turkish, *waqf* in Arabic). He switched from the Islamic to the Western calendar, established Sunday as the day of rest, and decreed that Turkish should be written in the Latin rather than the Arabic script. The Sharia was replaced by Turkish adaptations of European legal codes, and the veil for women and the fez for men were banned. Religious schools and sufi fraternal associations were outlawed. The Directorate of Religious Affairs was organized within the office of the prime minister, and given charge of the appointment and certification of religious leaders. It was staffed by civil servants, mostly secularists who in no sense considered themselves to be "spiritual leaders" of the Turkish people.

The Ataturk reforms did not involve a separation of church and state as in the West, but rather a government takeover of religious institutions and an attempt to reduce drastically the influence of religion on the minds of the people. Ataturk and his associates feared its influence, and were convinced that it should be militantly opposed. They believed it fostered superstition, inhibited change, and was incompatible with the modern world. Because Islam is a universal faith encompassing peoples of many nationalities, they felt that it detracted from Turkish nationalism, leading people to look beyond the nation to the world-wide community of Muslims. Since the call to prayer, ritual prayers, and holy scriptures (the Koran) were all spoken or written in Arabic, they feared the influence of Arabic civilization on Turkish culture.

After World War II the government started to relax its antireligious policies. In 1949, under the leadership of the Republican People's Party, the Turkish parliament passed legislation allowing for the establishment of schools to train imams (leaders of prayer in the mosque) and the establishment of a Faculty of Divinity at the University of Ankara. In a free election in 1950, the RPP was defeated by the Democratic Party, and one of the factors leading to its defeat was its harsh secularism.

Under the Democratic Party's leadership from 1950 to 1960, money was provided by the government for the construction of mosques, permission was granted for the call to prayer to be said in Arabic, religious instruction in the public primary schools was introduced on an optional basis, and sufi fraternal associations were allowed once more to function in public. Adult education courses on the Koran, some organized and financed by the Directorate of Religious Affairs, some sponsored and paid for by local initiative and voluntary contributions, were permitted to be offered.

Turks are divided over the social role of religion. Towns and villages are frequently split between a camp led by the public school teachers, graduates of teachers' colleges and universities, usually secularist and often Marxist, and one led by the muftis (interpreters of the Koran and the Sharia) and imams, who usually have only a primary education plus some religious training. The teachers more often than not grew up in a city, and the muftis and imams in a town or village. Each side feels that it is engaged in a struggle for the minds of the young and looks upon the other as the enemy. The teachers are convinced they are propagating science and knowledge and are fighting ignorance and superstition, and the religious leaders feel that they are defending divine revelation and opposing immorality and everything that threatens the way of life of the Turkish folk. It is also a struggle over who is to control the lives of the common people: the state centered in Ankara, of which the teachers are instruments, or the family and local leaders in the thousands of Turkish towns and villages.[12]

After about fifty years of official secularism, religious sentiment remains more widespread than the Kemalist reformers would have hoped or believed. Observers have spoken of the reemergence of Islam in Turkey, yet it never really disappeared. During the Republican period (1923-1950) it concealed itself to avoid official disapproval, but during the Democratic period and thereafter, given a more tolerant atmosphere, it has emerged once again. Permeating all of this is a modernization process—employment of Turks in European cities, movement from villages to towns and cities, industrialization—which increasingly attenuates the role of religion in society.[13]

Ataturkism

The founder of the contemporary Turkish nation-state, Kemal Ataturk, is continuously praised and glorified by his compatriots. His mausoleum in Ankara is a point of pilgrimage for people from all over the country, and his speeches, pronouncements, and random comments have assumed the aura of absolute truth. They are studied and commented upon with religious zeal. Except for extreme leftists who adhere to international sociialism, and extreme rightists

[12] See Arnold Leder, *Catalysts of Change: Marxist versus Muslim in a Turkish Community* (Austin, Tex.: University of Texas, Center for Middle Eastern Studies, Middle East Monographs, No. 1, 1976); Paul J. Magnarella, *Tradition and Change in a Turkish Town* (New York: John Wiley & Sons, Inc., 1974); and Binnaz Sayari, "Religion and Political Development in Turkey," (unpublished Ph.D. dissertation, City University of New York, 1976).

[13] Magnarella, *Tradition*, pp. 175-76.

who feel that they belong primarily to the universal community of Muslims, Turks accept the policies and programs of Ataturk as the guiding principles for their state and society.

Called Ataturkism in Turkey and Kemalism in the West, its meaning, significance, and purpose are argued about in newspapers, magazines, books, symposia, classrooms, mosques, and coffeehouses. In June 1971 a Special Commission on the Principles of Ataturk was created; its purpose was to perpetuate the image of Ataturk and spread Ataturkism.[14] The military officers who carried out the coup of 1960 and the "coup by memorandum" of March 12, 1971, justified their intervention in politics by saying that the government in power had deviated from Ataturk's principles.

Almost everyone in Turkey is in favor of Ataturkism, but as is typical of belief systems that enjoy such widespread support, it defies definition. It is about as vague and fundamental in Turkey as the "American system of free enterprise" or the "American way of life" in the United States. The real deviants and extremists in Turkish politics are those persons and groups that reject Ataturkism.

Ataturk was an officer in the Imperial Ottoman Army who led a number of Turkish troops at the Battle of Gallipoli (a town on the Dardanelles) in 1915. Under his leadership a British army that had as its objective the conquest of Istanbul was defeated. From 1919 to 1923 Ataturk led the Turkish people in a national liberation struggle to free the country from the humiliating Treaty of Sèvres imposed upon it by the victorious allied powers of World War I, and from a Greek invasion trying to restore a Greek empire on both sides of the Aegean. From 1923 until his death in 1938, he carried out a series of wide-ranging reforms that fundamentally changed the character of the Turkish state and had ramifications throughout its society.

The closest one comes to a formulation of the principles of Ataturkism is the famous "six arrows" (republicanism, nationalism, populism, étatism, secularism, and reformism) incorporated into the program of the Republican People's Party at its Fourth Congress in 1935 and made a part of the 1961 constitution.

Republicanism means that Turkey is no longer an empire, nor is it led by a hereditary ruler. Ataturk stressed the fact that the people were sovereign in the new Turkey, and that the republic was established as a result of the people's efforts, existing only for their good and not for the glory of any individual, group, or dynasty.[15]

Nationalism is probably the most powerful and dominant of the principles of Ataturkism. Kemal Ataturk repeatedly called upon his people to be vigilant

[14]Metin Tamkoc, "Stable Instability of the Turkish Polity," *Middle East Journal,* 27 (Summer 1973), 335, note 17.

[15]Suna Kili, *Kemalism* (Istanbul: Robert College, School of Business Administration and Economics, 1969), pp. 80-1.

in the defense of the fatherland. He evoked the memories of the historic battles of the Turks in premodern times, and reminded them of their heroism in the war of independence between 1919 and 1922.

Ataturk was against the cosmopolitanism of the Ottoman Empire, a political unit that was composed of peoples of diverse nationalities. He felt that the day of empires was gone and that of nations had arrived.[16] He wanted the Turkish people to live by themselves in a Turkish nation-state.

There are many controversies over what Ataturk really meant by populism, the third of the six arrows. One meaning is clearly the previously-mentioned idea that the state is based on the people. He also meant by it a Turkish people united regardless of social class. He vehemently rejected the Marxist concept that mankind is divided into warring social classes, and he even went so far as to argue that in Turkey there were no such classes. He believed that the reason for the Turkish victory in the war of independence was the united action of all the people. In particular he praised the simple peasants, whom he said contributed the most to this struggle.

Ataturk was in favor of the masses, but he believed that in order for their standard of living to be improved and their political capabilities to be developed, they needed to be led from above by a modern elite. In his time the peasants had not yet reached political consciousness and were not pressing for change, so the elite had to shake them out of their centuries-long traditional lethargy.

Today a major source of disagreement among Turkish politicians and writers is over the condition of the Turkish masses (the people) and whether political power and responsibility can be placed in their hands. Generally the RPP and persons on the political spectrum from center to left believe that the people are either exploited and need to be made aware of their exploitation, or that they are backward and need to be brought into the modern world. Ataturkism is sufficiently flexible to enable them to argue from it that the social order needs to be radically changed in order to improve the "status of the masses."[17] They believe in a centralized government and leadership from the top. The Justice Party (the successor of the Democratic Party) and persons from the center to the right are not so condemnatory of the condition and traditions of the people, and stress that in the fifty years since the foundation of the republic a lot of change has taken place. They favor a greater dispersal of power, with more authority resting in local governments, and are less committed to "radical social change" carried out in the name of the masses from the top.

The fourth principle of Ataturkism, étatism, mainly concerns economics. Kemal Ataturk was not enamored with either communism or capitalism. The former he rejected because of its class emphasis, and the latter he distrusted

[16] Ibid., pp. 81-5.
[17] Ibid., p. 93.

because of its association with imperialism in the Ottoman Empire. In a speech to the Grand National Assembly (the Turkish parliament) on December 1, 1921, he said, "We are a people who are convinced of the necessity of conducting our national struggle against an imperialism which wanted to destroy all of us . . . and against a capitalism which aimed to swallow us all."[18] His reference here was to the foreign capitalists who controlled many economic enterprises in Turkey prior to World War I. Ataturk wanted to free Turkey from their influence and make it economically strong without them. Therefore, under the policy of étatism, numerous Turkish state enterprises were established, especially in basic industries such as mining and steel.

Ataturk's economic views were related to his sense of nationalism. He wanted Turkey to be a strong nation-state, and that meant being strong economically. His bias was basically against foreign capitalists, not Turkish ones. The latter were tolerated so long as they accepted state direction of the economy with its emphasis on growth.

Secularism is the fifth of the six arrows, but since it has already been dealt with earlier in this chapter, the sixth, reformism, will be discussed. Ataturk abolished the Caliphate and Sultanate, abandoned the empire, adopted the nation-state, and changed from the Arabic to the Latin script, to mention only a few of his reforms. His changes have been called the greatest since the Turks converted to Islam, but these were largely limited to the state and government and had only a minimal effect on the way of life of the average Turk in the thousands of villages and towns.

Today in Turkey people argue about the meaning of the reformist principles of Ataturk. Some say that he did not go far enough, that Turkish society was little affected by what he did and that a radical transformation is needed. Others say that what he did was sufficient. Both claim to be "true Ataturkists." Those urging a continuation of the Ataturk revolution want to make up for the years of regression which they believe set in shortly after his death. "They emphasize the necessity of radical educational, cultural and socio-economic reforms which will bring about complete modernization" and "realize social and economic equality between all classes in Turkish society."[19] Since Ataturk instituted significant change, they argue that what they propose is not radical in the light of what he did.

The most significant aspect of Ataturkism is that it forms the basis of debate for the broad center of Turkish politics. Persons to the left and to the right of center argue about its meaning. That they can come to different conclusions about its interpretation simply illustrates its hold on the Turkish people. This is well illustrated in the excerpts that follow from two editorials in small-

[18]Ibid., pp. 94-5.
[19]Ibid., p. 110.

town newspapers, the first moderate, the second leftist, both on the "meaning of Ataturkism":

> Ataturk wanted to make Turkey a Western nation. . . . He was not against religion, but against religious exploitation. . . . An Ataturkist is bound by and loyal to the nation's customs, traditions, and religion. All true Ataturkists, regardless of your party affiliation, let us join together for a great Turkey.

> Ataturk did not want religion and the State to be tied together. He knew that religion was being used to exploit the people. . . . In the hands of the exploiters Islam has become a religion of superstition and myth. It was from this superstition and myth that he wanted to free the people. Did the people want the anticlerical reforms that Ataturk carried out? The answer is, "No!" But he still carried them out in the name of the national will, because he knew what was good for the people. A true Ataturkist is a secularist.[20]

POLITICAL GROUPS

The Army

Throughout their history the Turks have had a strong military tradition. From the ninth through the thirteenth centuries, they served the Abbasid caliphs in Baghdad as elite mercenary soldiers. In the eleventh century they produced a dynasty of their own, the Seljuqs, which from 1037 to 1092 ruled a sizable empire in western Asia. From the fourteenth through the twentieth centuries under the Ottoman dynasty they completed the conquest of Anatolia which the Seljuqs had begun, and expanded the domain of Islam into Europe. After the reign of Suleiman the Magnificent (1520-1566), the military power of the Turkish empire began a slow, steady decline, and the reputation of the Turks for bravery and military prowess was not restored until the twentieth century.

Led by ghazis and sultans in the past, the tradition of military leadership has continued into this century. The greatest figure in twentieth-century Turkish history is Kemal Ataturk. His successor in that office from 1938 to 1950 was Ismet Inonu, a close associate and also an army officer. Since 1950 the presidency of Turkey has continued to be held by military officers with one exception, Celal Bayar (1950-1960), who never served in the regular armed forces but did lead resistance forces in the War of Independence.

A deference towards military and civilian authority is deep-seated, and has been called the "most enduring feature of the Turkish statecraft."[21] Family,

[20]Magnarella, *Tradition,* p. 143.

[21]Tamkoc, "Stable Instability," p. 333.

school, party, and government all teach quietism, acquiescence, and obedience to the will of the powerful. The government is often referred to as *hukumet baba* ("father government").[22]

Because the Turks have frequently been engaged in combat against the peoples with whom they have come in contact, their leaders have considered foreign and military affairs to be primary. Ataturk's first concern was to rescue Turkey from the dismemberment and subjugation which were threatened after World War I, an effort in which he succeeded. He wanted to modernize Turkey so that it could stand by itself in a world of powerful industrial states. Since 1948 Turkey has held a critical position in the American-led Western defense system, guarding the southern flank of NATO against potential attack from the Soviet Union. Until the 1960s few political, journalistic, or intellectual leaders argued against the preoccupation of Turkish officials with foreign and military affairs, but since then many have said that because of it Turkey has become subordinate to the United States, and that the latter has come to meddle in Turkish internal affairs and prevent radical social change.

Service in the officer corps of the armed forces has always been a position of high status. In the Ottoman Empire the three most noble careers were the army, the civil service, and the higher clergy. Ataturk eliminated the prestigious religious positions, but he continued the tradition of power, life-time security, and generous pay for the corps of military officers and civil servants.

In the mid-1950s the Democratic government gave priority to business and agricultural interests and allowed inflation to continue, eroding the standard of living of military officers and civil servants on fixed salaries. Junior officers in particular felt the humiliation of having to scrimp and of being slighted in public places. However, after the coup of 1960, pay and fringe benefits increased rapidly, and military officers could once again live in comfort and enjoy the respect of other members of society.

An army career is one of the few ways by which a person from the lower middle class can rise to the top. Business has not been highly regarded as a career, and only in the Democratic era from 1950 to 1960 did business leaders have any influence on the government. The top ranks of the civil service have usually been closed to persons from the lower middle class because most villages and towns do not have the secondary schools that feed into the universities. Only the military has a system of schools which provide both lower and higher education and offer free tuition, board, room, clothing, and other basic needs, enabling poor boys from villages to attend them.

In a hierarchy of goals, most army officers put security from foreign attack first, internal order second, modernization third, and democracy fourth. A slogan coined by Ataturk and frequently repeated, "peace at home and peace in the world," succinctly states the first two goals. Modernization is third,

---

[22] Ibid., p. 334.

because it is necessary for a strong army and state. Democracy comes after these and earns qualified support.

When the Republican People's Party ruled from 1923 to 1950, there was a close relation between the army and both the RPP and the government. Ataturk and Inonu, victorious military commanders in the War of Independence (1919-1922), successively held the top positions in the state and the dominant political party. During his time in office, Ataturk was president of the republic and chairman of the RPP. Inonu followed him in both of these offices, holding the former from 1938 to 1950 and the latter from 1938 to 1972. Each urged upon the military officer corps a strict noninvolvement in politics and insisted that an officer resign his commission before running for elected office.

During that time, the armed forces trusted the civilian leadership because it was composed in large part of ex-soldiers. The top leadership of the state and of the armed forces had been born and bred in one of Turkey's larger cities, had gone to the same military academies and officer schools, shared common experiences from the War of Independence, and in military matters employed the tactics and strategy of the era of World War I. The state and military leaders ardently believed in the six arrows.

In 1948 American military assistance to Turkey began, and in 1952 Turkey joined NATO. Officers learned to operate advanced technological weapons, attended military schools in Europe and the United States, and had contact with their fellow officers in other NATO nations. They were taught the science of modern atomic and nuclear warfare and were knowledgeable about politics and social issues in countries other than Turkey. Especially for the younger officers, their horizons were broadened and their training became much more technological and scientific.

In 1950 the Democratic Party won in free general elections. While it had recruited some distinguished military officers to run for office under its banner and had attempted to show that it was just as patriotic and supportive of the armed forces as the Republicans, relations between it and the military were at best a détente. Throughout the ten years of Democratic rule, recurrent military conspiracies existed, and the Democrats were never able to exert civilian supremacy over the armed forces. The harmony of interests and values between the top military and civilian leaders that had existed in the Republican era existed no more. The hostility between the two was well illustrated by a widely quoted remark made in 1954 by Democratic Prime Minister Adnan Menderes to the effect that he could run the army with reserve officers if he chose.[23]

As inflation eroded the standard of living of military officers, they felt that they were no longer highly respected by Turkish society. The military budget did not receive the preferential treatment that it had in the past. In April 1960 the Democratic majority in parliament established a partisan anti-

---

[23] George S. Harris, "The Role of the Military in Turkish Politics," *Middle East Journal,* 19 (Spring 1965), 170.

Republican Committee of Investigation. It had extraordinary powers that superseded those of the legislature and of the courts, thereby violating the constitution
itself. In late April 1960 student demonstrations broke out in Ankara and
Istanbul. The government proclaimed martial law and ordered the military to
suppress them, which it did. In this tense atmosphere, a nearly bloodless coup
was carried out on May 27, 1960. Celal Bayar, president of the republic, Adnan
Menderes, prime minister, all the members of the cabinet, and the Democratic
members of parliament were arrested.

The leaders of the coup formed themselves into a National Unity Committee. It soon divided into a "moderate" faction overwhelmingly composed of
generals, and a "radical" one comprising junior officers up to and including
the rank of colonel. The former desired to hand power over immediately to
Inonu and the Republican People's Party, and the latter wanted the military
to hold onto power for a longer period of time in order that it might carry out
major social and political reform. The "moderates" led by Cemal Gursel won
out, and on November 13, 1960, it was announced that the fourteen "radical"
members of the National Unity Committee had been dismissed from it.

The National Unity Committee now moved quickly to return power to
civilians. In January 1961 it convened a Constituent Assembly to draft a new
constitution, which on July 9 was approved by the people in a referendum,
although almost 40 percent voted against it. General elections under the new
constitution were held on October 15, 1961, and again the military received an
electoral slap in the face, for its favorite, the Republican People's Party, received
only 37 percent of the vote and the parties that were successors to the overthrown Democrats, the Justice and New Turkey parties, received 35 and 14
percent respectively.

The new constitution institutionalized the military involvement in politics
and government. Members of the National Unity Committee were made life
members of the Senate, the new upper house. A National Security Council was
established consisting of "Ministers as provided by law, the Chief of the General
Staff, and representatives of the armed forces." Its function was to make recommendations to the Council of Ministers "with the purpose of assisting in the
making of decisions related to national security and coordination (Art. III)."
However, its recommendations have come to have considerable force, and it has
interfered in the deliberations and decisions of the cabinet.[24]

By carrying out the coup of May 27, 1960, having a new constitution
drawn up, and then quickly returning power to civilians, the armed forces
worked themselves into a dilemma from which they have not been able to extri-
cate themselves since. Acting as the "guardian of the republic," they intervened
when internal order broke down and the government became too dictatorial.
Yet the very act of intervention was illegal, undemocratic, and apt to promote

[24] Feroz Ahmad, *The Turkish Experiment in Democracy, 1950-1975* (Boulder, Colo.:
Westview Press, 1977), p. 181.

more public dissatisfaction and unrest. Since 1960 the armed forces have been unable to fully disengage from politics, and they have been actively involved in the most important governmental decisions.

From 1968 to 1971 the country was torn apart by strikes, demonstrations, assassinations, and kidnappings, and once again the leadership of the armed forces carried out a coup, this one on March 12, 1971. It is known as the "coup by memorandum." The commanders of the army, navy, and air force presented a memorandum to the president of the republic expressing a lack of confidence in the ability of Prime Minister Suleyman Demirel (Justice Party) to govern and maintain order. He resigned and a man agreeable to the military, Nihat Erim, became prime minister. Bulent Ecevit, secretary-general of the Republican People's Party, protested the military intervention and refused to cooperate with the army-sponsored government of Nihat Erim. The long period of collaboration between the army and the RPP was coming to a close.

In April 1971, at the instigation of the armed forces, a state of emergency was declared, and martial law was instituted in eleven of Turkey's sixty-seven provinces. Those affected contained the largest cities, and it was there that the student and worker population was the largest and the unrest the greatest. Armed with extraordinary powers, the army made thousands of arrests, and many persons were arrested and tried by military courts.

The two men who had held the office of the president of the republic since 1961 were Cemal Gursel and Cevdet Sunay, both generals in the army. In 1973 the latter's term was up, and the candidate of the military, General Faruk Gurler, chief of the General Staff, was rejected by the Grand National Assembly (the Turkish parliament), which is responsible under the constitution for choosing the president. Many of the civilian leaders in the Grand National Assembly were angered by the continuing military intervention in politics and were restive under the martial law regime. By turning down the candidate of the military, they asserted their authority. However, the candidates from the political parties could not receive a majority, and a deadlock resulted that lasted for twenty-four days. After protracted negotiations between the military and political leaders, a compromise candidate was elected on the fifteenth ballot. Fahri Koruturk, born in 1903, was an admiral and former chief of the navy, the least political of the three branches of the armed forces. He also had civilian experience as ambassador to Moscow and Madrid and had been in the Senate since 1968. Both the political parties and the armed forces felt they could live with him.[25]

Since 1960 the armed forces have been divided between "moderates" who desire, in collaboration with the political parties, to continue the gradual reformist policies begun by Ataturk, and "radicals" who want to carry out a

[25] Roger P. Nye, "Civil-Military Confrontation in Turkey: The 1973 Presidential Election," *International Journal of Middle East Studies*, 8 (April 1977), 226.

major social and political revolution through military rule alone. The former have been mostly generals and the latter mostly men of junior rank. The moderates have won out in all the internal military struggles, and under their leadership the Turkish armed forces have "set the boundaries within which the game of politics is played."[26]

The military is never completely "in" or "out" of politics. The president of the republic is a channel of communication between the military and political leaders, and in disputes between them acts as mediator. A neat civilian-military dichotomy does not exist, for the military has always had supporters among civilians, and civilians have been able to find supporters in the military. Soldiers in or out of uniform have not always displayed a "military mind," and some civilians have had more of a "military mind" than the soldiers. One result of the struggle over the presidency in 1973 was that "each side emerged with a better understanding of the other's 'proper' role in Turkish politics and of the parameters of 'fair play.' "[27]

Civil Bureaucracy

For centuries bureaucracy has been a distinguishing feature of Turkish society. The Ottoman Empire was ruled by a class of military officers, civil administrators, and religious officials beholden to the sultan whose mission was to maintain a divinely-inspired regime. In the period of one-party rule of the republic (1923-1950), the military and the bureaucracy under the direction of Ataturk and Inonu were the main instruments of rule, this time for the purpose of building a modern Turkish nation-state. Since 1950 bureaucratic domination has been nowhere near as great, with powerful political parties, a vigorous class of free intellectuals (journalists, students, writers), moderate-sized entrepreneurs, and prosperous farmers challenging its policies, power, and social status.

The Turkish bureaucracy has generally been free from popular control and has been more the people's master than their servant. The authorities have felt that they had a mission: in Ottoman times to defend and expand the House of Islam, and in the republican period to create a modern nation-state. Administrators were responsible upward to the authorities in the capital, and success was determined by the degree to which the official could maintain order in his area and earn compliance with central directives. It was assumed that the officials knew what was best for the people and had the right to rule over them. It was "we" the educated, against "them" the ignorant.

Prior to the early nineteenth century the ruling class agreed that the Koran and the Sharia were the basis of government and that all political institutions should be derived from them. In the nineteenth century a split developed

---

[26] Ibid.

[27] Ibid., p. 227.

between Westernizers (modernizers), who favored the introduction of European education, military organization, law, and government, and traditionalists, who were opposed to these changes, feeling that only by strengthening faith and reaffirming the old ways could the decline of the empire be checked.

For the most part the traditionalists were discredited by their part in the defeat of Turkey in World War I and their acquiescence to the demands of the victorious Western allies (Britain, France, and Italy). Ataturk and his followers, all of whom were Westernizers, saved the nation's honor, and until 1950 were dominant in the institutions of the state and the country at large. Since 1950 the nation has become much more fragmented, and religious-nationalist rightists, democratic socialists, and radical revolutionary Marxists vie with one another.

In the 1970s a major issue argued by Turks is whether the country should continue to be dominated by a military-bureaucratic elite. The Ataturk-style modernizers and the revolutionary Marxists agree that a powerful state and bureaucracy are needed to carry out reform and control "reactionaries." They support a strong central government, regulation of the press, control of the right to assembly, and state ownership and direction of the economy. They distrust the people, even though they say they are ruling in their name, because the people are "backward," "reactionary," or have been so duped and exploited that they do not know their own rights, needs, and interests.

A loose alliance of persons not employed by the state—private entrepreneurs, prosperous farmers, and traditional local leaders—have supported the Democratic and Justice parties, and are against the continued dominance of the military-bureaucratic elite. They seek greater pluralism in the political process and less state control of the economy, and desire that fewer decrees emanate from the capital to be enforced in every village in the country. Conservative, yet in varying ways affected by modernity, they desire to preserve the Turkish way of life, which has been a fusion of Islamic and Turkish practices. For them the military-bureaucratic elite has always been oppressive, arrogant, distant from the people, and subject to venality.

Education is the primary requirement for entrance into the top ranks of the bureaucracy. Prior to the nineteenth century one achieved a high position in society by being born into the right family, having private tutors, and attending one of the four educational institutions in Istanbul that fed graduates into the officer corps, the bureaucracy, the religious hierarchy, and court officialdom. In the nineteenth century, institutions modeled on those of Western Europe were established, such as the Imperial Ottoman Lycée at Galatasaray and the Civil Service School, later to become the Political Science Faculty, in Istanbul. They produced generations of Western-educated graduates who filled a preponderant share of positions in the cabinet, the higher levels of the bureaucracy, and parliament. After the founding of the republic, the Political Science Faculty was moved to Ankara where it became a part of the university there. Graduation from it and other university-level institutions of learning has remained the absolute prerequisite for appointment to executive positions in the bureaucracy.

In the period of one-party rule, from 1923 to 1950, Turkey was a bureaucratic polity (see the section, "The Bureaucratic Polity" in Chapter 4). A high percentage of the delegates to the Grand National Assembly were bureaucrats or military officers, and "there existed a sort of closed corporation of professional public servants who, acting as politicians, passed laws which they and their colleagues administered as bureaucrats."[28] The reforms of Ataturk, such as the law prohibiting the wearing of a brimless hat, were enforced by provincial administrators on a reluctant and often hostile peasantry.[29] Bureaucrats "quickly learned to appreciate their political and economic power,"[30] and came to be identified with the Kemalist policies and the semiauthoritarian methods used to administer them. They "grew accustomed to almost unchallenged power and to the social prestige which accompanied power."[31]

The Democratic victory in 1950 brought an end to this era. While the Republican People's Party was dominated by bureaucrats and the military, the Democratic Party appealed to the new groups and classes which had arisen as a result of the policies of modernization of Ataturk: professionals not employed by the state, independent businessmen, and traditional local leaders. The Democrats trimmed the power of the administrators in the provinces, towns, and villages, gave more power and prestige to locally-chosen political leaders, and inaugurated popular programs such as the building of roads and mosques. In this period an arrogant official faced the risk of being transferred to a less desirable area or position. The closed company of like-minded and similarly-educated politicians and administrators of the period of rule of the Republican People's Party was ended.

The military coup of 1960 is widely interpreted as a reaction of the military-bureaucratic elite to its decline in prestige and loss of power. Inflation eroded the purchasing power of state employees. Military officers and government officials were no longer looked upon with awe. State funds were spent on numerous "pork-barrel" projects that were popular with the people and helped local politicians but contributed only marginally to the modernization of the economy. University-educated officials were rankled that local leaders with no more than a primary education now had more access to cabinet ministers than they.

The coup of 1960 did not put the military-bureaucratic elite as firmly in power as it had been prior to 1950. The new constitution written at the instigation of the military received only 60 percent approval in the nation-wide referendum held in July 1961 and, as mentioned earlier, in the October 1961 general elections the RPP, preeminently the party of the modernizers and of the

---

[28] Richard L. Chambers, "Turkey," in *Political Modernization in Japan and Turkey*, ed. Robert Ward and Dankwart Rustow (Princeton: Princeton University Press, 1964), p. 326.
[29] Leslie L. Roos, Jr. and Noralou P. Roos, *Managers of Modernization: Organizations and Elites in Turkey (1950-1969)* (Cambridge, Mass.: Harvard University Press, 1971), p. 25.
[30] Ibid., p. 31.
[31] Ibid., p. 32.

military-bureaucratic elite, received only 37 percent of the vote, while the barely organized Justice and New Turkey parties won 35 percent and 14 percent respectively.

These events revealed that the military and the bureaucracy still had enormous power, but in free democratic elections they and their supporters could not win majority approval. Since the early days of the republic new groups had arisen in Turkey that were not going to permit Turkey to be ruled exclusively by the military and the bureaucracy. This was a totally new development in Turkish history.

Free Professionals, Private Entrepreneurs, and Modern Farmers

Ottoman society was composed of a military-bureaucratic elite, a peasantry, and a commercial class dominated by Greeks, Armenians, and Jews. Muslim Turks with aspirations for high social status and political power joined the military or the bureaucracy and shunned business.

Large numbers of Greeks left Turkey in 1923 and the years thereafter. The capitulations that had given economic privileges to foreigners living in the Ottoman Empire were abolished in the Treaty of Lausanne, signed by Turkey and the Allies in 1923. The exodus of the Greeks and other foreigners left a void in Turkey's commercial and business sectors which was filled by middle-class Muslim Turks. Ataturk's policies of economic growth and development further expanded this group and also produced a class of farmers who owned sizable pieces of good land, produced for the market, and used modern agricultural machinery and technology.

Unlike the minorities and resident aliens who could not participate in Turkey's internal politics because of their religion and nationality, this new class of professionals, entrepreneurs, and farmers has attained power, wealth, and social status in addition to a degree of support from the peasants. They have come to challenge politically the military-bureaucratic elite that formerly ruled Turkey exclusively. Among them are contractors, wholesalers, retailers, owners and investors in urban real estate, prosperous farmers, doctors, lawyers, and the proprietors of small factories. The enterprises or farms they run are almost always family-owned, employing few persons, if any, from the outside. Their education ranges from the elementary through the university levels. They can be classified as neither traditional or modern, and unlike members of the military and the civil bureaucracy they have not been shaped into a common mold by a similar education and institutional loyalties. They are diverse, and their political beliefs are vague and diffuse. They are proud to be Turks, responding readily to nationalist appeals, but to them much of the modernity which the military-bureaucratic elite has been pushing for a century in order to strengthen the nation-state, is destructive of the Turkish way of life. They are particularly resistant to militant secularism, and practice Islam with varying degrees of intensity.

Similar to the eighteenth- and nineteenth-century European middle class, they are independent and moderately prosperous. They do not include big business tycoons or robber barons, because large economic enterprises are monopolized by the state. As the corresponding middle class in Europe was opposed to mercantilism since it restricted trade and investment and favored the privileged feudal aristocracy, this class in Turkey has been less than enthusiastic about étatism, which benefits the bureaucratic class. It believes in economic policies that favor small and middle-range businesses and independent farmers rather than the large state economic enterprises. Its main political spokesmen have been the Democratic and the Justice parties. This class does not derive its livelihood from the state or receive from it security, wealth, or status. To the contrary, for them the state is quixotic and oppressive, taxing them, establishing new regulations, and removing old protections and subsidies.

The free professionals, private entrepreneurs, and prosperous farmers are not peasants whom state officials have for so long treated with disdain, because they were "in need of enlightenment" or "not yet capable of participating in the modern world." They form a new class that has risen between the peasantry and the military-bureaucratic elite, and they have profoundly changed Turkish society and politics.

Intellectuals[32]

All persons with a university education are classified in Turkey as intellectuals. In the Ottoman Empire they lived mostly in Istanbul, came from the same social background, and formed a homogeneous elite that was almost one and the same with the bureaucracy. Since the founding of the republic in 1923, the educational system has expanded enormously, with the result that intellectuals have become greater in number, more diverse, and more scattered around the country in cities and large towns. They are doctors, lawyers, teachers, professors, journalists, writers, engineers, architects, accountants, managers, and economists, and are employed in state schools and universities, state economic enterprises and government ministries, departments, and bureaus. Many are self-employed or work in firms in which they have a partial ownership.

In the late 1970s they are fragmented. Some are Ataturk-style modernizers who believe in secularism, strong central government, vigorous leadership from the top, large, well-supplied armed forces, continued membership in the American-led Western alliance, and economic development stimulated by the state. Others criticize Turkey's military dependence upon the United States and

---

[32] Kemal Karpat, "Social Groups and the Political System after 1960," in *Social Change and Politics in Turkey: A Structural-Historical Analysis,* ed. Kemal Karpat (Leiden: Brill, 1973), pp. 263-69.

its membership in NATO. They argue that the Turkish workers and peasants are exploited and can only be freed by radical social change under "enlightened" authoritarian leadership. They say that Turkey's political parties and parliament are manipulated and controlled by privileged cliques, and that the present system is not true democracy. Another group is against state power and authoritarianism, whether of the Ataturkist or socialist variety. It supports private property, free enterprise, civil liberties, limited government, and voluntary observance of religion without state interference. Significantly the first two viewpoints are argued primarily by intellectuals employed by the state, while the third is supported mostly by persons who are self-employed or work in private firms.

Labor [33]

Industrial workers are the largest social group created almost exclusively during the republic. Their fastest rate of increase occurred during the Democrats' period of rule through the expansion of private enterprise and industrialization. Thousands of villagers moved to towns and cities, found employment, and then voted for the Democrats who had brought about the new prosperity.

The intelligentsia, the bureaucracy, and the military showed little interest in labor problems until after 1960. This left the workers relatively free of ideological commitment to or association with political parties. Some labor legislation was passed prior to 1960, but it was more the result of government initiative than direct pressure by labor. The right to organize was granted in 1947, and the Confederation of Turkish Workers, founded in 1952, emerged as the largest national labor union.

Since the coup of 1960, labor has come to play an increasingly significant role in national life. It put pressure on the constitutional assembly convened by the military in January 1961 to give proper recognition to the rights of the working class. Eventually the assembly included in the new constitution the right of labor to establish unions, bargain collectively, and strike (Articles 46, 47). Then the Confederation of Turkish Workers advocated approval of the constitution and identified with the new political order.

The leftist-socialist element of the intelligentsia, which includes labor among the "energetic" forces, has hoped to lead it in a struggle against the military and the rightists in order to establish a new social order founded on justice and an absence of exploitation. It has produced a deluge of magazines, newspapers, books, and pamphlets glorifying the class struggle, revolution, and the workers' role as agents of change and progress. Intellectuals founded the Labor Party of Turkey, which between 1961 and 1971 attempted to rally the workers in the class struggle.

The main body of labor, however, has rejected the extreme left and

[33] Ibid., pp. 269-75.

supports the existing regime. It has used the newly-granted right to strike for economic, not for political, motives, bargaining with the military and the bureaucracy for specific rights and benefits. Labor is now one of the bases of Turkish society and a full participant in the political process.

POLITICAL STRUCTURES

The Constitution

The first constitution in Turkish history was promulgated in 1876. The result of pressure from the European powers and Westernizers within the Ottoman Empire, it attempted to restrict the hitherto autocratic powers of the sultan, guaranteeing civil liberties to all Ottoman citizens whatever their religion or nationality. Modeled on the Belgian constitution of 1831, it aimed to turn the sultan into a constitutional monarch and transform Turkey into a liberal democracy.

Turkey of the late nineteenth century, however, was not the same as Western Europe of that period. The Islamic society and political culture did not reinforce democratic values and processes. There was no autonomous local government, a Turkish Muslim middle class did not exist, and the class of Westernizers promoting the constitution was minute, mostly confined to Istanbul. The constitution never really took root.

In 1877 the sultan dissolved the parliament and ruled the country absolutely till 1908, when as a result of the revolution of the Young Turks, he was forced to restore the constitution. Constitutionalism and democracy again did not take hold, the Young Turk leadership became a dictatorship, and Turkey was sucked into World War I, emerging on the losing side.

In 1919 Kemal Ataturk went from Istanbul to Samsun in the interior of Turkey, led a movement of national liberation, and convened in 1920 in Ankara a Grand National Assembly which was the plenary body for the government he led in opposition to the one in Istanbul. On January 20, 1921, it passed ten fundamental articles as amendments to the constitution of 1876 and temporarily legitimized the government in Ankara.

In 1924 a new constitution was promulgated which concentrated authority in the Grand National Assembly, the voice and representative of the Turkish people. It was a unicameral legislature, endowed with both legislative and executive powers. It elected for a four-year term the president of the republic, and he in turn appointed the prime minister and the cabinet. In principle the president's powers were few and his office was ceremonial, yet because of his charismatic personality, Ataturk was able to impress his will on the cabinet and the legislature. He also led the only legal political party, the Republican People's Party.

In 1945 Ismet Inonu, president of the republic, allowed opposition political parties to begin to operate. In 1950, in the first completely free and honest elections in Turkey's history, the RPP was resoundingly defeated by the Democratic Party.

In the early years of the Democratic government, it allowed the voicing of opposing viewpoints and respected civil liberties. When the government passed restrictive laws and then established a one-sided parliamentary commission whose objective seemed to be the abolition of the Republican People's Party, the army staged a coup in 1960. A National Unity Committee was formed composed of high-ranking officers. It ruled until a civilian government was established.

On January 1, 1961, the National Unity Committee convened a Constituent Assembly composed of appointed and elected representatives to draft a new constitution. It was put to the people in a nation-wide referendum on July 9 and passed. On October 25, parliamentary elections were held, and formal power passed from the military back into the hands of duly-elected and duly-constituted civilian authorities.

In reaction to the concentration of power in the old constitution and its use by the Democrats for their purposes, the members of the Constituent Assembly created in the new one a government in which powers were separated and balanced. The legislature, named the Grand National Assembly, has two houses: the National Assembly and the Senate of the Republic. The president of the republic is chosen by the members of the two houses for a seven-year term not coterminous with that of the National Assembly. The prime minister is designated by the president from among the members of the Grand National Assembly. The other ministers are nominated by the prime minister and appointed by the president from among the members of the Grand National Assembly or from among those qualified for election as deputies. The Constitutional Court can declare unconstitutional laws passed by the Grand National Assembly.

The 1961 constitution also contains detailed sections on civil liberties, social welfare, and socioeconomic rights and duties. Rights are spelled out, and the grounds on which they can be curtailed are described.

Designed to protect civil liberties and prevent the concentration of power, the new constitution went far in the other direction. It allowed all kinds of groups to express themselves, thus fragmenting and weakening government power. From 1968 to 1971 there were so many assassinations, kidnappings, demonstrations, and strikes that the military staged its "coup by memorandum" of 1971.

Because of the unrest, the government of Nihat Erim that followed the coup proclaimed, and parliament approved, the imposition of martial law in eleven of the country's sixty-seven provinces, including its largest urban areas,

Istanbul, Ankara, and Izmir. This enabled military commanders to ban meetings or demonstrations, make searches without warrants, impose censorship on radio broadcasts and on the press, suspend associations, institute curfews, establish military courts, revoke the right to strike or to lock out, and detain suspects for up to one month. Beginning in January 1973 the government lifted martial law in some provinces, and by October 1973 it was totally removed.

In September 1971, under pressure from the military, the Grand National Assembly amended thirty-five articles of the constitution and added nine temporary articles. Generally they stressed that freedom could not be exercised in a manner that jeopardized public order or national security. They placed limitations on civil liberties and on the autonomy of the universities. They provided that the prime minister and the cabinet, with the approval of the Senate and the National Assembly, could declare martial law in part or all of the country for a period of up to two months, and that this could be extended every two months.

The 1961 constitution started out its life as a document designed to protect civil liberties, promote social welfare, and inhibit dictatorial concentration of power. It was backed by the military and was intended to justify its overthrow of the duly-elected and duly-constituted Democratic government. Charging that this government had become "dictatorial," and acting in its capacity as "guardian of the republic and of the nation," the military intervened to save freedom and democracy. The new constitution was proof of the nobility of its intentions.

The violence and unrest that began in 1968 caused the military to look upon the constitution in a new light. Freedom and democracy were being exploited by militant revolutionaries of the left, and the military felt that the higher need was for public order. The resulting amendments to the constitution limited civil liberties and strengthened state authority.

The President of the Republic

Elected for a seven-year term by the Grand National Assembly from among its own members, the president of the republic is required by the constitution to be at least forty years of age and to have received higher education. He is not eligible for reelection, and once elected, must disassociate himself from his party. Upon taking the oath of office he ceases to be a regular member of the Grand National Assembly.

He is the commander-in-chief of the armed forces, presides over the Council of Ministers "whenever he deems it necessary," appoints diplomatic representatives, receives those of foreign states, and ratifies and implements international conventions and treaties. As head of state he represents the "Turkish Republic and the integrity of the Turkish Nation." Subject to the approval of the lower house of the Grand National Assembly, he appoints the prime minister and the Council of Ministers. He may not dissolve parliament unless requested to do so by the prime minister. Informally he is the liaison between the high-ranking military leaders and the heads of the political parties.

The Cabinet

The prime minister and the other ministers form the Council of Ministers. The prime minister is designated by the president from among the members of the Grand National Assembly, and he in turn chooses the other ministers. After its formal appointment, the Cabinet presents its program before each house of the legislature; the lower house then takes a vote of confidence.

The prime minister is charged with implementing the general government policy with the assistance of the ministers. All members of the Cabinet are responsible collectively for it and individually for the acts of their own ministries.

In the most recent general elections of October 1973 and June 1977, no one party has achieved a majority of the seats in the National Assembly. Coalition governments have had to be formed, none of which has lasted very long, and government leadership, except for caretaker governments, has alternated between Suleyman Demirel, the head of the Justice Party, and Bulent Ecevit, head of the Republican People's Party.

The Grand National Assembly

The Turkish legislature is called the Grand National Assembly. Its lower house has 450 members elected directly by the people, and the upper one, 150 chosen in the same manner, in addition to 15 members appointed by the president. Members of the National Unity Committee, which ruled the country from 1960 to 1961, are *ex officio* members of the Senate for life, as are past presidents of the republic. The term of a member of the National Assembly is four years, that of a senator is six years. One-third of the membership of the Senate is elected every two years, and all of the members of the National Assembly every four years. Members of both houses are chosen on the basis of proportional representation.

The Grand National Assembly is empowered to enact, amend, and repeal laws, debate and adopt the state budget, and proclaim pardons and amnesties. While any member may initiate legislation, most bills originate from the cabinet. Each house may question the ministers, orally or in writing, on specific questions, but the cabinet is responsible only to the lower house.

Political Parties

From 1923 to 1945 Turkey was a one-party regime. Although Ataturk experimented with opposition parties (the Progressive Republican Party,

1924-25; the Free Republican Party in 1930), the country was really a guided democracy led and controlled by the RPP.

On November 1, 1945, opposition political parties were permitted to form, and the era of multiparty democracy began. In 1946 the Democratic Party (DP) was created by some men who had left the RPP, and since then it and its successor, the Justice Party (JP), have been the major political opponents of the RPP. Although the armed forces have repeatedly interfered in the political process since 1960, they have not attempted to govern without parties.

Since the adoption of the new constitution in 1961, the political mosaic has been very complex, and no one party has been able to dominate for very long. The results of the 1961 election have already been discussed. In the next election (1965), the JP surprised everyone by garnering 53 percent of the vote, while the RPP's share sank to 29 percent. In 1969 the JP received 47 percent as against 28 percent for the RPP, and the former was able to form a government by itself since it had a majority of the seats in the National Assembly.

The coup of March 12, 1971, deposed the Justice Party, and in the elections since then (1973 and 1977) the RPP has risen from its low of 1961, and the JP has fallen from its high of 1965. Both have suffered from competition by breakaway parties and from the rightist National Salvation and National Action parties; neither has been able to gain a majority. The RPP received 33 percent in 1973 and 42 percent in 1977, and the JP 30 and 37 percent respectively, in the same years. There have been several short-lived coalition governments and some periods without any government.

The Republican People's Party. The Republican People's Party is something of a paradox. It has been preeminently the party of the "center," led and supported by the modernists who live in the large cities and desire to raise Turkey to the level of Western European civilization, but it has also been supported by traditional village and regional leaders, the local notables, particularly in eastern Turkey, the most mountainous and less-developed part of the country. Since Ataturk was more a nationalist leader fighting a foreign enemy than he was a social revolutionary, in the 1920s he could mobilize these people to his cause. An implicit trade-off developed whereby the local leaders supported Ataturk's modernization program, which concentrated on institutional and legal change at the "center," in exchange for permission to retain their land, status, and local influence.[34]

The peasant masses were the objects of this alliance. Between 1923 and 1950 they received little in the form of economic and social benefits and were taxed and conscripted as they had been in the Ottoman era. Sharecropping was widespread, and most peasants were dependent on one local notable or another.[35]

[34] Arnold Leder, "Collaboration Politics and the Turkish Revolution" (Paper delivered at the Annual Meeting of the Middle East Studies Association, Los Angeles, California, November 11-13, 1976), p. 7.

[35] Ibid., p. 22.

The Kemalist ideology emphasized social harmony with the absence of class conflict. Populism, one of the six arrows, meant national solidarity and support for the nationalists from all elements of society. In founding the RPP, Ataturk stated:

> The aim of a people's organization as a party is not the realization of the interests of certain classes over against those of other classes. The aim is rather to mobilize the entire nation, called People, by including all classes and excluding none, in common and united action towards genuine prosperity which is the common objective of all.[36]

In the elections that have been held since 1950, when it has had to compete with other parties, the RPP has on no occasion won a majority. Particularly since 1965, its leaders have been searching for a formula to make it truly the "people's" party.

Two positions within the RPP have emerged. The first emphasizes national unity, harmony among social classes, and desires to carry out in the tradition of Ataturk. Its main spokesman has been Ismet Inonu. The second position carries the label left-of-center, and stresses change and reform for the benefit of the less privileged classes in Turkish society. It advocates land reform under the slogan, "land to the tiller and water to the user," restrictions on large-scale capitalism so that it does not adversely affect the peasants, workers, artisans, and small merchants, and a more equitable distribution of the national income through changes in the tax laws. It envisions Turkey adopting a form of socialism similar to that of Norway, Sweden, West Germany, and Britain. The left-of-center program is designed to appeal to new groups who have never before supported the RPP: workers, intellectuals influenced by the socialist and communist movements of Western Europe, and peasants.

Party secretary-general from 1965 to 1971 and chairman since 1972, Bulent Ecevit is the prime architect and proponent of the left-of-center program. He visualizes it as an alternative to the proposals of the extreme left and as a policy that could transform the RPP into an organization capable of meeting the challenge of the 1960s and 1970s. He believes that if the party is to win, it has to broaden its base in the working class and among the peasantry, even if that means losing the support of the shortsighted old-fashioned landowners. The left-of-center program is to Ecevit the only alternative to violent social revolution or anarchy.[37]

Ecevit feels that Turkey's relations with the United States have been a little too close. He criticized the 1959 Bilateral Agreement between Turkey and the United States because it allowed the government in power to request military intervention from Washington whenever it wished to prevent "internal,

[36] Ibid., quoted on p. 13.

[37] Ahmad, *Turkish Experiment,* p. 255.

unarmed aggression."[38] Ecevit was prime minister in July 1954 when Turkey decided to invade Cyprus after the coup on that island supported by the military junta in Athens and which overthrew President Makarios. This action was not favored by Washington, but in Turkey it transformed the public image of Ecevit from a well-intentioned, idealistic leader into a man of action comparable to Ataturk.[39] Ecevit does not feel that Turkey should leave NATO, but he does feel that it should pursue a policy designed to serve Turkish national interests and not those of other nations.[40]

Ecevit publicly denounced the 1971 coup by memorandum, fearing that it was directed more against the opposition left-of-center Republicans than against the Justice Party members in power. In disagreement with Inonu over his support for the "above-parties" government of Nihat Erim installed by the military in 1971, Ecevit resigned as secretary-general of the RPP. He opposed the 1971 amendments to the constitution and objected to the fact that they were not ratified by a popular referendum as the constitution in 1961 had been.[41]

The Democratic Party. Formed in 1946 by four dissidents from the RPP, the Democratic Party came to power in 1950 by promising less state control over the economy and more freedom from the government bureaucracy for the individual. By stressing the interests of the peasants and by appealing for their votes, the party involved them in the political process. It made them feel that they were being listened to rather than being told what to do. Prosperous farmers, free professionals, and moderate-sized entrepreneurs were the pillars of the party, supporting it financially and providing it with leadership.

As noted earlier, between 1950 and 1960 the Democratic government softened the harsh secularism of Ataturk. When the Democratic government was overthrown by the military in 1960, all Democrats in the parliament and cabinet were put in jail, and the party was banned. From October 1960 to September 1961, a trial of 528 Democratic leaders was held on the island of Yassiada in the Sea of Marmara. Three hundred ninety-eight were accused of violating the constitution by stifling freedom of the press and other civil liberties, and of trying to set up a one-party dictatorship. Three hundred fifty-two of these were found guilty. Former Prime Minister Adnan Menderes and former cabinet ministers Fatin Zorlu and Hasan Polatkan were hung. Former President Celal Bayar and 11 others received death sentences which were commuted to life imprisonment. About 100 were acquitted, and the balance were given long prison sentences.

The Justice Party. Formed in 1961, this party spoke to the widespread sentiment in Turkey that an injustice had been done to the leaders of the Demo-

---

[38] Ibid., pp. 158-59.
[39] Ibid., p. 343.
[40] Ibid., p. 419.
[41] Ibid., p. 314.

cratic Party. Its founders chose the name "Justice" in an obvious attempt to appeal to this feeling. It is the successor to the Democratic Party, and supported by the same groups and social classes. Likewise its platform has been roughly similar.

Its leader since 1964 has been Suleyman Demirel. Under his direction the party won a majority of the popular vote in the 1965 general election, and in the 1969 election it was able to retain a majority of the seats in the lower house of parliament though it did not have an absolute majority of the popular vote. Demirel was prime minister from 1965 to 1971, when he was forced to resign because of the coup. Toward the end of the 1960s the party began to divide into two factions, a relatively liberal one led by Demirel and a more conservative one. The conflict between the two reached a climax in February 1970, when five of the conservatives resigned from the General Executive Council of the party. Despite these divisions, this is still one of Turkey's two major parties, with strong support in the villages and towns; and since 1971 Demirel has frequently been prime minister in short-lived coalition governments.

The National Salvation Party. The predecessor of the National Salvation Party was the National Order Party, which was founded in January 1970 and led by Necmettin Erbakan. On May 21, 1971, the Constitutional Court ordered the latter dissolved on the grounds that its aim was to make Turkey into a theocracy contrary to the constitutionally-guaranteed secular character of the state. The leaders of the party, however, were not penalized in any way, and Erbakan was said to have gone to Switzerland until the situation calmed down.

In October 1972 the party reemerged, transparently disguised under a new name, the National Salvation Party, and Erbakan was again its leader. A party predominantly of the lower middle class, which is threatened by the ever-rising tide of modern capitalism and large-scale state economic enterprises, it argues that Turkey must leave NATO and cut its ties with the European Economic Community; otherwise small Turkish industries and businesses will be gobbled up or destroyed by the large, technologically advanced firms of Western Europe. The National Salvation Party members feel that Turkey must affiliate itself with Islamic countries and other states of the East, and that Islamic, not Western, values and standards should prevail in Turkey on moral issues.

In the 1973 general elections, the National Salvation Party emerged as Turkey's third largest party, with 11.8 percent of the vote; in 1977 it garnered 8.2 percent. In 1974 it served in a coalition government with the RPP and since 1975 has been part of various governments led by the Justice Party.

The National Action Party. Wielding influence far out of proportion to its very small size is the rightist National Action Party led by Alparslan Turkes, a former colonel in the army who was one of the leaders of the 1960 coup. One of the "radicals" in the National Unity Committee who did not want to turn the government back quickly to civilian rule, he and thirteen others were dismissed and exiled in November 1960. He returned to Turkey in February 1963, participated in an abortive coup in May of the same year, was arrested, and later freed. In March 1965 he joined the Republican Peasants' Nation Party, which he took over in June. Under his leadership it changed its name to the National Action Party and acquired a fascist character. It is militantly anticommunist and anti-Soviet, and has commando units that engage in street violence against leftist politicians and organizations.

POLITICAL LEADERSHIP

Between the two world wars, Turkey was led by a unified modernist elite headed by Kemal Ataturk. He rallied the people in a common struggle against foreign enemies and persuaded them to switch their loyalties from the multinational Ottoman Empire to the Turkish nation-state. He was loved, admired, and followed because he was the savior of the nation.

Ataturk's accomplishments in respect to internal social and economic reform were limited. After his death in 1938 and particularly after the hiatus created by World War II, Turkey underwent enormous social and economic change far greater than that of the Ataturk era. Turkey's alliance with the United States beginning in 1948 and its admission into NATO in 1952 meant that it participated in the rapid economic development of the Western world after World War II. Roads and factories were built, agriculture was modernized. Turkish laborers worked temporarily in Europe, and the Turkish armed forces received weapons and training from the United States. The result was the emergence of new social groups: an industrial working class, modern farmers, free professionals, and private entrepreneurs. Turkish society no longer consisted of simply a modern educated elite of bureaucrats and army officers at the top and a mass of illiterate peasants and artisans at the bottom, psychically and physically distant from one another.

In contemporary Turkey, leadership is infinitely more complex. Ataturk created a certain unity because most of the battles he was fighting were patriotic ones in which all social groups and classes could become involved and could sacrifice for a common cause. The issues which confront Turkey today, however, are mainly social and economic, and are bound to divide. They pit workers against capitalists and managers, peasants and farmers against city dwellers, military leaders with their concern for national security against political leaders who desire social justice, the university-educated elite with its deeply-ingrained feeling that it has a right to rule against the less well-educated masses who feel that they have been ignored for too long. The officer corps of the armed forces, the police, civil bureaucracy, political parties, courts, schools, and universities are all factionalized and politicized.

It is the declared goal of Turkish leaders to join the European Economic

Community around 1995, when it is hoped that the level of economic development in Turkey will equal that of the less-developed European nations. Italy in the 1970s is economically at the stage where Turkey hopes to be in the 1990s. Yet Italy in the 1970s is sharply divided politically, threatened by terrorist groups, suffers from enormous social cleavages and great irregularities in economic development, and is split over the social and political role of religion. The two countries are ironically and strikingly similar. Both are very difficult to govern.

POLITICAL POLICIES

Among the Islamic states of the Middle East, Turkey has been the one most influenced by Europe. The Westernizers in the nineteenth century were admirers of the liberal democracy of France and Britain, and since World War II the military officer corps and upper-level civil servants have been influenced by the United States, the left-of-center Republicans by the social democratic movements of Western Europe, and the far left by the French communist and socialist parties.

Turkey is the only Middle Eastern country that is a member of NATO and the only one that is planning to become a member of the European common market. Likewise it is the only Islamic country that has constitutionally established secularism as an official state policy.

Turkey further distinguishes itself from the other Islamic countries of the Middle East in that it has a well-established, functioning competitive party system. The Republican People's Party and the Justice Party have been in existence for decades, have a sophisticated, educated, and politically astute leadership, are well organized throughout the country, and own newspapers and magazines which disseminate their point of view. Each has a loyal following of voters who consistently support it. They are truly modern democratic political parties that are now firmly established.

Turkey lies predominantly in Asia, with most of its people believing to some degree in Islam. The popularity of the Democratic, Justice, National Salvation, and National Action parties, and the failure of the secularist-modernist RPP to win a majority in a free election, attest to the power of tradition and the people's eastern heritage. In the past, to be a Turk was to be a Muslim, and for most people today this still holds true. Western Europe is a predominantly secular society with a Christian heritage, and many Turks assume that as Turkey becomes more modern it will retain some of its Islamic heritage and unique qualities which make it different from Europe.

Ataturk's vision was of a totally secular, modern society knit together by feelings of national loyalty which emanated from a common language and history. For him Islam was not to be a part of the new Turkey. The leaders of the Democratic, Justice, National Salvation, and National Action parties, however, have challenged this vision. Under their direction the Islamic heritage and feelings of the masses have been recognized and the practice of their religion has been permitted. Even the Republican People's Party has come to grudgingly tolerate the Islamic dimension in Turkish society.

However, these issues remain the most fundamental ones for Turkey. Is it to become totally European—culturally, socially, economically, and politically? Or is it to remain in some way a part of the Middle East and of the world of Islam?

REVIEW OF THE MAJOR EVENTS IN THE MODERN HISTORY OF TURKEY

1876	Promulgation by the Ottoman sultan of the first constitution.
1877	Sultan dissolves parliament and rules absolutely.
1908	"Young Turks" carry out a revolution aimed at restoration of the constitution of 1876; after a brief period of freedom, their rule degenerates into a military dictatorship.
1914	World War I begins, and Turkey sides with Germany and Austria.
1915	At the Battle of Gallipoli, Colonel Mustafa Kemal (later to be known as Kemal Ataturk) plays a vital role in the Turkish victory over British forces attempting to occupy Istanbul.
1919	
May	Protected by British, French, and American warships, Greek armed forces land at Izmir. Mustafa Kemal leaves Istanbul for Samsum to rally Turks against the Greek invasion and imperial domination.
1920	
April	First Grand National Assembly meets in Ankara.
Aug.	Representatives of the sultan and of the Allies sign a peace treaty at Sevres, France depriving Turkey of much territory and limiting its sovereignty, but it is never implemented.
1922	
Sept.	Turkish forces complete the final drive against the Greeks and enter Izmir; Greek forces evacuate by ship.
Oct.	Turkish forces gain control of eastern Thrace from the British.
Nov.	Grand National Assembly abolishes the sultanate.
1923	
Jan.	Turkey and Greece conclude a treaty agreeing to the exchange of their respective Greek and Turkish minorities.

July   Representatives of Turkey and the Allies sign a peace treaty at Lausanne, Switzerland respecting Turkish territory and sovereignty.

Aug.   Inaugural congress of the Republican People's Party.

Oct.   Grand National Assembly declares Ankara the capital and proclaims the Republic of Turkey with Mustafa Kemal as President.

1924

March   Grand National Assembly abolishes the caliphate.

April   Grand National Assembly adopts a republican constitution.

1928

April   A secular state is declared.

Nov.   Grand National Assembly passes a law establishing a new Turkish script that uses modified Latin letters.

1934   Law of Surnames is adopted; Mustafa Kemal is given the name Ataturk ("Father of the Turks") by the Grand National Assembly. Women given the vote and the right to hold office.

1935   Fourth Congress of the Republican People's Party incorporates into its program the "six arrows" of Kemalism.

1938   Ataturk dies.

1945   Opposition political parties permitted to form.

1946   Democratic Party founded.

1948   American military assistance begins.

1950   In free general elections, the Democratic Party defeats the Republican People's Party.

1952   Turkey joins NATO.

1960   The armed forces carry out a coup d'etat against the Democratic Party government and arrest its leaders; the military officers form the National Unity Committee and rule the country.

1961

Feb.   Justice Party formed.

July   New constitution approved in a nationwide referendum.

Oct.   General elections held under the new constitution.

1965   Republican People's Party adopts a left-of-center program.

1971

March   The commanders of the army, navy, and air force carry out the "coup by memorandum," forcing Prime Minister Suleyman Demirel to resign.
            Martial law is proclaimed in 11 of the country's 67 provinces, including Istanbul, Ankara, and Izmir.

Sept.   Under pressure from the military, the Grand National Assembly adds numerous amendments and temporary articles to the constitution restricting civil liberties and giving more authority to the government.

1972   Ismet Inonu resigns as chairman of the Republican People's Party; Bulent Ecevit assumes the office.

1973   Struggle between military and civilian leaders over succession to the presidency ends with agreement upon a compromise candidate, Fahri Koruturk.

1974   A coup takes place against Cyprus President Makarios and is supported by the military government in Athens; Turkish forces invade the island by sea and air.

Glossary

Abbas I Shah of Iran from 1587 to 1629. He was the greatest of the Safavid monarchs.

Abbasid The name of an Arab Sunni Muslim dynasty that ruled an empire (capital, Baghdad) from 750 to 1258.

Achaemenid An ancient Persian dynasty that ruled over a large empire from 550 to 330 B.C.

Administered Territories The areas conquered by Israel in the war of 1967 and administered by the Ministry of Defense, comprising the West Bank, Gaza, the Sinai Peninsula, and the Golan Heights.

al-Afghani, Jamal al-Din A famous Muslim religious reformer who lived from 1838 to 1897.

Aguda Israel An Israeli political party to the right of the National Religious Party that advocates strict state enforcement of Jewish religious law. Its name means "Association of Israel."

Alawi Members of a Shiite sect who consider Ali the incarnation of the deity, hence the name Alawi. They inhabit mountainous regions of northern Syria and southeastern Turkey. In Turkish, their name is Alevi.

Ali Cousin and son-in-law of the Prophet Muhammad. He is especially revered by Shiite Muslims.

aliyah (plural, aliyot) A Hebrew word meaning literally "ascent," which in Israel is used to designate waves of Jewish immigration. The most critical one for the development of Israeli social and political institutions was the Second Aliyah (1905-1914), which was composed mostly of Eastern European Jews, many of whom became founders of the state.

anomic groups   Spontaneous, unplanned, and largely unorganized outbreaks in the political system, such as riots, demonstrations, strikes, and armed guerrilla activity.

Arab   Member of a group of people who live in the area from Morocco to Iraq and speak the Arabic language. They are predominantly Muslim but encompass a large number of Christian minorities.

Arab socialism   An ideology propagated by the Egyptian government from about 1961 to 1978.

Arab Socialist Union   The principal political party in Egypt from 1962 to 1978; it was founded by President Nasser.

Armenian   Member of a group of people who speak Armenian and are of the Christian faith. They live in the Armenian Soviet Socialist Republic and throughout the Middle East, Europe, North America, and South America. They formerly lived in an arc of villages interspersed with Turkish ones from the region of eastern Turkey near the border with the Soviet Union to the Mediterranean Sea. In the first quarter of this century, they fought with the Turks over the possession of a single homeland, were defeated, and dispersed.

Ashkenazi   (plural, Ashkenazim)   A member of one of the three divisions of Jews who lived in Europe and spoke Yiddish. In contemporary Israel the term refers to Jews born in Europe or of European descent.

associational groups   Organizations specifically created to articulate an interest in the political process.

Aswan High Dam   A dam across the Nile River near the city of Aswan built with Soviet assistance between 1958 and 1969.

Ataturk, Kemal   The great Turkish national leader and modernizer. Born Mustafa Kemal, he lived from 1881 to 1938. In 1933 the Turkish parliament gave him the surname Ataturk ("Father of the Turks"). He was a victorious military commander of Ottoman forces in World War I, the leader of Turkish forces in the War of Independence (1919-1922), and the president of the Turkish republic from its establishment in 1923 until his death in 1938.

Ataturkism   The ideology based on the reforms and policies of Kemal Ataturk; also called Kemalism, especially outside Turkey.

al-Azhar   Islamic seminary and university in Cairo founded in A.D. 972.

ayatollah   An honorific title that Iranians grant to mujtahids who have demonstrated exceptional learning and great dedication to Islam. The term literally means "sign of God."

Baath   A political party founded in Syria in the early 1940s that advocates Arab unity and socialism. Its name means "renaissance."

Baghdad Pact   A regional anti-Soviet military alliance formed in 1955 under the leadership of American Secretary of State John Foster Dulles. Its original members were Britain, Turkey, Iran, Iraq, and Pakistan. When Iraq withdrew after the revolution in 1958, the name was changed to Central Treaty Organization (CENTO).

Balfour Declaration   Statement issued in 1917 by Foreign Secretary Lord Balfour in the name of the British government. It "viewed with favor" the establishment in Palestine of a "national home for the Jewish people" and pledged not to "prejudice the civil and religious rights of the existing non-Jewish communities in Palestine, or the rights and political status enjoyed by Jews in any other country."

al-Banna, Hassan   Founder and leader of the Muslim Brotherhood. An Egyptian, he lived from 1906 to 1949.

basin irrigation   A method of irrigation in which a river is allowed to overflow its banks and the water is caught in basins made by building low dikes around fields. After the flood waters recede, seeds are planted in the wet soil. Since this method allows for only one crop a year, it has been replaced with perennial irrigation.

bedouin An Arab nomad.

Begin, Menachem Israeli political leader. Born in Poland in 1913, he immigrated to Palestine in 1942, where he became commander of Irgun Zvai Leumi ("National Defense Organization"), which was dissolved after the establishment of the state of Israel in 1948. Begin and other Irgun leaders then organized the Herut Party, which later became a member of the Likud coalition. In 1977 he became prime minister.

Ben-Gurion, David One of the founders of the state of Israel and its first prime minister. Born in Poland in 1886, he immigrated to Palestine in 1906 and died in Israel in 1973.

Ben Zwi, Itzhak Born in the Ukraine in 1884, he immigrated to Palestine before World War I. He was the president of Israel from 1952 until his death in 1963.

Berber Member of a group of people who live in the mountains of Morocco, Algeria, and Tunisia. They speak their own language (Berber) and are Sunni Muslims.

bey A Turkish title of respect widely used in the Ottoman Empire meaning "lord" and "ruler."

bureaucratic polity A political system in which bureaucracy and a powerful leader are dominant, with political parties, interest groups, the legislature, and the judiciary subordinate.

caliph One of the successors of Muhammad as the spiritual and temporal leader of the Muslim community. The last Abbasid caliph was killed by the Mongols in 1258. The Ottoman rulers used the title interchangeably with that of sultan. In 1924, upon the recommendation of Kemal Ataturk, the Turkish Grand National Assembly abolished the caliphate.

capitulation An agreement or treaty between two governments whereby one permits citizens of the other to live within its borders and not be subject to local law. In the nineteenth and twentieth centuries, these treaties became quite inequitable, giving resident foreigners in the Ottoman Empire, Iran, and Egypt a considerable advantage over the indigenous people, especially in business and commerce.

charisma Extraordinary power possessed by some leaders that enables them to elicit enthusiastic popular support.

Charter of National Action A document prepared under the direction of Gamal Abdel Nasser and endorsed in 1962 by a popular assembly that elaborates the principles of the revolutionary government.

Chief Rabbinate The supreme religious authority for Jews living in Israel. It is composed of two chief rabbis, one Ashkenazi, the other Sephardi, and a Supreme Rabbinical Council. Together they interpret the *Halakah* (Jewish religious law) and supervise the religious courts.

Circassian Member of a group of people from the Caucasus.

Copt Member of the principal Christian minority of Egypt, which makes up about 7 percent of the population.

culture (political) Ideas, attitudes, opinions, beliefs, and values relevant to politics and dominant in the society.

Cyrus the Great One of the most famous of the ancient Persian Achaemenid kings. He died in 529 B.C.

Darius I One of the most famous of the ancient Persian Achaemenid kings. He died in 486 B.C.

Demirel, Suleyman Leader of the Justice Party in Turkey and a prime minister.

Democratic Party   A Turkish political party founded in 1946 and banned by the military government that came to power in May 1960. It was the ruling party from 1950 to 1960.

Dhofar   A province in western Oman adjacent to the border with South Yemen.

Diaspora   Greek word meaning dispersion. It is used by Jews, Armenians, and Palestinians in reference to their expulsion from their homeland. For Jews, it also designates the Jewish communities outside Eretz Israel.

Druze   Member of an independent religious sect founded in the eleventh century that draws its beliefs from Judaism, Christianity, and Islam. Its adherents speak Arabic and are concentrated in mountainous areas of Syria, Lebanon, and Israel. Originally the faith was an offshoot of Shiite Islam.

East Jerusalem   The predominantly Arab sector of Jerusalem which from 1948 to 1967 was a part of Jordan. It contains the old walled city in which are sites of great historic and religious significance to Jews, Christians, and Muslims—the most important being the Western Wall, the Church of the Holy Sepulchre, and al-Aqsa Mosque. In 1967 the Israeli parliament extended the law and administration of the state to cover it, in effect annexing it.

Ecevit, Bulent   Chairman of the Republican People's Party of Turkey since 1972 and a prime minister.

Elected Assembly   Jewish elected legislative body during the British Mandate over Palestine. It was the predecessor of the Knesset, the parliament of Israel.

Eretz Israel   Hebrew term meaning "Land of Israel."

étatism   The economic policy of Kemal Ataturk. The word means "state socialism."

Faisal (King of Iraq)   Arab nationalist leader born in Mecca in 1883. He was the son of Sharif ("Prince") Hussein, who later became governor of the city and the region around it. During World War I, Hussein, in collaboration with the British, led the Arab revolt against the Turks. In 1919 Faisal represented the Arabs at the Paris Peace Conference and urged the Allies to recognize an independent Arab nation. Beginning in March 1920, he was king of an independent Arab kingdom with Damascus as its capital; it collapsed when the French conquered that city in July of the same year. From 1921 until his death in 1933, he was King of Iraq.

Farouk   King of Egypt from 1936 to 1952.

fellah (plural, fellaheen)   The Arabic word for peasant.

Gadna   Israeli paramilitary battalions for young people ages 14 to 18.

galut   Hebrew word meaning "exile."

Gaza   A strip of territory on the Mediterranean seacoast adjacent to the Israeli-Egyptian border. Formerly a part of the British Mandate of Palestine, it was administered by Egypt from 1948 to 1967 and has been under Israeli control since then. Its inhabitants are Arab.

ghazi   A Muslim warrior.

Golan Heights   A part of Syria adjacent to Lake Tiberias (the Sea of Galilee) conquered by Israel in 1967. It is sparsely inhabited.

Grand Liban   A term used by the French to indicate the enlarged territory that they created in 1920 by adding to old Mount Lebanon. The term means "Greater Lebanon," and its borders are the same as the present-day state.

Grand National Assembly (1) The plenary body of the nationalist movement led by Ataturk. It first met in Ankara in 1920. (2) The unicameral legislature under the constitution of 1924. (3) The bicameral legislature under the constitution of 1961, with the upper house being called the Senate of the Republic and the lower one the National Assembly.

Greek Catholic Member of a Christian community that broke away from the Greek Orthodox Church in the eighteenth century and affiliated with the Roman Catholic Church.

Greek Orthodox Member of one of the several related national churches that exist in the eastern Mediterranean region and throughout the world, each with its own patriarch and autonomous religious jurisdiction. All Orthodox churches are a part of Eastern Christianity, which developed from the split between Rome and Constantinople in the eleventh century. "Greek" is largely a historical designation, and increasingly the term Eastern Orthodox is being used.

groups (political) Social and economic formations that participate in politics and make demands on the political structures. Groups fall into four categories: (1) associational, (2) nonassociational, (3) institutional, and (4) anomic.

Gursel, Cemal A Turkish Army general who led the coup of May 1960. He was also head of the National Unity Committee in 1960 and 1961 and president of the republic from 1961 to 1966.

Haganah Jewish defense organization founded in Palestine in 1920. After the establishment of the state of Israel in 1948, it was transformed into the Israel Defense Forces.

Halakah Jewish religious law.

Herut A right-wing political party in Israel that grew out of Irgun Zvai Leumi. Since 1973 it has been allied with the Liberal Party in the Likud coalition. Its name means "freedom."

Herzl, Theodor The most important of the founders of the Zionist movement. Born in Budapest in 1860, he was educated in the German cultural milieu of the Austro-Hungarian Empire. In 1896 his book. *Der Judenstaat* ("The Jewish State") was published, and in 1897 under his leadership the first Zionist Congress was convened. He died in 1904.

Histadrut The giant Israeli labor union, which owns and manages numerous economic enterprises. It was founded in 1920 by some Labor-Zionist political parties.

Holocaust The murder of six million Jews by the Nazis during World War II.

iltizam A system of land ownership and administration in the Ottoman Empire whereby collection of taxes and supervision of agricultural production was delegated to a *multazim*, who received a percentage of whatever he collected from the peasants.

imam The leader of prayer in a mosque. For Shiite Muslims, one of the divinely inspired descendants of Muhammad through his daughter Fatima and his cousin and son-in-law Ali; to them the Imam is the spiritual and temporal leader of the Muslim community. For Shiites, imam also means simply a communal leader.

Inonu, Ismet A victorious military commander in the Turkish War of Independence and a close associate of Kemal Ataturk. He was president of the republic from 1938 to 1950 and chairman of the Republican People's Party from 1938 to 1972.

institutional group Organization composed of professionally qualified persons, formally organized for a purpose other than politics, yet which articulates interests and makes demands on the political structures.

Iranian   Member of a group of people who live in the plateau delineated by the Zagros and Elburz mountains and speak Persian.

Irgun Zvai Leumi   Jewish defense organization formed in Palestine in 1931. In 1948 it was disbanded and its members joined the Israel Defense Forces.

Islam   The faith based on the divine revelations transmitted to this world through the Prophet Muhammad. Ardently monotheistic, the fundamental credo is "There is no god but God."

Islamic fundamentalism   A term employed by Westerners to designate a number of modern Muslim movements, all of which desire to strengthen Islam as it adapts to the modern world. These movements are vigorously opposed to secularism and believe that Islam should continue to determine the social customs, mores, values, and beliefs of the people, the form of government, the structure of the legal system, the administration of justice, and the content of the law.

Islamic socialism   A system of beliefs and values that integrates traditional Islamic precepts with modern socialist thinking.

Ismail   Khedive of Egypt from 1863 to 1879, noted for his efforts to modernize and Westernize the country.

Israel Labor Party   Democratic, socialist, Zionist political party in Israel. It is the successor to Mapai and was formed in 1968.

Janissaries   An elite corps of soldiers and administrators in the Ottoman Empire who were first organized in the fourteenth century. It became a state within the state, and in 1826 was abolished by Mahmud II.

Jewish Agency   A branch of the World Zionist Organization with headquarters in Jerusalem that acted as a liaison with the British mandatory government. Since Israeli independence in 1948, it has been concerned with Jewish immigration to Israel and relations between Israeli and Diaspora Jews.

jihad   A religious war waged by Muslims. Today, the term has multiple connotations and can mean broadly a freedom struggle carried on with passion and willingness to sacrifice one's life. The person who engages in jihad is called a mujahid.

Justice Party   Turkish political party founded in 1961. It is the successor to the Democratic Party.

Kata'ib   A Christian political party in Lebanon. Its name means "Phalanges."

Kemalism   The ideology based on the reforms and policies of Kemal Ataturk. This is the term used outside Turkey and is the equivalent of Ataturkism, the term used in the country.

khan   The head of a tribe or the ruler of a region, especially in Iran, Afghanistan, and Soviet central Asia.

khedive   The title used by the monarchs of Egypt from 1867 to 1914 indicating that they were a semi-independent viceroy of the sultan of Turkey.

Khomeini, the Ayatollah Ruhollah   Iranian religious leader exiled by the government in 1963 because of his militant opposition to the shah's policies. While outside the country, he became a symbol and catalyst for opposition to the regime. He returned to Iran in February 1979, shortly after the shah's departure from the country, and was acclaimed by the people as their new leader.

kibbutz (plural, kibbutzim)   Israeli communal agricultural settlement that is cooperatively owned and managed.

Knesset   The unicameral Israeli parliament.

Koran   The sacred scripture of Muslims, who believe it to be the literal word of God transmitted to humankind through the Prophet Muhammad. It is written in Arabic, and usually Muslims do not translate it.

Kurds   Members of a group of people who inhabit a mountainous region overlapping Turkey, Syria, Iraq, Iran, and Azerbaijan and Armenia, both in the Soviet Union. They speak their own language (Kurdish) and are Sunni Muslims.

Labor Zionism   The Israeli political movement that combines democratic socialism and Zionism. The principal political parties that advocate it have been Mapai, the Israel Labor Party, and Mapam.

leadership (political)   Those persons who have more influence than others in the determination of political policies.

Levant   The lands bordering the eastern coast of the Mediterranean Sea. The term is now somewhat archaic.

Liberal National Party   A Christian political party in Lebanon.

Likud   A coalition of the Herut and Liberal parties in Israel.

Mahmud II   Ottoman sultan from 1808 to 1839 who introduced many modern reforms.

majlis   Word used in the Arab world and Iran to mean council or assembly. In Iran under the constitution in effect from 1906 to 1979, it designated the lower house of the parliament.

mamluk   An Arabic word literally meaning "owned," which came to designate an Egyptian dynasty (1250-1811) who were originally slaves.

mandate   A commission given by the League of Nations to a European power to rule over a certain piece of territory. Under the supervision of the League, the mandatory power was supposed to lead the mandated territory to independence.

Mapai   Democratic, socialist, Zionist political party in Israel. As a result of splits and re-mergers, in 1968 it became the Israel Labor Party.

Mapam   A Labor Zionist Israeli political party to the left of the Israel Labor Party.

Maronite   Member of a group of people who are concentrated in the mountainous region to the northeast of Beirut and to the southeast of Tripoli in Lebanon. They speak Arabic and are members of an Eastern rite of the Roman Catholic Church. Many are acculturated to French civilization.

Masada   A mountain and fortress in southern Israel where Jewish fighters made the last organized stand against the Romans in A.D. 73.

Meir, Golda   Israeli political leader. Born in Russia in 1898, she immigrated with her family to the United States in 1906, and in 1921 she settled in Palestine. She was prime minister from 1969 to 1974 and died in 1978.

Menderes, Adnan   Leader of the Democratic Party in Turkey and prime minister from 1950 to 1960. Removed from office by the military coup of that year, he was executed in 1961.

Middle East   As defined in this book, the region from Morocco to Iran that includes the Arab states, Turkey, Iran, and Israel.

millet   In the Ottoman Empire, a semiautonomous non-Muslim community organized under a religious head of its own.

Mongol   Member of a group of people who live in Mongolia and China. In the thirteenth century Mongol armies sacked Baghdad, capital of the Abbasid Empire, and marched as far as Palestine, where they were finally stopped.

moshav (plural, moshavim)   Israeli cooperative settlement of individual farms. The farms are individually owned, but work on them is organized collectively, equipment is used cooperatively, and produce is marketed jointly.

Mossadegh, Muhammad   Prime minister of Iran from 1951 to 1953 and leader of the coalition of parties called the National Front. Under his leadership the Anglo-Iranian Oil Company was nationalized. He was removed from office and arrested in the coup of August 1953.

Mount Lebanon   A mountainous region to the northeast of Beirut and to the southeast of Tripoli that is the traditional homeland of the Maronites and Druze. From 1861 to 1914 it was an autonomous territory within the Ottoman Empire (See Map 2).

Mu'awiyah   Umayyad caliph from 661 to 680.

mufti   A Muslim religious scholar who interprets the Sharia (Islamic law).

Muhammad   The Prophet and Messenger of God for Muslims. He was born in approximately A.D. 570 and died in 632, living his life in the Arabian cities of Mecca and Medina. Through him God transmitted to humankind revelations, which after his death were gathered together in the Koran. He was the political as well as the religious leader of the first community of Muslims.

Muhammad Ali   Ruler of Egypt from 1805 to 1849. Of Albanian descent, he came to Egypt in 1801 as an officer in the Ottoman army sent there to drive out the French forces under Napoleon Bonaparte. After their departure in 1801, Muhammad Ali established himself as the absolute ruler of the country. He modernized the army and administration, centralized power in his own hands, and expanded the irrigation system. His successors ruled Egypt until 1952.

Muhammad Reza Shah Pahlavi   Shah of Iran from 1941 to 1979.

Muharram   Month in the Islamic calendar during which Shiites mourn the death in 680 of Hussein, grandson of Muhammad.

mujahid   One who engages in jihad.

mujtahid   A man learned in religion and Islamic law who renders authoritative answers to legal and theological questions; an interpreter of the law.

mullah   An Islamic teacher and religious leader in Iran.

multazim   Ottoman tax collector and supervisor of agricultural lands who was allowed by the rulers to keep a percentage of whatever he collected from the peasants.

Muslim   A believer in the faith of Islam.

Muslim Brotherhood   An Islamic fundamentalist movement founded in 1928 by Hassan al-Banna, an Egyptian. It gained hundreds of thousands of militant supporters, struggled with the governments of King Farouk and of Gamal Abdel Nasser, and was suppressed by Nasser after an attempt was made upon his life in 1954. Muslim Brother cells and sympathizers have reappeared from time to time since then.

Nasser, Gamal Abdel   Leader of Egypt from the revolution of July 1952 until his death in September 1970.

nation   A group of people united among themselves by a feeling of oneness. Usually they speak the same language and live in a defined piece of territory (the fatherland). They share a common culture and history, and in some cases, a common religion.

National Action Party   A militant anticommunist party in Turkey.

National Bloc   A Christian political party in Lebanon.

National Democratic Party   The principal political party in Egypt since 1978. It was founded under the leadership of President Sadat.

National Pact   An agreement made in 1943 between the Lebanese Maronite and Sunni leaders. It allotted political offices according to sect and defined the basic policies of the state.

National Religious Party   Israeli political party that advocates state enforcement of Jewish religious law.

National Salvation Party   A right-wing Turkish political party in existence since 1972.

National Unity Committee   A group of Turkish military officers that led the country from the coup of May 1960 until October 1961, when it returned control to civilian leadership under a new constitution.

new middle class   Persons with a modern education at least through secondary school who live mostly on a salary derived from government employment, especially army officers and middle- and upper-level bureaucrats.

nonassociational groups   Communities of people tied together by kinship, race, nationality, language, or religion.

Oriental Jew   Member of one of the three divisions of Jews who lived in the Middle East and North Africa and spoke Arabic. In modern Israel the term is used interchangeably with "Sephardi" and designates a Jew of Middle Eastern or North African origin.

Ottoman   The name of a Turkish ruling dynasty that led an empire by that name from the fourteenth century until 1923. In 1453 they captured Constantinople from the Byzantines, named it Istanbul, and from that time onward it was the capital of their empire. At its height in the sixteenth century, the Ottoman domain stretched from Hungary in the north to the Arabian Peninsula in the south, excluding Yemen, and from Algeria in the west to Iraq in the east.

Pahlavi   The name that Reza Khan, ruler of Iran, gave to the dynasty he founded in 1925.

Palestinian   Member of a group of people or their descendants who lived in the British Mandate of Palestine prior to the establishment of Israel in 1948. During that year large numbers fled to the states bordering on Israel; in 1967, after Israel conquered East Jerusalem, the West Bank, and Gaza, another exodus took place. Today the term refers to Arabs who have their origins in Palestine but are scattered throughout the Middle East.

pasha   A title common in the Ottoman Empire which was made illegal in republican Turkey and revolutionary Egypt.

patriarch   A high ecclesiastical authority for Christian communities. In addition to his responsibilities as spiritual leader, he represents his members' interests vis-à-vis other groups and with the government.

perennial irrigation   A method of irrigation in which dams back up a river, and canals divert the water from it into fields. The advantage of this method is that two or three crops can be grown during a year where the weather is warm.

Persia   The name given to Iran by the ancient Greeks.

Poalei Aguda Israel   Israeli political party to the right of the National Religious Party that advocates state enforcement of Jewish religious law. Its name means "Workers of the Association of Israel."

pogrom   An organized and often officially instigated massacre of people, especially Jews, along with destruction of their property.

policies (political)   Decisions made by a government of long-lasting consequence and broad social scope.

protectorate   A form of colonialism in which the colonial power forces a weaker nation to sign a treaty whereby the former agrees to "protect" the latter. Usually the colonial power also controls the dependent country's taxation system, armed forces, and foreign relations.

Qajar   Iranian dynasty from 1794 to 1925.

Rabin, Yitzhak   Israeli political leader. Born in Palestine in 1922, he was commander of Israeli armed forces during the war of June 1967. As leader of the Israel Labor Party, he was prime minister from 1974 to 1977.

Ramadan   The month in the Islamic lunar calendar during which Muslims fast from sunrise to sunset.

Republican People's Party   Turkish political party founded by Ataturk in 1923.

Revolutionary Command Council   A group of military officers who ruled Egypt from the revolution of 1952 until the promulgation of a new constitution in 1956.

Reza Khan   Commander of the Persian Cossack Brigade who came to power in Iran in 1921 through a coup d'etat. In 1925 he assumed the crown, and ruled as Reza Shah Pahlavi from then until 1941.

al-Sadat, Anwar   A member of the group of military officers who carried out the Egyptian revolution of 1952. He has been president of the republic since 1970.

Safavid   An Iranian dynasty that ruled from 1501 to 1736. It was the first independent government after the Arab-Muslim conquest of the seventh century, and it strengthened Iranian national consciousness. Under it, Shiite Islam was established as the religion of the state.

Sassanid   A Persian dynasty that ruled over an empire from the third century A.D. to the Muslim conquest between 637 and 651.

SAVAK   Persian acronym for "State Organization for Intelligence and Security," established by the shah in 1957 and abolished by the revolutionary government in 1979. Its mission was to suppress opposition to the government.

Seljuq   A Turkish dynasty that ruled a sizable empire in Western Asia from 1037 to 1092.

Sephardi   A member of one of the three divisions of Jews who lived in the Iberian Peninsula and were expelled during the Grand Inquisition of the fifteenth century. They spoke Ladino, a mixture of Spanish and Hebrew. In modern Israel the term is used interchangeably with Oriental Jew and designates a Jew of Middle Eastern or North African origin.

Sèvres, Treaty of   A humiliating treaty imposed upon the defeated Ottoman government by the victorious Allies. It was signed at Sèvres, France in 1920 and was never implemented. The Treaty of Lausanne signed in 1923 by representatives of the Ataturk government and the Allies superseded it.

shah   The Persian word for king.

Shah Nameh   A great Persian epic poem written by Ferdosi about A.D. 1000 glorifying Persian kings and the Persian nation. The title means "Chronicle of Kings."

Sharia   Islamic law derived primarily from the Koran and governing in theory not only religious matters but also political, economic, civil, criminal, and domestic affairs.

Shariati, Ali Iranian religious leader who greatly influenced the youth of Iran through lectures and writings that integrated traditional Islamic belief with modern learning. He lived from 1933 to 1977.

Shazar, Zalman Born in Russia in 1889, he settled in Palestine in 1924. He was president of Israel from 1963 to 1973.

sheik A title commonly used in Arab countries with a variety of meanings: (1) the head of a family, tribe, clan, or village; (2) a Muslim religious leader of learning and distinction; (3) especially in the Arabian Peninsula, a ruler or prince.

Shiite Islam (Shiism) One of the two major divisions of Islam. It is the dominant religion in Iran.

social mosaic A society in which groups live next to one another but without a sense of common purpose or identity. The connecting links among them are few.

state An entity recognized by other states as being soverign and equal. It has a government that rules over a people in a clearly defined territory.

structure (political) Formal patterns of action whereby authoritative decisions are made.

Suleiman the Magnificent Ottoman sultan from 1520 to 1566 during whose reign the Turkish empire was at its height.

sultan A title for a Muslim ruler.

Sufi A Muslim of great religious devotion and piety, often a mystic.

Sunni Islam (Sunnism) One of the two major divisions of Islam. It is predominant among Arabs and Turks.

Taghout A pre-Islamic idol at Mecca that the Ayatollah Ruhollah Khomeini equated with the shah and his regime.

Torah The most important holy scriptures for Jews, comprising the first five books of the Christian Old Testament.

Tudeh An Iranian communist political party founded in 1942. It was outlawed in 1949 but continued to exist in the Mossadegh period and was not repressed until after the shah returned to power in 1953.

Turk Member of a group of people who speak Turkish and today comprise the overwhelming majority of the population of Turkey. The Turks originated in central Asia and migrated into the Middle East in successive waves beginning in the ninth century. They converted to Islam as they moved westwards. Turkish minorities exist in Iran and the Soviet Union.

ulama Islamic religious scholars who variously perform the roles of teacher, preacher, and judge.

Umayyad A dynasty of Arab Sunni Muslim monarchs who ruled an empire with its capital in Damascus from 661 to 750.

United Arab Republic A union of Syria and Egypt established in 1958. Syria seceded in 1961, but Egypt continued to call itself by this name until 1971.

waqf A Muslim charitable foundation used to support mosques, religious schools, and organizations that distribute aid to the poor. Its income is derived from agricultural land or urban real estate set aside for this purpose. (The Turkish spelling is vakf.)

Weizmann, Chaim   Zionist leader who lived from 1874 to 1952. He was born in Poland but settled in England in 1904. A chemist by profession whose research made a significant contribution to the British war effort, he was influential in persuading the government to issue the Balfour Declaration. He served as Israel's first president from 1949 to 1952.

West Bank   Territory on the west bank of the Jordan River controlled from 1948 to 1967 by the state of Jordan, and since 1967 by Israel.

Western Jew   An Ashkenazi Jew.

White Revolution   Program of reform in Iran launched by Muhammad Reza Shah in 1963.

World Zionist Organization   A movement founded in 1897 at the First Zionist Congress, which was called by Theodor Herzl at Basel, Switzerland. WZO advocates unity of the Jewish people and the centrality of Israel in Jewish life; it supports immigration to Israel and the preservation of Jewish education and culture.

Yazid   Umayyad caliph from 680 to 683 and bitter enemy of the Shiites.

Yiddish   A German dialect written in Hebrew script and spoken by Ashkenazi Jews.

Yishuv   The Jewish community in Palestine prior to independence.

Young Turks   Group of nationalist students and army officers who took power in Turkey in 1908 with the objective of restoring the constitution of 1876. After a brief period of freedom, their rule degenerated into a military dictatorship.

za^{c}im   Used especially in reference to Lebanon, where it means a powerful political leader whose authority is based upon loyalty of his followers. The supporters of a *za^{c}im* usually come from one sect and typically from a single region.

Zionism   The Jewish nationalist movement that began in the nineteenth century with the objectives of encouraging Jewish settlement in Palestine, establishing there a sovereign nation-state, reviving the Hebrew language, and creating a sense of identity.

Zoroastrianism   The religion of pre-Islamic Iran that was founded by the Prophet Zoroaster.

Bibliography

CHAPTER 2: THE INFLUENCE OF GEOGRAPHY ON SOCIETY AND POLITY

Geography

Cressey, George B., *Crossroads: Land and Life in Southwest Asia.* Chicago: J. B. Lippincott Company, 1960.

Fisher, William B., *The Middle East: A Physical, Social, and Regional Geography* (6th ed.). London: Methuen, 1971.

U.S. Government, Central Intelligence Agency, *Atlas: Issues in the Middle East.* Washington, D.C.: U.S. Government Printing Office, 1973.

Petroleum

Anthony, John Duke, ed., *The Middle East: Oil, Politics and Development.* Washington, D.C.: American Enterprise Institute, 1975.

Bill, James A., and Robert W. Stookey, *Politics and Petroleum: The Middle East and the United States.* Brunswick, Ohio: King's Court, 1975.

Engler, Robert, *The Brotherhood of Oil: Energy Policy and the Public Interest.* Chicago: University of Chicago Press, 1977.

____, *The Politics of Oil: A Study of Private Power and Democratic Directions.* New York: Macmillan, Inc., 1961.

Finnie, David H., *Desert Enterprise: The Middle East Oil Industry in Its Local Environment.* Cambridge, Mass.: Harvard University Press, 1958.

Issawi, Charles, and Mohammed Yeganeh, *The Economics of Middle Eastern Oil.* New York: Praeger, 1962.

Lenczowski, George, *Oil and State in the Middle East.* Ithaca, N.Y.: Cornell University Press, 1960.

Longrigg, Stephen H., *Oil in the Middle East: Its Discovery and Development* (3rd ed.). London: Oxford University Press, 1967.

Mosley, Leonard, *Power Play: Oil in the Middle East.* New York: Random House, Inc., 1973.

al-Otaiba, Mana Saeed, *OPEC and the Petroleum Industry.* New York: John Wiley & Sons, Inc., 1975.

Shwadran, Benjamin, *The Middle East: Oil and the Great Powers* (3rd ed.). New York: John Wiley & Sons, Inc., 1974.

Stephens, Robert, *The Arab's New Frontier.* Boulder, Colo.: Westview Press, 1976.

Stork, Joe, *Middle East Oil and the Energy Crisis.* New York: Monthly Review Press, 1975.

CHAPTER 3: THE NATIONS OF THE MIDDLE EAST

Nation and State

Emerson, Rupert, *From Empire to Nation: The Rise to Self-Assertion of Asian and African Peoples.* Cambridge, Mass.: Harvard University Press, 1960.

The Arab Nation

Antonius, George, *The Arab Awakening: The Story of the Arab National Movement* (4th ed.). Beirut: Khayat's College Book Cooperative, 1961.

Binder, Leonard, *The Ideological Revolution in the Middle East.* New York: John Wiley & Sons, Inc., 1964.

Carmichael, Joel, *The Shaping of the Arabs: A Study in Ethnic Identity.* New York: Macmillan, Inc., 1967.

Cleveland, William L., *The Making of an Arab Nationalist: Ottomanism and Arabism in the Life and Thought of Sati al-Husri.* Princeton: Princeton University Press, 1972.

Cremeans, Charles D., *The Arabs and the World: Nasser's Arab Nationalist Policy.* New York: Praeger, 1962.

Haim, Sylvia G., ed., *Arab-Nationalism: An Anthology.* Berkeley: University of California Press, 1962.

Khadduri, Majid, *Political Trends in the Arab World: The Role of Ideas and Ideals in Politics.* Baltimore: The Johns Hopkins University Press, 1970.

Nuseibeh, Hazem Z., *The Ideas of Arab Nationalism.* Ithaca, N.Y.: Cornell University Press, 1956.

Sayegh, Fayez, *Arab Unity: Hope and Fulfillment.* Old Greenwich, Conn.: The Devin-Adair Co., Inc., 1958.

Sharabi, Hisham, *Arab Intellectuals and the West: The Formative Years, 1875-1914.* Baltimore: The Johns Hopkins University Press, 1970.

Zeine, Zeine N., *Arab-Turkish Relations and the Emergence of Arab Nationalism.* Beirut: Khayat's College Book Cooperative, 1958.

———, *The Struggle for Arab Independence: Western Diplomacy and the Rise and Fall of Faisal's Kingdom in Syria.* Beirut: Khayat's College Book Cooperative, 1960.

The Turkish Nation

Balfour, John Patrick Douglas, Lord Kinross, *Ataturk: A Biography of Mustafa Kemal, Father of Modern Turkey.* New York: William Morrow & Co., Inc., 1965.

Berkes, Niyazi, *The Development of Secularism in Turkey.* Montreal: McGill University Press, 1964.

Gökalp, Ziya, *Turkish Nationalism and Western Civilization,* trans. Niyazi Berkes. New York: Columbia University Press, 1958.

Heyd, Uriel, *Foundations of Turkish Nationalism: The Life and Teaching of Ziya Gökalp.* London: Lusac, 1950.

Lewis, Bernard, *The Emergence of Modern Turkey.* London: Oxford University Press, 1961.

Mardin, Serif, *The Genesis of Young Ottoman Thought.* Princeton: Princeton University Press, 1962.

Ramsaur, Ernest E., Jr., *The Young Turks: Prelude to the Revolution of 1908.* Princeton: Princeton University Press, 1957.

Ward, Robert, and Dankwart Rustow, *Political Modernization in Japan and Turkey.* Princeton: Princeton University Press, 1968.

The Iranian Nation

Cottam, Richard, *Nationalism in Iran.* Pittsburgh: University of Pittsburgh Press, 1964.

Mustofi, Khosrow, *Aspects of Nationalism.* Salt Lake City: University of Utah Research Monograph No. 3, 1964.

The Jewish Nation

Buber, Martin, *Israel and Palestine: The History of an Idea,* trans. Stanley Gedman. London: East and West Library, 1952.

Elmessiri, Abdelwahab, *The Land of Promise: A Critique of Political Zionism.* New Brunswick, N.J.: North American Publishing Company, 1977.

Gal, Allon, *Socialist Zionism: Theory and Issues in Contemporary Jewish Nationalism.* Cambridge, Mass.: Schenkman Publishing Co., Inc., 1973.

Halpern, Ben, *The Idea of the Jewish State* (2nd ed.). Cambridge, Mass.: Harvard University Press, 1961.

Herzl, Theodor, *The Jewish State (Der Judenstaat),* trans. Harry Zohn. New York: Herzl Press, 1970.

Weizmann, Chaim, *Trial and Error: The Autobiography of Chaim Weizmann.* New York: Harper & Row, Publishers, Inc., 1949.

CHAPTER 4: SOCIAL, POLITICAL, AND ECONOMIC DEVELOPMENT SINCE 1798

Social, Political and Economic Development

Binder, Leonard, "Prolegomena to the Comparative Study of Middle East Governments," *American Political Science Review,* 51 (September 1957): 651-68.

Bonné, Alfred, *State and Economics in the Middle East: A Society in Transition* (2nd ed.). London: Routledge and Kegan Paul, 1955.

Dodd, Stuart C., *Social Relations in the Near East: A Text-book in Citizenship Prepared for the Freshmen at the American University of Beirut* (2nd ed.). Beirut, 1940. Reprinted, New York: AMS Press, Inc., 1975.

Dupree, Louis, "Democracy and the Military Base of Power," *Middle East Journal,* 22 (Winter 1968), 29-44.

Hudson, Michael C., *Arab Politics: The Search For Legitimacy.* New Haven: Yale University Press, 1977.

Huntington, Samuel P., *Political Order in Changing Societies.* New Haven: Yale University Press, 1968.

Issawi, Charles P., ed., *The Economic History of the Middle East:1800-1914.* Chicago: University of Chicago Press, 1966.

Landen, Robert G., comp., *The Emergence of the Modern Middle East: Selected Readings.* New York: Van Nostrand Reinhold Company, 1970.

Leiden, Carl., ed., *Conflict of Traditionalism and Modernism in the Muslim Middle East.* Austin: University of Texas Press, 1967.

Lerner, Daniel, *The Passing of Traditional Society: Modernizing the Middle East.* Glencoe, Ill.: Free Press, 1958.

Lutsky, V., *Modern History of the Arab Countries,* trans. Lika Nasser. Moscow: Progress Publishers, 1969.

M.I.T. Study Group, "The Transitional Process," in *Comparative Politics: Notes and Readings* (rev. ed.), ed. Roy Macridis and Bernard Brown, pp. 618-41. Homewood, Ill.: Dorsey Press, 1964.

Traditional Islamic Society

Gibb, Hamilton A. R., and Harold Bowen, *Islamic Society and the West: A Study of the Impact of Western Civilization on Moslem Culture in the Near East* (vol. 1, parts 1 and 2). London: Oxford University Press, 1950, 1957.

Modernizing Autocratic Society

Baer, Gabriel, *Studies in the Social History of Modern Egypt.* Chicago: University of Chicago Press, 1969.

Davison, Roderic H., *Reform in the Ottoman Empire, 1856-1876.* Princeton: Princeton University Press, 1963.

Holt, Peter M., *Egypt and the Fertile Crescent, 1516-1922, A Political History.* Ithaca, N.Y.: Cornell University Press, 1966.

Lewis, Bernard, *The Emergence of Modern Turkey.* London: Oxford University Press, 1961.

____, *The Middle East and the West.* Bloomington: Indiana University Press, 1965.

Polk, William R., and Richard Chambers, eds., *Beginnings of Modernization in the Middle East: the 19th Century.* Chicago: University of Chicago Press, 1968.

Colonial Society

Hourani, Albert, *Syria and Lebanon: A Political Essay.* London: Oxford University Press, 1946.

Memmi, Albert, *The Colonizer and the Colonized,* trans. Howard Greenfield. Boston: Beacon Press, 1965.

Monroe, Elizabeth, *Britain's Moment in the Middle East, 1914-1956.* Baltimore: The Johns Hopkins University Press, 1963.

Susa, Nasim. *The Capitulatory Regime of Turkey: Its History, Origin, and Nature.* Baltimore: The Johns Hopkins University Press, 1933.

The Bureaucratic Polity

Abdel-Malek, Anouar, *Egypt, Military Society: The Army Regime, The Left, and Social Change Under Nasser,* trans. Charles Lam Markmann. New York: Random House, Inc., 1968.

Be'eri, Eliezer, *Army Officers in Arab Politics and Society,* trans. Dov Ben-Abba. New York: Praeger, 1969.

Berger, Morroe, *Bureaucracy and Society in Modern Egypt: A Study of the Higher Civil Service.* Princeton: Princeton University Press, 1957.

Binder, Leonard, and others, *Crises and Sequences in Political Development.* Princeton: Princeton University Press, 1971.

Debbasch, Charles, and others, *Pouvoir et Administration au Maghreb: Etudes sur les Elites Maghrebines.* Paris: Editions du Centre National de la Recherche Scientifique, 1970.

Halpern, Manfred, *The Politics of Social Change in the Middle East and North Africa.* Princeton: Princeton University Press, 1963.

Hurewitz, J. C., *Middle East Politics: The Military Dimension.* New York: Praeger, 1969.

LaPalombara, Joseph, ed., *Bureaucracy and Political Development.* Princeton: Princeton University Press, 1963.

Riggs, Fred, *Thailand: The Modernization of a Bureaucratic Polity.* Honolulu: East-West Center Press, 1966.

Rustow, Dankwart, *A World of Nations: Problems of Political Modernization.* Washington, D.C.: The Brookings Institution, 1967.

CHAPTER 5: IDEOLOGICAL CHANGE SINCE 1798

General

Abdel-Malek, Anouar, *Anthologie de la literature Arabe contemporaine: les essais.* Paris: Editions du Seuil, 1965.

____, *La Pensée Politique Arabe Contemporaine.* Paris: Editions du Seuil, 1970.

Hourani, Albert, *Arabic Thought in the Liberal Age, 1798-1939.* London: Oxford University Press, 1962.

Karpat, Kemal, ed., *Political and Social Thought in the Contemporary Middle East.* New York: Praeger, 1968.

Laroui, Abadallah, *L'Idéologie Arabe Contemporaine.* Paris: François Maspero, 1967.

Rivlin, Benjamin, and Joseph S. Szyliowicz, eds., *The Contemporary Middle East.* New York: Random House, Inc., 1965.

Liberal Democracy

Baer, Gabriel, *Studies in the Social History of Modern Egypt.* Chicago: University of Chicago Press, 1969.

Berkes, Niyazi, *The Development of Secularism in Turkey.* Montreal: McGill University Press, 1964.

Davison, Roderic H., *Reform in the Ottoman Empire: 1856-1876.* Princeton: Princeton University Press, 1963.

Cottam, Richard, *Nationalism in Iran.* Pittsburgh: University of Pittsburgh Press, 1964.

Lewis, Bernard, *The Emergence of Modern Turkey.* London: Oxford University Press, 1961.

____, *The Middle East and the West.* Bloomington: Indiana University Press, 1964.

Marsot, Afaf Lutfi al-Sayyid, *Egypt's Liberal Experiment: 1922-1936.* Berkeley: University of California Press, 1977.

Safran, Nadav, *Egypt in Search of Political Community: An Analysis of the Intellectual and Political Evolution of Egypt 1804-1952.* Cambridge, Mass.: Harvard University Press, 1961.

Islamic Fundamentalism

al-Ghazzali, Muhammad, *Our Beginning in Wisdom.* Washington, D.C.: American Council of Learned Societies, 1953.

Husaini, Ishak M., *The Moslem Bretheren.* Beirut: Khayat's College Book Cooperative, 1956.

al-Husri, Khaldun S., *Three Reformers: A Study in Modern Arab Political Thought.* Beirut: Khayat's College Book Cooperative, 1966.

Kerr, Malcolm H., *Islamic Reform: the Political and Legal Theories of Muhammad Abduh and Rashid Rida.* Berkeley: University of California Press, 1966.

Mitchell, Richard P., *The Society of the Muslim Brothers.* London: Oxford University Press, 1969.

Smith, Wilfred Cantwell, *Islam in Modern History.* Princeton: Princeton University Press, 1957.

Socialism

Abu Jaber, Kamel S., *The Arab Ba'th Socialist Party.* Syracuse: Syracuse University Press, 1966.

Binder, Leonard, trans. and commentary, "The Constitution of the Arab Resurrection (Ba'th) Socialist Party of Syria," *Middle East Journal,* 13 (Spring 1959), 195-200.

Devlin, John F., *The Ba'th Party.* Stanford, Calif.: Hoover Institution Press, 1966.

Enayat, Hamid, "Islam and Socialism in Egypt," *Middle Eastern Studies,* 4 (January 1968), 141-72.

Karpat, Kemal H., "Socialism and the Labor Party of Turkey," *Middle East Journal,* 21 (Spring 1967), 157-72.

___, "The Turkish Left," *Journal of Contemporary History,* 1, no. 2 (1966), 169-86.

Kaylani, Nabil M., "The Rise of the Syrian Ba'th, 1940-1958: Political Success, Party Failure," *International Journal of Middle East Studies,* 3 (January 1972), 3-23.

Kerr, Malcolm H., "The Emergence of a Socialist Ideology in Egypt," *Middle East Journal,* 16 (Spring 1962), 127-44.

Hanna, Sami A., and George H. Gardner, eds., *Arab Socialism: A Documentary Survey.* Leiden, Netherlands: E. J. Brill, 1969.

Torrey, Gordon H., "The Ba'th: Ideology and Practice," *Middle East Journal,* 23 (Autumn 1969), 445-70.

Marxism

Abdel-Malek, Anouar, "Problématique du socialism dans le monde arabe," *L'Homme et la Société* (Paris), no. 2 (October-December 1966), 125-48.

Agwani, M. S., *Communism in the Arab East.* London: Asia Publishing House, 1970.

"Le Communisme et les problémes du monde arabe," *Orient* (Paris), no. 27 (3 Trimestre 1967) 195-208.

Daher, Adel, "Current Trends in Arab Intellectual Thought," RAND publication RM 5979-FF (Dec. 1969).

Harris, George S., *The Origins of Communism in Turkey.* Stanford, Calif.: Hoover Institution Press, 1967.

Ismael, Tareq, *The Arab Left.* Syracuse, N.Y.: Syracuse University Press, 1976.

Joyaux, François, "La Politique chinoise au moyen orient," *Orient* (Paris), no. 40 (4 Trimestre 1966), 25-44.

Karpat, Kemal, "Ideological Developments in Turkey Since the Revolution of 1960," *Turkish Yearbook of International Relations 1966.* Ankara: The School of Political Science, 1966.

Laqueur, Walter Z., *Communism and Nationalism in the Middle East.* New York: Praeger, 1956.

"Le Monde arabe cherche les leçons politiques de la défaite," special issue of *Democratie Nouvelle,* 21 (Feb.-March 1968).

Montasser, Adel, "La Répression anti-démocratique en Egypte," *Les Temps Modernes* (Paris), 16, nos. 173-174 (1960), 418-41.

"Le Parti communiste syrien et L'union arabe," *Orient* (Paris), no. 26 (2 Trimestre 1963), 151-59.

Sayilgan, Aclan, *Rifts Within the Turkish Left (1927-66).* (2nd ed.). Washington: Joint Publications Research Service, 1967.

"Unité arabe et socialisme en Egypte," *Orient* (Paris), no. 31 (3 Trimestre 1964), 185-204.

Yearbook on International Communist Affairs, 1971. Stanford, Calif.: Hoover Institution Press, 1971.

Zabih, Sepehr, *The Communist Movement in Iran.* Berkeley: University of California Press, 1966.

CHAPTER 6: ISRAEL

Abramov, S. Zalman, *Perpetual Dilemma: Jewish Religion in the Jewish State.* Rutherford, N.J.: Fairleigh Dickinson University Press, 1976.

Arian, Alan, *The Choosing People: Voting Behavior in Israel.* Cleveland, Ohio: Case Western Reserve University Press, 1973.

____, *Elections in Israel—1969.* Edison, N.J.: Transaction Books, 1969.

____, *Elections in Israel—1973.* Edison, N.J.: Transaction Books, 1973.

____, *Ideological Change in Israel.* Cleveland, Oh.: Case Western Reserve University Press, 1968.

Arkadie, Brian Van, *Benefits and Burdens: A Report on the West Bank and Gaza Strip Economies Since 1967.* Washington, D.C.: Carnegie Endowment for International Peace, 1977.

Avi-Hai, Avraham, *Ben Gurion: State Builder.* Edison, N.J.: Transaction Books, 1974.

Badi, Joseph, *The Government of the State of Israel: A Critical Account of its Parliament, Executive, and Judiciary.* New York: Twayne Publishers, 1963.

Bernstein, Marver, *The Politics of Israel.* Princeton: Princeton University Press, 1957.

Birnbaum, Ervin, *The Politics of Compromise: State and Religion in Israel.* Rutherford N.J.: Fairleigh Dickinson University Press, 1970.

Curtis, Michael, and Mordecai Chertoff, eds., *Israel: Social Structure and Change.* New Brunswick, N.J.: Transaction Books, 1973.

Daniel, Abraham, *Labor Enterprises in Israel* (2 vols.). Edison, N.J.: Transaction Books, 1977.

Deshen, Shlomo, and Moshe Shokeid, *The Predicament of Homecoming: Cultural and Social Life of North Africa Immigrants in Israel.* Ithaca, N.Y.: Cornell University Press, 1974.

Eisenstadt, Shmuel N., *Israeli Society.* New York: Basic Books, Inc., Publishers, 1967.

Elon, Amos, *The Israelis: Founders and Sons.* New York: Holt, Rinehart & Winston, 1971.

Etzioni-Halevy, Eva, and Rina Shapira, *Political Culture in Israel: Cleavage and Integration Among Israeli Jews.* New York: Praeger, 1977.

Fein, Leonard, *Israel: Politics and People.* Boston: Little, Brown & Company, 1968.

Halevi, Nadav, and Ruth Klinov-Malul, *The Economic Development of Israel.* New York: Praeger, 1968.

Horowitz, David, *The Economics of Israel.* Oxford, England: Pergamon Press, 1967.

Inbar, Michael, and Chaim Adler, *Ethnic Integration in Israel: A Comparative Case Study of Moroccan Brothers Who Settled in France and in Israel.* Edison, N.J.: Transaction Books, 1977.

Iris, Mark, and Avraham Shama, *Immigration Without Integration.* Edison, N.J.: Transaction Books, 1977.

Isaac, Rael Jean, *Israel Divided: Ideological Politics in the Jewish State.* Baltimore: The Johns Hopkins University Press, 1976.

Jiryis, Sabri, *The Arabs in Israel, 1948-1966.* Beirut: Institute for Palestine Studies, 1968.

Kraines, Oscar, *The Impossible Dilemma: Who is a Jew in the State of Israel?* New York: Bloch Publishing Co., Inc., 1976.

Landau, Asher F., *Selected Judgments of the Supreme Court of Israel.* Edison, N.J.: Transaction Books, 1971.

Landau, Jacob, *The Arabs in Israel: A Political Study.* New York: Oxford University Press, 1969.

Lissak, Moshe, *Social Mobility in Israel Society.* Edison, N.J.: Transaction Books, 1961.

Lissak, Moshe, and Emanuel Gutmann, eds., *Political Institutions and Processes in Israel.* New York: E. P. Dutton, 1974.

Lucas, Noah, *The Modern History of Israel.* New York: Praeger, 1975.

Medding, Peter Y., *Mapai in Israel: Political Organization and Government in a New Society.* Cambridge, England: University Press, 1972.

Nahas, Dunia Habib, *The Israeli Communist Party.* London: Croom Helm, 1976.

Pack, Howard, *Structural Change and Economic Policy in Israel.* New Haven: Yale University Press, 1971.

Patai, Raphael, *Israel Between East and West.* Philadelphia: Jewish Publication Society, 1953.

Peretz, Don, *The Government and Politics of Israel.* Boulder, Colo.: Westview Press, 1979.

Perlmutter, Amos, *Military and Politics in Israel: Nation Building and Role Expansion.* New York: Praeger, 1969.

Salpeter, Eliahu, and Yuval Elizur, *Who Rules Israel?* New York: Harper & Row Publishers, Inc., 1973.

Seligman, Lester G., *Leadership in a New Nation: Political Development in Israel.* New York: Lieber-Atherton Inc., 1964.

Selzer, Michael, *The Aryanization of the Jewish State.* New York: Black Star, 1967.

Smooha, Sammy, *Israel: Pluralism and Conflict.* Berkeley: University of California Press, 1977.

Zidon, Asher, *Knesset: The Parliament of Israel.* New York: Herzl Press, 1967.

Zohar, David M., *Political Parties in Israel: The Evolution of Israeli Democracy.* New York: Praeger, 1974.

Zucker, Norman L., *The Coming Crisis in Israel: Private Faith and Public Policy.* Cambridge, Mass.: The M.I.T. Press, 1973.

CHAPTER 7: LEBANON

Alouche, Richard, *Evolution d'un centre de villégiature au Liban (Broummana).* Beirut: Dar el-Machreq, 1970.

Barakat, Halim, *Lebanon in Strife: Student Preludes to the Civil War.* Austin: University of Texas Press, 1977.

_____, "Social and Political Integration in Lebanon: A Case of Social Mosaic," *Middle East Journal,* 27 (Summer 1973), 301-18.

Bashir, Iskandar, *Planned Administrative Change in Lebanon.* Beirut: Department of Political Studies and Public Administration, American University of Beirut, n.d.

Binder, Leonard, ed., *Politics in Lebanon.* New York: John Wiley & Sons, Inc., 1966.

Bulloch, John, *Death of a Country: The Civil War in Lebanon.* London: Weidenfeld & Nicolson, 1977.

Chiha, Michel, *Politique intérieure.* Beirut: Editions du Trident, 1964.

Corm, Georges G., *Politique economique et planification au Liban, 1953-1963.* Beirut: Imprimerie universelle, 1964.

Crow, Ralph, "Religious Sectarianism in the Lebanese Political System," *Journal of Politics,* 24 (August 1962), 489-520.

Dodd, Peter, and Halim Barakat, *River Without Bridges: A Study of the Exodus of the 1967 Palestinian Arab Refugees.* Beirut: Institute for Palestine Studies, 1968.

Dodge, Bayard, *The American University of Beirut.* Beirut: Khayat's College Book Cooperative, 1958.

Entelis, John P., *Pluralism and Party Transformation in Lebanon: Al-Katā'ib, 1936-1970.* Leiden, Netherlands: E. J. Brill, 1974.

Farsoun, Samih, and Walter Carroll, "The Civil War in Lebanon: Sect, Class, and Imperialism." *Monthly Review,* 28, no. 2 (June 1976), 12-37.

Frankel, Ephraim, "The Maronite Patriarch: An Historical View of a Religious Za'īm in the 1958 Lebanese Crisis," *Muslim World,* 66, nos. 3 and 4 (July and Oct. 1976), 213-25, 245-58.

Government of Lebanon, Ministère du Plan, *Besoins et possibilités de développement du Liban* (2 vols.). Beirut: Mission IRFED, 1960-1961.

____, Direction Centrale de la Statistique, *Recueil de statistiques libanaises.*

Grassmuck, George, and Kamal Salibi, *Reformed Administration in Lebanon* (2nd ed.). Ann Arbor: Center for Near Eastern and North African Studies, University of Michigan, 1964.

Gulick, John, *Social Structure and Culture Change in a Lebanese Village.* New York: Johnson Reprint Corp., 1968.

____, *Tripoli: A Modern Arab City.* Cambridge, Mass.: Harvard University Press, 1967.

Habash, George, *Laborers and the Palestinian Revolution.* Beirut: Kitab al-Hadaf, 1970.

Haley, P. Edward, and Lewis Snider, eds., *Lebanon in Crisis: Participants and Issues.* Syracuse, N.Y.: Syracuse University Press, 1979.

Harik, Iliya, "Political Elite of Lebanon," in *Political Elites in the Middle East,* ed. George Lenczowski, pp. 201-220. Washington, D.C.: American Enterprise Institute, 1975.

____, *Politics and Change in a Traditional Society: Lebanon, 1711-1845.* Princeton: Princeton University Press, 1968.

Hitti, Philip, *Lebanon in History.* New York: Macmillan, Inc., 1957.

____, *A Short History of Lebanon.* New York: St. Martin's Press, Inc., 1965.

Hottinger, Arnold, "Zu'amā' and Politics in the Lebanese Crisis of 1958," *Middle East Journal,* 15 (Spring 1961), 127-40.

Hourani, Albert, *Syria and Lebanon: A Political Essay.* London: Oxford University Press, 1946.

Hudson, Michael C., "Democracy and Social Mobilization in Lebanese Politics," *Comparative Politics,* 1 (January 1969), 245-63.

____, "The Electoral Process and Political Development in Lebanon," *Middle East Journal,* 20 (Spring 1966), 173-86.

____, *The Precarious Republic: Political Modernization in Lebanon.* New York: Random House, Inc., 1968.

Kewenig, Wilhelm, *Die Koexistenz der Religionsgemeinschaften im Libanon.* Berlin: De Gruyter, 1965.

Khalaf, Nadim G. *Economic Implications of the Size of Nations: With Special Reference to Lebanon.* Leiden, Netherlands: E. J. Brill, 1971.

Khalaf, Samir, "Primoridal Ties and Politics in Lebanon," *Middle Eastern Studies* (London), 4 (April 1968), 243-69.

Koury, Enver M., *The Crisis in the Lebanese System: Confessionalism and Chaos.* Washington, D.C.: American Enterprise Institute, 1976.

____, *The Operational Capability of the Lebanese Political System.* Beirut: Catholic Press, 1972.

Longrigg, Stephen, *Syria and Lebanon Under French Mandate.* London: Oxford University Press, 1958.

Meo, Leila M., *Lebanon: Improbable Nation: A Study in Political Development.* Bloomington: Indiana University Press, 1965.

Polk, William R., *The Opening of South Lebanon, 1788-1840: A Study of the Impact of the West on the Middle East.* Cambridge, Mass.: Harvard University Press, 1963.

Qubain, Fahim I., *Crisis in Lebanon.* Washington, D.C.: Middle East Institute, 1961.

Rilhac, Margaret, "Lebanon at School," *Middle East Forum* (Beirut), 36, no. 5 (May 1960), 11-18.

Rizk, Charles, *Le Régime politique libanais.* Paris: Librairie générale de droit et de jurisprudence, 1966.

Rondot, Pierre, *Le Institutions politiques du Liban: des communautés traditionnelles à l'état moderne.* Paris: Institut d'études de l'Orient contemporain, 1947.

Salem, Elie, "Cabinet Politics in Lebanon," *Middle East Journal,* 21 (Autumn 1967), 488-502.

____, *Modernization Without Revolution: Lebanon's Experience.* Bloomington: Indiana University Press, 1973.

Salibi, Kamal S., *Crossroads to Civil War: Lebanon 1958-1976.* Delmar, N.Y.: Caravan Books, Inc., 1976.

____, *The Modern History of Lebanon.* New York: Praeger, 1965.

Smock, David, and Audrey Smock, *Political Fragmentation and National Accommodation: A Comparative Study of Lebanon and Ghana.* New York: Elsevier North-Holland, Inc., 1975.

Suleiman, Michael W., *Political Parties in Lebanon: the Challenge of a Fragmented Political Culture.* Ithaca, N.Y.: Cornell University Press, 1967.

Vallaud, Pierre, *Le Liban au bout du fusil.* Paris: Hachette, 1976.

Yamak, Labib Zuwiyya, *The Syrian Social Nationalist Party: An Ideological Analysis.* Cambridge, Mass.: Harvard University Press, 1966.

Ziadeh, Nicola A., *Syria and Lebanon.* London: Ernest Benn, 1957.

Zuwiyya, Jalal, *The Parliamentary Election of Lebanon 1968.* Leiden, Netherlands: E. J. Brill, 1972.

CHAPTER 8: EGYPT

Abdel-Malek, Anouar, *Egypt: Military Society: The Army Regime, the Left and Social Change Under Nasser,* trans. Charles Lam Markmann. New York: Random House, Inc., 1968.

Ahmed, Jamal M., *The Intellectual Origins of Egyptian Nationalism.* London: Oxford University Press, 1960.

Akhavi, Shahrough, "Egypt: Neo-Patrimonial Elite," in *Political Elites and Political Development in the Middle East,* ed. Frank Tachau. New York: John Wiley & Sons, Inc., 1975.

American University, Foreign Area Studies, *Area Handbook for Egypt* (3rd ed.). Washington, D.C.: U.S. Government Printing Office, 1976.

Ammar, Hamed, *Growing Up in an Egyptian Village: Silwa, Province of Aswan.* New York: Octagon Books, 1966.

Ayrout, Henry Habib, *The Egyptian Peasant,* trans. John Alden Williams. Boston: Beacon Press, 1963.

Baer, Gabriel, *A History of Landownership in Modern Egypt, 1800-1950.* London: Oxford University Press, 1962.

Baker, Raymond W., *Egypt's Uncertain Revolution under Nasser and Sadat.* Cambridge, Mass.: Harvard University Press, 1978.

Barbour, Kenneth M., *The Growth, Location and Structure of Industry in Egypt.* New York: Praeger, 1972.

Berger, Morroe, *Bureaucracy and Society in Modern Egypt.* Princeton: Princeton University Press, 1957.

_____, *Islam in Egypt Today: Social and Political Aspects of Popular Religion.* Cambridge, England: University Press, 1970.

_____, *Military Elite and Social Change: Egypt Since Napoleon.* Princeton: Princeton University, Center for International Studies, Research Monograph no. 6, 1960.

Berque, Jacques, *Egypt: Imperialism and Revolution,* trans. Jean Steward. New York: Praeger, 1972.

Binder, Leonard, "Egypt: The Integrative Revolution," in *Political Culture and Political Development,* ed. Lucien Pye and Sydney Verba. Princeton: Princeton University Press, 1965.

_____, *In a Moment of Enthusiasm: Political Power and the Second Stratum in Egypt.* Chicago: University of Chicago Press, 1978.

Borthwick, Bruce M., "Religion and Politics in Israel and Egypt," *Middle East Journal,* 33 (Spring 1979), 145-63.

Burrell, R. Michael, and Abbas R. Kelidar, *Egypt: The Dilemma of a Nation, 1970-1977. The Washington Papers,* 5, no. 48. Beverly Hills, Calif.: Sage, 1977.

Cleland, Wendall, *The Population Problem in Egypt: A Study of Population Trends and Conditions.* Lancaster, Pa.: Science Press Printing Co., 1936.

"Constitution of the Arab Republic of Egypt," *Middle East Journal,* 26 (Winter 1972), 55-68.

Cooper, Charles A., and S. S. Alexander, eds., *Economic Development and Population Growth in the Middle East.* New York: Elsevier North-Holland, Inc., 1972.

Copeland, Miles, *The Game of Nations: The Amorality of Power Politics.* New York: Simon & Schuster, Inc., 1969.

Cremeans, Charles D., *The Arabs and the World: Nasser's Arab Nationalist Policy.* New York: Praeger, 1963.

Critchfield, Richard, *Shahhat: An Egyptian.* Syracuse, N.Y.: Syracuse University Press, 1978.

Dawisha, A. I., *Egypt in the Arab World: The Elements of Foreign Policy.* New York: John Wiley & Sons, Inc., 1976.

Dekmejian, R. Hrair, *Egypt Under Nasir: A Study in Political Dynamics.* Albany, N.Y.: State University of New York Press, 1971.

Fakhouri, Hani, *Kafr el-Elow: An Egyptian Village in Transition.* New York: Holt, Rinehart & Winston, 1972.

Farnie, D. A., *East and West of Suez: The Suez Canal in History, 1854-1956.* Oxford: Clarendon Press, 1969.

Hansen, Bent, and Girgis Nazouk, *Development and Economic Policy in the UAR (Egypt).* Amsterdam: North Holland Publishing Co., 1965.

Harik, Iliya, *The Political Mobilization of Peasants: A Study of an Egyptian Community.* Bloomington: Indiana University Press, 1974.

____, *The Road to Ramadan.* New York: Quadrangle, The New York Times Book Co., 1975.

Haykal, Muhammad Hasanayn, *The Cairo Documents: The Inside Story of Nasser and His Relationship with World Leaders, Rebels, and Statesmen.* New York: Doubleday & Co., Inc., 1973.

Hofstadter, Dan, ed., *Egypt and Nasser* (3 vols.). New York: Facts on File, 1973.

Holt, Peter M., ed., *Political and Social Change in Modern Egypt: Historical Studies from the Ottoman Conquest to the United Arab Republic.* New York: Oxford University Press, 1967.

Hopkins, Harry, *Egypt the Crucible: The Unfinished Revolution in the Arab World.* Boston: Houghton Mifflin Company, 1969.

Hussein, Mahmoud, *Class Conflict in Egypt, 1945-1970,* trans. Michel Chirman and others. New York: Monthly Review Press, 1973.

Ismael, Tareq, *The U.A.R. in Africa: Egypt's Policy Under Nasser.* Evanston, Ill.: Northwestern University Press, 1971.

Issawi, Charles, *Egypt in Revolution: An Economic Analysis.* London: Oxford University Press, 1963.

Jankowski, James P., *Egypt's Young Rebels: "Young Egypt" 1933-1952.* Stanford, Calif.: Hoover Institution Press, 1975.

el-Kammash, Magdi, *Economic Development and Planning in Egypt.* New York: Praeger, 1968.

Kerr, Malcolm H., "The United Arab Republic: The Domestic, Political, and Economic Background of Foreign Policy," in *Political Dynamics in the Middle East,* ed. Paul Hammond and Sidney Alexander. New York: Elsevier North-Holland, Inc., 1972.

Lacouture, Jean, *Nasser.* Translated by Daniel Hofstadter. New York: Alfred A. Knopf, Inc., 1973.

Lacouture, Jean, and Simmone Lacouture, *Egypt in Transition,* trans. Francis Scarfe. New York: Criterion Books, 1958.

Little, Tom, *Modern Egypt.* New York: Praeger, 1967.

Mahfouz, Afaf el-Kosheri, *Socialisme et pouvoir en Egypte.* Paris: Librairie générale de droit et de jurisprudence, 1972.

Mahmoud, Zaki N., *The Land and People of Egypt* (rev. ed.). Philadelphia: J. B. Lippincott Company, 1972.

Mansfield, Peter, *The British in Egypt.* New York: Holt, Rinehart & Winston, 1972.

_____, *Nasser's Egypt.* Baltimore: Penguin Books, 1965.

Mayfield, James B., *Rural Politics in Nasser's Egypt: A Quest for Legitimacy.* Austin: University of Texas Press, 1971.

Mead, Donald C., *Growth and Structural Change in the Egyptian Economy.* Homewood, Ill.: Richard D. Irwin, 1967.

_____, *Christian Egypt: Ancient and Modern* (2nd rev. ed.). Cairo: American University Press, 1977.

Meinardus, Otto F., *Christian Egypt: Faith and Life.* Cairo: American University Press, 1970.

Nagi, Mostafa, *Labor Force and Employment in Egypt: A Demographic and Socioeconomic Analysis.* New York: Praeger, 1971.

Nasser, Gamal Abdel, *Egypt's Liberation: The Philosophy of the Revolution.* Washington, D.C.: Public Affairs Press, 1955.

Neguib, Mohammed, *Egypt's Destiny.* New York: Doubleday & Co., Inc., 1955.

Nutting, Anthony, *Nasser.* New York: E. P. Dutton, 1972.

O'Brien, Patrick, *The Revolution in Egypt's Economic System: From Private Enterprise to Socialism, 1952-1965.* London: Oxford University Press, 1966.

Omran, Abdel R., ed., *Egypt: Population Problems and Prospects.* Chapel Hill, N.C.: University of North Carolina Press, 1973.

Owen, Edward R., *Cotton and the Egyptian Economy, 1820-1914.* New York: Praeger, 1968.

Perlmutter, Amos, *Egypt: The Praetorian State.* New Brunswick, N.J.: Transaction Books, 1974.

Rejwan, Nissim, *Nasserist Ideology: Its Exponents and Critics.* New York: John Wiley & Sons, Inc., 1974.

Saab, Gabriel S., *The Egyptian Agrarian Reform 1952-1962.* London: Oxford University Press, 1967.

al-Sadat, Anwar, *Revolt on the Nile.* New York: The John Day Co., 1957.

St. John, Robert, *The Boss: The Story of Gamal Abdel Nasser.* New York: McGraw-Hill Book Company, 1960.

Springborg, Robert, "Patterns of Association in the Egyptian Political Elite," in *Political Elites in the Middle East,* ed. George Lenczowski. Washington, D.C.: American Enterprise Institute, 1975.

Stephens, Robert, *Nasser: A Political Biography.* New York: Simon & Schuster, Inc., 1972.

Stevens, Georgiana, *Egypt: Yesterday and Today.* New York: Holt, Rinehart & Winston, 1963.

Tignor, Robert L., *Modernizations and British Colonial Rule in Egypt, 1882-1914.* Princeton: Princeton University Press, 1966.

Vatikiotis, Panayiotis J., ed., *Egypt Since the Revolution.* New York: Praeger, 1968.

_____, *The Egyptian Army in Politics: Pattern for New Nations?* Bloomington: Indiana University Press, 1961.

_____, *Nasser and His Generation.* New York: St. Martin's Press, 1978.

Warriner, Doreen, *Land Reform in Principle and Practice.* New York: Oxford University Press, 1969.

Waterbury, John, See his series of articles in *American Universities Field Staff Reports,* Northeast Africa Series (vols. 17-20; 1972-1975).

____, *Egypt: Burdens of the Past, Options for the Future.* Bloomington: Indiana University Press, 1978.

Wheelock, Keith, *Nasser's New Egypt.* New York: Praeger, 1960.

Wilber, Donald N., ed., *The United Arab Republic—Egypt: Its People, Its Society, Its Culture.* New York: Taplinger Publishing Co., Inc., 1969.

Ziadeh, Farhat, *Lawyers, The Rule of Law, and Liberalism in Modern Egypt.* Stanford, Calif.: Hoover Institution Press, 1968.

CHAPTER 9: IRAN

Abrahamian, Ervand, "The Crowd in Iranian Politics 1905-53," *Past and Present,* 41 (1968), 184-210.

Algar, Hamid, *Religion and State in Iran, 1785-1906.* Berkeley: University of California Press, 1969.

American University, Foreign Area Studies, *Area Handbook for Iran.* Washington, D.C.: U.S. Government Printing Office, 1971.

Arasteh, A. Reza, *Education and Social Awakening in Iran: 1850-1968.* Leiden, Netherlands: E. J. Brill, 1969.

____, *Faces of Persian Youth: A Sociological Study.* Leiden, Netherlands: E. J. Brill, 1970.

____, *Man and Society in Iran.* Leiden, Netherlands: E. J. Brill, 1964.

____, "The Struggle for Equality in Iran," *Middle East Journal,* 18 (Spring 1964), 189-205.

Armajani, Yahya, *Iran.* Englewood Cliffs, N.J.: Prentice-Hall, Inc., 1972.

Avery, Peter, *Modern Iran.* London: Ernest Benn, 1965.

Baldwin, George B., *Planning and Development in Iran.* Baltimore: The Johns Hopkins University Press, 1967.

Banani, Amin, *The Modernization of Iran, 1921-1941.* Stanford: Stanford University Press, 1961.

Bayne, E. A., *Persian Kingship in Transition: Conversations with a Monarch Whose Office is Traditional and Whose Goal is Modernization.* New York: American Universities Field Staff, 1968.

Bharier, Julian, *Economic Development in Iran, 1900-1970.* London: Oxford University Press, 1971.

Bill, James A., "Iran and the Crisis of '78," *Foreign Affairs,* 57 (Winter 1978/79), 323-42.

____, "The Patterns of Elite Politics in Iran," in *Political Elites in the Middle East,* pp. 17-40, ed. George Lenczowski. Washington, D.C.: American Enterprise Institute, 1975.

____, *The Politics of Iran: Groups, Classes and Modernization.* Columbus, Ohio: Charles Merrill, 1972.

____, "The Social and Economic Foundations of Power in Contemporary Iran," *Middle East Journal,* 17 (Autumn 1963), 400-418.

Binder, Leonard, "The Cabinet of Iran: A Case Study in Institutional Adaptation," *Middle East Journal,* 16 (Winter 1962), 29-47.

____, *Iran: Political Development in a Changing Society.* Berkeley: University of California Press, 1962.

____, "Iran's Potential as a Regional Power," in *Political Dynamics in the Middle East,* pp. 355-94, ed. Paul Y. Hammond and Sidney S. Alexander. New York: Elsevier North-Holland, Inc., 1972.

____, "The Proofs of Islam: Religion and Politics in Islam," in *Arab and Islamic Studies in Honor of Hamilton A. R. Gibb,* pp. 118-40, ed. George Makdisi. Cambridge: Mass.: Harvard University Press, 1965.

Brière, Claire, and Pierre Blanchet, *Iran: la révolution au nom de Dieu.* Paris: Editions du Seuil, 1979.

Browne, Edward G., *The Persian Revolution of 1905-1909.* Cambridge, England: University Press, 1910.

Cottam, Richard W., *Nationalism in Iran.* Pittsburgh: University of Pittsburgh Press, 1964.

Elwell-Sutton, L. P., *Persian Oil: A Study in Power Politics.* London: Laurence and Wishart, 1955.

English, Paul W., *City and Village in Iran.* Madison: University of Wisconsin Press, 1966.

Esfandiary, Fereidoun, *The Day of Sacrifice.* London: Heinemann, 1960.

____, *Identity Card.* New York: Grove Press, Inc., 1966.

Fallaci, Oriana, "Interview with the Shah of Iran," *New Republic,* December 1, 1973, pp. 16-21.

Farmayan, Hafez F., *The Beginnings of Modernization in Iran: The Politics and Reforms of Shah Abbas I (1587-1629).* Salt Lake City: University of Utah Middle East Center, Research Monograph No. 1, 1969.

Faroughy, Ahmad, and Jean-Loup Reverier, *L'Iran contre le Chah.* Paris: Editions Jean-Claude Simoën, 1979.

Firoozi, Ferydoon, "Demographic Review: Iranian Censuses 1956 and 1966: A Comparative Analysis," *Middle East Journal,* 24 (Spring 1970), 22-228.

Graham, Robert, *Iran: The Illusion of Power.* New York: St. Martin's Press, 1978.

Halliday, Fred, *Iran: Dictatorship and Development.* New York: Penguin Books, 1979.

Jacobs, Norman, *The Sociology of Development: Iran as an Asian Case Study.* New York: Praeger, 1966.

Kazemzadeh, Firuz, *Russia and Britain in Persia, 1864-1914.* New Haven: Yale University Press, 1968.

Keddie, Nikki R., "The Iranian Power Structure and Social Change 1800-1969: An Overview," *International Journal of Middle East Studies,* 2 (January 1971), 3-20.

____, "The Iranian Village Before and After Land Reform," *Journal of Contemporary History,* 3 (1968), 69-71.

____, *Religion and Rebellion in Iran: The Tobacco Protest of 1891-1892.* London: Frank Cass, 1966.

____, "The Roots of the Ulama's Power in Modern Iran," *Studia Islamica,* 1969, 31-53.

Laing, Margaret, *The Shah.* London: Sidwick and Jackson, 1977.

Lambton, Ann K. S., *Landlord and Peasant in Persia: A Study of Land Tenure and Land Revenue Administration.* London: Oxford University Press, 1953.

____, *The Persian Land Reform, 1962-1966.* London: Oxford University Press, 1969.

Lenczowski, George, *Russia and the West in Iran, 1918-1948.* Ithaca, N.Y.: Cornell University Press, 1949.

Looney, Robert E., *The Economic Development of Iran: A Recent Survey with Projections to 1981.* New York: Praeger, 1973.

____, *Iran at the End of the Century: A Hegelian Forecast.* Lexington, Mass.: Lexington Books, 1977.

Millward, William G., "Traditional Values and Social Change in Iran," *Iranian Studies,* 4 (Winter 1971), 2-35.

____, *The White Revolution* (2nd ed.). Tehran: Imperial Pahlavi Library, 1967.

Mohammed Reza Pahlavi, *Mission for my Country.* New York: McGraw-Hill Book Company, 1961.

Nirumand, Bahman, *Iran: The New Imperialism in Action.* New York: Monthly Review Press, 1969.

Ramazani, R. K., *The Foreign Policy of Iran—1500-1941, A Developing Nation in World Affairs.* Charlottesville, Va.: University Press of Virginia, 1966.

____, "Iran's Changing Foreign Policy: A Preliminary Discussion," *Middle East Journal,* 24 (Autumn 1970), 421-437.

Razi, G. Hossein, "Genesis of Party in Iran: A Case Study of the Interaction between the Political System and Political Parties," *Iranian Studies,* 3 (1970), 58-90.

Sangvi, Ramesh, *Aryamehr: The Shah of Iran: A Political Biography.* London: Macmillan Publishers Ltd., 1968.

Savory, Roger M., "Iran: A 2500-Year Historical and Cultural Tradition," in *Iranian Civilization and Culture,* pp. 77-89, ed. Charles J. Adams. Montreal: McGill University, Institute of Islamic Studies, 1972.

Sayeed, Khalid B., "Policy Making Process in the Government of Iran," in *Iranian Civilization and Culture,* ed. Charles J. Adams. Montreal: McGill University, Institute of Islamic Studies, 1972.

Shari'ati, Ali, *On the Sociology of Islam,* trans. Hamid Algar. Berkeley, Calif.: Mizan Press, 1979.

Soraya, H. I. H. Princess, *The Autobiography of H. I. H. Princess Soraya,* trans. Constantine Fitzgibbon. London: Arthur Barker, 1963.

al-Tabataba'i, Muhammad Husayn, *Shi'ite Islam,* trans. and annotated by Seyyed Hossein Nasr. Albany: State University of New York Press, 1975.

Upton, Joseph M., *The History of Modern Iran: An Interpretation.* Cambridge, Mass.: Harvard University Press, 1961.

Vieille, Paul, and Abol-Hassan Banisadr, *Pétrole et violence: terreur blanche et résistance en Iran.* Paris: Editions Anthropos, 1974.

Wilber, Donald N., *Contemporary Iran.* New York: Praeger, 1963.

____, *Iran: Past and Present* (8th ed.). Princeton: Princeton University Press, 1976.

Yar-Shater, Ehsan, ed., *Iran Faces the Seventies.* New York: Praeger, 1971.

Zabih, Sepehr, *The Communist Movement in Iran.* Berkeley: University of California Press, 1966.

____, "Iran's International Posture: De Facto Nonalignment Within a Pro-Western Alliance," *Middle Eastern Journal,* 24 (Summer 1970), 302-18.

Zonis, Marvin, *The Political Elite of Iran.* Princeton: Princeton University Press, 1971.

____, "The Political Elite of Iran: A Second Stratum?" in *Political Elites and Politics in the Middle East,* pp. 193-216, ed. Frank Tachau. New York: John Wiley & Sons, Inc., 1975.

CHAPTER 10: TURKEY

Ahmad, Feroz, *The Turkish Experiment in Democracy, 1950-1975.* Boulder, Colo.: Westview Press, 1977.

____, *The Young Turks: The Committee of Union and Progress in Turkish Politics, 1908-1914.* Oxford: Clarendon Press, 1969.

Akarli, Engin D., with Gabriel Ben-Dor, eds., *Political Participation in Turkey: Historical Background and Present Problems.* Istanbul: Bogazici University Publications, 1975.

American University, Foreign Area Studies, *Area Handbook for the Republic of Turkey* (2nd ed.). Washington, D.C.: U.S. Government Printing Office, 1973.

Aresvik, Oddvar, *The Agricultural Development of Turkey.* New York: Praeger, 1975.

Balfour, John Patrick Douglas, Lord Kinross, *Ataturk: A Biography of Mustafa Kemal, Father of Modern Turkey.* New York: William Morrow & Co., Inc., 1965.

Benedict, Peter, *Ula: An Anatolian Town.* Leiden, Netherlands: E. J. Brill, 1974.

Benedict, Peter, Erol Tumertekin, and Fatma Mansur, eds., *Turkey: Geographic and Social Perspectives.* Leiden, Netherlands: E. J. Brill, 1974.

Berkes, Niyazi, *The Development of Secularism in Turkey.* Montreal: McGill University Press, 1964.

Carey, Jane, and Andrew Carey, "Turkish Industry and the Five-Year Plans," *Middle East Journal,* 25 (Summer 1971), 337-54.

Cohn, Edwin J., *Turkish Economic, Social and Political Change: The Development of a More Prosperous and Open Society.* New York: Praeger, 1970.

1961 Constitution of Turkey, *Middle East Journal,* 16 (1962), 215-35. Also in Abid A. Al-Marayati, ed., *Middle Eastern Constitutions and Electoral Laws.* New York: Praeger, 1968.

Davidson, Roderic, *Turkey.* Englewood Cliffs, N.J.: Prentice-Hall, Inc., 1968.

Dewdney, John C., *Turkey: An Introductory Geography.* New York: Praeger, 1971.

Dodd, Clement H., *Politics and Government in Turkey.* Manchester, England: Manchester University Press, 1969.

Erim, Nihat, "The Turkish Experience in the Light of Recent Developments," *Middle East Journal,* 26 (Summer 1972), 245-52.

Frey, Frederick W., "Patterns of Elite Politics in Turkey," in *Political Elites in the Middle East,* pp. 41-82, ed. George Lenczowski. Washington, D.C.: American Enterprise Institute, 1975.

____, *The Turkish Political Elite.* Cambridge, Mass.: The M.I.T. Press, 1965.

Fry, Maxwell J., *Finance and Development Planning in Turkey.* Leiden, Netherlands: E. J. Brill, 1972.

Gallagher, Charles F., "Contemporary Islam: The Straits of Secularism: Power, Politics and Piety in Republican Turkey," *American Universities Field Staff Reports,* Southwest Asia Series, 15, no. 3 (1966).

Giritli, Ismet, "Turkey Since the 1965 Elections," *Middle East Journal,* 23 (Summer 1965), 351-63.

Gökalp, Ziya, *Turkish Nationalism and Western Civilization,* trans. Niyazi Berkes. New York: Columbia University Press, 1959.

Harris, George S., "The Causes of the 1960 Revolution in Turkey," *Middle East Journal,* 24 (Autumn 1970), 438-54.

____, *The Origins of Communism in Turkey.* Stanford, Calif.: Hoover Institution Press, 1967.

____, "The Role of the Military in Turkish Politics," *Middle East Journal,* 19 (Winter and Spring 1965), 54-66, 169-76.

____, *Troubled Alliance: Turkish-American Problems in Historical Perspective, 1945-1971.* Washington, D.C.: American Enterprise Institute, 1972.

Heper, Metin, "The Recalcitrance of the Turkish Public Bureaucracy to 'Bourgeois Politics': A Multi-Factor Political Stratification Analysis," *Middle East Journal,* 30 (Autumn 1976), 485-500.

Hershlag, Z. Y., *Turkey: The Challenge of Growth.* Leiden, Netherlands: E. J. Brill, 1968.

Heyd, Uriel, *Foundations of Turkish Nationalism: The Life and Teachings of Ziya Gökalp.* London: Luzac, 1950.

Hotham, David, *The Turks.* London: John Murray, 1972.

Howard, Harry N., *Turkey, the Straits and U.S. Policy.* Baltimore: The Johns Hopkins University Press, 1974.

Hyland, Michael P., "Crisis at the Polls: Turkey's 1969 Elections," *Middle East Journal,* 24 (Winter 1970), 1-16.

International Bank for Reconstruction and Development, *The Economy of Turkey: An Analysis and Recommendation for a Development Program.* Baltimore: The Johns Hopkins University Press, 1951.

____, *Turkey: Prospects and Problems of an Expanding Economy.* Washington, D.C.: The World Bank, 1975.

Karpat, Kemal H., *The Gecekondu: Rural Migration and Urbanization.* London: Cambridge University Press, 1976.

____, *Social Change and Politics in Turkey: A Structural-Historical Analysis.* Leiden, Netherlands: E. J. Brill, 1973.

____, "Socialism and the Labor Party of Turkey," *Middle East Journal,* 21 (Spring 1967), 157-72.

____, *Turkey's Politics: The Transition to a Multi-Party System.* Princeton: Princeton University Press, 1959.

Kazamias, Andreas M., *Education and the Quest for Modernity in Turkey.* London: George Allen and Unwin, 1966.

Kemal, Yashar, *The Wind from the Plain,* trans. Thilda Kemal. New York: Dodd, Mead & Company, 1963.

Kili, Suna, *Kemalism.* Istanbul: Robert College, School of Business Administration and Economics, 1969.

____, *Turkey: A Case Study of Political Development.* Istanbul: Robert College, School of Business Administration and Economics, 1968.

Krueger, Anne O., *Foreign Trade Regimes and Economic Development: Turkey* New York: Columbia University Press, 1974.

Kushner, David, *The Rise of Turkish Nationalism, 1876-1908.* London: Frank Cass, 1977.

Landau, Jacob M., "The National Salvation Party in Turkey," *Asian and African Studies,* 11, no. 1 (1976), 1-57.

____, *Radical Politics in Modern Turkey.* Leiden, Netherlands: E. J. Brill, 1974.

Leder, Arnold, *Catalysts of Change: Marxist versus Muslim in a Turkish Community.* Austin: University of Texas Center for Middle Eastern Studies, Middle East Monograph, no. 1, 1976.

Lerner, Daniel, and Richard D. Robinson, "Swords and Ploughshares: The Turkish Army as a Modernizing Force," *World Politics,* 3 (October 1960), 19-44.

Lewis, Bernard, *The Emergence of Modern Turkey.* London: Oxford University Press, 1961.

Magnarella, Paul, *Tradition and Change in a Turkish Town.* New York: John Wiley & Sons, Inc., 1974.

Makal, Mahmut, *A Village in Anatolia,* trans. Sir Wyndham Deedes. London: Vallentine, Mitchell and Co., 1965.

Mango, Andrew, *Turkey: A Delicately Poised Ally.* Beverly Hills, Calif.: Sage Publications, Inc., 1975.

Mansur, Fatma, *Bodrum: A Town in the Aegean.* Leiden, Netherlands: E. J. Brill, 1972.

Mardin, Serif, "Center-Periphery Relations: A Key to Turkish Politics?" *Daedalus,* 102, no. 1 (Winter 1973), 169-90.

____, *The Genesis of Young Ottoman Thought: A Study in the Modernization of Turkish Political Ideas.* Princeton: Princeton University Press, 1962.

____, "Ideology and Religion in the Turkish Revolution," *International Journal of Middle East Studies,* 2 (July 1971), 197-211.

Meeker, Michael E., "The Great Family Aghas of Turkey: A Study of a Changing Political Culture," in *Rural Politics and Social Change in the Middle East,* ed. Richard Antoun and Iliya Harik. Bloomington: Indiana University Press, 1972.

Nye, Roger P., "Civil-Military Confrontation in Turkey: The 1973 Presidential Election," *International Journal of Middle East Studies,* 8 (April 1977), 209-28.

OECD Economic Surveys: Turkey, Paris Organization for Economic Co-operation and Development, 1974.

Orga, Irfan, *Portrait of a Turkish Family.* London: Gollancz, 1950.

Özbudun, Ergun, "Established Revolution Versus Unfinished Revolution: Contrasting Patterns of Democratization in Mexico and Turkey," in *Authoritarian Politics in Modern Society,* ed. Samuel P. Huntington and Clement H. Moore. New York: Basic Books, Inc., Publishers, 1970.

____, *The Role of the Military in Recent Turkish Politics,* occasional paper in International Affairs, no. 14. Cambridge, Mass.: Harvard University Center for International Affairs, 1966.

____, *Social Change and Political Participation in Turkey.* Princeton: Princeton University Press, 1977.

Pierce, Joe E., *Life in a Turkish Village.* New York: Holt, Rinehart & Winston, 1964.

Ramsaur, Ernest E., Jr., *The Young Turks: Prelude to the Revolution of 1908.* Princeton: Princeton University Press, 1957.

Reed, Howard A., "The Religious Life of Modern Turkish Muslims," in *Islam and the West,* ed. Richard N. Frye. The Hague: Mouton, 1957.

Robinson, Richard D., *The First Turkish Republic: A Case Study in National Development.* Cambridge, Mass.: Harvard University Press, 1963.

_____, *High-Level Manpower in Economic Development: The Turkish Case.* Cambridge, Mass.: Harvard University Press, 1967.

_____, "Mosque and School in Turkey," *Muslim World,* 51 (September 1961), 107-10.

Roos, Leslie L., Jr., and Noralou P. Roos, *Managers of Modernization: Organizations and Elites in Turkey (1950-1969).* Cambridge, Mass.: Harvard University Press, 1971.

Rustow, Dankwart A., "Politics and Islam in Turkey, 1920-1955," in *Islam and the West,* ed. Richard N. Frye. The Hague: Mouton, 1957.

_____, "Turkey: The Modernity of Tradition," in *Political Culture and Political Development,* ed. Lucian W. Pye and Sidney Verba. Princeton: Princeton University Press, 1969.

Sayari, Sabri, "Aspects of Party Organization in Turkey," *Middle East Journal,* 30 (Spring 1976), 187-99.

Shaw, Stanford, *History of the Ottoman Empire and Modern Turkey* (2 vols.). London: Cambridge University Press, 1976, 1977.

Shorter, Frederic, ed., *Four Studies on the Economic Development of Turkey.* London: Frank Cass, 1967.

Srikantan, K. S., "Regional and Rural-Urban Socio-Demographic Differences in Turkey," *Middle East Journal,* 27 (Summer 1973), 275-300.

Sunar, Ilkay, *State and Society in the Politics of Turkey's Development.* Ankara: Ankara University Faculty of Political Science Publication no. 377, 1974.

Szyliowicz, Joseph S., *Education and Modernization in the Middle East.* Ithaca, N.Y.: Cornell University Press, 1973.

_____, "Elites and Modernization in Turkey," in *Political Elites and Political Development in the Middle East,* pp. 23-66, ed. Frank Tachau. New York: John Wiley & Sons, Inc., 1975.

_____, *A Political Analysis of Student Activism: The Turkish Case.* Beverly Hills, Calif.: Sage Publications, Inc., 1972.

_____, *Political Change in Rural Turkey-Erdemli.* The Hague: Mouton, 1966.

_____, "The Turkish Elections: 1965," *Middle East Journal,* 20 (Autumn 1966), 473-94.

Tamkoc, Metin, "Stable Instability of the Turkish Polity," *Middle East Journal,* 27 (Summer 1973), 319-41.

_____, *The Warrior Diplomats: Guardians of the National Security and Modernization of Turkey.* Salt Lake City: University of Utah Press, 1976.

Turham, Mumtaz, *Where Are We in Westernization?,* trans. David Garwood. Istanbul: Robert College Research Center, 1965.

Ulman, A. Haluk and Frank Tachau, "Turkish Politics: The Attempt to Reconcile Rapid Modernization with Democracy," *Middle East Journal,* 19 (Spring 1965), 153-68.

Vali, F. A., *Bridge Across the Bosporus: The Foreign Policy of Turkey.* Baltimore: The Johns Hopkins University Press, 1971.

Ward, Robert and Dankwart Rustow, eds., *Political Modernization in Japan and Turkey.* Princeton: Princeton University Press, 1964.

Weiker, Walter F, *Political Tutelage and Democracy in Turkey: The Free Party and Its Aftermath.* Leiden, Netherlands: E. J. Brill, 1973.

———, *The Turkish Revolution 1960-61: Aspects of Military Politics.* Washington, D.C.: The Brookings Institution, 1963.

Yalman, Ahmed Emin, *Turkey in My Time.* Norman: University of Oklahoma Press, 1956.

Yalman, Nur, "Some Observations on Secularism in Islam: The Cultural Revolution in Turkey," *Daedalus,* 102, no. 1 (Winter 1973), 139-68.

Index